Theology of Reconciliation in the Context of Church Relations

A Palestinian Christian Perspective in Dialogue with Miroslav Volf

Rula Khoury Mansour

© 2020 Rula Khoury Mansour

Published 2020 by Langham Monographs
An imprint of Langham Publishing

www.langhampublishing.org

Langham Publishing and its imprints are a ministry of Langham Partnership

Langham Partnership
PO Box 296, Carlisle, Cumbria, CA3 9WZ, UK
www.langham.org

ISBNs:
978-1-78368-772-5 Print
978-1-78368-799-2 ePub
978-1-78368-800-5 Mobi
978-1-78368-801-2 PDF

Rula Khoury Mansour has asserted her right under the Copyright, Designs and Patents Act, 1988 to be identified as the Author of this work.

All rights reserved. No part of this publication may be reproduced, stored in a retrieval system or transmitted, in any form or by any means, electronic, mechanical, photocopying, recording or otherwise, without the prior written permission of the publisher or the Copyright Licensing Agency.

Requests to reuse content from Langham Publishing are processed through PLSclear. Please visit www.plsclear.com to complete your request.

Scripture quotations, unless marked otherwise, are from The Holy Bible, English Standard Version® (ESV®), copyright © 2001 by Crossway, a publishing ministry of Good News Publishers. Used by permission. All rights reserved.

Scripture quotations marked (NIV) are taken from the Holy Bible, New International Version®, NIV®. Copyright © 1973, 1978, 1984, 2011 by Biblica, Inc.™ Used by permission of Zondervan.

British Library Cataloguing-in-Publication Data
A catalogue record for this book is available from the British Library

ISBN: 978-1-78368-772-5

Cover & Book Design: projectluz.com

Langham Partnership actively supports theological dialogue and an author's right to publish but does not necessarily endorse the views and opinions set forth here or in works referenced within this publication, nor can we guarantee technical and grammatical correctness. Langham Partnership does not accept any responsibility or liability to persons or property as a consequence of the reading, use or interpretation of its published content.

To:
The Arabic church
All this is from God, who through Christ reconciled us to himself and gave us the ministry of reconciliation.
2 Corinthians 5:18

For:
My sons
The world tells us to seek success, power and money; God tells us to seek humility, service and love.
–Pope Francis

Contents

Abstract xv

Acknowledgments xvii

List of Abbreviations xix

Chapter 1 1
  Introduction
    1.1 Research Question 2
    1.2 Palestinian Evangelicals in Israel: A Threefold Minority 3
    1.3 Palestinian Arab Culture 4
        1.3.1 Patriarchal Relations 5
        1.3.2 Honour and Shame 7
    1.4 Church Conflict 8
        1.4.1 The Nature of Church Conflict 8
        1.4.2 The Resolution of Church Conflict 9
        1.4.3 Conflict and Power 9
        1.4.4 Church Split/Exit: Impact of Congregational
              Characteristics 11
    1.5 Theology of Reconciliation 14
        1.5.1 Introduction 14
        1.5.2 Palestinian Protestant Theology of Reconciliation 17
        1.5.3 Miroslav Volf's Theology of Reconciliation 20
    1.6 Plan of the Thesis 21

Chapter 2 25
  Methodology
    2.1 Theoretical Framework and Epistemological Perspective 25
        2.1.1 Practical Theology 25
        2.1.2 Epistemological Perspective 26
    2.2 Choice of Qualitative Methodology and Methods Used in
        the Study 27
        2.2.1 Theology and Fieldwork 27
        2.2.2 Participant Observation 29
        2.2.3 Interviews 30
        2.2.4 Textual Resources 32
        2.2.5 Focus Group 32
    2.3 Research Plan 33

  2.3.1 First Phase: Field Mapping 33
  2.3.2 Second Phase: Case Studies...34
  2.3.3 Third Phase: Theoretical Analysis.......................................34
 2.4 Content Analysis..35
 2.5 Research Ethics 36
 2.6 My Own Position in the Field...37
 2.7 Reflexivity..41

Chapter 3 45
The Environment of the Palestinian Baptist Churches in Israel
 3.1 Introduction 45
 3.2 The Environment of the Palestinian Baptist Churches
  Before the Missionaries' Departure (1911–1990).........................46
  3.2.1 Historical Background 46
  3.2.2 Political, Social and Economic Factors..............................48
  3.2.3 Church Conflict between 1948 and 1990.........................53
 3.3 The Environment of the Palestinian Baptist Churches after
  the Missionaries' Departure (1990–2016)....................................54
  3.3.1 Identity...55
  3.3.2 Social Factors...62
  3.3.3 Economic Factors 64
  3.3.4 Cultural Factors 65
  3.3.5 Theological Factors 66
  3.3.6 Structural Factors...67
 3.4 Statistics of Splits and Exits in the Baptist Churches in Israel.......73
  3.4.1 Splits and Exits between 1990 and 2005...........................75
  3.4.2 Splits and Exits between 2006 and 2016...........................77
 3.5 Conclusion 79

Chapter 4 81
The Nature and Causes of Church Conflict in Three Case Studies of
Palestinian Baptist Churches in Israel
 4.1 Introduction 81
 4.2 Historical Background of the Three Churches and
  Their Conflicts..82
  4.2.1 Case Study A 82
  4.2.2 Case Study B 86
  4.2.3 Case Study C 89
 4.3 Primary Factors Contributing to the Conflicts........................95
  4.3.1 Theological Factor: Tension between Episcopalian/
   Sacramental versus Congregationalist/Functionalist 96

4.3.2 Socio-Cultural Factor: Tension between Traditional/
   Patriarchal versus Modern/Democratic Ethos 104
4.4 Secondary Factors Contributing to the Conflicts....................... 114
   4.4.1 Church Buildings 114
   4.4.2 Women's Informal Power 117
   4.4.3 Economic Factors 120
4.5 Conclusion 121

Chapter 5 123
Conflict Management Practices in Three Cases of Palestinian Baptist Churches in Israel
   5.1 Introduction 123
   5.2 Cultural Models: Tension between *Sulha* and Alternative-
      Legal Approaches 124
      5.2.1 The Middle Eastern Tradition of *Sulha*................... 124
      5.2.2 Alternative-Legal Approach................................. 130
      5.2.3 Comparison between *Sulha* and Alternative-Legal
         Approaches 132
   5.3 Christian Approach: Tension between Traditional
      Palestinian Churches and Western-Baptist Approaches 135
      5.3.1 Traditional Palestinian Church Approach................. 135
      5.3.2 Western-Baptist Approach 135
   5.4 Local Palestinian Baptists' Conflict Management Practices
      in the Three Case Studies 136
      5.4.1 *Sulha* Approach... 137
      5.4.2 Alternative-Legalistic Approach 148
      5.4.3 Hierarchical Approach 156
      5.4.4 Western-Baptist Approach 157
   5.5 Conclusion 167

Chapter 6 169
Theology of Remembrance
   6.1 Introduction 169
   6.2 Volf's Theology of Remembrance.................................. 171
      6.2.1 How Do We "Remember Rightly"?......................... 171
      6.2.2 How Long Should We Remember? 178
   6.3 Remembrance in the Case Studies................................. 183
      6.3.1 Hierarchical Approach 184
      6.3.2 *Sulha* and Alternative-Legalistic Approaches 187
      6.3.3 Western-Baptist Approach 189
   6.4 Challenges and Recommendations................................. 192

Chapter 7 199
Theology of Forgiveness
- 7.1 Volf's Theology of Forgiveness 199
  - 7.1.1 Understand God's Forgiveness 199
  - 7.1.2 How Should We Forgive? 201
  - 7.1.3 How Can We Forgive? 203
  - 7.1.4 A Cultural Critique of Volf's Theme of Forgiveness in Light of Local Culture (*Sulha*) 208
- 7.2 Theology of Forgiveness in the Case Studies 212
  - 7.2.1 Hierarchical Approach 213
  - 7.2.2 *Sulha* Approach 216
  - 7.2.3 Alternative-Legalistic Approach 221
  - 7.2.4 Western-Baptist Approach 223
- 7.3 Challenges and Recommendations 228

Chapter 8 235
Theology of Justice
- 8.1 Volf's Theology of Justice 235
  - 8.1.1 Seeking Justice 236
  - 8.1.2 Justice as a Dimension of Embrace 237
- 8.2 Theology of Justice in the Case Studies 241
  - 8.2.1 Hierarchical Approach 242
  - 8.2.2 *Sulha* Approach 244
  - 8.2.3. Alternative-Legalistic Approach 246
  - 8.2.4 Western-Baptist Approach 248
- 8.3 Challenges and Recommendations 252

Chapter 9 257
Theology of Embrace
- 9.1 Volf's Theology of Embrace 257
  - 9.1.1 The Social Construction of Identity 257
  - 9.1.2 The Self and Its Centre 259
  - 9.1.3 Embrace 261
- 9.2 Theology of Embrace in the Case Studies 263
  - 9.2.1 Hierarchical Approach 263
  - 9.2.2 *Sulha* Approach 266
  - 9.2.3 Alternative-Legalistic Approach 267
  - 9.2.4 Western-Baptist Approach 267
- 9.3 Challenges and Recommendations 270
- 9.4 Personal Agency 272

    9.5 Summary Analysis of the Four Approaches in Light of
        Volf's Model (Table) 275

Chapter 10 277
    Recommendations and Conclusion
    10.1 Findings and Recommendations 277
        1. Community 281
        2. Formality 283
        3. Venting 285
        4. Dignity restoration 285
        5. Nonlinear structure 286
        6. Conditional/unconditional forgiveness 286
        7. Justice as Restoration of Broken Relationships 287
    10.2 Contribution to Existing Body of Knowledge 288
    10.3 Limitation and Scope for Further Research 289

Appendix 1 291
    Arab Palestinian Baptists in Israel: A Threefold Minority

Appendix 2 293
    Parachurch Members in the Convention of Evangelical Churches in
    Israel (CECI) Established since 1985

Appendix 3 295
    List of Interviewees (In-depth Interviews)

Appendix 4 299
    Excerpts from the Constitution of the Association of
    Baptist Churches in Israel (ABC)

Glossary 311

Bibliography 313

List of Tables

Table 2.1: Field mapping interviews 31
Table 2.2: Case study interviews 31
Table 2.3: Categories used in case selection 34
Table 3.1: Generational typology of Ateek, Rabinowitz and Abu-Baker 49
Table 3.2: Splits/exits in the Baptist churches in Israel 75
Table 4.1: Members of church A 83
Table 4.2: Members of church B 87
Table 4.3: Members of church C2 91
Table 7.1: Forgiveness in Volf's theory and *sulha* model: A comparison 212
Table 8.1: Evaluating the four approaches in terms of Volf's theory of justice 251
Table 9.1: The results of the analysis of the four approaches in light of Volf's model 276

List of Figures

Figure 6.1: Remembering rightly in the case studies 192
Figure 7.1: Forgiveness in the case studies 227
Figure 7.2: Case C stages of forgiveness 227
Figure 7.3: Forgiveness in *sulha* model 231
Figure 7.4: Forgiveness in Volf's theory 232
Figure 7.5: Proposed model 232
Figure 9.1: Embrace in the case studies 270
Figure 9.2: Two stages of embrace in case C (reintegration and beginning of reconciliation) 270
Figure 10.1: Proposed rhombus model 282

Abstract

In the early 1990s, the International Mission Board of the Southern Baptist Convention, changed its global philosophy of ministry and withdrew from direct involvement in the Baptist churches it planted, including in Israel. Around the same time, local churches started to split.

This research project seeks to contribute towards a solution to this problem by asking and answering both a sociological and a theological question: Sociologically, what are the nature and causes of the splits and how do Palestinian Baptist churches manage such intra-church conflict? Theologically, what are the desirable conflict management practices and how should they be adapted to local cultural traditions? The primary purpose of this research is to generate a local theory regarding a Palestinian theology of reconciliation which is both theologically and culturally relevant.

This thesis argues that the primary factor for church splits is the clash between the pastors' legacy of a 'hierarchical-patriarchal' approach and the younger generation's 'congregationalist-democratic' approach, both grounded in, but each offering a different interpretation of Christian *theology* and Arab *culture*. It identifies four conflict management practices that are implemented by Palestinian Baptists in Israel and holds that the main reason that the conflicts have not been resolved effectively is the clash between contenders' interpretations of theology and culture. The pastors' cultural-theological approach is a combination of traditional *sulha* and hierarchical theology that was customary in traditional Palestinian churches. By contrast, the younger generation's cultural-theological approach is a combination of alternative-legalist and Western-Baptist.

The thesis examines the relevance of Miroslav Volf's theology of reconciliation for the cases at hand. It argues that the model is indeed pertinent to Palestinian Baptists in Israel, who are in the process of investing new meanings into their theology of reconciliation. Yet, in order to be applicable to this context it requires cultural translation in seven elements: (a) community, (b) formality, (c) venting, (d) dignity, (e) non-linear nature of the reconciliation process, (f) the focus on achieving reconciliation rather than focusing on whether forgiveness should be perceived as conditional or unconditional and (g) to view justice in terms of restoration of broken relationships, not only in terms of its socio-political understanding (rights).

Acknowledgments

For the final outcome of this thesis, many people must be acknowledged. Words cannot adequately express the debt I owe and feel towards them:

- First and foremost, the Palestinian Baptists who gave of their own time to share their lives and stories with me. Most of them would prefer not to be named; I hope that you are aware of how much I appreciate your partnership.
- I am indebted to both of my supervisors, Professor Miroslav Volf and Dr Amalia Sa'ar, and am particularly grateful for their friendship. They have encouraged me and passed on many words of wisdom as well as helpful and practical advice.
- Faculty members, staff, and colleagues at the Oxford Centre for Mission Studies, for their support, prayers, friendship and guidance. In particular, Dr Damon So, my House Tutor; Dr David Singh, the PhD Stage Leader; Dr Tom Harvey, the Dean; Dr Paul Bendor-Samuel, the OCMS Director; Dr Paul Woods; Dr Ben Knighton; Dr Bill Prevette; Dr Brainerd Prince; Ralph Bates, the Librarian; Nicky Clargo, the Finance Officer; Nadine Woods, the Development Officer; and Irim Sarwar and Rachel McIntyre, the Executive Officers.
- The Association of Baptist Churches in Israel (ABC) for their enthusiastic support and prayers.
- Nazareth Evangelical College in Nazareth for their prayers and encouragement throughout. In particular, the Academic Dean, Dr Yohanna Katanacho, for his insightful comments and continual encouragement and Dr Philip Sumpter for his helpful comments and support.

- Eastern Mennonite University, who invited me to be a visiting scholar for two years to work on my research. I am especially thankful to Daryl Byler, Dr David Brubaker and Dr Mark Thiessen Nation.
- Nancy Lively and Hannah Fox for their helpful proofreading.
- I also want to thank all who assisted me financially, especially Langham Partnership for their generous financial grant, prayers and the privilege of being called a "Langham Scholar." I am especially indebted to Dr Riad Kassis, Langham Scholars' Ministry Director; Dr Chris Wright, the International Ministries Director; Dr Ian Shaw, the former Associate International Director; and Dr Fred Gale and Liz McGregor, the Scholar Care Coordinators. I am also thankful to BMS World Mission and David Kerrigan, the former General Director, as well as Mennonite Mission Network and John Lapp, the Senior Executive for Global Ministries.
- Additionally, I am indebted to a small group of friends who have faithfully prayed for me and encouraged me through the ups and downs of this process.
- My parents, for their love, prayers and practical support, and my extended family, for their love, encouragement and help in a variety of situations.
- My three beloved young sons, Adi, Rami and Sami, who have been very supportive throughout the process.
- Bader, my dearest husband, who unreservedly sacrificed his own pursuits for me over the past several years and whose life is a model for reconciliation.
- Lastly and most deeply, I am indebted to my Lord and Saviour for all his goodness and guidance.

List of Abbreviations

ABC	The Association of Baptist Churches in Israel
ADR	Alternative Dispute Resolution
BCI	Baptist Convention in Israel
CECI	The Convention of Evangelical Churches in Israel
CSTC	Christian Service Training Centre
ESV	English Standard Version of the Bible
IMB	The International Mission Board of the Southern Baptist Convention in the US
NEC	Nazareth Evangelical College
OCMS	Oxford Centre for Mission Studies
TRC	The Truth and Reconciliation Commission

CHAPTER 1

Introduction

In the early 1990s, missionary organizations operating in Israel changed their philosophy of ministry and withdrew from direct involvement in the churches they had planted. This change, along with other cultural, theological and economic factors, led to splits and exits among more than 50 percent of the Palestinian Baptist churches in Israel.[1]

The Palestinian evangelical churches in Israel, as a multicultural minority,[2] have a growing potential to influence Israeli society by dialoguing effectively with non-Protestant Christians, Muslims and Jews and by playing an essential role in reconciliation between Palestinians and Israelis. Nonetheless, Christian disunity and divisions in Israel/Palestine raise questions about Christian credibility before Muslims and Jews.

The need in my country breaks my heart and has provoked me to contribute to the solution. As a public prosecutor with thirteen years of experience, I realize that the traditional legal system gives limited solutions, for it only deals with the symptoms of a conflict. There is a need to look for the sources of a conflict in order to fully resolve it.

It is my desire to see growth in healthy churches rather than churches immersed in pain, splitting over unresolved conflicts, as is the situation today within many Palestinian evangelical churches in Israel. As a Palestinian evangelical woman, I have seen many conflicts addressed unsuccessfully and without the contribution of women.

---

1. In this research, church *split* refers to the exodus of unsatisfied members and leaders resulting in a church splitting into two. Church *exit* refers to an unsatisfied leader who leaves church with his family and founds a new church or joins another church's leadership.

2. Palestinian Arab Christians in Israel are exposed to various cultures: Muslim Arab, Israeli Jewish and that of Western missionaries. See chapters 3 and 4.

A new approach for resolving intra-church conflicts between Palestinian evangelicals in Israel is needed. This is where a Palestinian theology of reconciliation becomes highly relevant and necessary.

My project is to understand the local causes and implications of church splits/exits,[3] and to articulate a culturally compatible theological model of reconciliation in Palestinian Baptist churches. I theologically evaluate the practices of Palestinian Baptist churches using Miroslav Volf's model and, in light of these practices, evaluate Volf's model in terms of its cultural suitability for the Palestinian context. This thesis is also an attempt to fill in some of the gaps in the academic body of knowledge on the theology of reconciliation. The local knowledge and practices of conflict management represented in the findings presented here inform Volf's theory.

1.1 Research Question

My research question is as follows: What are the nature, causes and managements of intra-church conflict within the Palestinian Baptist churches in Israel and how can they be handled in the most effective ways? How might Volf's theory further illuminate a Palestinian theology of reconciliation and how might a Palestinian theology of reconciliation inform his theory?

The first half of the thesis (chapters 2 to 5) is considerably contextual in form and content. I focus on the context of Palestinian Baptists and explore the environment, nature, causes and managements of intra-church conflict in three cases of church splits. In the second half (chapters 6 to 9) I relate the findings to Volf's theological model of reconciliation. I examine the existing practices of church conflict management in the Palestinian Baptist context (bottom-up models) in light of Volf's theory (a top-down model) and also critically evaluate its applicability in this context. My goal is to see how his theory might further illuminate or deepen the understanding of reconciliation in this context and how the context might inform his theory. The primary purpose of this research is to generate a local theory regarding a Palestinian theology of reconciliation which is both *theologically and culturally* relevant.

---

3. Splits or exits are not unique to Palestinians but actually characterize Baptist churches in general.

In this chapter I briefly describe the literature on the Palestinian Christian context in Israel, Palestinian Arab culture, church conflict, Palestinian Protestant reconciliation theology, and Volf's theology of reconciliation in order to provide an introductory theoretical background to this research. Nonetheless, rather than presenting a detailed "literature review" chapter, the literature will be discussed in more depth in the main body of the thesis, since the secondary literature plays a decisive role in the content of each chapter.

1.2 Palestinian Evangelicals in Israel: A Threefold Minority

Arab Palestinian Christians in Israel have been isolated from the majority of their culture through long centuries of Muslim rule, a situation exacerbated by the effects of the *millet* system under Turkish rule – a system which was then adapted by the British Mandate and later by the State of Israel.[4] In addition to this, Arab Palestinian evangelicals, in particular, have been further isolated three times over as a minority.[5] First, as Arab Palestinians they are an ethnic minority among Jewish citizens in Israel,[6] a "trapped minority" as

---

4. The word *millet* comes from the Arabic word *millah* and literally means "nation." It refers to the separate legal courts under which communities (Muslims, Christians or Jews abiding by *sharia*, canon or *halakha* law, respectively) were allowed to rule themselves under their own system. After the Ottoman Tanzimat reforms (1839–1876), the term was used for legally protected religious minority groups.

Under Muslim rule, Arab Christians survived by paying a special tax (*jizya*) which supposedly allowed Jews and Christians (*dhimmi*) to keep their religions. It did not always guarantee their safety, so times of relative peace alternated with times of persecution. Despite their minority status, Arab and Syriac Christians contributed in a significant way to the golden era of Arab civilization. Until, in 1917, the Ottoman authorities implemented the *millet* system, which gave Christian communities authority to administer themselves. However, this only isolated the Christian minority even further and was undoubtedly a political strategy to "divide and conquer" the Christian communities. The modernization of the Ottoman Empire led to a new era of Arab political activism. Christians were able to participate in a growing Arab nationalist movement. This offered them the means of escape from their *dhimmi* status (see Zaky, *Naḥwa lāhūt moāṣir*). Influenced to some extent by education conducted by missionaries, Christians were at the forefront of efforts to create secular, nationalistic political orders. See Yéor, *Islam and Dhimmitude*; Cragg, *Arab Christian*; Sharkey, "Christianity in the Middle East"; Jenkins, *Lost History of Christianity*; Bailey and Bailey, *Who Are the Christians*; Khūry, *A'rab masihiyūn*; and Mansour, *Narrow Gate Churches*.

5. Tsimhoni, "Christians in Israel." See appendix 1.

6. Twenty percent of the total population of Israel (8,680,000) are Arabs. Palestinians in Israel are discriminated against in practice in almost all aspects of life. They remained under military rule until 1966 and, even after that, suffered from lack of government funding

Rabinowitz describes them.[7] Second, as Christians they are a religious minority among Arab Muslims.[8] Third, as evangelicals they are a denominational minority among Arab Christians.[9] In all of life – political, social and religious – Palestinian evangelicals in Israel form a unique minority with a very complex identity: Arab, Palestinian, Israeli, Christian and evangelical.[10] Being a three-fold trapped minority with an identity crisis will be discussed in chapter 3 as one of the factors that has influenced the Palestinian Baptist response to church conflict.

1.3 Palestinian Arab Culture

"Culture means humanity" according to Barth's definition. "In other words, humanity does not live in culture, but its very being is actualized and concretized as culture."[11] If humanity is a gift from God, then culture is also a gift from God. Yu argues, "All culture, no matter how inadequate, aims to

---

and development opportunities. Furthermore, some laws are declaratively discriminatory on religious-ethnic grounds (see Benziman and Mansour, *Dayare mishneh*).

7. According to Rabinowitz, "The concept of 'trapped minority,' developed herein from an analysis of the Palestinian citizens of Israel, adds to this debate. A trapped minority is a segment of a larger group spread across at least two states. Citizens of a state hegemonized by others, its members are alienated from political power. Unable to influence the definition of public goods or enjoy them, its members are at the same time marginal within their mother nation abroad." Rabinowitz, "Palestinian Citizens of Israel," 64.

8. Of the non-Jewish population (which is predominantly Muslim Arab), 8.06 percent are Christians. See https://www.cbs.gov.il/he/mediarelease/DocLib/2017/113/11_17_113e.pdf and https://www.cbs.gov.il/he/mediarelease/DocLib/2018/384/11_18_384b.pdf.

9. At the beginning of the twenty-first century, the mainline Protestant churches still preserved a strong presence in Israel/Palestine, mainly through their education and health institutions. In Israel, the growing Protestant churches are the evangelical denominations: Baptist, Assemblies of God, Christian and Missionary Alliance churches, Nazarene churches and Brethren congregations. These denominations consist in general of independent congregations, connected together in an association called the Convention of Evangelical Churches in Israel (CECI). While missionaries were the main decision-makers in these churches until recently, missionaries now play either a smaller role or no role at all. It should be mentioned that these churches are not recognized officially by the state of Israel. Only 4 percent of the Christian Arabs in Israel are evangelicals, the others being Oriental or Greek Orthodox, Catholic or non-evangelical Protestants (Lutherans, Anglicans, etc.).

10. Palestinian Christians are a distinctive ethno-religious group in Israeli society and, to a large extent, in other Middle Eastern countries (Munayer, "Ethnic Identity"). Palestinian Christian differentiation has been accompanied in the last decades by considerable tension in their relationship with both Israeli Jews and Muslim Arabs.

11. Barth, "Church and Culture," 338, as cited in Yu, "Culture from an Evangelical Perspective," 82.

achieve a certain degree of wholeness for human existence. The wholeness of humanity however can only be found in the fulfilment of humanity as the image of God,"[12] namely, us.

I present two values of Arab Palestinian culture which are relevant to this research. Understanding these values helped me to understand how the participants in this study made certain decisions during, and post, conflict.

1.3.1 Patriarchal Relations

The family is the basic unit of social organization and production in traditional and contemporary Arab society. It is patriarchal, pyramidally hierarchical – particularly with respect to sex and age – and extended.[13]

Literature concerning Middle Eastern dispute resolution traditions has stressed the superiority of the family, with its strong patriarchal orientation, as a main social structure in many Arab cultures, including the Palestinian community in Israel.[14] The success or failure of an individual member becomes that of the family as a whole.[15]

This centrality of the family as the basic socioeconomic unit is now being increasingly challenged by the state and other social institutions, internal and external confrontations facing Arab families and the struggle for social transformation.[16] Nonetheless the network of interdependent kinship relations continues to prevail. The father continues to wield authority, assume responsibility for the family and expect respect and unquestioning compliance with his instructions.[17] Thus, the continued dominance of the family as the basic unit of social organization and production has contributed to the diffusion

---

12. Yu, "Culture from an Evangelical Perspective," 82.

13. Barakat, *Arab World*, 23; Dodd, "Family Honor."

14. See Joseph, "Gender and Family"; Joseph, *Intimate Selving*; Barakat, *Arab World*; Abu-Lughod, "Zones of Theory." See also Jabbour, *Sulha*, and Sa'ar, "Lonely in Your Firm Grip."

15. Dodd states, "Members of a family share responsibilities and duties, and enjoy its successes and failures. They feel proud when a member of the family achieves success, and feel ashamed when a member of the family fails. . . . If some member of the family . . . does something shameful, this is considered a disgrace to the whole family. Therefore, the relationships between members of the family are simply relations between interconnected members of a cohesive unit. Each member plays his/her role, but remains closely linked to roles of the other members." Dodd, "Family Honor," 43.

16. See Barakat, *Arab World*; Abu-Lughod, "Zones of Theory"; and Sa'ar, "Lonely in Your Firm Grip."

17. Barakat, *Arab World*.

of patriarchal relations into similar situations within other social, religious and political institutions, such as work, school and church. In all of these, "A father figure rules over others, monopolizing authority, expecting strict obedience, and showing little tolerance of dissent."[18] According to Barakat, those in leadership positions such as leaders, employers and supervisors fill the top of the pyramid of authority: "Once in this position, the patriarch cannot be dethroned except by someone who is equally patriarchal."[19] Hisham Sharabi claims that because of the prevailing patriarchy, modernization has failed to break down patriarchal relations and forms, creating the present neo-patriarchal society which is neither traditional nor modern and which limits the participation of its members because of the continued dominance exercised by single leaders.[20]

Regarding Palestinian families in Israel, Sa'ar states:

> The Israeli-Palestinian families tend to be nuclear units that are embedded to different degrees, within patrilineal kinship networks, in which new and old concepts of familial relations are constantly being renegotiated. These networks resemble the classic Middle Eastern patriarchy (Kandiyoti 1988: 278) in the dynamics of power relations and co-operation between their segments as well as in the values of honour, shame, and group solidarity.[21]

Yet, despite the predominance of patriarchy, it is noteworthy that solidarity to a hierarchical group exists alongside a seemingly opposing force: an egalitarianism that encourages competition within the group (individualism). Sa'ar points out that Arabs tend to view themselves as individually autonomous and egalitarian, while also remaining highly focused on group dynamics and loyal to their families.[22] This dual focus on both the individual and the group

---

18. Barakat, 23.
19. Barakat, 23.
20. Sharabi calls it "dependent modernization." Sharabi, *Neopatriarchy*, as cited in Barakat, *Arab World*, 23.
21. Sa'ar, "Lonely in Your Firm Grip," 728.
22. Sa'ar, "Lonely in Your Firm Grip," 729. See also Ginat, *Blood Revenge*, and Ibn Khaldūn, *Moqaddimah*.

can also be seen in the Israeli Palestinian community.²³ This is evident in the young laity's respect for their pastors (which leads to compromise and a desire to save face), and yet requires them to share power, as discussed in chapter 4.

1.3.2 Honour and Shame

Pierre Bourdieu claims that honour is mostly found in societies where relationships with others have primacy over relationships with oneself.²⁴ In cultures where family and community take precedence over individuals, honour will likely be the guiding norm for its members. Members of societies that value honour and shame will ask not if a given action is "right" but rather if it "looks good."²⁵

Western scholarship has often claimed that one of the differences between Arab and Western culture is the emphasis in Arab culture on shame versus Western culture's focus on guilt. Shame and guilt play an important role in conflict management by encouraging opposing parties to cease their fighting without dishonour and shame. However, contemporary scholarship now problematizes this simplistic dichotomy. Barakat suggests that Arabs exhibit both shame and guilt-oriented behaviour. They do not necessarily experience guilt feelings about the same issues that motivate guilt in Westerners, such as sexual conduct. Arabs experience great guilt when they violate internalized values and expectations such as disappointing their parents, neglecting their friends, harming innocent people or promoting themselves at the expense of others or of their country.²⁶ Although honour and shame are most frequently described in societies in the Mediterranean region, honour is valued in various parts of the world and plays a role in all cultures to varying extents and at different points in history.²⁷

---

23. Sa'ar points out that, in the case of men, "The seeming contradiction between the norms of group loyalty and individualism is resolved, Men's normative striving for freedom and their proud competitive spirit therefore frame their loyalty and sacrifice as investments rather than as altruism." Sa'ar, "Lonely in Your Firm Grip," 729.

24. Bourdieu, "The Sentiment of Honour in Kabyle Society."

25. Baker, *Arabs, Islam, and the Middle East*, 23; Kraft, "Community and Identity."

26. According to Barakat, many Arabs living abroad experience extreme feelings of guilt about forsaking their countries, particularly in times of distress. Barakat, *Arab World*, 196–197.

27. Slaughter, "Salman Rushdie Affair," 193; Smith, "Murder in Jerba," 110; Kraft, "Community and Identity," 136. Honour/shame sentiments are growing in importance in the West even as they lose their centrality in communities only now coming into increased contact with modernization (deSilva, *Honor, Patronage, Kinship and Purity*, 26–27).

Dignity is important to every human being and any threat provokes a strong reaction. When a relationship has been broken, affirmation of dignity in others is essential for releasing the pain, especially when conflict was caused by dignity violations.[28] Honour/shame is evident in the data, as seen in chapter 5, and in the theological discussion. However, the significance differs between the pastors – who viewed dignity/shame as a fundamental factor in conflict management – and young laity who focus more on their rights rather than on honour/shame.

The above presentation shows, perhaps against simplistic stereotypes, that Arab Palestinian culture is complex. While in some matters it gives prominence to the values of honour and shame (an indication of outward, collectivist orientation), in others it actually inculcates guilt (an indication of inward, individualistic orientation) – so, too, with respect to collectivism and individualism.

Barakat suggests that traditional values continue to prevail, but that prevalence is not what distinguishes Arab culture. While the ongoing struggle between opposing value orientations – such as shame versus guilt or collectivism versus individualism – continues, this is a transitional period,[29] the impact of which is clearly discernible in church conflict.

1.4 Church Conflict

1.4.1 The Nature of Church Conflict

The existing literature in the field of local church conflict reveals a lack of practical models available to researchers for understanding both what transpires during church fights and the fundamental nature of conflict.[30] The existing literature has helpful suggestions but does not fully examine the nature

---

28. Hicks, *Dignity*.
29. Barakat, *Arab World*, 197.
30. The definition of conflict has several elements: Conflict is an intense form of interaction. Conflict involves two or more parties who have opposed interests, and they engage in action directed to the defence of their interests. Conflict is a pattern of interaction that is personal, aware and intermittent (Weber, *Theory of Social and Economic Organization*). Conflict is a struggle over things that are perceived as important. These may include values, beliefs, claims of status, power and resources, which one individual wishes to gain over another individual. Another interesting definition: "Conflict is a group process that is shaped by members' understanding about the nature of authority and by their own commitment and

of conflict. Leas provides a framework for identifying the different levels of conflict intensity.[31] Friedman deals with church conflict from a psychological perspective.[32] Brubaker deals with structure and power in church.[33] Becker et al. have identified three broad domains for conflict: cultural, economic and administrative issues.[34] Becker distinguishes between two types of conflict: within-frame conflict and between-frame conflict.[35] Like Becker, Rothman and Olson mention the two types but they prefer the terms "interest-based conflicts" and "identity-based conflicts."[36]

1.4.2 The Resolution of Church Conflict

Various authors have written works on the resolution of church conflict, such as Leas and Kittlaus, Parsons, McCollough, Qualben, Halverstadt and Hausken. Some others deal with conflict from a biblical perspective, such as Flynn, Gunnink, and Sande. All are excellent works but are nevertheless conducted in a Western context. Most works used in an Arab context are simply Arabic translations of Western-oriented literature. There is therefore a need for research into the nature of church conflict that is conducted in an Arabic context, especially with regard to Arab Palestinian evangelical churches, about which no research has been done in the area of conflict and culture.

1.4.3 Conflict and Power

Regarding the relationship between power and conflict, Blalock states that it is not possible to separate power and conflict processes without doing injustice to one or the other side, because they are closely intertwined.[37] He adds that the concept of power is essential in analyzing social processes such

---

that in most cases articulates and reinforces a public consensus on 'how we do things here'" (Becker, *Congregations in Conflict*, 43).
31. Leas, *Moving Your Church through Conflict*.
32. Friedman, *Generation to Generation*.
33. Brubaker, *Promise and Peril*.
34. Becker et al., "Straining at the Tie that Binds."
35. Becker, *Congregations in Conflict*.
36. According to Rothman and Olson, in defining identity-based conflicts, "Issues are abstract, complex, and difficult to define. Desired outcomes are intangible and difficult to identify . . . involve interpretive dynamics of history, psychology, culture, values, and beliefs of groups that are often, at least initially, framed in ways that are mutually exclusive." Rothman and Olson, "From Interests to Identities," 297.
37. Blalock, *Power and Conflict*, vii.

as conflict.[38] Himes defines conflict in terms of power: "Purposeful struggles between collective actors who use social power to defeat or remove opponents and to gain status, power, resources and other scarce values."[39]

In the existing literature on church conflict, a few researchers have linked power to church conflicts.[40] Wallace makes the point that conflict is inevitable and suggests that it is important to understand the abuse of power in order to deal with conflict. There is an intrinsic link between conflict and power. Every conflict involves the use of power. And yet no organization can function without the use of power, and the church is an organization.[41] He proposes four different causes of conflict: (1) the abuse of power, (2) the assignment of power, (3) the assumption of power and (4) the absence of power.

Max Weber's typology of power authority is categorized into three types: (1) legal or rational authority (positional power),[42] (2) traditional authority[43] and (3) charismatic authority.[44] Oswald, Heath and Heath describe different forms of power within the church. They note that structural power (or authority) is formal power people have as long as they hold a certain office.[45] Members with important church roles have greater access to other currencies

---

38. Blalock, 26.

39. Himes, *Conflict and Conflict Management*, 14.

40. Russell has shown that understanding power is the key to understanding the nature of social actions (Russell, *Power*). In this way, power can be used to explain goal-oriented social activity in any culture, and it can also be seen within a church setting, where members take part in actions in order to achieve a certain purpose as a group or fulfil a desire as an individual. Therefore, the church needs to understand the nature of power and how it is used in order to understand the dynamics of social activity such as conflict.

41. Wallace, *Control in Conflict*, 47.

42. Legal or organizational authority is usually far more impersonal than the other forms of power and involves rules and policies that are set in place to enforce the will of the organization. Legal/organizational authority is the antithesis of traditional authority. Weber, *Theory of Social and Economic Organization*.

43. Traditional authority is based upon traditional rules and regulations that have been passed down between generations as cultural values. This type of authority is different to organizational power because its foundation is in personal relationships and loyalty that are grown over time, not through organizational hierarchy. In this way, the leader is perceived as a "chief." Weber, *Theory of Social and Economic Organization*, 341.

44. Charismatic authority can be found in certain individuals who have a personality which makes them stand out from other ordinary people, as they tend to be treated as having exceptional powers or qualities. This type of authoritative power is socially earned as the group recognizes and chooses to follow the charismatic leader. Weber, *Theory of Social and Economic Organization*, 358.

45. Oswald, Heath, and Heath, *Beginning Ministry Together*.

of power. Those who hold certain positions for many years are very powerful. It is often the case that church leaders cannot remove them from office because of the huge level of informal power that they hold within the system. Because they are well known (reputational power), they have access to many informal groups in the parish (coalitional power). Because they know most of the members of their church congregation, they know who to contact when their position faces threats (communicational power).

Brubaker notes structure is important in any organizational system because it formally situates power (authority). A clear decision-making structure communicates who has the right to make certain decisions. Thus, power that is seen as legitimate is less likely to be challenged. He adds that a healthy structure both confers power and limits its exercise and that bylaws exist in part to protect the church and congregants from the abuse of power by individual members. Structure allocates power, so when we mess with power arrangements, we should expect conflict.[46]

As will be demonstrated in chapters 4 and 5, pastors and laity misused power. The structural imbalance in power between the pastor and laity is a manifestation of the huge difference between their *theologies and cultures*.

1.4.4 Church Split/Exit: Impact of Congregational Characteristics

Chou explores factors that put congregations at a higher risk of developing conflict-related exit, including the characteristics of their leaders, the social composition of their members and their theological perspectives:[47]

1.4.4.1 Perceived legitimacy of leaders

Research has shown that religious leadership is a common cause of intra-congregational conflicts.[48] Leaders (pastors, priests, etc.) greatly affect the stability of their congregations. Whether or not the members of the congregation will be willing to follow these leaders depends on the leaders' legitimacy

---

46. Brubaker, *Promise and Peril*, 39–40.
47. Chou, "Impact of Congregational Characteristics."
48. Becker, "Congregational Models and Conflict"; Becker, *Congregations in Conflict*; Herman, "Conflict in the Church"; Shin and Park, "Analysis of Causes of Schisms"; Wood, *Leadership in Voluntary Organizations*.

in their eyes.[49] Based on all the research so far, older, male leaders with more experience and education have more legitimacy than younger, female, less-experienced and less-educated leaders.[50] Shin and Park discovered that in Korean American churches, the stability of congregations is positively related to the educational level of the head pastor.[51] This factor was similarly seen in one of the cases in this research, where the younger generation rebelled against their pastor who was less educated. The legitimacy of leaders also grows with age and tenure. Exit due to conflict is more likely to take place after the arrival of a young, newly ordained minister.[52]

1.4.4.2 Social homogeneity of members

Collins argues that members with similar cultural backgrounds are more loyal to their organizations.[53] Congregations with a diverse membership are more likely to experience conflict-related exit, since members of diverse social backgrounds have different lifestyles and expectations. There are two likely causes of group homogeneity in voluntary associations such as churches. First, new members are recruited mainly through the network ties of existing members particularly if their socio-demographic characteristics resemble those of older members. Second, members are more likely to stay if they are similar to the rest of the group, while those who are atypical are likely to leave.[54] Therefore, voluntary associations, including congregations, tend to be homogeneous.[55] Socially diverse groups are also less likely to reach consensus and are more likely to experience conflicts within the group.[56]

---

49. Collins, *Conflict Sociology*.
50. Chou, "Impact of Congregational Characteristics."
51. Shin and Park, "Analysis of Causes of Schisms."
52. Becker, *Congregations in Conflict*; Herman, "Conflict in the Church."
53. Collins, *Conflict Sociology*.
54. Popielarz and McPherson, "On the Edge or In Between."
55. Other research shows that there is more conflict in congregations with greater racial diversity (Emerson and Smith, *Divided by Faith*).
56. Becker examines intra-congregational conflicts by classifying congregations into different types: house of worship, family, community and leader models. Becker found that the quantity and quality of intra-congregational conflicts are associated with these congregational models. For example, community congregations have twice the number of conflicts as family congregations. Family congregations are more likely to fight over church buildings, while community and leader congregations tend to disagree on contemporary social issues. Becker argues that local congregational cultures reflected in these models explain intra-congregational conflicts better than other variables such as size, polity and liberal or conservative orientation

1.4.4.3 The charismatic movement

A congregation's members are more likely to submit to leaders who have important resources such as exclusive control over information in areas of uncertainty.[57] Therefore, congregations are more likely to experience internal conflict when certain members consider themselves to have access to "special revelations." The rise of the charismatic movement,[58] with its emphasis on the subjective experience of the individual, spontaneity and lay participation, and less emphasis on formal church regulation, has caused challenges for many congregations.[59] In this research the charismatic influence was found to have played a role in contributing to both tensions and conflict resolution.

There are several reasons why congregations affected by the charismatic movement may be more vulnerable to internal conflicts. First, the charismatic movement emphasizes individual, subjective experience. As individual experiences and interpretations may vary, congregations are more likely to experience conflict when each experience and interpretation is equally valued and a consensus cannot be reached. Second, the charismatic movement places less value on hierarchical or formal authority and supports lay participation.[60] This structure is more prone to intra-church conflicts than a centralized and hierarchical structure.[61]

Data from the National Congregations Study (NCS) shows that the probability of conflict-related exit is lower among racially and economically

---

that assume a homogeneous effect on intra-congregational conflicts. Becker, *Congregations in Conflict*.

57. Collins, *Conflict Sociology*.

58. The charismatic movement began around 1960 among Protestants and in 1967 among Roman Catholics. It refers to groups that emphasize the spiritual gifts of speaking in tongues and healing. They believe that miracles and other supernatural occurrences, such as prophecy and healing, are expected to be present in the lives of Christians.

59. Francis, Lankshear, and Jones, "Influence of the Charismatic Movement"; Jaichandran and Madhav, "Pentecostal Spirituality in a Postmodern World"; Poloma, *Charismatic Movement*. Although research has found that congregations affected by the charismatic movement show greater membership growth (Francis, Lankshear, and Jones, "Influence of the Charismatic Movement"), many experience conflicts (Starke and Dyck, "Upheavals in Congregations").

60. Some argue that the emphasis on shared eldership came from Brethren leaders who became charismatic in the 1960s.

61. Chou, "Impact of Congregational Characteristics."

homogeneous congregations and those with older leaders, while it is higher among congregations linked to the charismatic movement.[62]

1.5 Theology of Reconciliation

1.5.1 Introduction

What is a theology of reconciliation? Can we put such a theology into practice? What implications would it have for Palestinian Christian ministries and church conflicts in the midst of the ongoing Israeli-Palestinian conflict?[63]

Numerous scholars with experience of world conflict situations have contributed to the development of such a theology. I neither intend in this thesis to explore the biblical roots nor to list all contributions to this field. However, I will mention some of them.

Generally, theologians have focused on "vertical" reconciliation between humanity and God, with very little having been done on the "horizontal" reconciliation between peoples.[64] Understanding the social aspect of the theology of reconciliation to be a secondary result of personal salvation (vertical) as opposed to an inherent aspect of reconciliation with God (horizontal) has caused debates among theologians.[65]

Theologians such as Gunton and Webster discuss reconciliation primarily as a vertical concept with the horizontal seen as secondary.[66] Torrance offers a horizontal and vertical view of reconciliation theology, seeing the

---

62. Chou, "Impact of Congregational Characteristics." Researchers have argued that theologically liberal congregations are prone to intra-congregational conflicts (Hoge, *Division in the Protestant House*; Roof, *Community and Commitment*; Takayama, "Strains, Conflicts, and Schisms"), an argument which is supported by empirical research (Becker, "Congregational Models and Conflict"; Hoge, *Division in the Protestant House*). In this research, however, Zionist theology was identified as one of the main causes of conflict in one church, though not one of the case studies.

63. The situation in Israel/Palestine has been constantly shaped over the last century by violence and by economic, cultural and religious division. On both sides of the conflict there are Christians who have been living as minority groups, and who are not always acknowledged within wider Israeli and Palestinian society. This lack of recognition has increased their sense of feeling disconnected. While contemporary theological positions have attempted to voice the concerns of each cultural group, this has sometimes strengthened the division between the groups, particularly as the international community take different sides in the conflict.

64. Volf, "The Social Meaning of Reconciliation."

65. Robinson, *Embodied Peacebuilding*.

66. Gunton, "Towards a Theology of Reconciliation"; Webster, "Ethics of Reconciliation."

ministry of reconciliation as God's way of aiding humanity.[67] In these writings reconciliation is initiated by God alone. Schreiter agrees with this approach but sees it as extending to the community.[68] On the other side of the debate are theologians such as Volf, Tutu and De Gruchy, who see the horizontal aspect of reconciliation as being an undeniable part of the vertical and believe there is a danger that reconciliation's social implications are left to politics while its vertical ideals are exemplified theologically.[69]

Scholars use different terms to define their perspectives on reconciliation theology, including repentance, apology, forgiveness, justice, truth and peace. Some associate reconciliation with forgiveness and repentance. Liechty, in the Northern Ireland context, sees reconciliation as involving the complementary dynamic of *forgiveness and repentance*.[70] Schreiter takes the same approach, seeing reconciliation taking place with an initiation from God leading the victim who receives divine healing to forgive – and this forgiveness in turn inspiring repentance.[71]

Other scholars associate reconciliation with *justice and truth*. DeGruchy, in the South African context, sees justice as the primary element in reconciliation. For him, reconciliation is the restoration of justice, which means the reestablishment of broken relationships, and truth acts as liberator if it works alongside justice and reconciliation.[72] Isasi-Díaz also sees reconciliation under the category of justice. Volf argues against these approaches, believing a focus on justice only will eventually lead to injustice, which is why justice should be at work under the greater structure of reconciliation.[73] However, Volf and DeGruchy agree that the meaning of the main theological concepts within reconciliation are relative to the particularities of a social context, the South African for DeGruchy and the Croation for Volf.[74] Like DeGruchy in the South African context, Volf addresses the tension between liberation and reconciliation theologies by analysing the Kairos Document, which puts

---

67. Torrance, *Theological Grounds for Advocating Forgiveness*.
68. Schreiter, *Ministry of Reconciliation*.
69. Robinson, *Embodied Peacebuilding*.
70. Liechty, "Putting Forgiveness in Its Place."
71. Schreiter, *Ministry of Reconciliation*.
72. DeGruchy, *Reconciliation*.
73. Volf, "Social Meaning of Reconciliation."
74. Robinson, *Embodied Peacebuilding*.

justice and peace as opposing concepts within the larger pursuit of reconciliation as if seeking reconciliation equals giving up the struggle for liberation.[75]

Some scholars, such as Liechty and Clegg in the Northern Ireland context, use various concepts to explain the theology of reconciliation, seeing the uniting dynamics of forgiveness, repentance, truth and justice as interconnected. Volf adds the concepts of remembrance and embrace to these. Lederach also created a creative model that shows how certain elements work together in bringing reconciliation: truth, mercy, justice and peace.[76] Stevens and Liechty amended Lederach's model to include forgiveness and repentance as opposed to mercy and peace.[77] Liechty argues that the strength of Lederach's model is best when all components work together equally. Stevens discusses the inherent tensions between justice/truth and peace/mercy.[78]

Robinson, through her work on reconciliation in Northern Ireland, proposes a model that takes into account the influence of the social context on theological understandings of reconciliation. This model uses the four most common concepts from reconciliation theology: truth, justice, repentance and forgiveness. The concepts are divided into two tendencies: truth and justice (liberating tendencies) and repentance and forgiveness (atoning tendencies), all of which exist under the umbrella of reconciliation theology. Influenced by social context, the movement within the theology of reconciliation is seen in a modified version of Lederach's model that takes into account a sliding scale model of the swing from an emphasis on liberating tendencies (truth and justice), with a goal of freedom, to atoning tendencies (repentance and forgiveness), with a goal of peace. An emphasis on one tendency in any given context is based on the goal of those who are adhering to the theology. If the goal is freedom in a given context then there is a move towards liberating tendencies. If the desired goal is peace, then one sees a movement towards atoning tendencies. The above presentation shows that work is still ongoing within the field of the theology of reconciliation and its contested themes.

---

75. Robinson.

76. A model based on Psalm 85:10. Lederach, *Building Peace*.

77. Stevens, *Land of Unlikeness*; Liechty, "Putting Forgiveness in Its Place."

78. For more information about the history of theology of reconciliation in the academy, see Robinson, *Embodied Peacebuilding*.

1.5.2 Palestinian Protestant Theology of Reconciliation[79]

Katanacho finds that a Palestinian Protestant theology of reconciliation exists in five major forms: *biographies, apologies, liberation theology, reconciliation theologies* and *kairos theology*.[80]

First, *biographies*, such as those of Chacour, Rantisi and Raheb, provide personal reflections.[81] Raheb and Rantisi describe the hardships of living in the West Bank under Israeli occupation. These writings promote peace instead of war and are in favour of a loving God instead of a militant one. They raise thoughtful questions about the justice of God. The biographers, argues Katanacho, present the issues "in very general terms: Palestinians are the oppressed; Israelis are the oppressors." They over-emphasize cultural concerns and have limited insights into biblical interpretation, especially regarding militant Judaism.[82]

Second, the *apologies*, such as those of Shorrosh and Shehadeh.[83] These writings, argues Katanacho, "are theologically supportive of a national Jewish state and find it difficult to find a theological justification for a Palestinian one. This belief, accompanied by sharp criticism of Islam, hinders their effectiveness among Palestinians."[84] The spread of dispensationalism among Palestinian Evangelicals and its widespread influence in Israel have provoked a Palestinian Christian response, such as that provided by Katanacho and Isaac who advocate a Christological ownership of the land and provide a biblical study responding to dispensational Zionism.[85]

---

79. In the early 1990s, Palestinian contemporary theology started to be developed by pastors and activists who had mostly received their education in Western universities.

80. Katanacho, "Palestinian Protestant Theological Responses"; Katanacho, *Land of Christ*.

81. See Chacour, *We Belong to the Land* and *Blood Brothers*; Rantisi, *Blessed Are the Peacemakers*; and Raheb, *Bethlehem Besieged*.

82. Katanacho, "Palestinian Protestant Theological Responses," 290.

83. See Shorrosh, *Jesus, Prophecy & Middle East*; *Islam Revealed*; and *True Furqan*. See also Shehadeh, "Ishmael in Relation to the Promises of Abraham" and "A Comparison and a Contrast."

84. Katanacho, "Palestinian Protestant Theological Responses," 292.

85. See Katanacho, *The Land of Christ*, and Isaac, *From Land to Lands*.

Third, *liberation theology*,[86] such as that of Ateek and Raheb.[87] Ateek, in his book *Justice and Only Justice,* calls for his readers to "de-stereotype" Western images of the people of the Middle East, to "de-zionize" the Bible, and to "de-mythologize" the State of Israel.[88] Ateek focuses much of his attention on truth and justice as essential precursors to peace; for him peace begins by doing justice. Nonetheless, Ateek's socio-political justice does not present the full picture of biblical justice. Raheb is another important voice. He argues that post-Auschwitz theology has not paid attention to Palestinian suffering, due to hermeneutical flaws. Raheb proposes corrective interpretive principles that are more sensitive to Palestinian cultural concerns. He concludes that the Church must promote justice and righteousness in creative nonviolent resistance, which will hopefully lead to peace and coexistence between Palestinians and Israelis.[89]

Fourth, *reconciliation theologies*: *sulha* theology (*sulha* means peace or settlement, and it is the traditional Palestinian model) and *musalaha* theology (*musalaha* means reconciliation). *Sulha* theology focuses on Christian-Muslim relations. Abu El-Assal and Younan are examples of *sulha* theologians. They emphasize the common ground between Christians and Muslims, focusing on coexistence, dialogue and compromise, in order to avoid confrontations. Katanacho argues that by placing less emphasis on sin and the need for salvation, Younan attempts to provide an incarnational model that will be less likely to offend non-Christians.[90] *Sulha* theologians have contributed to building bridges with Muslims, but it seems that they tend to compromise their doctrine.[91]

Musalaha theology focusses on Messianic Jewish and Palestinian evangelicals' relationships, an approach adopted by Massad and Munayer.[92] Massad

---

86. According to Ateek, "Liberation theology is a way of speaking prophetically and contextually to a particular situation, especially where oppression, suffering, and injustice have long reigned." Ateek, *Justice and Only Justice*, 6.

87. See Ateek, *Justice and Only Justice* and *Palestinian Theology of Liberation*, and Raheb, *I Am a Palestinian Christian*.

88. Ateek, *Justice and Only Justice*, 159.

89. Katanacho, "Palestinian Protestant Theological Responses."

90. Katanacho, "Palestinian Protestant Theological Responses," 295.

91. Katanacho.

92. See Massad, "Theological Foundation for Reconciliation," and Munayer, "Relations between Religions in Historic Palestine."

focuses on forgiveness and repentance and makes justice *unnecessary* to reconciliation. He attempts to reconcile Palestinian Christians and Messianic Jews along the following lines: "Let us pursue not justice but a community of love. We will never reach perfect justice, but let us pursue confession, repentance, forgiveness, and love, which will prepare us to embrace one another as members of one body and will allow us to experience reconciliation."[93] Unlike Massad, Munayer asserts that justice is a necessary condition for reconciliation, agreeing with Volf that there can be no justice without embrace and no genuine embrace without justice.[94] Munayer clarifies that the cross "models a response" for reconciling Arabs and Jews. First, it transforms our identity from sinners, victims or oppressors into atoned and redeemed followers of Christ. Second, it transforms our interpretation to our reality and lead us to see others in relation to creation and redemption. It requires forgiveness, restitution, and a favourable socio-political atmosphere.[95]

Fifth, regarding *Palestinian kairos theology*, Katanacho sees that the Palestinian Kairos focuses on faith, love, hope and the mission of the church and the land, and it develops the political reading of the Bible into an ecumenical, post-liberal, theo-political reading. It starts by describing the current painful reality of Palestinians using biblical categories in a healthy dialogue between the contemporary reality and the biblical reality, and it unapologetically presents a theocentric reality, rooted in God the Creator and in our saviour Jesus Christ. It prioritizes and seeks socio-political justice.[96]

As we have seen, different voices from various contexts and cultures have contributed to the field of the theology of reconciliation. In this research, I will bring an additional perspective of reconciliation theology – namely, the Palestinian political context and culture. Nonetheless, it differs from the works of the Palestinian Christians listed above, in that I neither conduct my research with regard to the inter-ethnic conflict or Christian-Muslim or Messianic-Palestinian evangelical relations. I examine the way Palestinian Baptists perceive their theology of reconciliation in regard to church conflict.

---

93. Massad, "Theological Foundation for Reconciliation," 273–274, as cited in Katanacho, "Palestinian Protestant Theological Responses," 296–297.
94. Munayer and Loden, *Through My Enemy's Eyes*.
95. Munayer, "Reconciliation from a Palestinian Point of View."
96. Katanacho, *Land of Christ*.

In my discussion I look into the transportability of Miroslav Volf's model from an inter-ethnic conflict to one that takes place within a single church and a single ethnic group – one which is nevertheless embedded in an intractable ethno-national conflict. This indeed should be one of the contributions of the thesis: the transportability of the model to a different cultural setting and also the lessons that this particular theology can contribute to ethnic conflict resolution on a much deeper level. Additionally, my research generates a local theory regarding a Palestinian theology of reconciliation and also informs Volf's model.

1.5.3 Miroslav Volf's Theology of Reconciliation

My decision to draw upon Volf's theology of reconciliation implies the following: (1) that the analysis will be undertaken from a Protestant perspective; (2) that the horizontal element is intrinsic to the vertical element of reconciliation; and (3) that truth, justice, repentance and forgiveness are each significant concepts within the theology of reconciliation.

Volf's context has a uniquely blended perspective and identity. As a Croatian, he is well-placed to examine theology from a non-Western perspective, while, as an American, simultaneously speaking as an insider to the West.[97]

Among contemporary theologians, Volf has made a significant contribution to the topic of reconciliation.[98] Volf was reared in a Baptist tradition.

---

97. Miroslav Volf is the Henry B. Wright Professor of Theology at Yale Divinity School, as well as the Director of the Yale Centre for Faith and Culture. He has a BA from the Evangelical-Theological Faculty in Osijek, Croatia, an MA from Fuller Theological Seminary, and doctoral and post-doctoral degrees (with highest honours) from the University of Tübingen in Germany. He is the author of over fifteen books and more than seventeen academic articles. His books include highly regarded works such as *Exclusion and Embrace* (1996); *After Our Likeness* (1998); *Allah: A Christian Response* (2011); *Work in the Spirit: Toward a Theology of Work*; *A Public Faith: On How Followers of Christ Should Serve the Common Good* (2011); *Free of Charge: Giving and Forgiving in a Culture Stripped of Grace* (2005); and *The End of Memory: Remembering Rightly in a Violent World* (2006). http://faith.yale.edu/people/miroslav-volf.

98. Volf received the 2002 Grawemeyer Award for his book *Exclusion and Embrace: A Theological Exploration of Identity, Otherness and Reconciliation*, and this publication was also included among a list of the 100 best religious books of the twentieth century by Christianity Today. Writing this book came about as the result of a challenge Volf received from Moltmann in 1993 – "But can you embrace a četnik?" (in reference to the Serbian fighters who had violently attacked and killed his people) (Volf, *Exclusion and Embrace*, 9). Volf's response to this question has grown into an ongoing call to forgiveness and "embrace" in a violent world. http://faith.yale.edu/people/miroslav-volf.

He developed his theology of reconciliation in the context of the Balkan war and out of a deep concern for the implications of the Christian faith for the contemporary world.[99] He addresses the question of the social meaning of reconciliation from various angles and offers strong, biblical grounds for his theology.

I briefly present the key themes that emerge from Volf's work in relation to a theology of reconciliation between peoples: (1) *Remembrance*. Volf suggests that we need to remember wrongdoings rightly, an act which involves four elements – remembering truthfully, therapeutically, responsibly and in reconciling ways. (2) *Forgiveness*. Forgiveness is an unconditional divine gift; God forgives, and we make God's forgiveness our own and pass it on. (3) *Justice*. Justice can only be pursued adequately within the horizon of the will to embrace, yet embrace is conditioned by the realization of justice. (4) *Embrace*. Embrace involves the will to readjust our identity and make space for "the other." It encapsulates four requirements: opening arms, waiting, closing arms and the opening of arms again. These four themes are "easy to formulate, but complicated to fully understand and difficult to practice,"[100] and they will be discussed, applied and evaluated in the analysis of the conflict management approaches of Palestinian Baptists in chapters 6 to 9.

1.6 Plan of the Thesis

Following this introduction, which forms chapter 1 of the thesis, in chapter 2 I explain the three phases of my research plan, my methodological decisions and my own position in the field.

Chapter 3 gives an outline of the main features of the institutional field of Baptist churches in Israel, including structures of power, protagonists, main splits and the main discursive issues that preoccupy the community – identity being first among them. The flat structure and the absence of a patriarch in a patriarchal community, the low level of institutionalization and lack of assets, the pastors' struggle over livelihood and power and the young laity's "rebellion" against patriarchy "encouraged" splits/exits.

---

99. Volf was born in Osijek, Croatia, surrounded by different religions (traditional Christians and Muslims) and ethnicities (Serbs, Croats and Bosnians). Much of his reflection has grown out of his observation of the war that took place in his homeland for many years.

100. Volf, *Flourishing*, 175.

In chapter 4 I analyze the nature and causes of intra-church conflict in three case studies (case A, case B and case C) of churches that split. I argue that the clash between pastors and laity is in fact a clash between each side's strong combination of *theology and culture* working against the other side's. The pastors were influenced theologically by traditional, non-evangelical Palestinian churches and culturally by patriarchal, hierarchical tradition (which combined powerfully to strengthen their desire to maintain their dominant position at church). The younger generation who rebelled against their pastors were influenced culturally by secular, Western ideas of individual rights and democracy and theologically by Baptist theology, through which they justified their demands to share power in terms of the "priesthood of all believers."

In chapter 5, I argue that these same main factors of *theology and culture* contributed to the ways the conflicts were dealt with from the perspective of the pastor and the perspective of the laity. Again, because of the clash of those factors from each side, the conflicts were not resolved effectively. This chapter reveals that in resolving church conflict, Palestinian Baptists engage in four different practices, all operating in the field, each with a distinct (sometimes contradictory) perception, tradition and approach to conflict resolution. There are two *cultural* approaches – (1) Israeli litigation or an alternative legal approach and (2) a traditional Palestinian *sulha* approach, – and two *theological* approaches – (1) the hierarchical approach of traditional Palestinian churches and (2) a Western-Baptist approach. The pastors' *cultural-theological* approach is *sulha* combined with the traditional hierarchical approach of the Palestinian church. The laity's *cultural-theological* approach is alternative-legalistic and Western Baptist. In the case studies a shift is observed from the first generation (traditional), desiring to maintain the status quo, to the younger generation (modern culture), seeking change and power.

I also argue that pastors and laity held different implicit theologies of forgiveness and reconciliation which were all imperfect. *Sulha* lacks internal forgiveness and justice. Alternative-legalistic prioritizes justice over relationships. In the hierarchical approach the pastor is the one who implements justice and the laity is expected to obey. Western Baptist theology is more individualistic and lacks some aspects of Palestinian culture. This calls for a more comprehensive reconciliation theology. As I show in the second half of the thesis, Volf's theory might contribute to the solution.

In chapters 6 to 9, I progress to the theological discussion. In these chapters we see the fundamental significance of the combination of *theology and culture*. Nonetheless, this time the combination is necessary to the solution. I theologically evaluate the four conflict management approaches used by Palestinian Baptists during their church conflicts in terms of Volf's four themes. In chapter 6 I discuss remembrance; in chapter 7, forgiveness; in chapter 8, justice; and in chapter 9, embrace.

I also evaluate the applicability of these theological themes within the Palestinian Baptist context and argue that Volf's *theological* model needs *cultural* translation in order to be applicable to this context.

Finally, in chapter 10, I bring together the whole thesis, summarising the arguments and findings, presenting my recommendations, emphasising the contribution of this work, its limitations and imperfections, and recommending further research in some areas.

CHAPTER 2

Methodology

In this chapter, I first explain my epistemological perspective. Then I describe the methodological decisions made and why. After that I describe the three phases of my research plan. This is followed by a discussion of ethical concerns, including the choice to study a sensitive topic. Finally, I discuss my own position in the field and how this influenced my own reflexivity in collecting and analysing the data.

2.1 Theoretical Framework and Epistemological Perspective

2.1.1 Practical Theology

This research is located in practical theology. Practical theology is a complex theological enterprise.[1] It draws from the empirical research methods of the social sciences in order to explore and describe the nature of values, religious beliefs and practices.[2] While theologians working in the field of biblical studies interpret Scripture, and systematic theology is concerned with the interpretation of doctrine and tradition, practical theology is concerned with church practice. It examines theories and assumptions underlying a particular practice and points to alternatives.

Practical theology dialogues with the other theological disciplines. It provides a balance between theoretical inquiry (including understanding, evaluating and criticizing) and practical discipline (guiding and transforming

---

1. Swinton and Mowat, *Practical Theology*.
2. Kurian, *Encyclopedia of Christian Civilization*.

practices). It can be found within the tension between the script of revelation (scripture, doctrine and tradition) and the continuing innovative performance of the gospel.[3]

2.1.2 Epistemological Perspective

The epistemological position I take in this research is that of a Palestinian evangelical. Like Jones and Yarhouse, I advocate critical realism: "We are critical realists which means that we believe that there is a real world out there where it is possible to know and know truly ('realism'), but we also believe that our theories and hypotheses about that world, and our religious presuppositions and beliefs about reality, colour and shape our capacity to know the world ('critical realism')."[4]

I have a theocentric view of the natural world, and my evangelical understanding is affected by my experience, culture, personal belief and background.[5] I am neither a theologian nor a sociologist; I am a socio-theologian. Volf's approach works well with this perspective, for, to him, practice and belief are always interconnected, and Volf talks about both, calling for a specific practice in light of a Christian faith.[6]

Another issue to discuss is my bias, which is part of a conscious choice to do theologically-committed, action-oriented research. Researcher bias happens when the researcher's personal beliefs, experiences and values influence the study methodology and results. The insider-researcher should take care to avoid directing the researcher's own viewpoint onto interviewees or data analysis. When an insider-researcher overcomes personal bias, richer themes may be explored.[7] Multiple sources of data and methods of data collection, sharing and checking interpretations with informants and the support of my advisory team helped me to overcome my bias as an insider.

---

3. Swinton and Mowat, *Practical Theology*.
4. Jones and Yarhouse, *Homosexuality*, 14–15.
5. As someone whose childhood faith formation was in the Greek Orthodox Church, my theological agency is shaped by sacramental sense in a way that is different to my current Baptist church. I have carried that in my flesh from Orthodox tradition to Baptist tradition, and it has managed to stay alive despite the transition. Because *habitus* is not only generated by field practice but can also be transposed across them, similarities appear across different fields that have little or no relationship to each other. See Wigg-Stevenson, *Ethnographic Theology*.
6. Volf, "Theology for a Way of Life."
7. Smyth and Holian, "Credibility Issues in Research."

2.2 Choice of Qualitative Methodology and Methods Used in the Study

2.2.1 Theology and Fieldwork

In this research I want to understand how Palestinian Baptists relate to church conflict; I want to explore the complexity of their situation as a threefold trapped minority, and its impact on managing their church conflicts. Systematic theology is relevant for reflecting on their practices theologically but not as a way to frame the complex formation of their lived situation.[8] Volf argues that theologians have often done theology as a theoretical science, which has contributed to a sense that theology is unrelated to real life.[9] I agree with Volf that the purpose of theology is not simply to deliver knowledge about God but to serve as a way of life. Fieldwork has the potential to close the gap between what we say about the church and how we act as the church. When theologians look at the complex realities of local ecclesial situations like those of the Palestinian Baptists, this may help in doing theology that serves the church and God's redemptive work in the world.[10]

Scharen argues that the social science of Pierre Bourdieu suggests a way to do fieldwork in theology which may serve to get the church involved in what God is doing in the world.[11] Bourdieu's approach to fieldwork includes interviews, participation and other research methods. It also includes theoretical concepts such as *capital, field* and *habitus* and methodological frames such as *reflexivity*: "Yet it is grounded even for Bourdieu in a religious frame, making clear his openness to move in the direction of fieldwork in theology."[12]

---

8. See Fulkerson, *Places of Redemption*, 8–9.

9. Volf, "Theology for a Way of Life," 247.

10. In recent decades, there has been a tendency among theologians to turn to social science methodologies in order to better understand how cultural situations shape lived faith such as that found in the church. This has constructed new theological thinking for contemporary ecclesiology while also making it more complex. While a large amount of theological research has focused on systematic and philosophical theology as its primary discussion in the mid-twentieth century, it presents a new tension between the particular and the universal in theological reflection. A change to practice began in the 1980s as theologians began to think critically about the relationship between faith and action. Some suggest that a movement toward culture and practice might be able to bridge the gap between the world of academic theology and the lived experience of real life churches. See Snyder, "Theological Ethnography."

11. Scharen, *Fieldwork in Theology*.

12. Scharen, 112.

With regard to *habitus*, Paul Fiddes speaks about an interaction between the ecclesial model of the body of Christ and models of body developed in the social sciences, such as *habitus*, which are likely to be drawn on in empirical studies:

> For instance, there is the model of body *habitus*. The self is understood as an "embodied history" where the body is a site in which social structures are internalised over a length of time. Social customs and conventions are "written" on the body, and this *habitus* determines our response to the situation in which we are placed. What is learned by the body, Bourdieu comments, is not something that one has but something that one is. The *habitus* is thus an embodied "system of structured, structuring dispositions, which is constituted in practice and is always orientated towards practical functions" [Bourdieu, *The Logic of Practice*, 52]. Bourdieu aims to overcome the dualism between subject and object and there is obvious overlap here with the Christian model of the body of Christ, which is as we have seen a highly participative idea.[13]

For the last several decades, practical theologians, theological ethicists and liberation theologians have used ethnography for theological reflection; they use ethnographic research methods for creating thick descriptions that ground their projects, seeking to establish "what is" before engaging theological resources to argue for "what ought to be." There is a new theological-ethnography movement that claims a field of study can have "embedded and embodied within its life substantive contributions to theology and ethics."[14] I agree that the turn to fieldwork in the study of the church is an encouraging development in contemporary ecclesiology. According to Snyder, "Pluralism and modernity have challenged old lines of authority, a history of colonization

---

13. Fiddes, "Ecclesiology and Ethnography," 32.

14. Wigg-Stevenson, *Ethnographic Theology*, 167. In the early 2000s, some young scholars started to accept ethnographic methods as a way of grounding their theological work. They developed theoretical and theological arguments for theology as ethnography and not only applied from social science; they viewed ethnographic studies as theological work. See Snyder, "Theological Ethnography."

demands healthy practices of humility"[15] – but perhaps it also demands decolonization of the mind, as it were, by bringing power and history into the analysis.

The purpose of this research is to analyze the conflict management approaches used in Palestinian Baptist intra-church conflict in Israel and the development of a culturally compatible theological model of reconciliation in churches.

Bourdieu's theory of practice enriches the conceptual framework for understanding social and cultural practices in wider institutional and cultural contexts. I follow Bourdieu's approach by using multiple qualitative methods to create thick descriptions:[16] participant-observation, case studies, semi-structured interviews, in-depth interviews, recording, the writing of field notes, field mapping, relevant documents and a focus group. I will explain each data collection technique (field mapping and case studies will be discussed in section 2.3).

2.2.2 Participant Observation

Participant observation is an important tool in this research. In keeping with the holistic understanding of knowledge presented above, it allows one to trace non-verbal knowledge, including embodied, symbolic and practical knowledge. Juxtaposing these forms of knowledge against what I obtained from formal interviews and documents allowed me to see gaps and contradictions. According to Bourdieu, the language of the body is more ambiguous and overdetermined than ordinary language.[17] It reveals the multiple voices and interpretations that always exist within a single cultural setting and people's agency in negotiating meaning, interest and power. Hence, it opens a window into the culture's internal mechanisms of both change and reproduction. As I explain in chapters 3 and 4, participant observation attempts to understand the multilevel influences of the historical, theological, social, economic, cultural and ecological systems of subjects' perspectives and

---

15. Snyder, "Theological Ethnography," 5.
16. Qualitative research is referred to in social science as interpretive or descriptive research (Denzin and Lincoln, *Collecting and Interpreting*, 4) and involves the collection, study and analysis of empirical materials; it is phenomenological, inductive, explanatory and process oriented.
17. Bourdieu, *Outline of a Theory of Practice*, 120.

behaviours. Bourdieu suggests that we should examine actual performance and body movements and investigate the way in which nearly all important categories, such as ritual, are "based on movements or postures of the human body, such as going up and coming down . . . going to the left then going to the right, going in, coming out . . . sitting and standing."[18] He asserts that the dialectical relationship between the body and a socially structured space is important in the "embodying of the structures of the world. . . . Thus practices take on objective meanings, and classification schemes are embodied in the world of objects. . . . It is not that one causes the other, but that both are structured by dispositions."[19]

Keeping a field diary in which I also recorded my ongoing thoughts, informal conversations, visits to church services and attendance of church business meetings, conferences and meetings of the Association of Baptist Churches in Israel (ABC), as well as scattered events that are less directly related, allowed me to identify key symbols and contradictions in the field.

2.2.3 Interviews

The interviews began in February 2014 and continued through to January 2017. In the field mapping phase, I completed sixteen semi-structured interviews with current pastors. All these interviews took place at my office; some of them were face to face and the rest were through phone conversations. I wrote the answers in a notebook. I also conducted seventeen in-depth interviews with leaders, pastors and missionaries. The majority of interviewees were men. Further, I conducted another four open interviews with denominational leaders and pastors from other Arab countries such as Lebanon, Jordan and Egypt for comparison.

---

18. Bourdieu, 119.
19. Bourdieu, 89–91.

Table 2.1: Field mapping interviews

Semi-structured interviews	Pastors	16
In-depth interviews	Pastors	5
	Lay leaders	5
	Women	4
	Missionaries	3
Open interviews (other countries)	Pastors (1) and leaders (2)	3
	Women	1
	Total	37

Additionally, for the three case studies, I completed fifty-four in-depth interviews with those involved in church conflicts, ranging in age from thirty to eighty-five.

Table 2.2: Case study interviews[20]

	Case A		Case B		Case C	
Church	A	A2	B	B2	C3	C2
Pastors	7	2	1		1	
Lay people	1	7	1	2		2
Women	2	7	2	3	1	1
Missionaries	3					
Third-party	6		2		3	
Total	35		11		8	

Most case A in-depth interviews were conducted at my office or at the participant's house (this mainly applied to pastors and women of senior age). For case B and case C, I travelled to homes for interviews. I interviewed three people using Skype video call, two through phone calls and three via email. Most of the interviews were recorded, but three people preferred I took notes. Throughout the study, assurances of confidentiality and anonymity were given to all participants due to the sensitive nature of the topic within a small

---

20. I will give further details regarding the differences in the numbers of the interviews in section 2.2.3.

intertwined community. One leader requested that I delete his interview a few days later, explaining that his relationship with his pastor was very good and he did not want any written document to portray a different view.

I interviewed couples together mainly when I interviewed pastors and their wives in their homes. The wives' presence often helped to build trust quickly and develop a comfortable conversation. Some wives tended to add additional details and provided different insights. Sometimes important information was mentioned that the pastor would not have shared if we had been alone.

I chose an open-ended interview style, in which participants were asked to tell me about the conflict leading to the church split. Most of the topics I wanted to cover had been covered by the end of the interviews. I also pursued follow-up interviews to clarify emerging themes.[21] The interviews took from one to three hours to complete and were conducted in Arabic or in English for missionaries. The interview transcripts were typed. Shortly afterward I would typically write additional notes and observations while the interview was fresh in my mind.[22] My notes and the transcripts were written in Arabic, and the quotes presented in the thesis are my translation of the records. I was committed to remaining true to the narrative provided by participants in both transcribing and translating.

2.2.4 Textual Resources

Material collected from the field research included reports and church records, mission records, church and ABC business meeting protocols, letters, third-party reports, emails and sermons.

2.2.5 Focus Group

The focus group was held after the primary analysis of the data was collected via the interviews, observations and documents and served for triangulation. This was the last method; it enabled me to observe personal interactions between participants and assisted me in clarifying what had been said before.[23]

---

21. I had a few follow-up interviews during 2016–2017.

22. Miles and Huberman note that "write-ups usually add back some of the missing content; raw field notes stimulate remembering things." Miles and Huberman, *Qualitative Data Analysis*, 51.

23. See Morgan, *Focus Groups as Qualitative Research*.

The focus group meeting was held in a seminary. Six participants came: three seminary professors and three ABC leaders; all except one are Palestinian Baptist leaders. The meeting was held only to discuss the relevance of Volf's four themes to their context.

2.3 Research Plan

The research plan was designed to follow two main phases of fieldwork; a third phase of study involved a theoretical analysis.

2.3.1 First Phase: Field Mapping

Since there were no existent studies on conflict in the Palestinian Baptist church, the field mapping was exploratory and aimed at identifying factors affecting intra-congregational conflicts that result in the exit of members or the split of the church. Field mapping is also an effective and helpful method for identifying general patterns and categories to be used in case selection in the second phase. I focused on eighteen Baptist churches which are connected together under the Association of Baptist Churches in Israel (ABC) and represent 60 percent of Palestinian evangelicals in Israel.[24]

Topics discussed in the field mapping interviews:
1) Congregational demographics: size, church membership[25]/ attendance,[26] ages, gender and location (urban, rural or mixed town).
2) Congregational structure: plural/single elder leadership.
3) Types of capital: economic (building; local/foreign funds), cultural, symbolic and social.
4) Congregational change: projects, pastor/staff turnover, attendance and decision-making patterns.
5) Congregational conflict: personal differences, leadership style, lay/ clergy, building, finances, generational or new/old members.

---

24. The rest of the evangelicals in Israel are Assemblies of God, Christian and Missionary Alliance churches, Nazarene churches and Brethren congregations.

25. Baptist churches count members according to people who request membership and only after they are baptized as adults.

26. People who attend church on a regular basis include members, children (not yet baptized and therefore not members) and others who prefer to remain members in their traditional mother churches for different reasons.

6) Conflict outcomes: a split, pastor/leader exit,[27] resolution without damage, relationships damaged but no departure or new procedures/structure developed.
7) Third-party intervention: ABC, missionaries or other individuals.

2.3.2 Second Phase: Case Studies

Based on the field mapping, I selected three case studies from the eighteen churches according to the categories listed in the following table. Since the initial mapping revealed that a main element in church conflict is generational (the younger generation rebelling against older pastors), this became a criterion in the case selection. In this phase I analyzed the nature, causes and management of conflict in three cases. The following table presents the different cases.

Table 2.3: Categories used in case selection

Category	Case A	Case B	Case C
Generation of pastors	First generation	Second generation	Second generation
Generation of members	First, second and third generation	Mostly second generation; some third generation	Mostly third generation; some second generation
Church location	Town	Town	Town
Church Size	100 members 150 attenders	50–60 members	50–60 members
Age of conflict	Very old[28]	Fairly old	Recent
Property	Church building	Church building	No church building

2.3.3 Third Phase: Theoretical Analysis

This phase involved a theoretical analysis using Volf's theological model of reconciliation. His model is particularly relevant because he broadly belongs

---

27. Exit to another church or establish a new church/ministry.

28. Although the conflict took place many years ago, interviewees were able to describe many details of the conflict. In addition, many protocols and documents from locals and missionaries were helpful in providing information about this conflict.

to the same theological tradition as the churches I am studying – namely, Baptist. Additionally, his model emphasizes the issues so central to Palestinian evangelicals in Israel – namely, identity and culture. Volf's model is normative theology and proposes a way of reconciliation. As all theological discourse comes from cultural settings, I will examine the applicability of his model in the Palestinian context.

2.4 Content Analysis

Content analysis is described as a process of identifying patterns and themes in experiences of the nature of conflict and conflict management practices. As I did my analysis, I tried to deeply understand the given meanings and find hidden meanings.[29]

I followed a coding procedure to analyze the transcripts of interviews, field notes and relevant documents. I entered them into a qualitative data analysis program called MAXQDA-11. It is a functional program that works well as a filing system and helps by keeping interviews and documents reasonably organized with names and dates in the computer. MAXQDA-11 is useful for quickly accessing different parts of the interviews but not for actual analysis. Therefore, the main part of my analysis involved reading interview texts, taking notes both on the transcripts and in my notebook and drawing charts and tables to organize my thoughts in order to explore themes.

I started the coding by analyzing a whole sentence or paragraph.[30] While coding a sentence or paragraph, I asked, "What is the major idea brought out in this sentence or paragraph?," then gave it a name. Afterward I undertook more detailed analysis of that concept. According to Strauss and Corbin, this approach to coding is useful when the researcher already has several categories and wants to code especially in relation to them.[31] Using this approach, I identified many concepts and grouped them in subcategories and then in categories.

---

29. See Josselson, "The Hermeneutics of Faith," 21.

30. Coding began with selecting sentences, or ideas, from the interviews. Coding progressed to more abstract levels where text segments were integrated into working categories and concepts, establishing linkages between code and categories and arriving at one or several core categories that represent the central category.

31. Strauss and Corbin, *Basic Qualitative Research*, 120.

The delicate relationship with the interviewees does raise concerns about the conclusions of the research. I know there are people who are waiting for the results and desire to use the information to strengthen the churches. However, I also think they expect me to reach certain conclusions, and I am concerned about their reaction if I produce a conclusion that differs to their expectations. I have a good personal relationship with some of the participants – a few are close relatives or were even my pastors – and there is a natural preoccupation that this could affect our relationships. I am also worried about what constitutes a proper use of the trust they have placed in me, particularly those who shared openly, perhaps, because they expect me to consider their opinion. I tried to relate to the data with academic integrity, without damaging the trust given to me during the interviews, keeping in mind that helping churches in my community will involve raising questions of criticism. At the same time, I tried not to be judgmental.

2.5 Research Ethics

In fieldwork there are ethical considerations that must be taken into account, especially with a sensitive topic such as church conflict, and this was done in accordance with the regulations of the institution supervising the research. As an insider-researcher, I have taken this concern seriously, exercising maximal caution. Assurances of confidentiality were given to all participants. I have changed the names of the informants, churches and locations to protect the identities of those involved.

I believe this research has great potential to benefit the researched community. More importantly, perhaps, I decided to study this topic after hearing, a few years earlier, some leaders/pastors who expressed concern about the ongoing splits. Before starting this project, I consulted with the ABC about conducting the research within its eighteen churches. They were happy to give me permission. I was surprised by the openness of participants to share about their church conflict.[32] Most of them were sad about the last twenty-five years of church splits. Some of them were still hurt from such experiences. In

---

32. With two exceptions: one interviewee was not comfortable to be interviewed and only got back to me after three days, emphasizing the fact that she was ready to be interviewed only because of the benefit this research would bring. Another interviewee was hesitant to meet me; after we scheduled a date, he called and cancelled.

general, most expressed their wishes that these conflicts end and saw potential benefit in this research.

I considered all the ethical issues, such as honesty, privacy and responsibility, which are inseparable from any research. As a lawyer and mediator, I tried to avoid providing consultation to churches regarding current problems. I introduced my research at the ABC during a strategic planning conference in 2014. I was asked several questions about the research and its benefits to the ABC. Furthermore, during my observation in a meeting of the ABC committee regarding the conflict in case C, I sat at a distance taking notes without participating. As the only woman in the room, I believe my presence affected the meeting in some way. Later, I was asked by a member of the ABC committee to act as a mediator between Pastor C and the ABC. Following the policy I stated above, my response was negative.[33] I did not interfere with any situation relating to the cases throughout the research process.

2.6 My Own Position in the Field

In qualitative research, the researcher is an irreducible part of any study of social reality. As such, it is important that observers be clear about their own social and cultural location in order to make their research credible. Researchers take on a variety of roles in the research setting. These roles can extend from an insider to an outsider.[34] In general, insider-researchers study a group to which they belong, while outsider-researchers do not belong to the group.[35] Nonetheless, I agree with Hellawell that instead of worrying over whether one is more of an insider or outsider, researchers should insist on being both.[36] There is much to be gained from being close to one's research and also from keeping one's distance and having an outside perspective. Narayan suggests that writing texts that mix lively narrative and rigorous analysis

---

33. However, I had mixed feelings: should not that have been a great opportunity to observe conflict management practices closer? After consulting my supervisor, I decided not to accept the position and remained an observer.
34. Adler and Adler, "Observational Techniques."
35. Breen, "The researcher 'in the Middle.'"
36. Hellawell, "Inside-Out."

involves enacting hybridity, regardless of our origins or whether we are either an insider or outsider.[37]

Chavez argues that unlike traditional training for outsider researchers that starts with "getting to know the field," insider-scholars need to get into their own heads first to know in which ways they are similar/different from their participants and which of their social identities can advantage or complicate the process.[38] I approach this study as a Palestinian Baptist woman who lives in Israel. I am thus an *insider* to this community, politically, culturally and religiously. Since the late 1980s, I have attended a Baptist church, though not one included in this research.

There are both advantages and disadvantages to being an insider-researcher. Bonner and Tolhurst identified three key advantages of being an insider-researcher: (1) having a better understanding of and sensitivity to the culture, speaking the same language and understanding local values; (2) not changing the flow of social interaction unnaturally; and (3) having a profound established closeness which assists the telling and the judging of truth.[39] Further, insider researchers generally know the politics of the institution, the formal and informal power structures and how and where to reach the right people and get easy access to documents.[40]

I know many of the participants; thus, during the data collection process, my requests were almost never rejected. Additionally, being married to an ABC leader was beneficial in establishing a good position and, of course, having excellent access to textual resources. For example, leaders of the ABC and the churches that split very generously gave copies of different documents and forwarded many relevant emails. When I wanted to set interview times, they reacted positively and quickly, showing respect by sharing their narratives and expressing willingness to be observed in their churches. Many church members shared information and allocated time for this project on

---

37. Narayan, "How Native Is a 'Native' Anthropologist?"
38. Chavez, "Conceptualizing from the Inside," 491.
39. Bonner and Tolhurst, "Insider-Outsider Perspectives."
40. Unluer, "Being an Insider Researcher"; Smyth and Holian, "Credibility Issues in Research." Unlike outsider-researchers, insider-researchers are accepted as political allies. They are working in the midst of long-term relationships which extend beyond a research relationship since they involve their families, communities, organizations and local networks. See Smith, *Decolonizing Methodologies*, 15.

a voluntary basis. I could easily complete the missing data by asking for clarification. I had spontaneous conversations with leaders and members which enriched the data.

Another important advantage was knowledge of the personality of participants, which assisted the interactions between us.[41] Additionally, knowing what was happening in the ABC in general, as an insider, helped me to give meaning to implicit messages and provide clarification.

I believe I made good use of these advantages, which an outsider in such a study might not have experienced, and, in this manner, succeeded in collecting valid data.

Although there are various advantages to being an insider, there are also disadvantages. One clear disadvantage is the lack of detachment from the field which can cause issues, including the following: overlooking certain routine behaviours, making assumptions about the meaning of events, not seeking clarification and assuming one knows participants' views and issues. Participants may also tend to assume an insider already knows what they know, while closeness to the situation can hinder the researcher from seeing all dimensions of the bigger picture while collecting data. Greater familiarity can lead to a loss of objectivity.[42]

An insider will likely have more difficulty in being objective in analyzing a community than an outsider, yet many native researchers question such an assumption. Gatson and Zweerink, native researchers, suggest there is a difference between compartmentalizing their roles as researcher and insider, and denying the one to excel at the other.[43] As an insider, I do not claim to be objective but rather strive to have two roles.

Smith recognizes that no indigenous researcher is fully an insider.[44] The critical issue with insider research is the constant need for reflexivity. Based

---

41. For example, one of the interviewees has a hearing problem and was not responding to my questions directly himself. His wife often jumped in and answered "for him." If I had not known his disability, I would probably have had a different analysis.

42. Unluer, "Being an Insider Researcher"; Smyth and Holian, "Credibility Issues in Research."

43. Gatson and Zweerink, "Ethnography Online." See also Kraft, "Community and Identity," 68.

44. According to Smith, "Indigenous research approaches problematize the insider model in different ways because there are multiple ways of both being an insider and an outsider in indigenous contexts" (Smith, *Decolonizing Methodologies*, 137). Narayan argues, "Given the

on my experience in this research, I propose that defining researchers as insiders or outsiders is less significant. On the one hand there may be contexts in which the researcher is fully an outsider. On the other, as Smith suggests, when insiders becomes the researchers, they are no longer truly insiders.[45] My position in this research was certainly as an insider, but there were elements in which I became an outsider which were crucial to the effective development of this project.

Personally, I am not originally from the same town as the cases I am studying, nor was I a member of these churches during the conflicts. I know many of the members and church participants in most churches but did not have close relationships with most of them. As a researcher, my knowledge about the conflicts in the three cases was general and minimal. I thus do not consider myself an insider-participant-observer. I carried out the research from within only in the sense that I was on site.

Professionally, as a lawyer and mediator, I did not have any mediation or administrative role at any church or in the ABC. I did not have power or authority which could affect the data collection process negatively.[46] This actually gave me an element of an outsider status.

I tried to overcome some of the disadvantages by taking a preventative approach. I did not reveal any observations that I made to any participants. This guaranteed participants' confidence in me. When participants assumed I already knew what they knew, I asked for more clarification. Furthermore, advisors play a role in supporting the research while conducting insider research. In my study, my two supervisors, an evangelical Croatian-American

---

diversity within cultural domains and across groups, even the most experienced of 'native' anthropologists cannot know everything about his or her own society.... By opening up access to hidden stores of research materials, the study of anthropology can also lead to the discovery of many strange and unfamiliar aspects of one's own society" (Narayan, "How Native Is a 'Native' Anthropologist?," 678–679).

45. I agree with Narayan that "the process of doing fieldwork involves getting to know a range of people and listening closely to what they say. Even if one should already be acquainted with some of these people before one starts fieldwork, the intense and sustained engagements of fieldwork will inevitably transmute these relationships" (Narayan, "How Native Is a 'Native' Anthropologist?," 679). In fact, I was amazed to realize that my knowledge about the participants after the interviews became much deeper.

46. See Smyth and Holian, "Credibility Issues in Research."

theologian and an Israeli Jewish anthropologist, provided significant input, and I believe they could criticize my "insider" work.[47]

2.7 Reflexivity

Bourdieu explains the importance of a reflexive sociology in which sociologists conduct their research with a great awareness of the influence of their own position and power and how these may distort or prejudice their objectivity.[48] Mauthner and Doucet argue that situating oneself socially and emotionally in relation to participants is a crucial part of reflexivity since "our emotional responses to respondents can shape our interpretations of their accounts."[49] This requires the researcher to determine what that appropriate level of distancing is, which is no easy task. Taylor notes, "Where the researcher-self is a part of the other's narrative, the narrative of the researched and the researcher become entwined. The researcher, then, is forced to look both outward and inward, to be reflexive and self-conscious in terms of positioning, to be both self-aware and researcher-self-aware and to acknowledge the intertextuality that is a part of both the data gathering and writing processes."[50]

There are multiple methods by which insider-researchers can develop reflexivity. Diaries and external perspectives stimulate reflexivity; that is, their importance as a form of "self-triangulation." Lincoln and Guba suggest triangulation as a technique that may be employed to establish credibility in research.[51] Triangulation refers to the researcher's use of multiple theories, methods and sources.[52]

---

47. Another aspect important to evaluating a project involving fieldwork, suggested by Cassell, is the quality of the interaction between the researcher and the researched (Cassell, "Ethical Principles for Conducting Fieldwork"). I feel our relations were characterized by honesty and openness. Before I started each interview, I informed the participants that I had ABC permission to do this research. I was open to answer their questions but insisted on confidentiality, especially when we both knew the same people. Additionally, I let the participants choose where they wished to meet. Most of them seemed happy to have someone interested in their story.

48. Bourdieu and Wacquant, *Invitation to Reflexive Sociology*.
49. Mauthner and Doucet, "Reflexive Accounts," 418.
50. Taylor, "Intimate Insider," 9, cited in Greene, "On the Inside Looking In," 9.
51. Lincoln and Guba, *Naturalistic Inquiry*.
52. Lincoln and Guba, 305.

I employed a multiple methods approach in my research. Additionally, several theoretical frameworks, primarily in the areas of peace studies, sociology and theology, influence my interpretation of the findings. Being an outsider during these conflicts, I kept reminding the informants to explain what happened from the beginning as if I knew nothing. This approach helped me to be more reflexive. This is also the reason I chose in-depth interviews, where I only interrupted when I needed more explanation. I also asked some questions to which I knew the answers in an effort to act like an outsider.

Another important issue is the researcher's power. According to Smith, "Researchers have the power to distort, to make invisible, to overlook, to exaggerate and to draw conclusions, based not on factual data, but on assumptions, hidden value judgments, and often downright misunderstandings."[53] It is important that the researchers insure that their power is no greater than it should be while conducting the research.

While there is no racial or class tension in my context, it should be noted that being connected to an academic institution might cause the participants to feel a sense of my authority as a researcher.[54] On the one hand, in the Middle Eastern context, being a woman from a younger generation decreased my power position. I felt that participants placed emphasis on my femaleness more than on my identity as a researcher, particularly as most of the participants were men aged fifty to eighty-five. I also asked my husband to initially talk to a few pastors before I approached them to make sure it was acceptable for them to be interviewed regarding their churches' splits. Because of that, many participants met me as the wife of my husband (which might have given me some power) and not as a university researcher in my own right. On the other hand, I feel that my extensive knowledge in conflict resolution, the experience I have as a lawyer and my position as a public prosecutor earned me the respect and trust of the participants, and thus I did not face the challenges associated with being a woman doing sensitive research in a patriarchal community. I believe that this helped to significantly

---

53. Smith, *Decolonizing Methodologies*, 176.

54. Edwards, "Education in Interviewing." Merriam et al. state that "during fieldwork the researcher's power is negotiated, not given" (*Power and Positionality*, 409, cited in Greene, "On the inside Looking In," 6). Thus, as an attempt to minimize the power between insider researchers and participants, insider researchers can present themselves as advocates. See Breen, "The Researcher 'in the Middle.'"

balance the power dynamics. As a woman, I had the privilege of being able to gain deeper insight in situations where I met other women, which a male researcher would have found more challenging due to the patriarchal nature of Arab culture. It was of great importance to me that those I met felt I was approaching them from a position of equality.[55]

Finally, I had to reflect constantly on how my actions might affect the people I was researching. I tried to be "reflexive in real time."[56] I was aware that I was interviewing pastors in a patriarchal community where there are obvious power dynamics (man/woman, old/young, pastor/member). Sometimes, I felt that I would not ask confrontational questions so I would not harm our relationship. At other times, I felt I was treated with a great deal of respect, perhaps due to my background as a public prosecutor. Some participants even consulted me, after the interview, regarding personal legal issues, and I was happy to help. Another matter I had to manage was to hide my investigation techniques. In this regard I insisted on having in-depth interviews to overcome my desire to ask investigational questions. Additionally, being aware of the dialogue in the context of the patriarchal culture, I treated the pastors with great respect and sensitivity.

Reflexivity continued throughout the analysis. I shared my analysis with a few of the participants as Josselson suggests research conducted with the purpose of distilling, elucidating and illuminating must involve a good deal of dialogue with the researched and careful reflexivity on the part of the researcher.[57] During the process of my research, I also had the opportunity to test some of the proposals and arguments of this thesis by presenting papers at a number of conferences.[58]

With that being said, I believe I am uniquely placed to research the topic of Palestinian Baptists in Israeli and their intra-church conflicts. I approached the analysis of the data not from the unsympathetic lens of an outsider nor from the uncritical lens of an insider. I am neither solely a woman, wife and mother, nor just a Palestinian Christian, cultural Middle Easterner, British

---

55. Kraft, "Community and Identity."
56. Nagar-Ron, "Al dibor."
57. Josselson, "The Hermeneutics of Faith," 5, 11.
58. In January 2013, I presented a paper on generational conflict at the Hebrew University in Israel. I also presented some of my chapters several times at my college (OCMS) and at the Langham consultation in Cambridge.

academic, Israeli citizen and lawyer who studied in secular Jewish universities and worked as a public prosecutor in the Israeli establishment. I am all of those identities together.[59] I navigate between them. Some of them, without my control, are more dominant than others. It is not easy to evaluate to what extent each identity influenced my fieldwork. However, I believe my professional identity affected my fieldwork both while doing the investigating and in giving me the passport to enter the field freely.

When analyzing the data, I tried to look at it from all of these perspectives and even from an outsider perspective as best I could. As Ruth Behar has said, "I am here because I am a woman on the border . . . between identities, between languages, between cultures. . . . One foot in the academy and one foot out."[60] The portrait presented in this thesis, therefore, reflects that unusual combination. I believe the combination of these characteristics, as well as my normative motivation in doing this research within my own community, helped me to become even more reflexive.

From the discussion above I do not claim that my analysis is "pure," but I want to explain the reflexive position from which I have written. I do intend for the findings of this research to be used to help improve the practices of church conflict management.

I felt comfortable being away from the field for two years (in the United States) after finishing the data collection to continue working on the analysis. The distance helped me to be more reflexive and self-critical.

It seems that through this research I also tried to answer questions that I find personally frustrating, even when I did so unconsciously. I sought to undertake this research from the secure distance of researcher and critical observer to understand beyond stereotypes and the struggle between identities. Being personally involved and culturally close, yet constantly maintaining distance within my researcher's mind throughout the process of questioning and analysis, was an enjoyable experience for me.

---

59. Kraft, "Community and Identity."
60. Behar, *Vulnerable Observer*, 162.

CHAPTER 3

The Environment of the Palestinian Baptist Churches in Israel

3.1 Introduction

Having described the context, presented a brief literature review and explained my methodology, I now move to describe the environment and map the field of the Palestinian Baptist churches in Israel.

A church "split" or member "exit" from a church is a dramatic decision leading to a member's withdrawal from relationship with, and active participation in, the congregation. Since conflict-related splits/exits are easier to observe and measure than voice (an attempt to repair or improve the relationship through communication of the complaint, grievance or proposal for change),[1] I examined factors affecting intra-congregational conflicts resulting in the exit of leaders or a church split. In this research *church split* refers to the exodus of unsatisfied members and leaders resulting in a church splitting into two. *Church exit* refers to an unsatisfied leader who leaves the church with his family and founds a new church or joins another church's leadership.

In this field mapping I visited churches and completed thirty-seven interviews (semi-structured and in-depth). The interviews were analyzed to identify the following: (1) the environment and nature of the conflict, (2) general patterns, (3) categories to be used in case selection, and (4) processes and types of conflict management.

---

1. Voice is manifested in democratic institutions. It is especially important when exit is costly. As Hirschman noted, "This is very nearly the situation in such basic social organization as the family, the state, or the church." Hirschman, *Exit, Voice and Loyalty*, 33.

The findings in this phase provide evidence of two distinct periods of time in Palestinian Baptist life, which influenced responses to conflict. The first period (1911–1990) was before the missionaries' departure: during eight decades no splits and only a few exits were recorded. The second period (1990–2016) was after the missionaries' departure: during two decades thirty-two church conflicts ended with church splits or leaders' exits, and twelve churches were founded after these splits/exits.[2]

This differentiation between the two periods led me to conduct additional interviews with some first-generation Palestinian Baptists and missionaries to explore why splits/exits happened mainly after the missionaries' departure. Seemingly, the missionaries' departure left the field with no centralized authority and funding, contributing to church splits/exits.

It is not possible to understand the present situation of Baptist churches in Israel without taking the missionary legacy and other factors into account. Therefore, I will present (separately for each period) several factors identified based on literature and the interviews as contextual background for the examination of intra-church conflict. These factors are historical, political, economic, social, structural, theological and cultural.

3.2 The Environment of the Palestinian Baptist Churches Before the Missionaries' Departure (1911–1990)

3.2.1 Historical Background

Baptist work in the Holy Land was started in 1911 by Shukri Mosa, a Palestinian from Safed. Mosa (1870–1928) was born into a Catholic Melkite family and travelled to the United States in 1909 due to the difficult economic, social and political situation in the Ottoman Empire.[3] While in Dallas, Texas, he was touched by Baptist teachings and received adult baptism from George W. Truett at the First Baptist Church in Dallas. Mosa was ordained and, with the support of Southern Baptist churches in Illinois, returned as

---

2. I will discuss and map church splits/exits in more depth in section 3.4.

3. Another account states that Shukri was converted by Presbyterian missionaries in Palestine before travelling to the United States. The only thing that changed while he was in the United States was that he became Baptist.

an indigenous missionary to the Holy Land.[4] He arrived in 1911, began his ministry in Safed, and later that year moved to Nazareth where he founded the first Baptist church in the Holy Land.[5] He was at first harassed by some priests from the Greek Orthodox and Catholic churches but, with support coming from churches in the United States, was able to found a church that met in rented facilities.[6]

Additional indigenous leaders were raised up, and in the 1920s American missionaries from the Southern Baptist Convention started to arrive, and Baptist work was established in several places.[7] After the establishment of the State of Israel, the Baptist Mission was organized under the Baptist Convention in Israel (BCI), a legal entity including all Southern Baptist missionaries, which still exists today. Furthermore, in 1965 Baptists established the ABC with the aim of representing local Baptists working in partnership with the BCI. Until the 1970s the ABC included Jewish, Palestinians and American Baptists. In the 1990s, Southern Baptists changed their policy regarding the goals of their missionary work and withdrew from direct involvement in the Palestinian Baptist churches, stopping their financial support.[8]

---

4. Baker, *Baptist Golden Jubilee*.

5. Watts, *Palestinian Tapestries*, 14–15.

6. Makdisi, *Teta, Mither and Me*; Mansour, *Baptist History in the Holy Land between 1867 and 1950*.

7. After World War I, the Foreign Mission Board of the Southern Baptist Convention in the United States adopted the church in Nazareth, together with a few other churches operating in Lebanon. They founded the Near East Mission Board and sent their first American missionaries in 1923. The first church building was erected in Nazareth in 1926. With more missionaries coming, Baptist work developed, and new work was established in Jerusalem in 1932 and in Haifa in 1936. A church building was built in Jerusalem, but a rented apartment was used for meetings in Haifa (referred to as "The Upper Room" in missionary correspondence). The Baptist mission in Palestine employed locals to help, and a few missionaries came to serve for short periods of time. In 1936, a primary school was established in Nazareth but had to stop in 1941 due to all the missionaries going back home when the United States entered World War II (Rowden, *Baptist in Israel*). In 1944, missionaries began to come back and a care institution was established in Nazareth. The churches in Nazareth, Haifa and Jerusalem were still alive at that time. For more information on this history see Mansour, *Baptist History in the Holy Land between 1867 and 1950*.

8. On the one hand, this put most of the local ministry under serious financial pressure, but, on the other, it "forced" some, especially larger churches, to support their own work. Furthermore, this caused the ABC to become not merely a fellowship of churches but an important body responsible for supporting, encouraging and representing Baptist churches in Israel.

3.2.2 Political, Social and Economic Factors

The creation of Israel in 1948 came, among other reasons, as a response to the Jewish experience of anti-Semitism in Europe. A milestone leading towards its creation was the Balfour Declaration of 1917. From that point on, Jewish immigration increased, using the protection of the British Mandate to prepare for the establishment of a Jewish state in Palestine. During the 1948 Palestine war, an estimated 700,000 Palestinians fled or were expelled, and hundreds of Palestinian towns and villages were destroyed. Those who left were not allowed to return when the war ended and became refugees in the surrounding countries; the small percentage of Palestinians (approximately 150,000) who managed to stay became Israeli citizens. This event is known in the Palestinian narrative as the *nakba*.[9]

Ateek's evaluation of the history of the Palestinian community in Israel between 1948 and 1989 identified three different stages of response: shock, resignation and awakening.[10]

1) During the first stage (1948–1955), Palestinians were characterized as a "people in shock."[11]
2) During the second stage (1956–1967), they were characterized as a "community of resignation."[12]
3) The third stage (1968–1989) was characterized as a "nation awakening."[13]

Rabinowitz and Abu-Baker describe the first stage as the "survival generation," and the second and third stages as the "worn-out generation."[14] After 1990 is what they describe as the "stand-tall generation."[15]

---

9. The term *nakba* also refers to the period of war itself and events affecting Palestinians from December 1947 to January 1949. See Pappé, *Forgotten Palestinians*, and Khalidi, *All that Remains*. See also two different perspectives and narratives regarding the *nakba* in Munayer and Loden, *Through My Enemy's Eyes*.
10. Ateek, *Justice and Only Justice*.
11. Ateek, 33–36.
12. Ateek, 36–38.
13. Ateek, 38–44.
14. Rabinowitz and Abu-Baker, *Door Zakoof*, 25, 36.
15. Rabinowitz and Abu-Baker, 63.

Table 3.1: Generational typology of Ateek, Rabinowitz and Abu-Baker

Periods	Ateek, *Justice and Only Justice* (1989)	Rabinowitz and Abu-Baker, *Door Zakoof* (2002)
1948–1955	shock stage	survival generation
1956–1967	resignation stage	worn-out generation
1968–1989	awakening stage	worn-out generation
1990–2015		stand-tall generation

For each stage I explain the political, social and educational factors and also present the missionaries' contributions.

3.2.2.1 First stage (1948–1955): "survival generation"

In 1948, Palestinians in Israel were stunned when within a short period they became a minority and refugees in their own land. Two actions by the Israeli government contributed to their nightmare. First, there was the imposition of martial law aimed at controlling the movement and limiting the rights of Palestinians. The new government retained the Emergency Defence Regulations created by the British Mandate, which enabled them at will to enter, confiscate or even destroy Palestinian houses. Second, in 1950 the government introduced an "absentee property law" under which the state was able to confiscate Palestinian land, even the land of those who had never been displaced from their homes.[16]

Missionary work: relief work, involvement in churches, care and educational institutions

In 1948, when the State of Israel was established, most mission work was destroyed because most Palestinian Baptists became refugees. The Baptist church in Haifa ceased to exist and the membership of the Nazareth Baptist Church diminished to only five members.[17] However, mission work was kept alive by three missionary ladies who ran a care institution and also managed the church and relief work after the Palestinian *nakba* when many Palestinian refugees from evacuated towns and villages found shelter in

---

16. Ateek, *Justice and Only Justice*, 33–36.
17. Rowden, *Baptist in Israel*.

Nazareth.[18] Baptist work in West Jerusalem lost its Palestinian members and had to be rebuilt with its few Jewish members and a handful of expatriates who remained in Jerusalem after 1948.

In 1950, the Baptist mission in the United States sent missionary families to revive Baptist work in Israel. Missionaries arrived to pastor the Nazareth Baptist Church, run a care institution and reopen an educational institution. Others were sent to Jerusalem and other places to work among the Jews. In terms of academic education, during this period there were only some Palestinian students enrolled in Israeli universities.

3.2.2.2 Second stage (1956–1967): "worn-out generation"

For the Palestinian community in Israel, this period was characterized by an attitude of acceptance towards the unresolved conflict and life as an unwanted minority that was considered foreign to the new state it inhabited. Even their identity was threatened; new identity cards were issued with the word "Palestinian" deleted and replaced with "Arab."[19] Some argue it was an attempt to delete their history as Palestinians and change their loyalty.[20] The state also issued cultural and educational restrictions. Palestinian children spent more time studying Jewish history than their own. However, many Palestinians were impressed by the development and progress of the new state.

The state had developed a sophisticated "system of control," by which to manipulate the Arab minority and control it effectively, through three components: segmentation, dependence and co-option.[21] Some scholars claim that the failures of the Israeli-Arab community to "organize itself" are due to the presence of a highly effective system of control which, since 1948, has operated over Israeli-Arabs.[22] During the shock and resignation period, the Israeli-Arab workforce was largely blue-collar. At the end of the 1950s it was

---

18. Palestinians in Israel live mainly in small towns and villages in the north of the country. The biggest Palestinian town is the city of Nazareth (seventy-five thousand residents), which has become the political, economic and cultural centre of the Palestinians in Israel. This town survived in 1948.

19. Golda Meir, the Israeli prime minister declared, "It was not as though there was a Palestinian people in Palestine . . . and we came and threw them out and took their country. . . . They didn't exist." June 15, 1969; quoted in Avnery, *Israel without Zionism*, 262.

20. See Ateek, *Justice and Only Justice*, and Rabinowitz and Abu-Baker, *Door Zakoof*.

21. Ateek, *Justice and Only Justice*, 38.

22. Lustick, *Arabs in the Jewish State*.

easier to receive a scholarship from an American school and to study abroad than to be accepted into an Israeli university.

Missionary work: planting and building new churches
Before 1965, missionaries were the main decision-makers in church affairs. After the establishment of the ABC in 1965, missionaries were influential in church life, both indirectly through funding and through the position of ABC "field representatives" (who were responsible for church planting and management). Some missionaries were members of the executive of the ABC.[23]

Socially, most of the interviewees who were aware of this period mentioned that their church was the centre of their spiritual, social, financial and educational life, due to the connection between the church, the care institution and the educational institution.[24] An American missionary who pastored the Nazareth Baptist Church launched a team of key young leaders called the Village Team to plant churches in Arab towns and villages. Every Sunday afternoon the Village Team visited villages and towns to provide Sunday school and church activities, which resulted in the establishment of new Baptist churches in Akko, Haifa, Cana of Galilee, Tooran, Rama, Eilaboun and Yaffa of Nazareth.[25] Missionaries were responsible for these churches and locals helped in the ministry. Those joining the Baptist churches tended to be from poor backgrounds, often refugees, in contrast with the prominent Palestinian families who held remarkable status in traditional churches (Catholic/Orthodox).[26]

From an economic perspective, during and after the *nakba*, the Baptist mission provided jobs and employed many church members to work at the care and educational institutions, as well as offering scholarships to those who wished to study abroad.[27]

---

23. Jack, interview with author, November 2014.
24. Jack, Ron, Paul, Ramiz, Amal, Suhad, Dan, Tamer, Hiyam, Emily and Nabil in interviews with author.
25. Baker, *Baptist Golden Jubilee*.
26. Pastor A, interview with author, April 2014.
27. Nabil, Jack and Pastor A in interviews with author.

3.2.2.3 Third stage (1968–1988): "worn-out generation"
The following elements helped to raise the consciousness of Israeli-Arabs as Palestinians:[28]

1) The Palestinian Liberation Organization, which was recognized by the Arab League in 1964, was created as a political body whose purpose was to bring together the fragmented segments of Palestinians scattered around the world. It created a framework that integrated the cultural, social, economic, political and military activities of Palestinians.

2) At the end of 1960 the presence of educated Palestinians in Israel began to be felt in the community. A new generation of Palestinian university graduates returned from Eastern Europe, having been sent under the joint sponsorship of the Communist Party in Israel (RAKAH) and the host countries. Together they formed the backbone of thinkers, organizers and conceptualizers for the Palestinian community in Israel. Because of the lack of a channel to express their views they turned to the Communist Party (the political force in Palestinian society in Israel). The decline in the Party's power affected the Christian community, as it had served as their political voice. Gradually, many left and organized themselves with some left-wing Jews into the Progressive List for Peace, which first appeared in the 1984 Israeli election.

3) After the battle of *Karameh* in 1968, where Palestinians for the first time engaged in direct battle with Israelis and inflicted heavy losses on them, there was a rebirth of Palestinian consciousness.

4) The "Land Day" of March 1976, when Israeli authorities revealed their intention to expropriate 1.5 million dunams of Palestinian land,[29] caused an awakened consciousness among Palestinians in Israel that has lasted into the present day.

5) The new consciousness-raising of the Israeli-Arabs steadily increased throughout 1980 with the Israeli invasion of South

---

28. Ateek, *Justice and Only Justice*.
29. One dunam equals 0.245 acres.

Lebanon, a disaster that killed nineteen thousand Arabs in Lebanon, mostly Palestinian refugees, and at least 654 Israeli soldiers.

6) The *Intifada* (uprising) in the West Bank and Gaza in 1987 continued the increase of consciousness. After twenty years under occupation, Palestinians began to purposefully resist the forces of occupation.

7) Finally, the failure of the strategic initiatives of Jewish-Arab cooperation and coexistence in some political parties led to the idea becoming "worn-out" and the next generation starting to look for alternatives.

During this stage, missionaries started appointing indigenous pastors to churches and providing some pastors and leaders with houses.[30] Some pastors were appointed merely because they were available, even if they were not particularly qualified. They were sent to study theology abroad or were trained in leadership courses based on Western perspectives and culture.[31] These leaders were ordained as pastors by the missionaries and/or the ABC.[32]

3.2.3 Church Conflict between 1948 and 1990

Until the missionaries' departure in the early 1990s, they planted churches, appointed local pastors and were responsible for funding. In most cases the authority of the missionaries was not questioned by locals. Conflicts and their management were as follows.

---

30. Jack, interview with author, November 2014; Pastor A, interview with author, April 2014.

31. Such as Christian Service Training Centre (CSTC), an American Baptist College. The teachers were Americans.

32. Jack, interview with author, November 2014; Samir, interview with author, April 2014. Besides being influenced by Western theology and American missionaries who grew up in a culture that takes statistical and objective measurement seriously, Palestinians evaluate ministry differently to contemporary Western/American missiology. This can be seen in the bias with which Westerners discuss evaluative criteria, as contemporary Western/American missiology focuses on measurable goals, accuracy and predictability. Church growth statisticians are concerned with numerical growth; this justifies the requirements of Western agencies that results be measurable, at least in numbers. Some Western observers noted that church growth statistics were influential, as it fed the rationale to begin more projects. This might explain why some local observers felt that missionary concerns were mainly on the numbers attending the church and the number of church plants created. Pastor Samir complained, "One missionary cared only for numbers. He did not consult locals in decision-making; his main goal was to show larger numbers." (Samir, interview with author, April 2014).

3.2.3.1 Issues of conflict

Churches were very small and led by pastors who were a "one man show." Most of the conflicts were about personality differences between members of the laity and pastors rather than leadership style and structure. However, some tensions between church leaders and missionaries were mentioned by interviewees.[33]

3.2.3.2 Conflict management

Missionaries who owned the church properties and provided pastors' salaries were indirectly the main decision-makers; some interviewees said missionaries did not really consult locals. When there were problems with a pastor, they "encouraged him to leave" or helped him get another job.[34] Additionally, there were a few exits from members who were not satisfied with a pastor; most of these members went back to their original churches. However, during this period no church splits were recorded and no pastors/leaders exited to found new churches.

3.3 The Environment of the Palestinian Baptist Churches after the Missionaries' Departure (1990–2016)

The findings of the field mapping indicate that several factors shaped the environment of the Palestinian Baptist churches: the issue of identity and social, economic, cultural, theological and structural factors. As these factors were subjected to change, they influenced Palestinian Baptist responses to church conflict. As change might induce conflict,[35] these factors in the environment need to be explored as they could potentially combine together in a powerful way to contribute to church splits/exits.

---

33. Open interview with missionaries Paul and Ron.
34. Samir, interview with author, April 2014.
35. Brubaker, *Promise and Peril*.

3.3.1 Identity

3.3.1.1 *The "stand-tall generation" (1990–2016)*

Rabinowitz and Abu-Baker describe the period between 1990 and 2016 as the "stand-tall generation."[36] The grandparents of this generation were children in 1948, their parents were involved in the "Land Day"[37] and they, the grandchildren, (i.e. the "stand-tall generation") witnessed a violent incident against Palestinian citizens of Israel in October 2000 (the Israeli police killed thirteen young Palestinians), as well as the failure of the Oslo Accords.[38] In the 1990s, new Palestinian voices started to demand a "country for all its citizens." Instead of asking for coexistence as their parents had, they demanded full equal rights as a condition for coexistence. This period was characterized by a new generation that had experienced a shift in its identity. Many were proud Palestinians, being aware that their residency in Israel did not make it their country.[39] They did not accept being second-class citizens, and they sought to fight for their rights using different means from those of their parents. Their struggle could be seen in Israeli campus demonstrations in which many female students became more dominant. They were more educated and many of them sought to work in various human rights organizations and professional civil or community organizations. The main experience of the "stand-tall generation" has been the struggle against inequity in their country of residence – whether positional, religious or gender based – a struggle between generations and ideologies. Coincidentally, during recent years more Palestinian Christians have joined the Israeli military/national service.[40]

Each of the generations I have described ("survival," "worn-out" and "stand-tall") is building on the experience and accomplishments of those who came before them. Thus, I do not claim that the "stand-tall generation" is either stronger or more qualified in this struggle.

---

36. Rabinowitz and Abu-Baker, *Door Zakoof*.
37. See section 3.2.2.3.
38. One positive dimension of the peace process was that Palestinians gained recognition of their right to self-determination.
39. Despite the fact that there are some Palestinian voices who would not agree, the majority seek an end to the conflict.
40. This is related to the fragmentation of Palestinian identity along religious lines (Christian/Muslim), especially as witnessed in Nazareth in the 1990s. Some argue that one major motivation for young Christians to join the army is the desire to defend themselves against Muslims.

3.3.1.2 Political/cultural identity

Palestinian Arab Christians in Israel are exposed to various cultures (Muslim-Arab, Israeli-Jewish and that of Western missionaries) and are required to find their place within this complex, and often conflicted, cultural arena[41] – while at the same time facing the longstanding "divide and conquer" policy of the state of Israel. Several models have been suggested for the study of ethnic identities of Palestinians in Israel.[42]

In regard to Palestinian Christian identity during this period (1990–2016), Sa'ar examines how Palestinian Christians navigate their affiliation with nation, state and religion.[43] According to Sa'ar, Palestinian Christians' practices include both conformity and resistance. They tend to be politically conformist to avoid national issues and emphasize the cultural distinctions between themselves and Muslims. Sa'ar has interpreted this as a social reproductive orientation because it reinforces the state's policy of control over the Palestinian minority.[44] She suggests that their political conformism and Christian ethnocentrism weaken their status within the national community; however, the social reproductive orientation has empowered them to borrow power from the political centre. At the same time another attitude exists, as Palestinian

---

41. Nagel sees identity and culture as two fundamental building blocks of ethnicity. It is through interaction both inside and outside of ethnic communities that cultures are formed and defined. Culture is constructed as we select particular items from the shelves of our past and present. In this way cultures can be seen to change; they are borrowed, blended, rediscovered and redefined. Nagel, "Constructing Ethnicity."

42. Hofman and Rouhana ("Young Arabs in Israel") set national (Palestinian) and civic (Israeli) identities in opposition to one another arguing that the strengthening of one identity is conversely proportional to the weakening of the other identity. Others claim that the Israeli and Palestinian components in Palestinian Arab identity are independent of one another and therefore must be analysed separately. Smooha believes that a parallel process of "Palestinization" and "Israelization" is occurring (Smooha, "Yaḥasy A'raveim yehodeim"). See Munayer, "Ethnic Identity."

43. Sa'ar, "Feminine Strength." Sa'ar argues that Palestinian Christians are marginalized within an encompassing state. Although a minority within their own nation, they constitute a majority and elite among the local Palestinian community. Her research was conducted between 1991 and 1993.

44. *Social reproduction* refers to the processes that ensure the self-perpetuation of a social structure over time, in rough analogy to biological reproduction for a population. The idea of social reproduction has its origins in Karl Marx's analysis of capitalist society. Bourdieu associates social reproduction with his concept of *habitus* which he defines as something that "ensures the active presence of past experiences, which, deposited in each organism in the form of schemes of perception, thought and action, tend to guarantee the correctness of practices and their constancy over time." Bourdieu, *Logic of Practice*, 54.

Christians are increasingly participating in political criticism and national activity – both unconscious oppositional behaviour and conscious resistance.

Another study was conducted in 1998 showing that Palestinian Christians in Israel perceive themselves as a distinct ethnic group who have a positive evaluation of their cultural group.[45] Contributing factors to their positive collective self-esteem seem to be the educational and economic level Christians have been able to achieve in spite of the difficulties of being a minority. They show a higher preference for integrating with Israeli Jewish society (i.e. for adopting aspects of its culture without giving up their traditional culture) and being separate from Muslim Arabs (participating in relatively little intercultural contact). Other results suggest that Palestinian Christians tend to regard Israeli Jewish society as a vehicle for Westernization, yet it seems clear that they are not willing to adopt every Western value and are selective of which values they choose to adopt.[46]

A decade later, after the second *Intifada* (2000), the second Lebanese War (2006), and the Israeli military operation of Gaza (2008), Munayer and Horenczyk conducted a similar study.[47] It shows a strengthening of Christian identity and culture among Palestinian Christians in Israel, with separation emerging as the strongest attitude with regard to both Muslims and Jews. Such a process can be better understood within a broader view of cultural identities and intergroup processes in Israel.[48] It has been argued that ethno-religious identities are gaining visibility and influence in the conflicted society.[49] The delicate situation of Palestinian Christians in Israel has deteriorated; they feel

---

45. Horenczyk and Munayer, "Acculturation Orientations."

46. The *Westernization* of Palestinian Arab Christians is a process that began in the nineteenth century, before the formation of the State of Israel, and applies to the Middle East in general. The Western church schools that were established in Palestine by different churches during the Mandate period were major vehicles for Westernization. There the students were exposed to Western teaching, languages and study materials. Another important aspect of this relationship was that the Palestinian Arab Christians, and Arab Christians in the Middle East in general, were looking for Western powers to stand beside them as a minority in order to protect them and help them maintain their religious and civil rights (Munayer, "Ethnic Identity").

47. Munayer and Horenczyk, "Multi-Group Acculturation Orientations."

48. According to Smooha, "These years were a lost decade for Arab-Jewish coexistence. Instead of improvement, there was deterioration. Arab-Jewish relations worsened and Arab attitudes hardened." Smooha, *Arab-Jewish Relations in Israel*, 27.

49. Jewish Israeli society is also undergoing a process of fragmentation along ethnic, religious and cultural lines.

increased pressure from Muslim Arabs as well as from the Israeli political establishment.[50]

The above outcomes have been influenced over the last two decades by several factors. The emergence of radical Islamic parties,[51] the decline in the Communist Party's power which had served as Christians' political voice,[52] Palestinian Christians' demographic decrease and the rise of an exclusionary nationalist discourse in Israel have increased the sense of marginalization among Christians.[53]

The identity of Palestinian Christian in Israel has recently been even more shaken with the dramatic changes of the 2010s.

First, during the Gaza war in the summer of 2014,[54] several Israeli senior politicians and public figures made statements that questioned the loyalty of Palestinian citizens of Israel because many of them sympathized with the people of Gaza and held demonstrations against the war.

Second, the Israeli establishment has been promoting the idea of Christians volunteering for civil service and the army (Christians and Muslims have been exempted from serving in national service since 1948). In 2012, the state recruited a senior Greek Orthodox priest to advocate for this cause.

Third, a new bill was passed in 2014 allowing Christians to change their nationality in their identification cards from "Arab" to "Aramaic." Even though very few people have decided to do this, this development could be seen as yet another attempt by Israel to divide its Christian and Muslim minorities.

---

50. Ramon, *Christianity and Christians*. According to Munayer and Horenczyk, in the majority of cross-cultural studies, the first way minorities relate to majority groups is typically integration. They attribute the inconsistency in relation to Palestinian Christians to their characteristics of being highly religious, supported by a strong church and school structure, and having a long history of survival in the Middle East. Perhaps their heightened investment in Arab Nationalism would have played an important role, at least in the early days. Munayer and Horenczyk, "Multi-Group Acculturation Orientations."

51. This was the first political movement among Arabs to exclude Christians.

52. See section 3.2.2.3. Regarding the Communist Party, Ateek has claimed that the silence of the Palestinian Church during the Israeli-Palestinian conflict has caused many Christians to leave the church and become active in the Communist Party. See Ateek, *Justice and Only Justice*.

53. In 2000, there was conflict in Nazareth over building a mosque next to the Church of Annunciation, known as the *Shihab el-Din* crisis. Some argue that this was a turning point in Christian-Muslim relations in Israel, causing Christians to feel vulnerable and thus damaging the former Christian-Muslim solidarity.

54. Operation Protective Edge.

Finally, the recent political unrest in the Middle East (after the so called "Arab Spring" started in 2010) has resulted in radical Islamist groups gaining power.[55] These groups have resulted in the exodus of many Christian populations in Syria and Iraq who have lived in the Middle East for hundreds of years. The situation in Lebanon and Egypt has also been unstable for Christians. All this has caused Christians in Israel to feel the pressure and question their existence in the Middle East. More Christians are advocating for aligning with Jews in Israel, separating from their historical alliance with Muslims, while others are considering immigration to a country in the West where Christianity is the majority religion.

These dramatic changes have made the issue of identity an immediate problem for the fourth generation of Palestinian Israelis, born in the 1990s. The urgent question of serving in the national service has deepened their identity crisis even more.

Third and fourth generation Baptists, who are struggling with these questions in their churches, are questioning their pastors about Christian Zionism.[56] This has caused degrees of tension and conflict in some churches. This kind of conflict is new as it is related to theological conviction rather than conflicts over power. Based on this study's findings, this kind of conflict was identified in three Baptist churches.

It is likely that the identity crisis of Palestinian Baptists, and their living in a legally uncertain environment (being threefold minorities and second-class citizens), might cause their insecure feelings to reflect in church life as well.

3.3.1.3 Evangelical identity as shaped by missionary legacy

The term "evangelical" is not widely used in the non-evangelical Christian community. Evangelicals might have been labelled as *motajadideen* (the renewed) by Eastern Palestinian Christians, but, if asked to identify themselves, they use the term "believer." Research conducted in 2014 shows that their identity is centred on their Christian faith more than nationality or ethnic

---

55. Such as ISIS (the Islamic State of Iraq and Syria), which kills Christians who refuse to convert to Islam or pay the *jizya*.

56. Christian Zionism is a belief among some Christians that the establishment of the State of Israel in 1948 was in fulfilment of Biblical prophecy. They believe that the gathering of Jews in Israel must precede the second coming of Jesus, and that Christians should actively support the return of the Jews to the Land of Israel, along with the idea that the Jews ought to convert to Christianity.

origins; many of them appear to build their identity primarily around evangelical doctrinal commitments.[57]

Every effort to do Christian mission also involves some form of cultural and civilizational transformation. The interaction that occurred between two strong societies and traditions (Western/Eastern) was bound to produce positive and negative results. It was inevitable that, in many cases, religious, missionary and educational motives would be mixed with cultural, civilizational, ideological, economic, political and even military motives.[58] Evangelical missionaries brought several aspects of their culture and civilization that were very enriching (establishing schools, orphanages, churches, funding, jobs and so on). Nonetheless, some Arab evangelical scholars argue that there is a tendency by some in the Western church to understand itself as normative and anything which deviates from this theological or ecclesial framework as unacceptable.[59] There are several aspects of Palestinian evangelical presence in Israel that have had an unintended negative impact: cultural legacy, legacy of Zionism and legacy of pietism.

Cultural legacy
The cultural, social and political alienation that the evangelical community experiences has led some evangelicals (perhaps influenced by missionary indoctrination) to further alienate themselves from their Eastern roots in favour of Western cultural forms of expression, such as less respect for Eastern liturgy, symbols and the Virgin Mary.[60] Another example is the dress code of the pastor in and out of church; wearing a suit and tie is so typically Western American, in a context where Christian clerical clothing is important. This has alienated the evangelicals from many of their fellow Eastern Christians and non-Christians, though a few attempts at contextualising theology have been made and an increasing number of evangelical pastors are interested in wearing clerical collars.

---

57. Ajaj, Miller, and Sumpter, *Arab Evangelicals*.
58. Badr, "Involvement of the Evangelical Church."
59. Munayer, "Beyond Bells and Smells"; Badr, "Involvement of the Evangelical Church."
60. This is a theological issue rather than cultural, though theology is influenced to some extent by culture.

Legacy of Zionism: ideological conflict reflects the Israeli-Palestinian conflict

Some evangelical missions have mixed the preaching of the gospel with the transmission of certain Western political-ideological presuppositions related to the interpretation of the Old and New Testaments. This is especially evident in the case of the propagation of Zionist ideology in light of biblical interpretation concerning the theology of the promised land and the return and conversion of the Jews. This issue has caused increasing criticisms by traditional Palestinian Christians towards Palestinian evangelicals. Furthermore, major conservative evangelical denominations in the West openly support Zionism and the State of Israel, without any consideration for the implications that this support has. This ideology can be seen as a key contributing factor to the tremendous amount of injustice experienced by both Christian and non-Christian Palestinian communities in Israel/Palestine.

Christian Zionism has substantially influenced the level of political and financial support given to the State of Israel, which has in turn impacted the Israeli-Palestinian struggle and caused a great tension among Palestinian Christians regarding their identity as Palestinians. Many Palestinian evangelicals have tended to feel both misunderstood and ignored by many Western Christians.[61] However, in research conducted in 2014 with evangelical Palestinian pastors and ministers in Israel on the issue of eschatology, many were neither for nor against Zionism and did not think the issue was relevant. This shows that Palestinian evangelicals in Israel are characterized by diversity, which also demonstrates the complexity of their reality.[62]

Legacy of pietism: tendency to look inward as opposed to social engagement

Palestinian evangelical churches trust Christ for personal conversion and the gift of grace to lead a victorious life in Christ – a life possible after conversion but not before, as sin and the fallen nature must be dealt with in the new birth experience. Most churches preach against carnality and worldliness, and personal piety means obedience to Scripture, prayer and regular fellowship with other believers. They have the tendency to be *apolitically pietistic*, a type

---

61. Sabella, "Arab Christian Presence."
62. Ajaj, Miller, and Sumpter, *Arab Evangelicals*.

of personal "flight from the world," with their hopes focused on the bodily return of Christ or escape from the present world.[63] Churches hold deeply pietistic values but few contextualize theological resources. Evangelicals retain a commitment to personal and corporate piety.

Some argue that this has separated Palestinian evangelicals from their community and its struggle against injustice done to the Palestinian community. This contributes to the church's tendency to look inward as opposed to outward in any form of social engagement. This might be one of the reasons why many Palestinian evangelicals focus their ministries inside the church buildings, resulting in churches becoming crowded with pastors and leaders seeking to become pastors but with no place for them – especially as churches are small and concentrated in a small area. Obviously, this leads to conflicts around leadership. According to Brubaker, when churches look outward to their community and initiate programmes, conflicts at church lessen.[64]

3.3.2 Social Factors
3.3.2.1 *Newly educated young generation*
For Palestinian Christians in Israel, education has come to replace land as a major element of an individual's socioeconomic status. Christians who have had the benefit of a higher education and occupational profile constitute the middle class. Palestinian Baptist churches are rich in social and cultural capital. One church is associated with an educational institution, another with a care institution and another is linked to a prominent Christian website. More than 50 percent of the attendees are highly educated and of a younger generation, with careers outside the church. This generation does not come from prominent families (no ascribed power) and works hard to succeed (achieved power).

---

63. Research conducted between 1999 and 2000 in Palestine revealed that three tendencies emerged between Palestinian Christians: (1) a secular-nationalist tendency – these individuals had usually undergone thorough mobilization and consciousness formation within the political factions; (2) a religio-communal revival tendency – these individuals increasingly looked inward to the religious community, seeking its revival through more stringent religious education to better counter Islamization in the wider society; (3) an apolitical pietistic tendency – a type of personal "flight from the world," seeking succour away from the depredations of occupation and the ravages of political contestation in the alternative domains of church liturgies and personal piety. For these individuals, the kingdom is not of this world. Lybarger, "For Church or Nation?," 777–813.

64. Brubaker, *Promise and Peril*.

Baptist churches in Israel have grown significantly over the last thirty years, from two hundred members in 1970 to three thousand in 2016. Growth came from a younger, educated generation requesting more reforms in church life, wanting to take churches from being "mission centres" to churches with constitutions, shaped by decisions made by members.[65] This has resulted in tensions with older generation pastors, many appointed by missionaries. In some churches, many members have a higher level of education than their pastor, sometimes leading to laity/pastor conflict. Serious splits were led by young laity against dominant pastors who resisted change (see section 3.4).

Many intra-congregational conflicts are related to church growth and the legitimacy of its religious leadership through members' eyes.[66] Shin and Park argue that the stability of congregations is positively related to the educational level of the head pastor.[67]

3.3.2.2 *Openness to the outside world*

The situation following the 1967 war has allowed Palestinians from Israel to fellowship with Palestinians from the West Bank and Gaza. Peace with Egypt in 1979 opened the Arab world to Palestinians in Israel. In 1994, Israel made peace with Jordan causing more openness. With the influence of satellite television and the internet, the average church member is more aware of how churches should be run, challenging pastors and traditional leadership to change. It is likely that reconnecting with Christians in the larger region also helped to alleviate the sense of isolation felt by many Palestinian Christians in Israel.

---

65. Research indicates that conflicts are more likely to occur in socially heterogeneous congregations (Leas and Kittlaus, *Church Fights*), groups with socio-economically diverse membership (Shin and Park, "Analysis of Causes of Schisms"), groups with a mixture of young and old members (Herman, "Conflict in the Church"; Hoge, *Division in the Protestant House*), and groups with a mixture of older and newer members (Becker, "Congregational Models and Conflict"; Becker, *Congregations in Conflict*; Becker et al., "Straining at the Tie that Binds").

66. Brubaker, *Promise and Peril*; Becker, "Congregational Models and Conflict"; Becker, *Congregations in Conflict*; Herman, "Conflict in the Church"; Shin and Park, "Analysis of Causes of Schisms"; Wood, *Leadership in Voluntary Organizations*; Collins, *Conflict Sociology*. See chapter 1, section 1.4.4.

67. Shin and Park, "Analysis of Causes of Schisms." See chapter 1, section 1.4.4.

3.3.3 Economic Factors

In the early 1990s, the International Mission Board of the Southern Baptist Convention in the United States (IMB) decided to stop supporting local Baptist churches and institutions around the world and instead focus on "unreached groups." They halted all financial support provided to Baptist churches in Israel. This step, even though done gradually over a period of ten years, left the churches unprepared. Suddenly, Baptist churches became independent and pastors had to secure their monthly salary. These financial challenges were one potentially important factor for causing splits/exits.[68]

Palestinian Baptist churches lack material capital. Only seven churches have their own church buildings, and those were built by missionaries more than fifty years ago; the rest meet in rented halls. Churches are very small and usually provide the pastor with a modest salary if any. In 2015, 80 percent of the churches had an annual operating budget of between seven thousand and twenty thousand dollars. This leads to the question: when a pastor/leader exits and starts a new church, how can a small church provide his salary? Four of the pastors I interviewed do not get a salary from their churches. Some pastors have joined a parachurch organization or started a new one which provides their livelihood.

NGO-ization is a phenomenon in Israeli society in general and in the Arab community in particular. It relies on social/political, local/international funding. The Baptist churches are non-profit for organizational and practical reasons. Some leaders who exited and founded new churches established non-profit philanthropist ministries – "start-ups," as Rami, an ABC leader, calls them.[69] During the last two decades around nine parachurches were established.[70]

Sometimes, pastors who receive funding from various parachurch organizations may become loyal to these groups sometimes at the expense of their own churches; donors might influence the perceptions and expectations of ministries and churches.[71] As an example, Christian Zionist groups that are very active among evangelicals in Israel have also been trying to influence

---

68. Open interview with Paul, a missionary, and Rami, an ABC leader.
69. Rami, interview with author, 2014.
70. See a list in appendix 2.
71. Rami, interview with author, 2014.

Palestinian evangelical churches, causing conflict within churches that are naturally hesitant towards such groups.

At least 80 percent of Palestinian Baptist churches rely on foreign funds. Half of these churches experienced a split or leader's exit, after which the leader started a new church, a new ministry alongside the church or joined another parachurch ministry. Phil, a retired Palestinian pastor, claimed that dependence on Western funding and theology contributes to Palestinian Christian disunity. He added that adopting certain Western theology that contradicts local theology would cause divisions.[72]

It is not clear whether there is causation between parachurches and exits. However, it is likely there is a correlation between the economic factor and exits.[73]

3.3.4 Cultural Factors

What is unique to Palestinians is the socio-cultural understanding of leadership, which some have attributed to the Arab authoritarian style of leadership.[74] This question of how to deal with power was the key issue faced by local churches, as I will discuss in chapter 4.

Another cultural element is the communal component within the Palestinian Christian community. While theology and church practice are more individualistic in the West, in the Eastern traditional church (from which almost all Palestinian Baptists were converted) the emphasis on liturgy and sacraments is based on communal identification whereby these traditions bind Christians to the global church and the saints in heaven.

The loyalty of members to their organizations is another element that affects whether individuals will leave when their expectations are not met. Collins argues that members who share similar cultural backgrounds are more loyal to their organizations. In binding organizations (such as classical Judaism and Catholicism) extreme loyalty was demanded; voice was prohibited and exit was impossible.[75] In Protestantism, loyalty has been a matter of

---

72. Phil, interview with author, July 2014.
73. Some pastors and church leaders see parachurch ministries as competitors and a source of negative influence. This perception creates a confrontational dynamic instead of cooperation.
74. See chapter 1, section 1.3.
75. Collins, *Conflict Sociology*.

individual commitment; more voice is permitted, and exit (schism) relatively easy.[76] In Arab culture, loyalty and identity are intimately connected within a communal community. When missionaries came, most Palestinian Baptists were loyal to their traditional churches (Catholic or Orthodox). This is evident in the struggle that took place between the Orthodox Church and missionaries.[77] Those who left their traditional churches were harassed by their church or family.[78] First-generation Baptists who left traditional churches continued to feel deeply loyal to their communities and families, so leaving their traditional church was both painful and very costly for them.

Most Baptist churches have no teaching regarding loyalty and belonging to church, having instead a strong individualistic focus.[79] Some Baptists attend church for the benefits it gives them. If they do not like one church, they can easily move to another.[80] As such, second-generation converts have a crisis in their sense of belonging, while third-generation converts have a very weak sense of loyalty to their Baptist churches; they are more loyal to ideology. Seemingly, this is another factor that has increased church exits among the third generation.[81]

3.3.5 Theological Factors

In the early 1990s, a young, charismatic Palestinian-American pastor came to Israel to serve with the Baptist churches. In 1999 he conducted a two-year leadership programme, which was joined by around twenty-five to thirty young educated men and women. The programme included a charismatic emphasis which encouraged lay participation in leadership and placed less value on hierarchical authority. This caused an influx of young lay leadership influenced by charismatic teachings, some of whom sought to become pastors

---

76. Smelser, *Social Edges of Psychoanalysis*, 188.

77. Register, *Back to Jerusalem*.

78. A few first-generation pastors were excluded and boycotted by their families after their conversion.

79. Individualism in this context means individual salvation in Jesus with a focus on a vertical relationship to God and less emphasis on the "horizontal" relations among members of the church – or an ecclesiology that sees the church as a collection of Spirit-filled individuals who do not really need each other.

80. My personal observation.

81. This factor is discussed in section 3.4 and chapter 4.

or become involved in ministry in the following decade. However, only four young leaders were ordained as pastors between 1990 and 2010.

The findings show that many of the Baptist churches have charismatic teachings. Although 30 percent of the pastors are not charismatic, many of their church members are open to charismatic teaching. Additionally, many churches have been influenced by visiting charismatic Arab pastors who gained their theological education in Western seminaries. Based on my personal observations, it appears many Palestinian Baptists rely on well-known charismatic pastors, whom they often invite to their annual church conferences, for church growth and revival.

The rise of the charismatic movement, with its emphasis on individual subjective experience, spontaneity and lay participation, and its lesser emphasis on formal church regulation,[82] has caused challenges and conflicts for many churches in other contexts.[83]

3.3.6 Structural Factors

Split or exit is not unique to Palestinian Baptists but actually characterizes Baptist churches in general. Some even claim that the Baptist church worldwide grows through splits. It is likely that the main strategy of conflict management used in Western Baptist churches is splits and exits. Nonetheless, splits/exits within the Palestinian Baptist churches have their own unique characteristics. Several structural elements affected the Palestinian Baptist environment: The ABC, Palestinian Baptists' perceptions on ordination, the shortage of trained pastors and church buildings and the establishment of the Convention of Evangelical Churches in Israel.

3.3.6.1 The Association of Baptist Churches in Israel (ABC)

Before 1965, missionaries were the main decision-makers in Baptist churches in Israel. After the establishment of the ABC, missionaries continued to be influential in church life through funding and the position of "field representative." After the missionaries left, the ABC tried to take their place. When

---

82. I have met some "lay elders" who believe in having great spiritual authority but who dismiss formal training and ordination.

83. See chapter 1, section 1.4.4.3. Bax, *Good Wine*; Francis, Lankshear, and Jones, "Influence of the Charismatic Movement"; Jaichandran and Madhav, "Pentecostal Spirituality in a Postmodern World"; Poloma *Charismatic Movement*; Starke and Dyck, "Upheavals in Congregations."

the ABC tried to intervene during church conflicts, some pastors opposed the ABC, claiming that churches are independent according to Baptist doctrine. Some Palestinian Baptist leaders argued that this attitude contributed to church splits/exits.[84]

The ABC consists of eighteen churches.[85] Most of these churches have relatively few members, averaging between thirty to sixty persons; only two churches have close to two hundred. During the last twenty years, twelve new churches were founded and two small churches have ceased to exist (one could not provide the pastor a salary).

The results show that the ABC has a low level of institutionalization, with no clear guidelines about succession process, pension and church committee assignment. The primary source of struggle in many churches is over control and power between the pastor and young laity. Some leaders who have a theological education are not offered any leadership positions within their church. In small churches, the pastor and his family are usually the main decision-makers. In churches that have church committees there is usually some rotation between committee members who support the pastor, with some of them remaining for a long time (see section 1.4.3 on power).[86]

There is no clear leadership structure within these churches; some churches have a pastor (sometimes not ordained) with or without a church committee. Other churches have only elders or deacons or both. There are no clear criteria on how to become a pastor, elder or deacon. There is no succession process or clear understanding about the roles of elders and deacons and their assignments.[87]

---

84. Rami, Sami, David in interviews with author.

85. Members in each church share the same cultural background. Most of the churches include many families and some individuals. Exceptions are one church with many youth and another church with many women in their seventies. The approximate median age of church attendees is between forty and fifty. Thirty percent of the churches are middle-class with many professionals.

86. Oswald, Heath and Heath argue individuals who have certain roles for many years are very powerful. Often, congregational leaders are not able to remove them from office because they possess huge amounts of informal power within the system. Oswald, Heath, and Heath, *Beginning Ministry Together*.

87. The Baptist theology of ordained ministry has been rather misunderstood by pastors, and the charismatic influence on members might have displaced the authority of pastors practised in the churches of Israel.

Another important element is pensions. If there were a good pension system for pastors this might encourage earlier retirement or leaving their church after retirement, especially since there are limited career options within this context for pastors after leaving their pastorates.

Regarding church constitution and decision-making at church, findings show only 70 percent of the Baptist churches have constitutions. Half of these churches do not use them, justifying this with the following statements: "We try not to work against the constitution"; "I don't know if we are working according to the constitution"; "We don't ignore it but we walk according to God's guidance." Three churches mentioned that they are changing their constitution, mainly after a split. Only two churches work according to their constitution.

In relation to decision-making, more than 50 percent of the pastors said they were the main decision-makers; most were also founders of their churches.[88] Fewer than 50 percent of the pastors consult the church committee or elders and meet every two to three months; those that do are usually young pastors who were ordained by the ABC, or are those who pastor a big church.

3.3.6.2 Perceptions on ordination: Palestinian Baptist practice

Baptist churches in Israel were influenced by three evangelical movements:[89]

1) *Southern Baptists* founded the Baptist ministry in Israel and thus have had a powerful influence on local theology and practice. In 1953 the Nazareth Baptist Church was officially reorganized as a single-elder congregationalist church. The churches that were planted later on had similar styles.

2) *The charismatic movement* has had its impact on Baptist life. Charismatics tend to emphasize that all believers receive spiritual gifts for active service but also that ministers have a special anointing; that is, there is a divine source of the pastor's calling. Some say that the pastor alone is responsible for the ministry of Word and Sacrament; others say that, because of the "priesthood of all believers," the laity can also take on these responsibilities.

---

88. The "founder's syndrome" as Kassis and Costa call it. Kassis and Costa, *Secret to Successful Governance*.

89. See Farraj, "Analysis of Differences."

Furthermore, some churches just have a single pastor and a board of deacons under the pastor, whereas others have plural eldership, in which one elder functions as the pastor.[90]

3) *Recent British Baptist theology* emphasizes the plural eldership style as addressed in the ABC's new constitution. Between 2007 and 2013, a British pastor played an important role in writing this new constitution. Part of this constitution involves the question of the ordination of pastors and allows for greater influence by the ABC over churches experiencing conflict. Previously, the ordination decision was made entirely by the local church with the ABC's formal blessing.[91] The new constitution (2007) recognized two offices: elder (*sheikh*)[92] and deacon (*shamas*).[93] Among the elders, the pastor is regarded as having a special role in teaching and presiding over the congregation and the officers of the church. The new constitution represents a shift that has taken place in the relationship between the individual congregation and the ABC. Now the ABC interviews the candidate to check his suitability and thus has more authority.[94] Nonetheless, the ultimate decision still remains with the local church.[95]

On the issue of singular versus plural eldership there is ongoing debate, much as with other Baptists elsewhere. Some churches fear the abuse or loss of power, and this leads to a reluctance to elect a single pastor or even an eldership board.

In Israel, since the new constitution, the ABC has been taking an increasingly active role in the process of ordination, not only in examining

---

90. Beasley-Murray, *Radical Believers*.

91. The old constitution made no reference to ordination, but there were unwritten, implicitly agreed procedures.

92. An elder in the free church is a lay person who serves as an administrator; he preaches and/or has pastoral roles in a local church, and sometimes he is ordained to such an office. There is a difference between ordained elders and lay elders.

93. A deacon in the free church is a laity administrative role, not a clerical office.

94. Before the new constitution (2007), seven pastors were ordained by missionaries, and three pastors were ordained by their churches' initiative and the ABC. After the new constitution, only three pastors were ordained by the ABC (in 2009 and 2013). Eight non-ordained pastors are pastoring churches.

95. To be an ordained ABC pastor, the candidate must satisfy not only his local church but also the ABC.

candidates, but also leading ordination services with only ordained pastors invited to lay hands on the ordinand.[96] This is an example of the Baptist concern for interdependence, with the ultimate decision resting with the church. The ABC can also recommend pastors to vacant churches or recommend a probationary period to monitor suitability. It is not, however, involved in the process of ordaining elders, but only pastors. This leads to the pastors having a special role among the elders.[97]

3.3.6.3 The shortage of trained pastors

Education of clergy for churches was virtually non-existent, as only several selected individuals were sent to study in seminaries in Western countries. Some others, from the 1970s to the 1990s, studied in an American extension department (CSTC) in Haifa, which served as a pre-university-level theological education centre for people interested in ministry. These leadership courses contained uncritically imported theology based on American perspectives and culture. Some of these leaders were ordained as Baptist pastors.

A small number of pastors with basic theological (pastoral) training meant that each church relied on local lay leadership. This strengthened congregational leadership but caused a great tension in leadership between pastors and young laity who were very often highly educated. Findings show that only one-third of the pastors (including non-ordained pastors) are well educated (having an additional degree to their theological training). Another one-third have diplomas from a local Bible College, one-sixth have a master's degree in theology from Western seminaries and one-sixth are still working on their Bachelor of Divinity from Western seminaries. The foundation of the Nazareth Evangelical Seminary in 2007, that merged into Nazareth Evangelical College (NEC) in 2013, has come to fulfil the need for local theological education and well-educated leaders.

3.3.6.4 Church buildings

Based on the Baptist principle of the autonomy of the local church, missionaries in Israel desired to register buildings in the name of local congregations, but some opposing voices claimed that this could result in the abuse of the

---

96. Internationally, Baptist associations and unions have varying levels of influence on the local church.
97. Farraj, "Analysis of Differences."

property, particularly when a church was controlled by a certain prominent family. As the price of land and property is very high, the use of church property has been a key issue in church splits, which resulted in the need for a mechanism to decide church property ownership when a church is split. Serious splits have happened in congregations with church owned buildings.[98]

Until 2018, church buildings remain registered under the name of the BCI (the local branch of the International Mission Board of the Southern Baptist Convention in the United States), yet BCI involvement is minimal.

3.3.6.5 *The Convention of Evangelical Churches in Israel (CECI)*

The Convention of Evangelical Churches in Israel (CECI) was established in 2005, when representatives from five evangelical denominations and some parachurch organizations united together in order to gain recognition as an "official religion" in Israel – a unified entity entitled to the same rights and responsibilities as Israel's other officially recognized religions.[99] Nonetheless, because of the diverse theologies represented by the five denominations, the Israeli government has posed the CECI with some challenges for recognition as a single "recognized community." A further advantage of establishing the CECI is that it would improve visibility and legitimacy in the broader society, especially among traditional Christians, Muslims and Jews who are often confused at the many denominations that are all called "evangelical." Grouping the denominations in one body in faith and practice would help them be recognized by the broader society.[100]

Based on my observation and interviews, openness to other denominations was available after the convention was founded. This openness, however, encouraged the mobility of pastors/leaders who, as a result of conflict, would easily leave for another denomination. Between 2010 and 2017, three Baptist pastors/leaders left the ABC and joined other denominations.

---

98. This factor is discussed in depth in chapter 4, section 4.4.1.

99. The various churches that constitute the CECI amount to thirty-four individual congregations: eighteen Baptist churches, seven Assemblies of God, three Church of the Nazarene, two Christian Missionary Alliance and four Open Brethren. One can add to this the five Plymouth Brethren churches not members of the convention. See Ajaj, Miller, and Sumpter, *Arab Evangelicals*.

100. For more information, see Ajaj, Miller, and Sumpter, *Arab Evangelicals*.

In sum, the evangelical movement in the Holy Land is relatively new, being approximately one hundred years old. Since the 1990s, Palestinian Baptists in Israel have been in the process of indigenization through running their own institutions and churches, and many basic elements of church life and theology are still in formative stages. This also explains the low level of institutionalization in the Baptist denomination. Palestinian Baptists have also started to engage in contextualization, determining their own areas of interest and action, such as changing the ABC constitution, obtaining official recognition from the State of Israel and establishing their local seminary.

3.4 Statistics of Splits and Exits in the Baptist Churches in Israel

The results of the field mapping show that the generational factor (mentioned in section 3.2.2) explains the different strategies each generation uses in handling church conflict. Ateek, Rabinowitz and Abu-Baker's typologies suggest that the attitude of the three generations towards political conflict is different.[101] The "survival generation" refers to those who became refugees in their own land in 1948: they gave up and accepted reality; the "worn-out generation" refers to those who sought coexistence and struggled to get into leadership but failed; and the "stand-tall generation" refers to those who demanded their full rights as a condition for coexistence. On the basis of my research, my thesis is that these generational characteristics can also be identified among the Palestinian Baptists during congregational conflict. The first generation accepted reality and kept the status quo without resolving the church conflict; the second generation fought for change, splitting the church when this failed; the third generation exited, starting new churches.[102]

---

101. Ateek, *Justice and Only Justice*; Rabinowitz and Abu-Baker, *Door Zakoof*.

102. In order to evaluate this result, I interviewed two Jordanian pastors: one, a Palestinian pastor who lived in Jordan for many years and is familiar with the three case studies; the second, a Jordanian pastor living in Israel pastoring a Palestinian church. According to them, Baptist churches in Jordan, which include many Palestinians, have very few splits for three reasons. First, Jordanians have deep respect for their king; in the same manner, Jordanian Baptists (both younger and older generations) have respect for people in authority, such as pastors; it is likely that this is a reflection of their national Jordanian identity in their church practice. Second, Jordanian society is more unified than the deeply divided Israeli-Palestinian society. Third, the Jordanian state does not allow people to randomly found a church; each church should be registered legally. Additionally, I interviewed two Lebanese evangelical leaders, and, according

However, I am aware that these are only generalizations and cannot be used to characterize everyone born in each generation.[103]

As mentioned previously, I find two different periods of time in Palestinian Baptist life in Israel which have influenced their responses to conflict: (1) Before the missionaries' departure (1911–1990) – in eight decades no splits were recorded. There were exits both from unsatisfied members and a few pastors who were encouraged by missionaries to leave their position. The first generation, who belong to the "survival" group, were more evident during this period; they tended to accept reality rather than seeking change. One first-generation deacon told me, "Leaving the church was not seen as an option during the conflict; even after the pastor fired us [the deacons], we kept attending the church hoping to convince him to change his attitude."[104] (2) After the missionaries' departure (1990–2016) – at least thirty-two church conflicts which were resolved through three different strategies of conflict management: (a) the church split into two; (b) the church leader exited with his family and founded a new church; and (c) the church leader exited with his family and joined another ministry/church.

Between 1990 and 2005 the common strategy for handling church conflict was *splitting*. Between 2006 and 2016 the common strategy for handling church conflict was *exiting* – founding a new church or joining a new ministry. It seems that in the last decade, conflict has been more often resolved by exiting rather than splitting. This is similar to the strategy used in the Baptist churches in the West.

These results are portrayed in the following chart (the numbers in the chart are by decade).

---

to them, Lebanese Baptist churches face frequent splits, and they have three conventions. Their society is also deeply divided like the Israeli-Palestinian society.

Seemingly, the excessive deference of Jordan's younger generation Baptists towards pastors (possibly because of their monarchical form of government) is similar to that of first-generation Palestinian Baptists in Israel, who also defer to pastors but for different reasons (the sacramental theology of the converts' traditional mother traditional churches). However, younger generation Palestinian Baptists in Israel, who live in different political conditions, handle intra-church conflicts differently. We can conclude that the political situation affects the attitude of each generation towards church conflict. However, I am aware that this argument needs further research; space limits further discussion.

103. Some second-generation members might have a "stand-tall" attitude, and some third-generation members might have a "worn-out" attitude.

104. Jack, interview with author, April 2014.

Table 3.2: Splits/exits in the Baptist churches in Israel

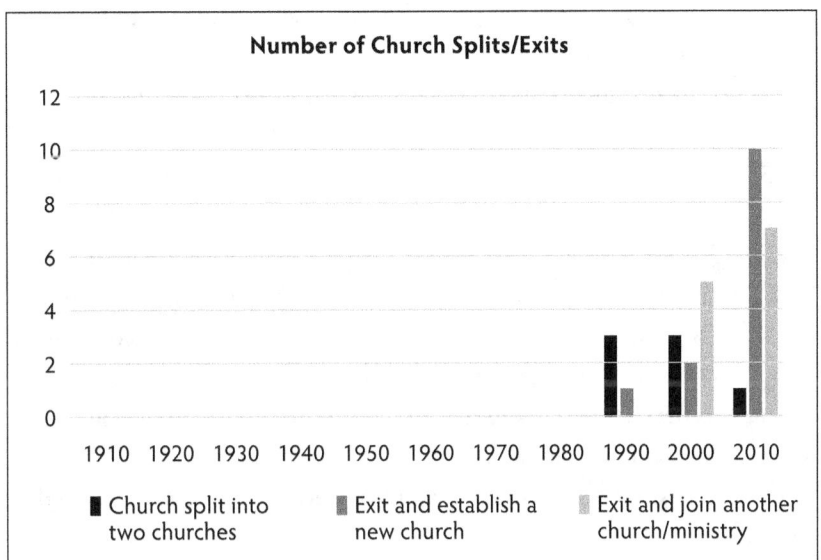

It is important to understand the nature (conditions) of the relationship between the factors (political, social, structural, theological, cultural and economic) mentioned above and the strategies (processes) that have been used to handle the conditions that pertain to the phenomenon of church splits (consequences) over the last two decades. Giddens discusses the importance of studying the processes by which actors, in specific contexts, reproduce or change social structures through their interactions.[105] This helps generate a better understanding of conflict in local Palestinian Baptist churches in Israel.

I briefly present the findings of this research regarding splits/exits, conditions, processes and consequences separately for each decade.

3.4.1 Splits and Exits between 1990 and 2005

During this decade six splits and one exit took place.
1) A split: a youth leader with several families left and started a new church.
2) A split: a youth leader left his church with several families and started a new church.[106]

---
105. Giddens, *Constitution of Society*.
106. He was also recruited by the ABC to pastor a small church.

3) An exit: a young pastor, who was in conflict with the former pastor who refused to pass on power, was encouraged to leave the church to lead another one.
4) A split: young leaders left the church with many families and started a new church.
5) A split: young leaders left with some families and started a new church.
6) Two splits: a pastor from a non-Baptist denomination joined two rural Baptist churches. In one church he became the pastor; after a short time the church split. In the other church he tried to take over as pastor; when he did not succeed, the church split as well.

During this period the splits were public and acrimonious, irreversible, foreseen and had widespread impact.

Conditions related to splits during this decade can be summarized as follow:

1) The leadership that split was an educated new generation (those belonging to the "worn-out generation") seeking for change and wanting to be part of church leadership.
2) Most of the pastors of these churches were first-generation Baptists (those belonging to the "survival generation") and were ordained as pastors during the 1960s;
3) Most of the pastors had basic theological education and felt threatened by the younger, more educated generation;
4) Most of the pastors were the main spiritual authorities and were often "in charge of everything" – they hardly shared or passed on power to the younger generation;
5) The splits took place in churches that owned church buildings and institutions (economic/cultural/social capital);
6) The ABC was weak due to its voluntary nature and lack of a clear structure to handle church splits – also, some ABC leaders were involved in these splits;
7) During this period pastors did not have the mobility to join another denomination because the convention (CECI) which facilitated such movement was only established in 2005.

Processes and consequences during this decade show that younger leaders who belonged to the "worn-out generation" were more evident in this decade. They sought change but failed to get into leadership as pastors hardly shared or passed on power. Young leaders left with half of the church after a dispute. The consequences were splits.[107]

3.4.2 Splits and Exits between 2006 and 2016

During this decade twenty-four exits and one split took place. It is clear that there were more exits in this period than in the period 1990–2005, but less splits.

1) Eight young leaders exited their churches and founded new ones.
2) Eight leaders exited their churches and joined another church's leadership.
3) Two leaders exited their churches and joined another ministry.
4) Four young leaders, in conflict with their pastor, were encouraged by the ABC to leave and lead other small churches.
5) Two young female leaders exited their churches and started their own ministry.
6) A split: a pastor left his church with half of the members and established a new church.

Regarding conditions related to this decade, I find that this decade is characterized by the emergence of a new style of churches which I call *personalized churches*, where each church was recognized by the pastor's name. People attended the church because of the pastor's charisma. This left younger people in the church with no hope of taking part in leading the church (unless they were part of the pastor's family),[108] leading them to silently leave the church to start their own new churches. This kind of conflict and outcome was identified in more than 50 percent of the churches. It is reasonable to

---

107. In one church the "worn-out generation" split the church several years into the conflict. In their opinion, this was the only way to deal with the conflict. One of them explained, "The business meetings were aggressive and full of accusations. They hurt us deeply and accused us of trying to fire the pastor. However, we decided to leave the church only after the pastor changed the constitution and dismissed the deacons from office" (Sami, interview with author, Feb. 2014).

108. In rural areas, churches are small and have family leadership. Some churches started as home churches, and the pastor is in control. The pastor's family somehow control the church and do not share power outside the family realm.

conclude that pastors who had established a church themselves could cause other leaders to leave – the "founder's syndrome" as Kassis and Costa call it[109] – unlike the situation when a pastor was not the founder of the church, in which case it was easier to make him leave.

Furthermore, the findings show that churches that went through a split experienced splitting again. Additionally, churches that split from the mother church would be more likely to experience a further split. One pastor whose church split twice, first from the mother church and second from the new church he founded, said, "If some Baptist churches were recognized by the ABC after splitting, then it is legitimate for other churches to split too."[110] Unresolved conflict in the first decade (1990–2005) gave legitimacy for contemporary churches to split, as this became an accepted norm.

Processes and consequences were different in this decade. The "stand-tall generation" was evident in this period; they were less traditional and more loyal to ecclesial ideology; they discovered a new sense of pride in themselves; and they thought and acted differently. If the pastor was not willing to share power/pass on power, they exited and founded their own church. They did not even struggle for change within the existing church.[111]

During this period the common strategy for handling church conflict was exits. Most of these exits happened when the pastor attempted to ensure that an ambitious young leader understood that he was not welcomed as a decision-maker. Generally, the official statement for leaving the church would be that the young leader was "guided by the Lord to start a new ministry" and left peacefully, even though many knew that he left unhappily. Unambitious leaders would leave and join another church or denomination hoping to be welcomed by another leadership.

---

109. Kassis and Costa, *Secret to Successful Governance*.

110. Pastor C, interview with author, 2014.

111. During the conflict of one of the churches, the youth were having their own youth meetings outside the church building. One leader explained, "We did not feel welcomed at church, with all the conflict going on we decided to focus on our youth ministry outside the church" (open interview with author).

3.5 Conclusion

The missionaries' departure, along with other changes in the social, economic, cultural, theological, structural and generational factors, influenced Palestinian Baptist responses to church conflict. It is likely that a combination of these factors contributed to church conflicts that led to splits/exits among Palestinian Baptists.

The findings show that splits within these churches arose from multiple characteristics – characteristics which are unique to a church that does not act like the traditional churches in its community. The Palestinian Baptists' identity crisis and living in a legally uncertain environment (as threefold minorities and second-class citizens) –which mirrored their insecure feelings in church life – the scattered field of very small churches, the flat structure and the absence of a patriarch in a patriarchal community, the lack of economic capital, the low level of institutionalization, the pastors' struggle over livelihood and power (which was constantly being threatened by lay leaders), the influx of educated young leaders with commitment to individual rights and their "rebellion" against patriarchy, all combined to encourage splits/exits.

Furthermore, the power that has kept Palestinian Baptist churches together has weakened. The new generation is more individualistic, and churches focus on the vertical dimension and less on the communal. At the same time, churches are personalized, have no assets, have poor accountability to the ABC, and splits/exits have become an option.

The results also show that the generational factor explains the different strategies used in handling church conflict during the two decades after missionary departure. While in the first decade (1990–2005) the main strategy was splitting, in the second decade (2006–2016) the main strategy was exiting. It is likely that in the Palestinian Baptist churches there are three different generational attitudes: "survival," "worn-out" and "stand-tall." Each attitude used a different strategy to handle church conflict. The first generation with its "survival" attitude tried to maintain the status quo, even if that left the conflict unresolved, and thus until the early 1990s no splits/exits were recorded. In the first decade after the missionaries' departure the second generation, with its "worn-out" attitude, split the church after they failed to become part of the leadership. In the second decade after the missionaries' departure, the third generation, with its "stand-tall" attitude, exited their churches to start new ones when their pastors did not share power. It seems the different generations that have been identified in the Palestinian society in Israel as a whole can also be found in Palestinian Baptist churches in Israel.

Second- and third-generation Baptists, who are more open to the outside world than the previous generation, have integrated secular, Western values, affecting the way they dealt with church conflict. They have adopted a common Western-Baptist conflict management practice – namely, splits and exits – which is not recognized as a conflict management practice within traditional churches in their community.

Finally, since the 1990s, Palestinian Baptists in Israel have been in the process of indigenization, running their own churches and organizations, while also engaging in contextualization, shaping their own theology. Most Baptists have identified some aspects of their imported theology which they like, such as church autonomy, single-pastor churches, ecclesiastical polity, pietism, individualism and the focus on the vertical dimension. However, they have also identified certain things to leave behind, such as the cessationist teaching they received from some American Baptists. They prefer charismatic theology. Regarding Zionist theology, Palestinian Baptists have diverse opinions; there is a strong debate around this issue that causes tension between them. This process of contextualization is ongoing, as Baptists struggle to obtain official recognition as a religious body from the State of Israel. Additionally, the foundation of Nazareth Evangelical College is an example of local Baptists having identified a need for local theological education.

After exploring the different potential factors that contributed to conflict in the Palestinian Baptist churches in Israel, in the next chapter I will examine the primary factors that led to splits/exits in three case studies.

CHAPTER 4

The Nature and Causes of Church Conflict in Three Case Studies of Palestinian Baptist Churches in Israel

4.1 Introduction

Having described the context, mapped the field, and explained the environment and the potential factors that contributed to conflict in the Palestinian Baptist churches, I will now examine the nature of the conflict and main factors that caused splits in three case studies.

This chapter reveals that Palestinian Baptists are navigating between their affiliations to different communities with competing worldviews and identities: (1) secular, Western rationality acquired through their involvement in Israeli institutions, (2) Palestinian cultural deference to patriarchal authority, and (3) dual religious commitment to episcopalian and congregationalist traditions.[1]

I begin with a brief description of the churches, providing pertinent background information needed to understand the dynamics of occurrences before and during the conflict. Then I analyze the nature and causes of conflict explaining the primary and secondary factors that led to church splits/exits.

---

1. Many Palestinian Baptists whom I interviewed used English and Hebrew words as part of a fluent conversation in Arabic, and some of the more educated even switched back and forth between Arabic and English/Hebrew. This might indicate how Palestinian Baptists in Israel are affected by three different cultures.

4.2 Historical Background of the Three Churches and Their Conflicts

4.2.1 Case Study A
4.2.1.1 Background

Church A is located in a town in Israel. It is surrounded by larger traditional Christian churches in terms of both membership and property owned. These churches have buildings and a hierarchical form of government, which is very different from church A and its relative lack of congregational property. It is to be expected that this environment would influence the way the church perceives itself.

Church A was founded a few decades before 1948. After the 1948 war it was greatly weakened, but the congregation was revived by the arrival of American Southern Baptist missionaries, with Pastor Mike pastoring church A for nine years until he resigned and informed the church that it was time for an indigenous pastor.[2] According to the church constitution, a new pastor had to be recommended by the church and his name brought to all members for voting; however, the personal preference of Pastor Mike was to play an important role in determining whose name would be brought for voting.

Pastor A was elected pastor and ordained after he returned from a year's study abroad. There was community disagreement regarding Pastor A's ordination. After he was ordained two large families left the church. Pastor A enjoyed a team of helpers, including deacons and some American missionaries, who helped lead the church while other leaders were busy with church plants and other activities. A few became pastors in new Baptist church plants, and some held leadership roles in an educational institution established by American Southern Baptist missionaries to serve the local population.[3]

During the late 1980s and into the early 1990s, church A had an influx of young people. Evangelistic gatherings in the church, programmes in the educational institution and Baptist summer camps attracted this group.[4] These

---

2. Mansour, *Baptist History in the Holy Land between 1950 and 2020*.

3. For more information on this history see Mansour, *Baptist History in the Holy Land between 1950 and 2020*.

4. During the 1970s and 1980s, the church saw growth mainly as a result of people coming to church to hear these charismatic speakers preach, which led many people to join the church.

young people came from medium socioeconomic families and were cared for by young Baptist missionaries living in the town. This newer, younger group did not have strong ties with the pastor, which led to some leaving the church.

Table 4.1: Members of church A

	First generation born in 1930s-1940s	Second generation born in 1950s-1960s	Third generation born in 1970s-1980s	Miss-ionaries
Pastor	1			
Deacons: 4	3	1		
Church committee: 7	3	3		1
Church members: 100	30%	30%	30%	2 families

4.2.1.2 Conflicts, splits/exits in church A
A youth exit: a group in their early twenties left church
This group felt they did not belong in the church, even though they had attended it for years. They felt they were not pastored properly by Pastor A and left the church. Kareem, who attended church A for fifteen years, said, "One Sunday, Pastor A greeted me and asked me about my name; I felt humiliated and decided not to come back to church A."[5] Nora, a church A member, invited Pastor A to speak at an ecumenical student conference. He was very excited to see many young Christians, so he invited them to come to his church, not realising that many of them had attended for some years.[6] Some of this group left the church, and others looked for other evangelical churches to join.

---

5. Open interview, Kareem, 2014.
6. Nora, interview with author, Mar. 2014.

A split: a ministry leader and some families left church A and established a new church

Jonathan was an influential young leader in church A. According to the church's constitution, each ministry leader must be re-elected after a certain period of time. It was time for Jonathan to finish his term, and he strongly felt he should continue. Pastor A insisted Jonathan should be replaced. The deacons also tried to convince Jonathan to stay and work alongside the new ministry leader.[7] Jonathan believed Pastor A was threatened by his influential ministry at church. He asserted, "I was shocked to hear that some people from the pastor's side said that I was leading a conspiracy to replace Pastor A!"[8] Backed by one of the missionaries, Jonathan decided to leave the church and begin a home group. One year later, Jonathan founded a new Baptist church.

A split: young members and deacons left church after a conflict with Pastor A

When Pastor A reached pension age, the church committee decided to extend his time as there was no replacement. Two years later, Pastor A and the deacons invited Pastor George to be assistant pastor for six months and then replace Pastor A.[9] Pastor A's wife claimed that George was invited without Pastor A being informed. After six months, surprisingly, Pastor A informed the deacons he was not ready to resign and wished to continue. He suggested George could work under his authority, but George refused. This resulted in a dispute and many heated meetings. In one meeting, Pastor A overrode the constitution and dismissed the deacons and finally the church split and church A2 was founded. The power dynamics between Pastor A, the deacons and the younger generation are discussed in section 4.3.

The founding members of church A2 were some of the young people from the 1980s revival and the deacons. The mission's area-director allowed church A2 to begin using an educational institution's auditorium a few metres away from church A. Later, George was invited to pastor church A2 on a part time basis. Church A2 attracted new members and quickly grew to one hundred

---

7. Jack, interview with author, Apr. 2014; Tamer, interview with author, Mar. 2014; Jonathan, interview with author, Apr. 2014.

8. Jonathan, interview with author, Apr. 2014.

9. Church protocol, 23 Feb.

members. In subsequent years, church A2 was attractive, but later on this church, too, experienced a few exits. Church A2 went through four different exits of leaders who were not satisfied; two of them became pastors of new churches, and the other two joined another church leadership team.

Third-party interventions in this conflict were mainly informal individual initiatives by respected figures in the evangelical community. These interventions took place during and after the split and were not successful. Another important intervention was done by the BCI and the ABC who initiated a retreat between disputants and were able to draft a preliminary agreement. This initiative also failed later on, as I will explain in chapter 5.

Five exits: Leaders left church A and founded a new church or ministry

Church A also grew with two dynamic young pastors helping Pastor A – namely, Mark and Majd. Pastor A continued to recruit young pastors to work alongside him, but, according to them, they decided to leave when they discovered that he was not willing to share power.

1) Majd joined the church upon Pastor A's request and became assistant pastor. He left after a few years.[10]
2) Another young leader, ambitious to become a pastor, left the church and started a new one.
3) Adam, a deacon, left and joined church A2.
4) Victor joined church A, hoping he would be ordained as a pastor.[11] Pastor A agreed but had him sign an agreement that this ordination did not mean that he would replace Pastor A at any future given time. Victor left and founded a new church.
5) Samir joined church A and became assistant pastor.[12] After a few years, he decided to leave and joined another church.

According to interviews with the above leaders,[13] seemingly Pastor A had a perpetual pattern of behaviour to protect his position. He would enlist a young assistant pastor to help him. Then, when church members became

---

10. Majd was previously the pastor of another Baptist church.
11. Victor was previously the leader of another Baptist church.
12. Samir was a veteran pastor who was previously a pastor of another Baptist church.
13. Samir, Mark, Majd, Adam, George, Jonathan and Victor in interviews with author.

excited about the new assistant, Pastor A "encouraged" him to leave using various means, such as telling the assistant that he was no longer welcome,[14] seeking to control the assistant's behaviour,[15] and refusing to let him be part of the church decision-making team.

In 2017, Pastor A is still the pastor of church A. Church A has an average attendance of twenty members every Sunday and some guest speakers come to visit and preach. I have attended several services. The building is large and can contain three hundred attendees, but only twenty come regularly and most are in their seventies. There are only three families. Members sit separately as if there is no connection between them. In August 2015, I attended a service at church A. Pastor A preached about salvation. His wife played the piano and another woman sang from her place. Nizar, an old member, led the worship from the pulpit without singing himself; the songs were also about salvation. At some point a few members left before the end of the service after they fulfilled their roles (worship and collecting the offering). Immediately after the service everybody walked towards the door and left without fellowship time. I did not feel welcomed to stay as no one greeted me except Pastor A and his wife who knew I was coming, but even their direction was towards leaving the church. I joined another service where Pastor A spoke about judgment. A group of tourists had joined that service. Surprisingly, that same day an elder in church A2 told me that they were expecting a group to come to their church. Apparently they had mistakenly gone to church A since it is located on the main street and has a church sign, whereas church A2 meets in a hall and is not identifiable as a church from the outside.[16] This misunderstanding has happened several times.

4.2.2 Case Study B
4.2.2.1 Background
Church B, established before 1948 by American Southern Baptists, is located in a town in Israel. The church halted operations twice: first, before World War II, when the Lebanese pastor went back to his home country and many members of the church were scattered due to the conflict; and second, in

---

14. Pastor B, interview with author, Apr. 2014.
15. Majd, interview with author, June 2014; George, interview with author, Mar. 2014.
16. Field note, Aug. 2015; open interview with Rami.

1972.[17] In the 1980s, an American veteran Baptist missionary revived the church, starting with a few members, including two local ordained pastors. At the time, a few young people joined the church, and it did well for a few years until the missionary left to take a position overseas. Pastor B, a promising young Palestinian leader, came back after he finished his master's in theology from a western country. With missionary support,[18] he became pastor of church B. Pastor B, charismatic with a strong personality, was successful in rebuilding the church, attracting families and many middle-class professionals, and, at certain times, it had over seventy members.[19]

Table 4.2: Members of church B

	First generation born in 1930s-1940s	Second generation born in 1950s-1960s	Third generation born in 1970s-1980s	Miss-ionaries
Pastor		1		
Deacons				
Church committee		7		
Church members: 70	10%	80%	10%	1

---

17. Mansour, *Baptist History in the Holy Land between 1950 and 2020*. Up until this period American Baptist missionaries had been working with Jews and Arabs together, trying to develop Arab-Jewish churches. The Baptist Church was re-opened in 1965 and had three pastors: a Jew, a Palestinian and an American missionary. This church was not functional because of theological differences between Jews and Palestinians, mainly after the six-day war. This then led to the closure of the church in 1972.

18. Missionaries were indirectly the main decision-makers during this period, as they owned the church buildings and funded part of the pastors' salaries.

19. For more information on this history see Mansour, *Baptist History in the Holy Land between 1950 and 2020*.

4.2.2.2 Conflicts, splits/exits in church B
An exit: A leader left church B
Yasmin was a ministry leader at church B. She claimed that the pastor did not share power. Although, according to some interviewees, her ministry at church was successful, she left and joined another church.[20]

An exit: A leader left church B
Nadia was a ministry leader at church B for many years. Pastor B claimed that he was dissatisfied with her style of leadership over the final few years and asked her to leave her church ministry. Nadia left the church.[21] When the church committee questioned Pastor B regarding his conflicts with Yasmin and Nadia, he became upset and conflict escalated.

A Split: Five church leaders left church after a conflict with Pastor B
As a result of Yasmin and Nadia's exits, the church committee requested for church B to be led by a council alongside Pastor B and to have a constitution. Pastor B could not handle this request well and viewed this as a conspiracy to fire him; his condition was, "I, the pastor, lead the meetings and I, the pastor, have the primary individual responsibility and privilege to lead the church."[22] The church committee worked in creating a constitution without Pastor B being involved. This led to heated business meetings between the committee members and the pastor. When they called for a general meeting, ignoring Pastor B, Pastor B dismissed the church committee.

After a few months of turmoil, the church split. Around 60 percent of its members (mainly professionals) left and established church B2. The dynamics between Pastor B and the church leaders are discussed in section 4.3.

The attempts of the ABC to reconcile the parties were in vain; Pastor B did not encourage any third party to intervene.[23] The other group, led by

---

20. Yasmin, interview with author, Sept. 2016; Elias, Rana, interviews with author, Aug. 2015.
21. Elias, Nadia, Rana, and Pastor B, interviews with author, Aug. 2015.
22. Pastor B's letter to the ABC, 9 Dec.
23. Which would have been the traditional thing to do.

Elias, decided to withdraw all their requests to use the church building and established a new church.[24]

In August 2015, I attended a service at church B. The building can hold one hundred people, but there were about thirty people in attendance, many of them family and relatives of the pastor. In this service two of his family members led the worship with two other young women, the worship theme was "God rebuilds broken relationships." His sermon about David's repentance was short, whereas in the past he had preached with more enthusiasm and for a much longer time.[25]

Church B2 meets in an auditorium. Initially it grew and doubled its attendance. It is led by a committee and has no pastor. A few years later, Nadia, who joined church B2 and became a committee member, felt at some point that she was not being given enough power and decided to begin a new ministry. She left with her family. In August 2015, I attended a service at church B2; the attendees were the same group that split the church ten years ago, except they were ten years older and without their children. At this service there were two sets of guests, a pastor (who was invited to preach) and his family and another family. Church membership was only eleven. The church has no new generation of children/youth, and it is run by the same church committee from a decade ago. They have no meetings except the weekly main service. Immediately after the service everybody left with no fellowship time.[26]

4.2.3 Case Study C
4.2.3.1 Background
Church C, established after 1948 by American Southern Baptists, is located in a town in Israel. A decade later, an indigene was appointed pastor of church C.[27] In the early 1980s, church C decided to build a care institution on its premises which later became an integral part of the church.[28]

---

24. Open interview with Rami, an ABC leader; a letter church B2 sent to the ABC, 15 Dec.; Pastor B's letter to the ABC, 23 Apr.

25. Field note, Aug. 2015.

26. Field note, Aug. 2015.

27. Register, *Back to Jerusalem*; Mansour, *Baptist History in the Holy Land between 1950 and 2020*.

28. Missionaries' report.

A young man from this town became a Baptist and was eager to serve. He travelled to a Western country to study theology. He returned after a few years and led a ministry at church C. Meanwhile, the pastor became busier developing the care institution, which was beginning to show signs of incompatibility with the church mission. Many young church members became excited about the young leader, which created tensions between him and the pastor. The ABC intervened and decided to ordain the church leader (hence, Pastor C) and appointed him to pastor a Baptist church in another town.[29] Many of the youth and families left church C and joined him; he also led a home group in the original town.

The old pastor tried to revive church C in the town, but he was too busy with the care institution. From then until his death only a few people attended church C which had shrunk to near non-existence.

4.2.3.2 Conflicts, splits/exits in church C2
The creation of church C2
Pastor C decided to resign from the church he was pastoring and moved back to his town. He established church C2 to meet the need there for a Baptist ministry. The church rented a facility and was successful in attracting many young people and families and quickly grew to sixty members. It became a member of the ABC. Later, the ABC decided to halt the membership of church C in the ABC as the church basically ceased to exist. Prior to his death, the pastor of church C was asked by the ABC to allow church C2 to use the church building, but all requests were in vain.

---

29. The ABC can ordain pastors according to its constitution. See appendix 4, section 2.6, "Ordination," in the constitution.

The Nature and Causes of Church Conflict in Three Case Studies

Table 4.3: Members of church C2

	First generation born in 1930s-1940s	Second generation born in 1950s-1960s	Third generation born in 1970s-1980s	Miss-ionaries
Pastor		1		
Deacons				
Church committee: 4			4	
Church members: 50–60	10%	20%	70%	

The conflict in church C2

Church C2, with many young educated members, began an evangelistic ministry to reach the Arab world. The ministry became successful and was run as a church ministry led by Pastor C and managed by Bishara, a young church leader.

The success of the evangelistic ministry was phenomenal, nonetheless, a few years later, a dispute erupted between Pastor C and Bishara concerning the management of the evangelistic ministry and who was in charge. Pastor C explained, "This ministry became the vision of our church; I started to work hard on issues of fundraising for this project and I involved young members in it. It became the 'baby' of the church and here was the mistake!"[30] However, Bishara claimed that he started this project as a church ministry, and when Pastor C became involved the project became successful. Bishara added, "When we did strategic planning, Pastor C wanted to become the manager of this project."[31] Pastor C told me that his suggestion was to have two managers, one to manage the ministry and one for development.

Interviewees claimed this evangelistic ministry was the source of conflict in church C2. The church was divided into two parties: (1) Pastor C, his extended family, friends and new church members; (2) Bishara, his family

---

30. Pastor C, interview with author, July 2015.
31. Bishara, interview with author, Aug. 2015.

and some church leaders. This conflict grew and people spoke unsympathetically about each other. A third-party intervention failed to resolve the dispute. Pastor C decided to leave the evangelistic ministry to Bishara as an independent project unrelated to church C2.[32] Although this project left the church, its problems remained and conflict between the pastor and Bishara escalated.[33] Consequently, Pastor C became angry and Bishara was asked to leave the church.[34]

Six years before the conflict, a charismatic American-Arab pastor became a close friend of Pastor C and church C2. He visited church C2 several times, influencing it with charismatic teaching. During the conflict he mentored members and tried to help Pastor C. Based on the interviews it seems his ideology influenced the way church members handled this conflict, as I will explain in the next chapters.

A few church leaders exited from church C2

During the conflict at church C2, three church leaders left. One leader, Albert, admitted, "I could not submit spiritually to Pastor C any more. My wife and I prayed, and we felt we should leave; if I couldn't submit spiritually to my pastor then I would risk myself and the church."[35]

A year later, Pastor C decided to resign from church C2. He appointed a leader from a different church to pastor alongside him for six months before he would leave to pastor church D.[36] This action caused more disagreements in the church, resulting in a serious dispute during one Sunday meeting, where members confronted Pastor C and argued with him. Shortly after this, Pastor C decided to leave church C2.[37]

Pastor C left church C2 and the ABC intervened

Pastor C asked the ABC to take over the ministry in church C2. The ABC met with Pastor C and the leaders exited from church C2. The ABC recommended

---

32. Third-party report, 20 Dec.; Bishara, interview with author, Aug. 2015.
33. Bishara, Albert, and Shirin, interviews with author, Aug. 2015.
34. Pastor C, interview with author, July 2015.
35. Albert, interview with author, Aug. 2015.
36. Where he has been pastoring for the last several years.
37. Pastor C, interview with author, July 2015; Albert, Shirin, interviews with author, Aug. 2015.

that they return and support Pastor C.[38] Pastor C insisted on leaving and the Ministry Committee of the ABC (hence, the ABC committee) became responsible for pastoring the church in its transition period. It tried to bring about reconciliation between Pastor C and Bishara. The ABC committee met with them and they apologized to one another. Bishara, on the request of the ABC committee, apologized in front of the church. Pastor C, who was not present in that meeting, became angry at not being included in this process as he was the pastor and felt he was the one who was wronged.[39]

Pastor C agreed to focus on pastoring church D, but refused to drop his membership in church C2 for his family's sake.[40] The ABC insisted Pastor C drop his membership and requested that his family stay at church C2. When Pastor C left the church, his family and friends, who were not happy that he was leaving, left with him. The ABC worked to bring back the people who left church C2, and Bishara returned after being absent for over three years.[41]

Pastor C established church C3

Pastor C decided to begin a "home group" for people who left with him and later established church C3. When the ABC informed Pastor C that this was unacceptable, he decided to resign from the ABC. At the same time, the ABC appointed Boulus, a young man with a Bachelor of Divinity, as the interim pastor; he pastored church C2 until the reintegration took place.[42]

Reconciliation

One year later Pastor C started some efforts to reconcile and reintegrate with church C2. He contacted the ABC committee which was positive about leading the reintegration.

The findings reveal two important stages in the reconciliation process. First, the reconciliation retreat conference (titled "I Am About to Do a New Thing"). Pastor C, with church C3, visited a retreat church C2 was holding;

---

38. Letter from the ABC committee, 18 June.

39. Letter, 18 Dec.

40. In the beginning, the ABC committee agreed to him keeping his membership but then changed its attitude (Pastor C, interview with author, July 2015; letter, 27 Dec).

41. ABC records, Pastor C, Bishara, interview with author, Aug. 2015.

42. ABC committee report; Boulus, interview with author, Aug. 2015; David and George, interview with author, Aug. 2015.

Pastor C went to the pulpit and tearfully apologized to church C2. Worship continued for hours and different groups joined to pray together for healing and forgiveness. All interviewees told me that during that meeting an unexpected and very powerful reconciliation took place. This was followed by the reintegration of the two churches a few months later. Second, the American-Arab pastor's conference (titled "The Complete Love") which took place a year after the reintegration. Some interviewees said during the conference another barrier to real reconciliation fell down.[43]

Boulus, the interim pastor, was appointed to pastor another church. He left church C2 and Pastor C returned to church C2 as a member but refused to become the official pastor. He functioned as the acting pastor of church C2, and his presence in the church made it difficult for the ABC and church C2 to bring in a new pastor.[44] Later, Pastor C insisted on pastoring church C2 for two years, during which he would train a leader from the church to pastor the church after him.[45]

The three case studies present the phenomenon where pastors, in a congregationalist polity, were the main authority with power to dismiss church deacons/church committees or leaders from office. What was the source of their powerful authority? Why did pastors cling to power and destroy any form of competition to their position? Why were deacons/leaders unable to use their authority as church leaders to replace the pastor or take part in leadership? Why did dissatisfied members compromise and leave church? To answer these questions, it is necessary to understand the nature and causes of conflict in Palestinian Baptist churches in Israel.

After presenting the background of churches A, B and C in the three cases, for case A I will focus on the main split that led to the creation of church A2; for case B, I will focus on the split that led to the creation of church B2; and, for case C, I will focus on the split that led to the creation of church C3.

The three cases have many common characteristics: a similar context, all are in the same country, members are Palestinian Baptists converted from traditional churches, the churches were planted by the same mission and

---

43. The two stages will be discussed in chapter 7.
44. Shirin, Albert, and Boulus, interviews with author, Aug. 2015.
45. ABC committee report, 8 Oct.

they are all members of the ABC. Nonetheless, they differ in location, age of conflict,[46] generation of pastors/members[47] and material capital.[48]

As I will elaborate in the next section, it is evident that the theological and socio-cultural factors are the primary factors contributing to the conflicts in the three cases. Secondary factors are church buildings, women's informal power and economic issues.

4.3 Primary Factors Contributing to the Conflicts

The recurrent main feature of the conflicts in the three cases is the struggle between the pastor and the younger laity who sought power to influence and shape the church's future. In explaining the causes of the conflicts from the perspectives of both the pastor and the young laity, we can see the combination of the following factors operating from either side. From the pastor's side, the *theological* factor (from traditional, non-evangelical Palestinian churches) and the *cultural* factor (patriarchal and hierarchical) combined powerfully as the key fundamental factors (of principle) to strengthen his desire to maintain his dominant position in the power structure of the church. The structural imbalance in power between the pastor and laity is therefore a manifestation of the above two factors and is not a fundamental factor in itself. From the young laity's side, the *theological* factor (Baptist ecclesiology) and the *socio-cultural* factor (their education) combined powerfully as the fundamental factors in strengthening their desire to share power with the pastor. The laity's dislike of structural imbalance is merely a manifestation of the more fundamental factors and is not a fundamental factor in itself, as seen in the further elaboration below.

Both pastors and laity can misuse power once they have it; if they do not have it, they may struggle to get it. It is worth noting that the new churches resulting from a split (church A2 and church B2) were led by a committee of lay people for a long time (ten to twelve years). In both churches, some leaders exit because they were not included in the leadership team. This pinpoints a central nature of church conflicts, which is the use, misuse or abuse of power.

---

46. Old and contemporary.
47. First-, second- or third-generation Baptist.
48. Church building, educational institution.

Seen in this way, the pastors and young laity do not share the same *theology and culture*, and the resulting clash between them reflects a deep generational clash in worldviews that encompasses theology, cultural values and social relations.

4.3.1 Theological Factor: Tension between Episcopalian/Sacramental versus Congregationalist/Functionalist

The findings indicate that the clash between the theologies of the pastors and the young laity is mainly around episcopal/sacramental versus congregationalist/ functionalist views of the clergy and the church.[49] In theory, the churches are congregationalist; in practice they many times act as "episcopal," as I will elaborate below. In the three cases, seemingly, Palestinian Baptists who converted from traditional churches did not fully internalize and practise a congregationalist polity for three main reasons: first, the limited knowledge regarding how congregationalist polities work; second, the pastors' high view of ordination; third, the deep respect members have for clergy.

According to Volf, "People make Christian beliefs their own and understand them in particular ways partly because of the practices to which they have been introduced- in which their souls and bodies have been trained- in the course of their lives."[50] He also adds that beliefs relate to sacraments. Core Christian beliefs are, by definition, normatively inscribed in sacraments but not in practices, and thus sacraments enact normative patterns for practices. The fact that the Palestinian Baptists' former church background is episcopal/sacramental, while their current churches are congregationalist/functionalist, sheds light on the tension and the contradictory way commitments occur as seen in the behaviours of pastors and laity, as I will explain.

4.3.1.1 Tension in the way Baptists view ecclesiastical polity

There is a difference between the way Baptists view the significance of the congregationalist form of government and the hierarchical view held by the traditional church denominations where almost all Palestinian Baptist

---

49. A sacrament is a Christian ritual regarded as an outward and visible sign of inward and spiritual divine grace instituted by Christ for our sanctification, such as baptism, confirmation, the Eucharist, penance, anointing of the sick, ordination and matrimony among Roman Catholic and many Orthodox churches, and baptism and the Eucharist among Protestants.

50. Volf, "Theology for a Way of Life," 256.

converts were formerly members. According to congregationalist polity, authority is ultimately held through membership of the organization based upon a theology of "the priesthood of all believers." For the traditional churches, only bishops have the exclusive right to ordain priests and deacons, and the hierarchy is sacramental as I elaborate below (however, there are different episcopal systems and some have considerable "democracy," as in the Anglican Church). In this theology, the priesthood is a lifelong sacrament, while in the Baptist churches it is functional. This will help to explain some of the contradictions in behaviour.[51]

Volf presents some distinctions between free church ecclesiology and that of episcopal churches.[52] First, the free church has a democratic character that is generally unknown in episcopal ordered churches: "a church organization in which 'power' is held by the entire congregation represents an indispensable condition of ecclesiality."[53] Second, in the free church, Christ's presence is unmediated and direct, both to individual believers and local churches. In episcopal churches it is mediated sacramentally and dependent on the concrete relation of any given local church to all other churches. The third distinction concerns "the subjective dimension of the conditions of ecclesiality."[54] In the episcopal model, the church is constituted through the performance of objective activities; the free church tradition also recognizes subjective conditions like genuine faith and obedience to God's commandments.[55]

In the episcopal model, Christ's own subject is active in the church, and so the presence and actions of Christ can be discerned in the acts of the church and its agents, such as bishops, priests and deacons. The relationship of the individual bishop and his diocese to the church is hierarchical. The individual is asked to surrender to the church and its authorities (not directly to Christ); this is an aspect of the trust implicit in the act of faith. The Catholic model considers a bishop as representing the one Christ as the head of the church. Unlike the Orthodox, ordination in the Catholic Church does not involve

---

51. For example, a pastor continues to be addressed as such for ever, regardless of his actual current job. This actually contradicts most Baptist theology, which maintains that "pastor" is a *functional* category and not an *ontological* one.

52. The term "free church" refers to churches sharing congregationalist polity.

53. Volf, *After Our Likeness*, 133.

54. Volf, 134.

55. Volf, 135.

an ontological change; to be ordained is to be ordered to a particular *ordo*. Hierarchy is a result of differing ordos and the tasks assigned to each. This is not the case in free church polity, where Volf makes the case that while ordained clergy may be appropriate, perhaps even important or normative, they are not necessary for a church to be a church. According to Volf, a free church is not a human creation but a community gathered together by the Spirit, possessing the ministries necessary to fulfil the tasks given to it by Christ. Formal ministers serve in positions of leadership, but their authority rests in their contractual relationship with the congregation as a whole. Each local free church is viewed as autonomous with no ecclesiastical authority in the form of a person or organization presiding over it.[56]

There are two primary organizational structures seen within the congregationalist polity: single-pastor churches and plural-eldership congregations. In a single-pastor form of government, one individual runs the church with the support of a team of elders or a board who are lower in authority. In a plural-eldership congregation, a board of elders lead a church together.

Most of the Palestinian Baptist churches (except church A2 and church B2) follow a single-pastor form of government.[57] The offices are separated into three categories: clergy positions, church committee/board (including the pastor, treasurer, elders and/or deacons) and lay positions centring around various church functions that are still considered official (the head of women's ministries, Sunday school teachers and others).[58] This form contrasts with the episcopal form of government, which is the one followed by traditional Palestinian churches and holds to a threefold hierarchy in its leadership structure: bishops, presbyters (or priests) and deacons. Bishops have the right to consecrate other bishops and ordain priests and deacons. There is provision to ensure a succession of bishops to rule over those underneath them. Given

---

56. Volf, *After Our Likeness*. However, some of these congregations choose to associate themselves with a denominational association. In terms of the structures of power, perhaps Palestinian Baptist churches are closer to Orthodox patriarchs rather than Catholic ones who must submit to a higher authority.

57. As of 2015. This approach has its roots in the Southern Baptist form of church government which tends to have single-pastor churches.

58. Because some churches use a variety of boards as a part of their decision-making process, there can obviously be an overlap in terms of the categorizations of board positions as opposed to lay positions, and all of these can overlap in various ways or take other forms if the culture dictates.

Palestinian Baptists' original backgrounds and their current theological commitments, there appears to be tension in the way members of churches A, B and C2 relate to ecclesiastical polity.

4.3.1.2 Tension in the way Baptists view clergys' ordination and authority

Most Palestinian Baptists came from traditional churches and therefore brought with them a view of clergy as the primary leaders with ultimate spiritual authority and decision-making power. Similarly, many Baptist pastors understand their position this way and also expect to remain in their positions until death. In the case studies, it is likely pastors had internalized that tradition and applied it, probably seeing themselves as specially anointed to a lifelong sacrament. As a result, the pastors did not fully understand or accept congregationalist polity, which gives authority to church members to lead the church together. The following examples demonstrate how this created considerable clash between pastors and laity.

In case A, after two years of discussions, the deacons and Pastor A agreed with the suggestion that Pastor George was to replace Pastor A. However, during the annual meeting with all members in attendance, Pastor A surprisingly, instead of informing the church about his retirement and appointing Pastor George, made the following official statement: "After praying, I decided to remain the pastor as long as I can serve God."[59] Pastor A's wife asserted, "The constitution says nothing about retirement or the age of the pastor. . . . As long as the pastor can serve God, and if there is nothing against his morality, he will stay the pastor of this church until death."[60] Many members from Pastor A's party referred to him as the "anointed" from God and felt this should not be questioned.

In case B, when the committee tried to change the form of church leadership from single-pastor to plural-eldership, Pastor B viewed this as a conspiracy to "fire" him from the church. He insisted, "The pastor has the primary individual responsibility and privilege to lead the church."[61] He asserted, "I

---

59. George, Sami, Jack and Dan, interviews with author, 2014.
60. Suhad, interview with author, Apr. 2014.
61. His letter to the ABC, 9 Dec.

will leave when God tells me to leave. If God does not tell me to leave, then I will not move from this church."[62]

This issue was not relevant to case C for several reasons. First, Pastor C was feeling frustrated with church C2 and planned several times to leave church C2. Second, Pastor C was always involved in other "start up" ministries. Shirin, a church leader, confirmed, "Pastor C used to say that he cannot see himself solely as a pastor; he sees himself involved in many other ministries."[63] Third, he does not rely on church C2 for his living. Finally, he was pastoring church D in a village nearby, so losing his position as the pastor in church C2 would not affect him.

The model of Bercovitch, Kremenyuk, and Zartman defines the issues at stake in conflicts in terms of conflicting evaluations, rewards and content.[64] In terms of this model, it is likely that, for the three pastors, the issue of conflict is a matter of belief and identity (theology) rather than interest.[65] Conflicts over beliefs and values are much less amenable to a compromise solution than conflicts of interests. Pastors believe they are ordained to a lifelong sacrament; in terms of identity, Pastor A is deeply related to the church he has pastored for many years. He and the building are recognized as capital symbols, even for the broader Palestinian community and international evangelicals. For him, the position, the building and he himself all symbolize Baptists in the Holy Land;[66] leaving his position would have meant sacrificing a central part of his identity. George, who was supposed to replace Pastor A, noted, "Pastor A told me that he cannot leave the church, because this church is his life, and he is deeply attached to it."[67]

---

62. Pastor B, interview with author, Aug. 2015.

63. Shirin, interview with author, 18 Sept. 2016.

64. Bercovitch, Kremenyuk, and Zartman, "Introduction." They define the issues at stake in conflicts in terms of: (a) Conflicting evaluations of the nature of the issue; i.e. does the conflict concern issues of interest or issues of values? (b) Rewards associated with the various issues; i.e. is it a win/win situation or a zero-sum conflict? (c) Content – is the issue about survival, scarcity, resources, status, prestige, etc.?

65. Issues of values characterize conflict situations where the parties disagree even on what they want. Such differences in the parties' definition, or evaluation, of the issues in conflict have a significant effect on the process of conflict management.

66. Bryan, interview with author, June 2014; Nizar, interview with author, June 2014; Samir, interview with author, Apr. 2014; Mark, interview with author, Aug. 2014.

67. George, interview with author, Mar. 2014.

Pastor B was offered a visiting scholar position in a Western institution but preferred to remain pastor of the church he rebuilt. Pastor C planned three times to leave church C2 but was deeply attached to it; even after he finally left, he made repeated efforts to return. We can argue that the pastors became deeply connected to the churches they built/rebuilt as pastoring a church becomes a matter of identity, honour and authority. It is noteworthy that Palestinian Baptist pastors continue to wear clerical collars and are called pastors even when they no longer pastor a church.

In sum, the pastors' high theology of ordination, according to which one remains a pastor forever after ordination, escalated the conflict, finally leading to splits.[68] In this regard we can conclude that pastors could not fully practise a congregationalist polity.

4.3.1.3 Tension in the way congregants defer to clergy

Another form of tension identified in the cases indicates that the members did not fully internalize and practise a congregationalist form of government because of the excessive deference given to the clergy. While, in the traditional churches, clergy are respected even if they are not qualified, in the congregationalist polity in general pastors may feel threatened by the ability of members to vote them out of office.

Most of the Palestinian Baptist churches in Israel have small memberships; the pastor is easily accepted as the primary leader, spiritual authority and decision-maker. In theory the churches are congregationalist in polity, but in practice the lead pastor is often "in charge of everything." The pastor may have a worship leader and elders to help him, whom he may consult when he considers it necessary. Even in churches where there is a church committee, the head of the committee is the pastor, and members would not vote against him because they respect him as a spiritual leader. One church leader told me, "In the church committee, although each one of us individually does not agree with the pastor's suggestion, all of us as a group agreed with the pastor's suggestion because he is the pastor."[69] In case C, Albert, a leader of church C2, pointed out that it would not be practical after the reintegration

---

68. Until the day I interviewed the pastors, they seemed not to understand why the splits occurred (Pastor A, Pastor B, interviews with author, Aug. 2015; Suhad, interview with author, Apr. 2014).

69. Bilal, interview with author, Nov. 2014.

to have Pastor C back on the church committee as an equal because members would continue to respect his opinion as being the spiritual authority.[70] This is typical behaviour of many Palestinian Baptists.

My findings indicate that in most churches, business meetings take place once or twice a year, mainly for announcements and often after decisions have been made. The church committee does not check the pastor, because its "main role" is to give legitimacy (the "amen") to pastoral decisions. Church members accept this style for several reasons. First, it is familiar to them from their former traditional churches where members are not involved in decision-making. Second, there are no teachings in churches about the congregationalist polity where authority is ultimately held by the membership. Third, churches are not used to consulting the constitution. This explains why many members are passive and tend to vote according to the pastor's suggestion – though the younger generation who split/exited were exceptions, as demonstrated in the following examples.

In case A, during the conflict that led to the split and the creation of church A2, church A's committee included Pastor A, deacons, lay people and a missionary (who left two years before the split).[71] This committee used to meet every month for church affairs. Twice a year there would be a business meeting for all members. Although it seems that this church had a congregationalist polity working according to protocol, the interviews with the deacons provide a different picture. Pastor A, who was in control, enjoyed the backing of the deacons. Even when the church committee made a decision, the next day Pastor A could change or cancel it. His behaviour became a habit and the deacons compromised for over thirty years, seldom confronting him. Even after they were dismissed from office, the deacons continued to attend the church hoping that Pastor A would change his attitude. Although both the deacons and Pastor A were from the first generation, they deferred to him as the spiritual authority. Another example is Pastor A's response letter to the younger generation's petition letter. Pastor A's letter was signed by forty-one people, many of whom were not active members at church A but were asked to sign as an *act of loyalty* to Pastor A. However, problems started when

---

70. Albert, interview with author, Oct. 2016.

71. Missionaries appointed Pastor A, and they stayed involved in church leadership until the early 1990s. They were on church committees and are the owners of church buildings.

ambitious young leaders wanted to gain power through becoming part of church leadership, in order to bring about a change. When they failed, they left church, compromising their right to bring in a new young pastor and to use the church building.

Similarly in case B, for around ten years members were content to have a pastor whom they loved and trusted and who was also the main decision-maker,[72] only having a few lay positions such as a leader of women's ministry, a youth leader and a treasurer. However, problems started when two leaders left church after a conflict with Pastor B.[73] Not happy about this, some church leaders approached Pastor B to bring them back. Pastor B, who was not happy with their approach, did not cooperate and instead dismissed the church committee from office. In their opinion, a split was the only way to deal with the conflict. Elias, a church leader, explained, "We cannot work together. Pastor B's philosophy in managing the church is different from ours; we want the church to be managed by a council or elders and not individually by a pastor."[74] As in case A, they left the church, compromising their rights to introduce a constitution and use the church building after the split.

In case C, Pastor C (like Pastor A and Pastor B) was also the sole decision-maker; he enjoyed having professional and gifted members who loved him. Nonetheless, when a disagreement took place, he would immediately dismiss the person from office in a gentle way. We can see the deep respect held towards clergy in the way that the church compromised for Pastor C when he made a decision concerning his successor without consulting the members, despite the fact that he was leaving the church and this decision should have been left to the members. Bishara told me, "Pastor C used to say, 'even if I do mistakes you have to obey me and God will reveal the truth.'"[75] In the above three cases the opposition groups justified their claim for power in terms of the Baptist theology of the "priesthood of all believers."

In sum, it can be concluded that churches A, B and C did not fully practise a congregationalist polity in three respects: first, the limited knowledge and experience pastors and many members had regarding how congregationalist

---

72. Pastor B was second generation, like most church members.
73. Elias's letter, 26 Nov.; Rana, interview with author, Aug. 2015.
74. Elias's letter to a pastor (friend of the church), 17 Dec.
75. Bishara, interview with author, Aug. 2015.

polity works (4.3.1.1); second, the pastors' high view of ordination as lifelong sacrament (4.3.1.2); third, the respect members had for clergy limited them from practising their authority at church (4.3.1.3). The educated younger laity were the exception as they requested that churches should be managed according to the constitution.

4.3.2 Socio-Cultural Factor: Tension between Traditional/Patriarchal versus Modern/Democratic Ethos

The findings indicate that there was a clash between the pastors' culture (traditional-patriarchal) and the younger generation's culture (modern-democratic). The connection between people's values, behaviour and historical situation is articulated in Bourdieu's concept of *habitus*.[76] Bourdieu asserts that people are predisposed through their *habitus* to produce and reproduce objective meaning.[77] I argue that the pastors' *habitus* oriented them to act according to their traditional-patriarchal culture and hierarchical theology. The younger generation's *habitus* oriented them to act within the limits of their culture by embracing some values of secular Israeli society and Baptist theology while still retaining some values from their culture. Stated differently, their *habitus* oriented them to play an active part in social reproduction.

4.3.2.1 Tension between tradition and modernity

Based on the interviews, it seems the first generation associates authority with position and age, characterized by a tendency to compromise, accept reality and save face; the younger generation associates authority with education and knowledge.[78] Many members of church A, and most in churches B and C, are younger generation. They are more open to the outside world, having studied in Israeli universities and internalized the secular, Western cultural values represented therein. As a result, they have incorporated into their culture new values that set them apart from the older one; they have taken separate paths within the same mother culture by adopting a modernized

---

76. See chapter 2, section 2.2.1
77. Bourdieu, *Outline of a Theory of Practice*.
78. Conflicts are more likely to occur in socially heterogeneous congregations such as a mixture of young and old members (Leas and Kittlaus, *Church Fights*; Herman, "Conflict in the Church"; Hoge, *Division in the Protestant House*). Also, the stability of congregations is positively related with the educational level of the pastor (Shin and Park, "Analysis of Causes of Schisms").

version of the same culture. Seemingly, this has caused tension in how they view pastoral authority. They respect clergy as authority figures based on their traditional cultural values, while, at the same time, critiquing them for two reasons based on their modern cultural values: First, the younger generation are more educated; second, Palestinian Baptist churches are non-profit corporations with a secular corporate form and organizational structure, allowing church laity to gain power over their pastors.[79] I present some examples of how education and modernity influences the younger generation's response to church conflicts.

They insisted on change
Younger generation members in churches A and B tried different ways to achieve change. When they failed, they split their churches, starting their own and leading them in their desired style. Since its inception, church A2 has been led by a committee of elders for twenty years, while two pastors led for a few years each. Church B2 has been led since its beginning by a committee with no pastor.

They used legalistic means to communicate with the pastor
In case A, the younger generation drafted a petition letter to Pastor A asking for immediate action to again discuss securing a new pastor.[80] The letter hinted that not taking steps in this direction would cause further problems and even a split. Nineteen young members signed this letter and sent it via delivery service to Pastor A's house. In case B, church members (mainly professionals) required Pastor B to introduce a constitution; they confronted him in one meeting and sent him invitations to join committee meetings. When Pastor B did not cooperate, they called for a general meeting without consulting him. In case C, Pastor C claimed some church members complained against him to the ABC. These actions dramatically escalated the conflict.

---

79. See chapter 3.

80. The letter emphasized that the church had not taken any steps towards doing this and that it had not brought the topic to the general church members to discuss, although it was supposed to be the whole church's decision (letter, 15 Aug).

They appealed for their right to use the church building

In case A, the opposition stopped attending church A and requested permission to hold a service in the church building at a separate time,[81] but Pastor A refused to allow them use of the building. This letter escalated tension and resentment between the two groups. The deacons convinced the younger generation not to use legal means against Pastor A. In case B, the opposition began meeting on the church's first floor. Pastor B immediately changed the lock, contacted the mission and got their support that, as the pastor, he was the only one with the right to use the church building. The ABC convinced the opposition not to use legal means against Pastor B.

The younger generation's behaviour did not necessarily indicate theological integrity or faithfulness to the Bible as the main driving factors for their actions. They engaged in power politics, sometimes using manipulation to move into positions of influence, and drew on strategies that were sometimes similar to ones used by the pastors. It is noteworthy that when Pastor B and Pastor C established churches B and C2, they were viewed by the members as loving spiritual fathers; Pastor B wrote, "I baptized them and nurtured them with the best that God had given me."[82] He felt betrayed. Anita, a member at church B2, said, "When we left the church we were young; we were stubborn and insisted on change. Today we are older; we see things differently and are ready for compromises."[83]

To summarize, the tension between young members' respect for and rejection of the pastor can be seen in their use of confrontational letters and asking pastors to leave (rejection), yet their willingness to compromise and themselves leave the church without using legal means to enforce a sharing of the building (respect). Nonetheless, this action (split) was taken only after years of conflict when they had failed to convince the pastor to share power and bring about change. The younger generation's *habitus* oriented them to act within the limits of their culture by embracing some values of modern

---

81. In their letter they explained that these meetings would be led by the deacons and aimed to protect the members from leaving the church. Additionally, they would join the church services again after the leadership resolved the conflict in the church. They urged Pastor A to work together with them for peace, and warned if this did not happen they would have to take inevitable steps.

82. Pastor B's letter to ABC, 9 Dec.

83. Open interview with Anita, Aug. 2015.

culture, such as those of secular Israeli society and the values of Baptist theology, while simultaneously keeping a certain degree of respect according to their traditional culture.

4.3.2.2 Tension between patriarchal ethos and democratic ethos

The congregationalist form of government poses a challenge to Middle Eastern culture where democracy, rule of law and individual rights, according to the common Western understanding, are not so well practised. This, I argue, explains why the pastors and church members misuse or struggle with practising their authority in decision-making at church.[84] Although voting in congregationalist polity is an expression of democracy – namely, the will of Christ speaking through the will of the members – in the three case studies the process, action, interaction and results failed to achieve this goal. It is noteworthy that the relationship between secular democracy and the congregationalist polity are two distinct yet overlapping influences upon the thought and behaviour of the younger generation.

I identify three cultural perceptions that contributed to defeating the requirements of the constitution: leadership style, loyalty to the authority figure and avoidance of confrontation.

Palestinian leadership style in the church

The traditional Palestinian authoritarian style of leadership is another factor that affects the authoritarianism of Baptist leaders.[85] For example, when Pastor A initiated a business meeting although there was no quorum,[86] he decided to vote on changing the quorum for this specific meeting. This special business meeting changed the status of deacon in the constitution from being a position for life to a position for a limited term voted on every three years. He decided to dismiss the current deacons and elect family and new people, loyal to him, to a new system in the form of a church committee. Upon Pastor

---

84. According to Brubaker, a healthy structure both confers power and limits its exercise, and bylaws exist in part to protect the church and congregants from the abuse of power by individual members. Brubaker, *Promise and Peril*.

85. See chapter 1, section 1.3.1.

86. Pastor A refused to postpone this meeting at the request of one of the deacons for organizational reasons.

A's request, people who had not attended the church for a long time came to this meeting and voted in support of his resolutions.

Pastor A, in most cases, was the sole decision-maker; questioning his authority was seen as "unfaithfulness to the church." When the younger generation insisted on change, Pastor A and his family interpreted this as a betrayal and rejection. This led to hard feelings such as disappointment, offence, rejection and anger. Pastor A's wife said in tears, "What causes the deepest sorrow for us during this conflict is the lack of appreciation for Pastor A, who has served the church in faithfulness for many years; disrespect to a clergyman is something very unacceptable."[87]

This attitude affected the way Pastor A and his family interacted with the younger generation's request to bring in a young pastor, since the request was labelled as a "conspiracy against the pastor." However, Pastor A's attitude was perceived by many church members as authoritarian. As Rima put it, "I felt that we were prohibited to come close to this authority [Pastor A].... He was like a patriarch and everybody had to obey him – I don't think we still have such things even in this town!"[88] Mary noted, "The patriarch stays in authority until death! The only way out is that people leave."[89] Even the deacons finally wrote, "Since we were not allowed to express our opinion freely at church we decided to write you [Pastor A] a letter."[90]

This style of individual leadership was also seen in case B. Although Pastor B agreed unwillingly to have a church committee, he did not cooperate. Elias, a committee member, told me, "I resigned from the council of the church because the pastor did not want to meet with us, despite me visiting him twice and asking him to work with us; the third time, four committee members visited him but his answer was *no*."[91] When the committee insisted on calling for a general meeting, Pastor B initiated another meeting. His relatives and long-time non-attendees came to this meeting and voted in support of the pastor. In this meeting the committee was dismissed and declared no longer

---

87. Suhad, interview with author, Apr. 2014.
88. Rima, interview with author, Mar. 2014.
89. Mary, interview with author, Apr. 2014.
90. Letter, 14 Apr.
91. Elias's letter, 26 Nov.

part of the church. Today, church B has no committee; church business meetings take place only when needed.[92]

Pastor B, in most cases, was the main decision-maker. He felt that questioning his spiritual authority and decision-making amounted to distrust and disrespect for the pastor. In his words: "They have no respect for a pastor. . . . They forgot all the blessings God bestowed on them through me. My humble conditions were to affirm their *trust and respect* for me as a pastor; the pastor leads the meetings and has the primary individual responsibility."[93]

This attitude affected the way Pastor B interacted with the laity's request to introduce a constitution and to take part in decision-making, for he labelled it a "conspiracy to fire the pastor." Pastor B told me, "Till this day, I don't know why they did this conspiracy; they wanted to fire the pastor but God fired them from the church."[94] Nonetheless, Pastor B's attitude was perceived by many of the church members as authoritarian.

In case C, Pastor C appointed members to positions in the church committee. He would give them freedom to work, but, if tension or disagreement arose, he would immediately dismiss them.[95] Albert, a youth leader, told me that during the conflict Pastor C sent him a note informing him he was dismissed.[96]

The findings show common patterns of pastoral behaviour during church conflict: rebuking of members from the pulpit indirectly and through preaching, dismissing leaders/committees from office and claiming to follow God's directions ("God told me to") to indicate that they have the spiritual authority at church. Furthermore, interviewees complained that most of the pastors did not recognize leaders to lead and preach. Many times, when they were away, they would arrange for an external guest to preach; in church retreats they would bring in guests to lead the worship and to preach.

More importantly, in these cases the process and the results of voting failed to practise the congregationalist polity. Most pastors acted in an authoritarian

---

92. Pastor B, interview with author, Dec. 2014.
93. Pastor B's letter to ABC, 9 Dec.
94. Pastor B, interview with author, Aug. 2015.
95. Shirin, a church leader, explained, "When there is disagreement, Pastor C cannot differentiate between personal relationship and ministry" (interview with author, Sept. 2016).
96. Albert, interview with author, Aug. 2015.

way; some overrode the constitution and others fired church leaders and elected family and friends to various church positions.

Loyalty

Hirschman talks about how members' loyalty to a group affects the ease with which members may leave when dissatisfied.[97] This in turn affects people's willingness to engage in behaviour leading to conflict (such as the younger generation voicing their dissatisfaction in the case studies) or people's unwillingness to voice complaints – stemming from their desire to repress conflict before it threatens membership or the survival of the group (such as the older generation).[98]

In terms of loyalty, the findings indicate there is a contradiction between older generations who are loyal to family and tradition and younger generations who follow Baptist ideology which is inherently democratic and therefore anti-traditional. Four types of attitudes were identified in the case studies.

First, loyalty to tradition. This applies to some first-generation members in church A who would not leave the church or pastor under any circumstances. They remained in church A following the conflict and left only after they were fired. The deacons' attitude was also influenced by pastoral loyalty more than concerns for the health of the church. When Pastor A turned sixty-five, they suggested keeping him as pastor until a "suitable" replacement was found.[99] All deacons except an American missionary agreed.[100] This is an example of an encounter between an American missionary's worldview (influenced by American culture and Baptist practice) and Palestinian practices. In churches B and C there were only a few first-generation women observers during the conflict, and they also had a similar attitude to stay.

---

97. Hirschman, *Exit, Voice and Loyalty*. Scholars such as Simmel, Coser, Kriesberg, and Hirschman look at conflict as something that flows out of certain patterns of group life and culture. They focus on questions such as boundaries, loyalty, and commitment. How do people interact with one another? How do they think and talk about the group's identity and purpose? See Simmel, "Conflict"; Coser, *Functions of Social Conflict*; Kriesberg, *Sociology of Social Conflict*; and Hirschman, *Exit, Voice and Loyalty*.

98. Becker, *Congregations in Conflict*.

99. Samir, interview with author, April 2014.

100. This decision empowered the pastor to decide what was "suitable" and what was not. At the time of writing this thesis (2018), the pastor has still not agreed on a suitable replacement.

Second, loyalty to family. In the three cases, the pastors' respective families and relatives were involved in keeping the pastors in position.

Third, loyalty to both tradition and ideology. This was evident in churches A and B, mainly with second-generation ("worn-out") members who respected authority figures and age (tradition), up to the point that the pastor ignored and then rejected them. When they failed to achieve power using the constitution (ideology), they split the church.

Forth, loyalty to ideology. Third-generation members ("stand-tall") do not share this same respect for authority. They are more committed to congregationalist principles of ecclesiology than the first and second generations. They justified their demands in terms of the Baptist theology of the "priesthood of all believers" and took matters into their own hands. For example, in case A, during the conflict they held their youth meetings outside the church building. In case C, where most members were third generation, they *questioned* both the attitudes of Pastor C and the ABC committee during conflict management and were loyal to their ideology during the dispute. Their ideology conducted them *not to split* but to *exit* without starting a new church (three leaders exited during the conflict). Additionally, they left silently and *did not fight* Pastor C, although they confronted him. This attitude differed from the third generation in case A in two aspects: first, leaders of church C2 did not leave with their entire families (Bishara left with his wife, but his mother and daughter continued to attend church C2), and, second, they did not start a new church.

Two reasons influenced church C2's attitude. (1) Throughout the conflict, and even before the escalation, many members were mentored by the American-Arab pastor.[101] Some interviewees told me they updated him with every step during the conflict and tried to follow his instructions. He instructed them to stay submissive to Pastor C as long as they were in church C2. If they could not, it would be better to leave peacefully (and not start a new church) since opposition would cause division.[102] (2) The ABC intervention during the conflict influenced Pastor C's behaviour. It is my thesis that the American-Arab pastor's ideology and ABC's intervention were important

---

101. An old friend of church C2, see section 4.2.3.
102. Albert, interview with author, Oct. 2016.

factors leading to reintegration in case C.[103] This ideology has *space for the pastor as authority figure*; however, it differs from the first generation's deference to clergy. In case B, the third generation was still too young to take action.

Avoidance of confrontation or confrontation as the last attempt[104]

In case A, the deacons compromised for years. Although they were very supportive of people who wanted change, they tried to act neutrally and keep good relationships with Pastor A. George claimed, "The deacons preferred to leave church instead of confronting the pastor; they didn't take responsibility as church leaders to resolve the conflict biblically."[105]

After the deacons were dismissed by Pastor A, they sent him a letter expressing their resentment concerning the last meeting, for it involved violation of the constitution. They said they did not confront him during the meeting as they did not want to cause more tension and provide a poor witness. This is a trait of Arabic culture – namely, not confronting people in public. The deacons and most of the younger generation gave up and left the church. They felt they were driven to leave by Pastor A's attitude. They did not want to seek help in secular courts, where this kind of behaviour would not be a good witness for their community. However, some interviewees believed starting a church on the doorstep of the mother church was even worse.[106]

This attitude differs in case B, where most of the church was second generation and confronted Pastor B directly as their *last attempt* to deal with him. Two months before the split, the committee confronted Pastor B directly in a meeting and tried to convince him to introduce a constitution and reconcile the leaders who exited. During the first meeting, Pastor B came prepared to lecture on how the church should be led. One of the committee members asked him to stop, since this meeting was for him to listen to what the church wanted to say. Two of the committee spelled out what they had against Pastor B, who left angry. The committee met four times without Pastor B to work on

---

103. As I will explain in the next chapters.

104. Culturally, since open conflict is to be avoided, confrontation is done through an intermediary. This is where a neutral third party is used to communicate that which cannot be said in a face-to-face context. This intermediary allows unpleasant things to be said without being direct and causing confrontation, thus maintaining smooth interpersonal relationships while still communicating the unpleasant.

105. Mar. 2014.

106. Majd, interview with author, Mar. 2014; Mark, interview with author, Aug. 2014.

these issues – he was invited but did not appear. Pastor B issued conditions that they should trust him, and *he* would lead the meetings, and *he* would build the constitution. A few days before the split, they announced a general meeting in a church service, ignoring Pastor B's presence and without asking his permission.[107]

In case C, the third generation viewed Pastor C as their spiritual father; they loved and respected him. However, the conflict sounded like a family quarrel. He also rebuked them from the pulpit.[108] Some leaders confronted Pastor C privately about his attitude, and he occasionally listened. They did not insult him but asked him to leave.

The above analysis of the *theological* and *cultural* factors explains why pastors could not handle the younger generation's request to share power well, viewing it as a conspiracy against them and therefore causing them to cling to power and demolish any form of competition for their positions. It also explains how pastors in a congregationalist polity were able to fire deacons and church committees, thereby causing the younger, educated generation to leave the church.

Pastors cling to power because of a combination of theological and socio-cultural factors. Theologically, pastors are influenced by episcopal churches in believing that they are called by God to a lifetime position; that it is God's will for the church to be led absolutely by one monarchical shepherd anointed by God; that laity are to say "amen" and members are to be submissive; and that questioning authority is viewed as sinful. Socio-culturally, they believe religious communities in general must be hierarchically structured to function effectively. Both point in the same direction of claiming power.

The findings also reveal that the younger generation do not share the same theology and culture as their pastors. The younger generation who rebelled against their pastors were influenced culturally by secular, Western ideas of individual rights and democracy (having adapted these ideas to their

---

107. Elias, interview with author, Aug. 2015; letter, 26 Nov; Rana, interview with author, Aug. 2015; Pastor B, interview with author, Aug. 2015.

108. Albert, a church leader, said, "Pastor C told me, 'When the church stops following me I will leave the church.' Pastor C was not the reason for the problems, but the members. The issue of gossip is everyone's responsibility, not only Pastor C's. . . . Eventually, Pastor C took responsibility with the help of the ABC and the church; the members did not take responsibility yet" (interview with author, Aug. 2015).

traditional culture). Theologically influenced by Baptist theology, they justified their demands to share power in terms of "the priesthood of all believers." However, they showed respect for clergymen when they decided to surrender to their pastors by leaving the church, as mentioned earlier. Again, both point in the same direction of claiming power.

In sum, the clash between the pastors and younger laity can be seen as a clash in *theology and culture* between their view of and claim for *power*.

4.4 Secondary Factors Contributing to the Conflicts

The church buildings, women's informal power and economic issues are very important factors which contributed to the splits in these cases. Nonetheless, out of principle the pastors would not consider these aspects to be a factor in order to maintain their stance. While they may serve as consequential factors, this is difficult to gauge as it concerns motivation. Therefore, I decided to classify these factors not as fundamental but as secondary factors.

4.4.1 Church Buildings

There is a difference in the way that Baptists view the significance of their church building compared to the view of traditional church denominations from which almost all Palestinian Baptists originally converted. For the traditional churches, land and buildings are highly significant, both as symbols of power and as representations of the theological commitments of these churches.[109] In Baptist ecclesiology, however, the building itself has very little theological significance. What matters are the "living stones" of the church – the congregants themselves – with the building largely being understood in functional terms. Given their original backgrounds and current theological commitments, and based on the data, there appears to be a tension in the way Palestinian Baptists relate to church buildings.

On the one hand, Baptists are committed to the functional view of a church building.[110] Yosef, a young leader who exited from his church, implemented

---

109. For example, Orthodox believe that heaven itself is made present within the building and that is a reason why the building must be beautiful – in order to represent that reality symbolically.

110. One American missionary told me, "we need 'church-growth eyes'; in the early church there were multiple house churches.... Buildings can limit the growth of the church" (Ron, July 2014).

the alternative of starting three home groups. He claimed, "The church should grow this way as it did in the early church; churches are becoming more traditional and hierarchical."[111] This commitment to a functional view of a church building can also be seen in the fact that many churches meet in rented halls, with decoration largely being limited to a cross on the wall.[112]

On the other hand, the issue of controlling space in a socially hostile and legally uncertain environment,[113] as well as the symbolic meaning of the church building, played a significant role in the development of the conflict that led to splits in each of the three case studies. This can be demonstrated by the following observations.

In case A, the church building is large and conspicuously located near a number of traditional church buildings. Although the entire pre-split congregation contributed to the reconstruction of this building, Pastor A maintained control of it and refused to let others hold meetings within the building, even changing the locks. This was the final straw causing them to leave.[114] As Ron, a missionary, put it: "I believe the building eventually caused the final split in leadership when the opposing group was not allowed to use the new building for meetings. Somehow there was a difference over who controlled the new building when it became apparent Pastor A did."[115] Nonetheless, Waleed, a leader from Pastor A's party, had a different viewpoint. He thought it was unreasonable to give the opposing group the right to use the building since cooperation would be hard and might escalate the conflict.[116]

Seemingly, the reason Pastor A refused to share control of the building was because of its prestige and significance in the aforementioned context.

---

111. Yosef, interview with author, Apr. 2014. Seemingly, many Palestinian Baptists only feel a need for a place to worship. They may not view the building as symbolic or economically relevant to their vision of institutionalising their Baptist denomination.

112. Only seven Baptist churches have their own church building (these buildings were built by missionaries fifty years ago; all of them are halls except one church); eleven churches meet at rented halls.

113. As discussed in chapters 1 and 3.

114. Both theoreticians and practitioners have argued that major building projects produce conflict. From a theoretical perspective, the significant change in physical structure that accompanies most building projects should be enough to engender conflict. Becker found that family congregations are more likely to fight over church buildings (Becker, *Congregations in Conflict*).

115. Ron, interview with author, July 2014.

116. Waleed, interview with author, June 2014.

It was a status symbol that granted him honour and respect in the broader community. According to a third party: "I think Pastor A has not responded to the reconciliation attempts to unite the church, in order to 'protect' the building. He is also angry that the church that split meet next door in the same site. . . . His condition for reconciliation is that their church moves to another venue."[117] Here we see that Pastor A did not even want the new church to meet near the building, possibly because it implied shame, rejection and a public testimony to their inability to reconcile. Importantly, however, the new church consciously chose a nearby location; where they meet is only a few metres from church A. When I asked some elders of church A2 why they still meet in the same location after twenty years and do not rent a different place, their response was, "We did not find a suitable place yet."[118] This issue continues to cause tension between the churches; for instance, when preachers/groups are invited to church A2, they often mistakenly attend church A and only realize their mistake during the service.

In case B, we see similar behaviour in relation to church B's building. During the conflict, the church committee announced a general meeting for the whole church, including Pastor B, to vote on three issues: (1) adoption of the new constitution, (2) a change from an individual pastor to a pastor-and-council-led church, and (3) bringing back the leaders who exited. Pastor B, who was not happy with their approach, arranged another meeting inviting loyal church members, his family and friends.[119] In this meeting, a letter was drafted confirming that they were the "church members" and Pastor B was their pastor. Therefore, they asked the ABC and the mission (the BCI owner of the church building) to consider this a formal statement authorizing them to use the building and not allow the opposing group use of it.[120] When the opposing group tried to use the first floor for their meetings, the lock was changed.[121] Pastor B's identity was connected with the building; for him, if the opposing group had the right to use the building, it would be a rejection of

---

117. Bryan, interview with author, Mar. 2014.
118. Sami, George, Dan, interviews with author, 2014.
119. Elias, Rana; Michel, interviews with author, Aug. 2015.
120. Letter, 26 Nov.
121. Pastor B, interview with author, Aug. 2015. He mentioned the same idea in another email sent to the ABC in 7 Dec.

himself. For him to have absolute use of the building amounted to recognition of him as the legitimate pastor.

As for case C, although the church had no building and met in a rental place, a "church building" contributed indirectly to the conflict. First, Pastor C twice planned to leave church C2 because of the conflict. However, on one occasion he changed his mind and decided to remain as the pastor when the former pastor who controlled the town's Baptist church building became very ill. The other time was when a missionary told him that the issue of the building would be resolved soon in court. Second, Pastor C tried to initiate reconciliation with the former pastor. He tried to convince him to become one church again and renovate the neglected church building.[122] The old pastor, who had refused to allow church C2 to use the building, refused any attempt at reconciliation. Some referred to his desire to hold onto his position because of the building, even after his church ceased to exist. It is likely that Pastor C's desire to remain pastor because of the building increased the tension in church C2. Pastor C held on because of the building the former pastor controlled. He hoped that church C2 could use it in the near future. This issue shows how the building is an important factor in church conflict.

4.4.2 Women's Informal Power

Middle Eastern women, including Palestinians in Israel, are influenced by patriarchy in different spheres of life: the family, nation, religious community and state. However, they do have informal power. Sa'ar argues that resourceful Palestinian women in Israel, who are commonly referred to as *qawiyyi*, "strong" (Sa'ar also offers the term "feminine strength"), are preoccupied with modernity, cultural morality and collective identity; they are heroic, informal, individualistic and not radical. They are not feminists but are strong in dealing with two feminine positions: the traditional and the modern-normative. While balancing between conflicting powers, they are ambitious to oppose cultural norms without losing cultural consensus. This is usually made possible when they have a supportive husband, father or family.[123]

---

122. Pastor C, interview with author, July 2015.
123. Sa'ar, "Feminine Strength." There is literature that examines different viewpoints of the lives of Palestinian women in Israel, including the duality of subordination and empowerment (Ginat 1982; Kanaaneh 2002; Herzog 2004).

The Palestinian Baptist Church in Israel continues the legacy of many Baptist churches in the world, and the Middle Eastern Church in particular, in being patriarchal.[124] Although, in the congregationalist system, women have the right to vote, women may only have, at most, small roles at church – such as children's, women's or charity ministries.[125] Lately, however, some evangelical churches have allowed women to have positions such as membership on church committees.[126]

I argue that women were a further factor (alongside theology, culture, the church buildings and economic aspects) in shaping the way church conflict played out. I found two scripts of femininity: *wives of pastors* represent one script and *activist* female members represent another. This can be seen in the following examples.

In relation to *pastors' wives*, in case A most interviewees felt that Pastor A's wife had a significant influence on decisions involving her husband. For example, the unofficial record says that she believed that Pastor A should remain in his position and should not leave the pastorate of church A. Interviewees said that, while Pastor A's wife was away abroad, Pastor A and the deacons proposed making George his replacement, but when his wife returned from her trip, Pastor A seemed to change his mind, claiming that the Lord revealed to him that he would remain the pastor as long as he could serve God. Pastor A's wife felt that the deacons tried to manipulate Pastor A and brought George without consulting him. She believed that she received confirmation for her theory through visions and dreams, and she therefore held a level of power as someone who claimed a high spirituality. In Sa'ar's terms, we can refer to her "feminine strength," which was supported by her husband and son. In case C, the wife of Pastor C provided a different type of influence as, after the split, she gathered a group of women, praying and fasting for the reconciliation that eventually took place a year later.

In relation to *activists*, opinionated and professional females were identified in each of the three cases. In case A, three young educated women with

---

124. There are also Baptist churches and Protestant denominations in the West, such as Anglicans, Methodists and Lutherans, that now accept female ordination, although within these streams there are individual movements which continue to reject female ordination.

125. In the ABC, between 65 percent and 75 percent of church attendees are women. Seventy-five percent of the people who are active at church are also women.

126. In the beginning of 2017, in Lebanon, two Lebanese women were ordained as pastors in the Presbyterian Church.

presence and influence stopped attending the church six months before their husbands (who were church leaders) decided to leave. Rima explained, "It became impossible to attend church A because of the ongoing conflict; on Sundays we leave the church sad and frustrated. I told my husband I would stop attending the church for now."[127] We can argue here that the women's attitude influenced that of their husbands, as well as having a direct influence on the community. They had agency since they were also clearly communicating to other couples. Along with other factors, this attitude probably affected their husbands' decision to leave.

Another example of "feminine strength" was displayed when some women from the group that left church A complained they would not have a Christmas service as they did not belong to any church. These women convinced their husbands to initiate a Christmas service. This service initiated the idea of founding a new church. One year later, church A2 was founded. Similarly, in case B, this type of female power was also identified during the conflict and after the split, as leaders' wives put pressure on their husbands to initiate reconciliation with Pastor B after their children left the church. In case C, Shirin, a young, influential leader, was involved in many church activities. Five years earlier she had also been another church attendee and observer during a church split and was therefore determined that church C2 would not also experience a split, having seen the sorrow and pain the split caused both sides. Shirin was the unofficial mediator between church members and Pastor C; when she herself struggled with Pastor C's attitude, she sought guidance from the American-Arab pastor who mentored many church members during the conflict. We can argue that Shirin's attitude (along with other factors) influenced church members' decision not to engage in church split. These were examples of "feminine strength" (*qawiyyi*).

Another type of female power was identified in the cases – namely, the "powerful" woman. Sa'ar classifies this kind of strength as having obtained "masculine power." The "powerful" woman differs from the strong woman (*qawiyyi*), in that her energies are invested mostly in the public domain (career/social life), and she resists any attempts to either break her power or devalue her femininity.[128]

---

127. Rima, interview with author, Mar. 2014.
128. Sa'ar, "Feminine Strength," 404.

Nadia is a talented, well-educated woman with a very strong personality. She served inside and outside the church. Many interviewees said she was the pastor's right-hand woman, very helpful and protective of the pastor. A few interviewees claimed the problem was that Nadia started to see a gap between her spirituality and her pastor; she left church after a conflict with him. Immediately after Nadia left, some church leaders decided to stand beside her; intensive meetings took place to convince the pastor to bring her back. The pastor, who felt that they should support him, was not happy with these endeavours, and he did not cooperate. A month later the split took place, and a new church, church B2, was established. The council of this church included Nadia.

A few years later, Nadia left the church and decided to begin her own new ministry. Nadia is the on-site leader of this ministry and, as preaching is forbidden for women in evangelical Palestinian churches, she preaches in conferences for women within the same ministry. This ministry is not well accepted among pastors as it is accused of not coordinating its work with them. Nonetheless, it attracts many members to its meetings.[129] Nadia told me the Convention of Evangelical Churches in Israel (CECI) boycotts her ministry: "They have a problem with a woman leading a ministry by herself, but they have no problem with women cleaning tables."[130] At the time of our interview, she continues to lead her successful ministry preaching to women. We can conclude that Nadia is a "powerful" woman who confronted pastors publicly in a patriarchal community and continues to achieve her goals despite the obstacles.

In sum, women's informal influence extended throughout the conflicts in the case studies, even though they did not hold formal leadership positions. There was a significant shift in women's position, style, and influence in the passage between the three cases; this is also closely tied to generation and education.

4.4.3 Economic Factors

Since I discussed the economic factor in chapter 3 (section 3.3.3), I briefly present this factor here. Pastor A, and some first generation church members

---

129. Nadia, interview with author, Aug. 2015; open interview with Rami and David.
130. Nadia, interview with author, Aug. 2015.

who had become internally displaced refugees in their home country during the *nakba*, viewed church A as the main source of material security during the 1948 war. Missionaries provided them with jobs and salary. In light of this, Pastor A's control is probably grounded in his position. For Pastor B and Pastor C, although they are second generation, the issue of conflict was also a matter of material security and controlling the church building.[131] Pastor C did not have the threat of losing everything since he was pastoring another church; nevertheless, the church building was crucial for him.[132]

For the young laity, the issue was not one of material security; they had their own careers outside the church and were enthusiastic to create change using their professional skills. Their goal was to gain power in order to influence and shape the church's future.

4.5 Conclusion

In this chapter, I argue that the clash between the pastors and laity, which led to church splits, had its root in the way each side construes its identity, *theologically and culturally,* in light of the will of God. Stated differently, the clash was between each side's strong combination of its *theology and culture* working against the other side.

Theologically, churches A, B and C were seen to face several challenges: first, the pastors' high view of ordination understood as a lifelong calling and sacrament, and their belief that it was God's will for the church to be lead by them absolutely; second, the excessive deference many congregants have for clergy, which limits them from practising the authority they have through their membership; and third, the limited knowledge and experience pastors and many members have regarding how congregationalist polity works. *Culturally,* due to Arab culture, with its strong emphasis on individual male leadership, and the unconditional support of their blood relatives, pastors acted in an authoritarian manner. While overriding the constitution, pastors fired deacons, committees and church members, electing their families and friends to various positions to control the church. Since the pastors' authoritarian manner, derived theologically, is also encouraged in the culture, their

---

131. Pastor B, Elias, Rana, interviews with author, Aug. 2015.
132. As mentioned in section 4.4.1.

authoritarian stance is entrenched *theologically and culturally*, but it is not clear which element dominates.

The pastors' *theological and cultural* identity created conflict with that of the younger generation's *theology and culture*. They rebelled against their pastors and were influenced by several factors. *Socio-culturally*, the younger generation was influenced by secular, Western ideas of individual rights and democracy. They adapted these ideas to their traditional culture when they required pastors to operate according to the constitution, persisted to demand their rights, called for a general meeting, requested a separate service in the church building and finally split the church. *Theologically*, they justified their demands in terms of the Baptist theology of the "priesthood of all believers." Since their claim for power, derived theologically, is also encouraged by modern cultural components, their claim is also entrenched *theologically and culturally*, but it is again not clear which element dominates.

Besides the primary factors of theology and culture, I identified three important secondary factors which contributed to the splits in these cases: the church buildings, women's informal power and economic factors. The symbolic meaning of church buildings (power and its theological commitments) and its location grant the pastors honour and respect in the broader community. The informal power of women extended throughout the conflict and process in the three cases. The economic factors also influenced the way conflict was handled.

I also showed that the polity of Palestinian Baptist churches embodies democracy in more than one aspect: no central authority, secular organizational structure as a non-profit corporation, female participation in committees and other values of Baptist theology such as the priesthood of believers. Meanwhile, the local culture involves a centralized hierarchical, patriarchal authority structure and most churches are inclined this way.[133] Thus, this is a central tension bound to have implications for the nature of conflicts and their management practices which is the subject of the next chapter.

---

133. This makes Palestinian Baptist churches more similar to civil society organizations than other religious ones such as traditional Palestinian churches.

CHAPTER 5

Conflict Management Practices in Three Cases of Palestinian Baptist Churches in Israel

5.1 Introduction

After exploring the fundamental factors that caused splits in the three case studies – that is, the combination of theology and culture on the pastors' side working against the combination of theology and culture on the younger generation's side – in this chapter I argue that these same main factors of *theology and culture* contributed to the ways the conflicts were dealt with from the perspectives of the pastors and the younger generation. Again, because of the clash of those factors from each side, and the newness of Palestinian Baptist churches, the conflicts were not resolved effectively.

This chapter reveals that, in resolving church conflicts, Palestinian Baptists engage in four different approaches, each with a distinct tradition, perception and method of conflict resolution. Two approaches are cultural: (1) the Israeli alternative-legalistic approach and (2) the Palestinian traditional *sulha* approach; and two approaches are theological: (1) the traditional Palestinian church approach and (2) the Western-Baptist approach. The pastors' *theological-cultural* approach is a combination of hierarchical theology known from traditional Palestinian churches and *sulha* ("hierarchical-patriarchal"). The younger generation's *theological-cultural* approach is a combination of Western-Baptist and alternative-legalistic ("congregationalist-democratic").

More importantly, I argue there is a shift in the practices of conflict management that disputants and third parties used in the three cases.[1] It is the shift between the older generations who desire to maintain the status quo versus a younger generation's will for change. It is a shift from traditional patriarchy to modern culture, involving everything from different rationalities to styles and management of conflict.

I begin by explaining the approaches used in the Palestinian society in Israel, highlighting the contradictions, and then I move to explore the local Palestinian Baptist conflict management practices as demonstrated in the three case studies.

5.2 Cultural Models: Tension between *Sulha* and Alternative-Legal Approaches

There are three major approaches to conflict resolution in Palestinian society in Israeli: the Arab Palestinian traditional *sulha* model, litigation, and Alternative Dispute Resolution (ADR). *Sulha* in Arabic means peace (it also means "resolution" or "settlement" or "fixing," generally in problem solving). This approach is used throughout the Palestinian community in Israel and is perceived by community leaders as a ritualized process of conflict resolution to manage a wide range of conflicts.[2] Sometimes *sulha* is used in the absence of state jurisdiction; at other times it is combined with state judicial procedures.

This modern adaptation of *sulha* reflects its ongoing societal importance and flexibility. Brown emphasizes the unique relationship between modern state justice mechanisms and *sulha*, noting that ultimately it is the court that offers the final verdict.[3] *Sulha* offers a culturally relevant mechanism for long-term reconciliation in ways that address the need for honour.[4]

5.2.1 The Middle Eastern Tradition of *Sulha*

Sulha makes use of a unique mix of local variants of mediation and arbitration techniques to help transform inter- and intra-communal conflicts

---

1. The three cases are described in chapter 4.
2. Irani and Funk, "Rituals of Reconciliation."
3. Brown, *Rule of Law*.
4. Shihade, "Internal Violence."

from revenge to forgiveness.⁵ *Sulha* does not recognize the Western-based differentiation between mediation and arbitration but rather makes use of both approaches when needed.⁶ Furthermore, *sulha* does not replace an individual's responsibility, which is subject to trial by the state legal system. Jabbour emphasizes that the communal approach to conflict is based on the view that hurting an individual means hurting the entire community.⁷ Said, Funk, and Kadayifci write that, *sulha* "stresses the close link between the psychological and political dimensions of communal life through its recognition that injuries between individuals and groups will fester and expand if not acknowledged, repaired, forgiven and transcended."⁸ Irani and Funk state that *sulha* as ritualized behaviour produces the space for retrieving dignity when lost.⁹ As an interpersonal strategy, *sulha* allows for micro-level relationship repair with the capability for macro-level impact.¹⁰ *Sulha* does not address the source of conflict but does readjust communities for peaceful coexistence and *keeping the status quo*. Such views of social order are represented and retold repeatedly in the minds of *sulha* participants.¹¹

5.2.1.1 *The stages of the* sulha *process*
Jaha: Forming the sulha committee (third party)

The *jaha* includes only elderly men and is based on *patriarchal habitus*. The *jaha* draws its power from its members' positions in the community and from a disputant's authorization.¹² The *jaha* includes an "unbiased insider with ongoing connections to the major disputants as well as a strong sense of the common good and standing within the community."¹³ They are not neutral

---

5. Jabbour, *Sulha*. On the "mediation side," *Sulha* strives to reconcile differences between the disputants' clans; on the "arbitration side," the decision of the *jaha* is final and binding.

6. According to Pely, what initially appears to be a similarity of functions between similarly named elements of Western ADR and those in *sulha* are similar in name alone. For example, similarly named tools, such as venting, neutrality and confidentiality, are actually used differently in the two practices. Pely, "Where East Not Always Meets West," 428.

7. Jabbour, *Sulha*. Jabbour is a long-time dispute resolution practitioner within the Palestinian community of northern Israel.

8. Said, Funk, and Kadayifci, *Peace and Conflict Resolution*, 182.

9. Irani and Funk, "Rituals of Reconciliation."

10. Gellman and Vuinovich, "From Sulha to Salaam."

11. Lang, "*Sulha* Peace-Making Process."

12. Pely, "Resolving Clan-Based Disputes."

13. Irani and Funk, "Rituals of Reconciliation," 61.

outsiders, since they are familiar with the history, norms and customs of the community.[14] They can also create political capital through the process, which is important for building prestige and moral authority.[15] They are selected for their honesty,[16] experience, intelligence, status, leadership in the community and age – as older community members are highly respected in Arab society.[17]

Women are not allowed to serve in the *jaha*, and the *sulha* does not contain any formal mechanism designed to provide for the concerns of women. However, Pely examines the role of women within *sulha* and finds that women's informal influence extends throughout the process, from the pre-*sulha* stage of venting to the *sulha* agreement.[18]

The role of the *jaha* is to urge the offended family, on behalf of the offender, to seek reconciliation through *sulha* instead of revenge. Jabbour states that a unique characteristic of the *jaha* is its ability to act as "anger or shock absorbers," with great tolerance and patience, when listening to the family members of disputants who are often filled with sadness and bitterness. Jabbour explains the importance of *venting* in *sulha*, asserting, "Grief work must be enabled by the *jaha* to make way for peace."[19]

Hodna: Ceasefire agreement

The *sulha* process begins after the *taffwid* is given. The *jaha*'s first goal is to convince the families of both the offended and offender to accept a temporary ceasefire and promise not to take revenge or confront the other side.[20]

Taffwid: Initiating the jaha

To act officially, representatives of the offender's family contact a member of the local *jaha* and provide the *jaha* with a *taffwid* – that is, an irreversible written authorization to act on their behalf to contact the victim's family and conduct the *sulha*. The *taffwid* contains the commitment of the offender's

---

14. Abu-Nimer, "Conflict Resolution Approaches."
15. Lang, "*Sulha* Peace-Making Process."
16. Smith, "Reward of Allah," 388.
17. Gellman and Vuinovich, "From Sulha to Salaam."
18. Pely, "Women in *Sulha*." For more details about women's informal power in the case studies, see chapter 4, section 4.4.2.
19. Jabbour, *Sulha*, 46–47.
20. Jabbour, *Sulha*, 34.

family to obey whatever verdict the *jaha* reaches.[21] By giving written authorization, the psychological, emotional and communal burden of the conflict is shifted from the parties to the *jaha*.

Atwa: Payment of good faith

The *sulha* process demands a symbolic payment from the offender's family to the offended's, as determined by the *jaha*. The *atwa* is in addition to any payment made by the offender's family to secure its agreement to obey the *jaha*'s final decision. When the victim's family receive the *atwa*, the *hodna* goes into effect.[22]

The jaha's investigation

Investigation generally takes place via private discussions with representatives of the disputants and witnesses. The *jaha* must not expose information given by witnesses as it could damage the reputation of the *jaha* and the community's trust in them as credible mediators.[23]

The *sulha* ceremony

The verdict is determined and participation in post-ceremony activities is required to ensure the durability of the agreement. If the offender has already taken responsibility, the *jaha's* only determinations are the amount of compensation to be paid and conditions for reconciliation.[24] This includes paying a huge amount of compensation for the victim's family and many times (in murder cases) the offender's family is asked to leave the village for some years or even permanently. If the dispute did not arise out of violence, the *jaha* does not assign guilt. A mediated agreement, agreeable to each side, is crafted and memorialized in writing;[25] it is then read at a public ceremony and signed by representatives from each side. Afterwards, the *jaha* and notable community members sign the agreement as well. A rejection of the verdict is considered a severe infraction of the process, an insult to the *jaha* and a loss of face

---

21. Pely, "Resolving Clan-Based Disputes."
22. Jabbour, *Sulha*, 35.
23. Pely, "Resolving Clan-Based Disputes."
24. The compensation is called *diya* in a murder case, meaning "blood money," and *taawid* in a non-murder case.
25. At this point, there are no further negotiations or appeals allowed in relation to its contents.

for all involved.[26] The final ceremony is centred on forgiveness, peace and compromise for the greater good of society. *Sulha* ceremonies involve three symbolic acts: (1) *Musafaha* – a handshake between the disputants validates the peace for all those present and absent;[27] (2) *Musamaha* – a declaration of forgiveness by the victim's father; and (3) *Mumalaha* – a ceremonial meal that ends the *sulha* process.[28]

5.2.1.2 Key assumptions in **sulha**

Honour and forgiveness are the main basis of the socio-cultural assumptions employed within *sulha*.[29] When the *sulha* agreement is ready, disputants' families and the wider community are invited to the final *sulha* ceremony outdoors in the village centre, as the restoration of honour requires public viewing.[30] The final *sulha* ceremony is usually punctuated by a "heavy silence" and is a scene of temporary humility for both parties:[31] the offender's family humbly accepts the wrongdoings and offers compensation on behalf of their family member, and the bereaved family respectfully forgives the offender's family as an act of humility. The sharing of a meal indicates the reversal of the tragedy and the restoration of peace.[32]

In *sulha, venting* is equally important to resolving problems. This venting ritual aims to start the process of channelling the emotions of the victim's family; it is given large cultural support in order to help position them into the communally preferred option of conciliation and forgiveness.[33] Lang describes the venting process and the underlying social rationale as "reverse *musayara*" (reverse social etiquette and ingratiation). This refers to the practice whereby the *jaha* treat the victim's family, from the beginning to the end of the *sulha* process, with the great respect normally given to high status persons. Lang explains this process as a performative reversal of the standard patron-client

---

26. Jabbour, *Sulha*; Pely, "Resolving Clan-Based Disputes"; Gellman and Vuinovich, "From Sulha to Salaam."

27. The larger community are taking the role of observer, rather than active witness to the resolution.

28. Smith, "Reward of Allah."

29. Jabbour, *Sulha*, 56.

30. Lang, "*Sulha* Peace-Making Process," 58.

31. Jabbour, *Sulha*, 55.

32. Irani and Funk, "Rituals of Reconciliation," 65.

33. Jabbour, *Sulha*.

relationship common in Arab society. She adds, "In relationships of patronage (*wasta*), the client's request for a favour is flattering for the patron, and each *wasta* favour can be seen as a transaction wherein *sharaf* [honour] flows from the client to the patron."[34] In the venting, process the *jaha* symbolically turn this relationship on its head (reverse *musayara*) by pleading with an ordinary family to grant them a favour – namely, to forgive rather than to revenge. This reverse positioning is exceptionally flattering for the offended, humiliated family. The family is temporarily placed in a position of "patronage" over the most respected men in the community. Such a process calms the feelings of humiliation further and, in a sense, contributes to honour restoration.

Gellman and Vuinovich argue that *sulha* provides a culturally appropriate means for restoring values and that cultural symbols and rituals such as *sulha* are necessary for societal construction of peaceful coexistence.[35] According to Smith, in Palestine *sulha* is a method of communicating the need to "resolve a conflict," as well as creating a future-oriented socio-political relationship in which different communities can live together in harmony.[36] Even if done with resentment, the final sharing of a meal as the ritualized performance of sharing vital nutrients is what counts. Lang comments that "sincerity is irrelevant because by participating in the *sulha* the actors enmesh themselves in a web of social relations that will constrain them to observe the peace."[37]

The connection between the *internal cohesiveness* of the Arab family and *sulha* is crucial. As Jabbour argues, "The collective responsibility of the extended family (*hamula*) in Arab culture toward all its members is one of the main factors that makes *sulha* work."[38] It is important to recognize that, in the same manner that the family may be the key to resolving conflicts, they could also cause the eruption or quick expansion of conflicts.[39]

Sulha is the only culturally authorized means to provide an alternative to the vengeance path. In *sulha*, *honour* plays a major functional, ritualistic and emotional role. Interveners and disputants use honour tools during

---

34. Lang, "*Sulha* Peace-Making Process," 55.
35. Gellman and Vuinovich, "From Sulha to Salaam."
36. Smith, "Reward of Allah."
37. Lang, "*Sulha* Peace-Making Process," 64.
38. Jabbour, *Sulha*, 69.
39. See chapter 1, section 1.3.1.

each of *sulha's* stages so that the option to forgive gradually replaces the drive to avenge. If, eventually, honour is increased and forgiveness replaces revenge, there will be an agreement. The use of honour tools continues after the agreement, with honourable figures noticeably used in actions designed to guarantee the endurance of the agreement.[40]

Sulha has become less practiced in Palestinian society in Israel for several reasons: first, *jaha* intervenes only after the conflict has exploded; second, *jaha* lacks the resources and professional background to fully understand the causes of disputes and treats the symptoms instead; third, the same values that underpin the *sulha* (honour and forgiveness) can also "prevent or obstruct the process of reaching a just resolution; instead it may contribute to the preservation of an asymmetrical power relationship that exists between the parties."[41]

5.2.2 Alternative-Legal Approach

There are two other ways to solve conflicts in Israel: litigation and ADR (Alternative Dispute Resolution). ADR is a generic term referring to various means of settling disputes outside the courtroom, such as conciliation, facilitation, negotiation, neutral evaluation, mediation and arbitration.[42] ADR methods are informal and attached to official judicial mechanisms. The methods, tools and skills used are similar to negotiation. I will not discuss litigation since this was not used in the case studies.

Fisher and Ury have developed the method called "principled negotiation" or the problem-solving approach. This method is based on five principles: (1) separate people from the problem, (2) focus on interests, not positions, (3) invent options for mutual gain, (4) insist on using objective criteria and (5) know your BATNA (Best Alternative to Negotiated Agreement).[43] This approach assumes people to be calculating and cost-benefit oriented. It has several characteristics that make its use problematic in conflicts involving Middle Eastern culture. First, it is designed primarily to satisfy individual

---

40. Pely, "Honor."

41. Abu-Nimer, "Conflict Resolution in an Islamic Context," 32, and "Conflict Resolution Approaches."

42. Some Western ADR practices, such as arbitration and mediation, have developed into separate approaches. Disputants who choose (or are instructed) to seek a solution outside the courtroom can use one of these separate methods (Abu-Nimer, "Conflict Resolution Approaches"; Barrett and Barrett, *History of Alternative Dispute Resolution*).

43. Fisher and Ury, *Getting to Yes*, 1st ed.

needs. This is in contrast to Middle Eastern tradition which conceptualizes people as selves-in-relationship.[44] Second, problem-solving suggests that participants "separate the person from the problem." This is in contrast to Middle Eastern conflict processing in which individuals are integral parts of the conflict and its solution. Fisher and Ury's approach has also been criticized for its claims of cultural universality.[45] Third, emotions (or venting) are acknowledged and respected in the process, but it is not universally accepted as a legitimate and/or constructive tool of conflict resolution within some strands of Western ADR.[46] Nevertheless, their approach seems to be one of getting the emotions out of the way so a settlement can be reached.[47] Middle Eastern approaches see emotional expression (or venting) as equally important or more important than resolving specific problems.

Galtung argues that the basic needs approaches of resolving conflict such as Burton's (recognition, security and identity) are culturally biased in assuming that non-negotiable human needs are universally applicable to all cultures.[48] Galtung stresses that people of differing cultures meet those needs in different ways. Burton's basic human needs approach is individualistic rather than communally based in that it defines the human needs of the individual, not the human needs of societies. For example, human needs for honour are fundamental in many communal cultures.

---

44. Walker, "Concepts of the Self."

45. See Avruch and Black, "Ideas of Human Nature."

46. Grillo, "The Mediation Alternative." In Western-style ADR, venting can serve a dual purpose when used as a tool of mediation: it allows the parties to vent their feelings of anger and frustration, and it allows each party to realize that they are not alone in their feelings of anger and frustration. Sometimes, venting is even seen as a therapeutic process which allows the move to possible resolution (Silbey and Merry, "Mediator Settlement Strategies").

47. Avruch, *Culture and Conflict Resolution*, 78.

48. Galtung, "International Development"; Burton, *Resolving Deep Rooted Conflict*. In *Violence Explained*. Burton makes the argument that a need for recognition, security, and identity are an essential part of being fully human and therefore cannot be bargained away. This means that in Burton's analysis, negotiating over basic human needs is not effective in decreasing conflict and may even make it worse. This is in contrast to Fisher and Ury's approach, which argues that basic human needs are security, economic well-being, belonging, recognition and control over one's life and should be taken into consideration in negotiations (Fisher and Ury, *Getting to Yes*, 2nd ed).

5.2.3 Comparison between *Sulha* and Alternative-Legal Approaches

I briefly compare *sulha* and alternative-legal approaches in terms of their assumptions, worldviews, third-party interventions and processes.

5.2.3.1 Assumptions underlying both models

The *sulha* assumption is that conflict is a negative interaction, and the focus is on the damage conflict can bring. Conflict resolution aims to maintain status quo, restoring social order and a disrupted balance of power, rather than to change power relationships. The group, not individuals, is the central locus of action, and future relationships are very critical elements. Norms such as honour, saving face, dignity, social status and religious beliefs are social codes utilized to evaluate an individual's status and operate as a pressuring tool to reach a mutual agreement.[49]

The alternative-legal assumptions are that conflict is not necessarily a negative interaction. Interest-based negotiation and a cooperative approach can be relied on to achieve a task, with laws accepted as a framework for intervention in a dispute.[50] People who are not directly connected to a conflict have minimal involvement (individualism). Behaviour is calculated according to rational measures and norms such as "behaving according to professional codes."[51]

5.2.3.2 The worldviews underlying both models

The *sulha* characteristics reflect a worldview distinctly different from that underlying the alternative-legal model frequently imposed on Palestinian communities.[52] In the alternative-legal system, humans are autonomous

---

49. Abu-Nimer, "Conflict Resolution Approaches"; Merry, "Mediation in Non-Industrial Societies"; Nader and Todd, *Disputing Process*; Witty, *Mediation and Society*; Irani and Funk, "Rituals of Reconciliation"; Jabbour, *Sulha*; Gellman and Vuinovich, "From Sulha to Salaam"; Lang, "*Sulha* Peace-Making Process"; Shihade, "Internal Violence."

50. Bellah et al., *Habits of the Heart*.

51. Abu-Nimer, "Conflict Resolution Approaches.

52. With the establishment of Israel, the Palestinian community became a minority after having been the majority. The *sulha* worldview and techniques grew naturally from the community, bottom up, while the Israeli worldview, which is frequently imposed on Palestinian communities, is top down. Thus, seeking help in the Israeli courts is considered to be going against the social codes of this community and hurts their honour by disrupting the balance of social order.

individuals. Techniques are emphasized; intellectual experiences are used; and an analytical method is employed, with time perceived as linear. In the *sulha* system humans are communal, interconnected beings. Processes are emphasized; emotional expression is encouraged; and a holistic method is employed, with time considered in relation to interconnections between the conflict, participants and society.[53]

5.2.3.3 Third-party intervention in both models

In *sulha*, the *jaha* may suggest an intervention, but they officially act only after authorization from a family representative. In the alternative-legal system, the disputants' primary expectations are directed towards the legal system. In *sulha*, the third party has authority in the process, and both disputants have to respond to the values and norms of the society (dignity, religion and patriarchal identity), which is different from the alternative-legal model where the process is based on joint decision-making.

In the alternative-legal approach, interveners lack the connectedness to the disputants that is a natural characteristic of the interveners in *sulha* – interveners who are involved in the day-to-day life of the disputants. This connectedness often enables pressure to be placed upon disputants to resolve the conflict, but in the alternative-legal model such pressure might come from the courts. In *sulha*, interveners are involved emotionally in the dispute, often because they have actual kin relationships with the disputants. In the alternative-legal approach, interveners are expected to be committed to the process itself.

5.2.3.4 The process in both models

The alternative-legal method utilizes a voluntary process of private mediation, in which a neutral third party helps the parties negotiate a mutually acceptable agreement. The process usually involves a mix of joint and private meetings with the parties. The parties determine the outcome and can cancel it at any given moment.

The *sulha* process differs in that once the disputants agree to participate, they are obligated to agree with the *sulha* verdict. *Sulha* rarely uses joint

---

53. Galtung, "International Development"; Fisher and Ury, *Getting to Yes*, 1st and 2nd eds.; Avruch, *Culture and Conflict Resolution*; Bush and Folger, *Promise of Mediation*.

caucuses (meetings); it frequently uses private caucuses, seemingly because of the anger disputants feel towards each other. Furthermore, the *jaha* can freely use coercion when required to push the process forward.[54] The *sulha* process also differs from mediation (and arbitration) in that, although it cannot be used without the parties' agreement, there could be strong pressure from the community or the *jaha* to participate in it.[55]

During the investigatory stage, the *jaha* also use some mediation-like techniques. For example, they discuss prior precedent, reframe aggressive statements and allow disputants to express their emotions. In *sulha*, venting of grief/anger is heard only by the *jaha*, and disputants meet only at the *sulha* ceremony. In the alternative-legal approach, the mediator often holds a joint session to facilitate expression of emotions.[56]

In *sulha*, the investigation, deliberations and verdict stages are more like arbitration, with touches of mediation. For instance, although the *jaha* decide the facts and the verdict (arbitration),[57] the *jaha* negotiate the verdict with the disputants so that it will be acceptable to both. As with mediation, the *jaha*'s goal is to create a narrative that both sides agree with.[58] In the alternative-legal approach, communications with the mediator during private caucuses are strictly confidential. The main reason for *sulha* confidentiality is the desire to increase harmony between the disputants.[59] The *sulha* agreement is not confidential and can be submitted to a court.[60]

---

54. Pely, "Resolving Clan-Based Disputes."

55. One stage of the *sulha* process that is similar to mediation is the process of bargaining the *hodna* (ceasefire).

56. Pely, "Resolving Clan-Based Disputes."

57. It should be mentioned that the instruments of coercion in the *sulha* process are the written and verbal commitments (*taffwid*) that the disputants give the *jaha*, obliging them to abide by the *jaha*'s verdict.

58. Pely, "Where East Not Always Meets West."

59. Since revealing positive things the parties said about each other could promote resolution, *jaha* members are permitted to testify about such things if they are not incriminating.

60. The *sulha* agreement can be submitted to a court even though the agreement could contain incriminating information. Additionally, the settlements are declared in a public forum. Pely, "Where East Not Always Meets West"; Gellman and Vuinovich, "From Sulha to Salaam."

Neutrality is essential to both alternative-legal and *sulha* processes. A tool that can promote neutrality is the right of the parties to veto members of the *jaha*.[61]

5.3 Christian Approach: Tension between Traditional Palestinian Churches and Western-Baptist Approaches

The tension between episcopal/sacramental versus congregationalist/functionalist polity was discussed in depth in chapter 4. In this section, I briefly describe the two approaches.

5.3.1 Traditional Palestinian Church Approach

According to Israeli law, the traditional Palestinian churches have juridical autonomy in the area of personal status and family law.[62] However, when church conflict arises, it is dealt with by a decision made by the bishop or a specific committee appointed for that matter. In some cases, conflict remains unresolved for years.

5.3.2 Western-Baptist Approach

Theoretically, as churches are independent, conflict should be dealt with according to each individual church constitution. This could involve bringing the dispute to church meetings where members could vote on its resolution, or the constitution could demand the appointment of a mediator or arbitrator. When churches have no constitution, or if the constitution does not include instructions on how conflict should be managed, then the most powerful figure is able to impose his own solution and the unsatisfied party may leave church.[63]

---

61. Pely, "Where East Not Always Meets West"; Gellman and Vuinovich, "From Sulha to Salaam."

62. See chapter 1, footnote 4 page 3.

63. For more details about the tension over power between pastors and laity, see chapter 4, section 4.3.2.

5.4 Local Palestinian Baptists' Conflict Management Practices in the Three Case Studies

I have found that the conflict management processes in the three case studies consist of the above four different approaches with contrary commitments.[64] Two of them belong to either *sulha* or alternative-legalistic *cultural* models, the rest derive from local *theological* practices found in traditional Palestinian churches and in Western-Baptist practices.[65] The pastors' cultural-theological approaches are a combination of *sulha* and the hierarchical theology known from traditional Palestinian churches. The younger generation's cultural-theological approaches are a combination of alternative-legalistic and Western-Baptist.

Palestinian Baptists in Israel mix these practices as they deal with church conflict. Nonetheless, no party consciously adopted any one of the four approaches for conflict management. It merely happened that *some elements* of these various approaches can be found in the way the pastors and laity dealt with conflicts, and it is likely that they had been influenced by these approaches, albeit unknowingly or sometimes knowingly.

I argue that these practices have been unproductive because of the traditional power of the pastor in a traditional, patriarchal community, the movement towards more democratic principles within society and the newness of the Palestinian Baptist churches that have not yet institutionalized their church-conflict management practices.

In the following analysis, I characterize the attitudes of congregants, pastors and third parties with respect to each approach. My ascription of one of these approaches to each interviewee does not mean that they exhaustively practice everything the approach would recommend. It is to say that this particular approach was more characteristic of this particular person. The four different approaches are *sulha*, alternative-legalistic, hierarchical and Western-Baptist.

I offer the term "*sulha* approach" to talk about a compromising and non-confrontational approach in which the elements of *sulha* are obvious. Conflict

---

64. People are generally complex and live with contradictory commitments. It can be argued that nobody lives strictly according to one worldview.

65. It is noteworthy to distinguish between approaches and practices. Approaches are the sources, and practices are the actual outworking of different elements from different approaches.

management that is more legally oriented – one involving confrontation, formality and a perception of entitlement – I call an "alternative-legalistic approach." I suggest the term "hierarchical approach" to explain the pastors' way of dealing with conflict within their churches. Finally, I offer the term "Western-Baptist approach" to explain Western missionary and Western-minded Palestinian pastors' approaches.

I begin by providing, from the case studies, examples of the *sulha* approach, and I then move to the alternative-legalistic approach, where I dwell on the underlying need for balance between patriarchy and modernity. After that, I move on to the hierarchical approach. Finally, I expand the descriptions to include the Western-Baptist approach. The discussion is dedicated to the ways in which the alternative-legalistic and Western-Baptist approaches echo ongoing collective efforts to balance opposing forces and differing worldviews that operate in this community.[66] Bridging the gap between practical knowledge and formal knowledge reveals a range of creative negotiations that make the local articulations of Palestinian Baptist conflict-management more complex than they may seem.[67]

5.4.1 *Sulha* Approach

Sulha elements seemed right to many participants, especially the older, more traditional congregants. Some elements of *sulha* were used or combined with other approaches during conflicts and after splits by both disputants and third parties. I identify several *sulha* social codes in the case studies which were pressuring tools in conflict management.

5.4.1.1 Sulha *social codes identified in the case studies*
Future relationships and restored social order
To promote future relations with Pastor A and restore social order in case A, deacons continued to attend church A even after the split. Although the deacons emphasized, in their letter to Pastor A, that all members run church affairs and pastors are not church owners, they admitted their compromise

---

66. Rabinowitz, "Palestinian Citizens of Israel."
67. Palestinian Baptists in Israel are shaped by different cultural forces. Their approaches to texts are a result of habituation as well. What we might call "biblical habituation" is partly a function of the religious tradition that formed them, but it is also a result of many other places that produce them, as mentioned above. Fulkerson, *Places of Redemption*, 160.

was driven by beliefs that relationships are more important than ministry and change, and restoring the church's social order was a priority. Courtesy and saving face of the clergy were issues at stake.[68]

Additionally, most third parties discontinued interventions. They did not want to confront Pastor A and aimed to keep good future relationships with him, although they disagreed with his attitude. Their suggested resolutions therefore included keeping Pastor A but adding an associate pastor.

Furthermore, when church A2 applied for ABC membership, the ABC was divided in its loyalties between either Pastor A or the deacons (who later joined church A2). Mark, an influential leader, succeeded in convincing Pastor A not to vote against church A2's membership in the ABC.[69] Mark asserted this conflict influenced the whole denomination and could easily have caused a split in the ABC itself. In this case, the focus was on social stability in the ABC and honour in the eyes of the broader community.[70] In case B, church B2 – upon the ABC's request – agreed to give up the right to use the church building in order to maintain a good future relationship with the ABC.

Focus on damage, not change, and the codes of shame, honour, saving face, and good witness

Most members from both churches in case A recognized the split as a stigma and a poor witness within the community.[71] A sentiment backed up by sentences such as, "You become like the other traditional churches that have lots of conflicts";[72] "You Baptists, although you are very small in number, you nevertheless split."[73] When I asked about their prayers during the conflict, participants said, besides praying for Pastor A, they prayed they would continue to be a good witness and not be shamed in their community. Mark

---

68. Letter to Pastor A, 14 Apr.

69. Mark, interview with author, Aug. 2014. It is claimed the decision was made when it was agreed that church A2 would seek a different location. Church A2's leaders claimed that they promised to move only when they found a suitable place, but they never found one.

70. Future relations were important for both church A and church A2. Seven years after the split, they came together in joint services as an initiative of former missionaries.

71. Seemingly, the phrase "not to be a poor witness," repeated by many interviewees, seems to mean not to be an obstacle to others' faith and also to protect one's reputation in the face of others.

72. Dan, interview with author, Mar. 2014.

73. Jonathan, interview with author, Apr. 2014.

argued that this conflict was not dealt with properly since the focus was on "our reputation in the community" and not really on solving the problem.⁷⁴

Additionally, even within the evangelical community, this split caused a poor reputation for church A2. Some pastors stated they would not accept an invitation to preach at church A2 until it moved away from the doorstep of church A. As Majd explained: "It is a bad witness because it is a ministry on the doorstep; the geographic place of worship is critical to determine blessing. If a church splits and worships on the doorstep of the mother church, this is unacceptable culturally, biblically and logically. We heard comments even from Muslims about that."⁷⁵ In *sulha,* a split or divorce was not an option. Majd blamed the mission for the split since they immediately provided church A2 with a place for its meetings. He believed that they indirectly encouraged the split as "they did not realize the sensitivity of founding a church on the doorstep after a split within Palestinian culture, where saving face is so important." According to him, the mission should force reconciliation and not allow splits (*sulha* attitude).

Although the split happened more than twenty years ago, its associated shame continues due to the location of church A2. Every Sunday, members of both churches remember the split as they meet at the same time, physically side by side. Often this requires explaining to visitors why there are two Baptist churches in the same venue.

Another example of shame and saving face was when the deacons, along with most of the younger generation, gave up and left the church, since they did not want to keep fighting at every meeting or to seek help in a secular court – in their culture this would be unacceptable and would be a poor witness, bringing shame on them.⁷⁶

The younger generation's attitude, mixed with their feeling of entitlement, created a different rationality of honour and shame; they put emphasis on confrontation and finally split the church.⁷⁷ In case B, we saw a clear shift in

---

74. Mark, interview with author, Aug. 2014.
75. Majd, interview with author, Mar. 2014.
76. Another example of saving face was when the dismissed deacons sent Pastor A letter expressing resentment concerning the last heated church meeting instead of confronting him during the meeting to prevent more tension and poor witness.
77. This is an example of using the alternative-legalistic approach.

attitude, with the younger generation focusing more on their rights to have their own church than on shame and saving face.[78] There are two reasons for this shift: first, case A set a precedent for splits in cases B and C; second, during case B many of ABC's leaders were from the younger generation.

In case C, third parties focused on the damage conflict would bring to the community. They tried to "force" Pastor C and Bishara to continue to work together on the evangelistic ministry despite the conflict. David, a third party, stated: "We forced them to stay together. We told them it is unacceptable to divorce; your decision would influence the broader community, you are ministers and this would hurt the church. . . . We focused on the damage that their decision would bring; we also focused on the benefit the reconciliation would bring."[79]

Another third party tried to bring about reconciliation between Pastor C and Bishara.[80] The third party met with them and they apologized to one another. Bishara told me the third party "forced" him to apologize at church although he was not convinced he should. Saving face is implicit in these two examples.

Compromise

Compromise was another dominant element in the cases. In case A, deacons were able to convince the second generation not to use the legal system to force Pastor A to share the church building. As Jack, a deacon, explained:

> The church's constitution doesn't provide a way of dealing with conflict. . . . We tried hard to find the right biblical way and thought that it was best to leave the church. . . . I don't know if this was biblical except we *compromised* and left so we wouldn't be poor witnesses. . . . During the conflict, we prayed our witness would remain good in the eyes of our city.[81]

---

78. See chapter 1. This supports Barakat's argument that what characterizes Arab cultural identity in this transitional period is the ongoing struggle between opposing values. Barakat, *Arab World*.
79. David, interview with author, Aug. 2015.
80. A delegation from the ABC (before the formal intervention of the ABC committee).
81. Jack, interview with author, Mar. 2014.

Rima, a member at church A2, argued, "the deacons and many others were dissatisfied, but they accepted this reality because they got used to being silent at church since this is the way 'it should be.'"[82] In case B, the ABC attitude was to convince church B2 to compromise and give up the building for Pastor B's sake, to prevent escalation of the conflict. In case C, third parties put pressure on Bishara to make more compromises for Pastor C's sake, hoping this would solve the conflict.

Religious beliefs such as submissiveness to clergy
Most interviewees had mixed feelings, believing that splits were wrong but unable to see an alternative route out of situations where they felt powerless. Splits therefore seemed the only solution, but some respondents reported that they lived with a sense of shame after the split. Third parties in case A accused members who left church of not being submissive enough to their pastor. Speaking of Pastor A, the ABC president during and after the conflict said, "Do not harm the 'anointed' from God."[83] Rima thought it was very painful when third parties were judgmental towards them; as she explained, "It was painful for us too to leave but we had no choice. . . . Many others told us you had to stay and bear everything, and there should be a solution. . . . Eventually, none of them could do anything to solve the conflict."[84] She added that some members from Pastor A's party would accuse them of being "against the 'anointed' of God," since God had appointed him as pastor and everybody should be submissive and loyal. Some old women were afraid to leave church A to join church A2 as they might lose the privilege of being buried respectfully, "as if Pastor A had the authority to remove this privilege from them."[85] Some members felt Pastor A's preaching was judgmental and were hesitant to take communion at church.

---

82. Rima, interview with author, Mar. 2014.
83. Where does this idea of the "anointed" come from? I am aware that the word "anointed" can be used in different senses. In the Bible, anointing was related to accountability and service. This might be related to David and Saul who were anointed as kings and Jesus who was anointed as servant. Seemingly, Palestinian Baptist local culture developed a theology over the perception of the word "anointed" to give more privilege to leaders in hierarchical (untouchable) positions rather than a theology of service. This theology might have its roots in charismatic theology.
84. Rima, interview with author, Mar. 2014.
85. Rima, interview with author, Mar. 2014.

Deference to clergy was evident in case A when first-generation deacons did not confront Pastor A for years. Majd, a pastor who exited from church A, said, "The deacons were tolerant with Pastor A even on 'unbiblical issues'; eventually they themselves were harmed by their attitude."[86] In cases B and C, younger generations were loyal to their pastors; when pastors did not share power, they confronted them.

The following quote summarizes the *sulha* approach, delineating social codes (of future relations, saving face, compromise and submissiveness to clergy) which directed the attitude and actions of disputants and third parties:

> The church waited a long time without real confrontation because of special relationships, courtesy, saving the face of the pastor and not hurting his feelings. Compromise for many years is the reason for today's hardship. . . . The members' Arab-Christian perspective hindered them from confrontation and frankness. . . . As Arabs we were not frank and as Christians we respect clergy and age.[87]

5.4.1.2 *The reason for the* sulha *approach failure*

There are several external and internal reasons *sulha* seems to have failed to solve these conflicts.

External reasons (related to broader community)

First, the traditional nature of the *sulha* can be a weakness because disputes today differ from the past. For example, the *jaha* is unable to address the source of conflicts, since its goal is to preserve the status quo. In the case studies, the younger generation was interested in change and dissatisfied with keeping the status quo. The result was frequently that, when the underlying roots of the conflict were unresolved, the conflict continued.

Second, the *sulha* model has become less effective and less practiced in Palestinian society in Israel because massive loss of land to the state hastened the decline of patriarchal control and contributed to critical changes in family relations.[88] Another important reason is the younger generation's exposure

---

86. Majd, interview with author, Mar. 2014.
87. Jack's letter to Pastor A, 14 Apr.
88. See chapter 1, section 1.3.1 and chapter 3, section 3.2.2.

to secular Israeli rationality, ideas of secular justice and individualism. They have developed a sense of rights to lead and shape the church. Accordingly, their understanding and deference to elders has weakened.[89]

Third, the susceptibility of the process to becoming dominated by socially powerful participants often leads to unsustainable resolutions and to a contradiction of the value of justice and individual rights. This was indeed true in the case studies with the unbalanced power between pastors and congregants. *Sulha's* ability to mend relationships is strong but is weak when challenging the patriarchal structure because of its patriarchal *habitus*.[90]

Fourth, due to lack of resources and compensation, it is hard to find volunteers to enter into the *jaha*.[91] This results in a greater tendency to appeal to the Israeli legal system. One of the main complaints of interveners and disputants in the cases was the inability to find volunteers able to allocate considerable time to dispute resolution.

Fifth, since *jaha* intervenes only after the conflict has become violent, the situation becomes more complicated and the goal of reconciliation harder to achieve.[92]

Finally, church splits are a new challenge facing the Palestinian Baptist community, and *sulha* would need to *adapt to the changes* the community is experiencing. This requires new techniques and professionals.[93] Based on the data, disputants complained third parties lacked professional knowledge to deal with church conflicts.

---

89. While Arab societies are undergoing rapid changes throughout the world, the *sulha* and its place in these societies may also be undergoing some change.

90. See section 5.2.1. One of the weaknesses of the *sulha* is that intervention is based on a hierarchical system of mediators and procedures.

91. *Jaha* members are traditionally unpaid.

92. Amal, a deacon's wife told me, "The conflict should be dealt with immediately – it is easier to solve when it is small – so people will not get used to it and accept it" (interview with author, Mar. 2014). Jack asserted, "When the solution becomes a split (divorce), this means that the conflict has already been there for long time" (Jack, interview with author, Mar. 2014).

93. In general, there is a lack of documentation in the many meetings held during *sulha* processes. This lack hinders the *sulha* from improving a body of precedence for promoting the conflict resolution process (Tarabeih, Shmueli and Khamaisi, "Towards the Implementation of Sulha").

Internal reasons (related to case studies)
One main reason for *sulha*'s failure in the case studies is that its stages were not fully applied by third parties, and it was not practised explicitly.

First, third parties had no *authority* since they were not authorized by the disputants as in *sulha*, and thus they did not have the power of *jaha*. In case A, third parties involved informal individual initiatives by respected evangelical community figures: two elderly ABC pastor representatives, two elderly respected figures from the wider evangelical community, and two second-generation pastors from church A who tried to initiate talks with church A2.[94] Two missionary pastors from each church initiated a joint prayer meeting. Other third parties and joint friends initiated joint worship services. Two other additional attempts at reconciliation by church A2's leadership were rejected by Pastor A.[95]

In case B, after the split, an ABC-delegation met with the disputants separately, but the disputants insisted that there was no way to reconcile. Another attempt from the ABC failed since Pastor B was very upset by its stance. Despite strong pressure from the Baptist community to participate in reconciliation attempts (similar to the kind of social pressure operating in *sulha*), Pastor A and Pastor B, who felt betrayed and rejected by their church members, were uncooperative.

Second, the element of neutrality is essential to the success of a *sulha*, because the *jaha* actually imposes a settlement, making it crucial that all sides of the dispute feel that the *jaha* is completely neutral in its approach.[96] However, in the case studies, many of the interveners (who also lacked the *jaha* power since they were not formed and authorized accordingly) could not continue as they were afraid of losing friendship with the pastors.

Third, in *sulha*, interveners meet separately with disputants to convince them to choose reconciliation; private meetings are important because of the anger each side feels. Joint meetings take place at the end, during the *sulha* ceremony. In case A, third parties initiated a joint meeting with disputants, hoping to resolve the problem in one session. Phil, a senior pastor, and Peter, an evangelical leader, met with the parties. Phil told me, "When

---

94. When Pastor A knew about this initiative, he became angry.
95. Rami and John, interviews with author, 2014.
96. Pely, "Where East Not Always Meets West," 437.

we arrived at the meeting we did not know what the problem was, and we asked the parties to explain.... We were hoping by the end to build bridges between them, to drink coffee and shake hands... but we did not get to this point."[97] Peter added, "We were not prepared; we went spontaneously, and we said to ourselves 'they are believers.' We would share with them what the Bible teaches us about solving problems, and they would agree... but they did not want to apply it."[98] Because of the interveners' attitude (skipping the private meetings), no venting took place, no truce agreement,[99] no honour restoration and no investigation – and therefore no agreement was achieved, as would have been the case in *sulha*.

Fourth, another third party started the process with a verdict to solve the problem, skipping all *sulha* steps. Two elderly, respected pastors, both ABC-representatives, were asked to try to solve the conflict in a biblical way. On their agenda were three issues: (1) cancel the last vote in the business meeting, (2) the pastoral candidate, and (3) the need to stop using the pulpit to pass negative messages.[100] This attempt also failed.

Fifth, some third parties started the process with a *sulha* ceremony, skipping the prior *sulha* stages. Seven years after the split, this process was started with joint church services at church A, which can be seen as parallel to a *sulha* ceremony. Many interviewees focus on externality; for them the purpose of joint services was to publicly restore social order and good witness. Amal, a deacon's wife, viewed joint services as a kind of reconciliation, "since we showed willingness to be together."[101] She added, "Only the building can unite us again: each church would have its own services in the building, and the building unites the body of Christ since we will be together, and everybody can see we are together."[102] In this attitude (externality), we can

---

97. Phil, interview with author, July 2014.

98. Peter, interview with author, May 2014. This attitude was close to the ADR model where the mediator often holds an early joint session for the expression of emotions.

99. Truce agreement means the promise not to take revenge and not to confront the other side.

100. ABC records.

101. Amal is a member in church A2. Amal, interview with author, Mar. 2014.

102. Amal, interview with author, Mar. 2014. According to church A2, since Pastor A had not yet attended their church service this would mean that there is still a problem. These joint meetings in fact would provide them with legitimacy in the broader community as they were perceived as the one who did wrong.

see appearance is important; the whole community should be able to observe the "peace" by "being together" in a joint service. For Amal external forgiveness can lead to reconciliation (*sulha* attitude).[103] I would call this kind of reconciliation "diplomatic reconciliation." "Diplomatic reconciliation" focuses on the external aspect of reconciliation and might overlook the need for genuine forgiveness and justice and is aimed at keeping the social order despite unresolved conflicts.

We also see a different viewpoint, a focus on internality, from some younger members. For example, Rima did not attend the joint services at church A, since she felt it was not sincere and that church A members were not welcoming, and they never agreed to join services at her church (church A2). Rima perceived internal forgiveness as a condition to real reconciliation.[104] It is noteworthy that Pastor A rejected church A2's invitation to join their services because of the church's location.[105] He wrote, "Having your church located a few metres from ours after the split . . . causes resentment to many people . . . in addition to ongoing friction and competition to attract members." He ended his letter by praying for them to find another place soon.[106]

Starting the process with a *sulha* ceremony, after skipping the prior *sulha* stages, was also seen in case C. Albert, a church leader, told me, "Before the split, when we had tension at church, we would arrange a trip and have a barbeque all together, but we did not discuss the problem. . . . We tended to minimize the problem and ignore it."[107] It seems "sincerity" is less relevant to this attitude because, by participating in joint services or sharing a meal,

---

103. External forgiveness is an external process aimed at restoring social order and is realized in the broader community. This will be discussed in-depth in chapter 7, section 7.2.

104. Internal forgiveness is an internal process of overcoming negative attitudes and emotions (revenge, resentment, avoidance or anger) towards the offender. This will be discussed in-depth in chapter 7, section 7.2.

105. Letter, 4 May.

106. Letter, 20 May. As of 2018, the situation in case A is a ceasefire (analogous to a *hodna*); the conflict is still unresolved. In the first years after the split, most people did not interact and people still talked about their hurt and hard feelings. Slowly, and mostly after joint services, people began to greet one another. Pastor A also agreed to allow the use of the church building for funerals and weddings of church A2 members. However, some misunderstandings still arise because of church A2's location. This is a ceasefire until a new spark takes place, such as discussing the church building again. However, as Bryan, a missionary, put it, "There was no willingness to pay the cost . . . to meet and become completely honest with each other" (interview with author, Mar. 2014).

107. Albert, interview with author, Aug. 2015.

the congregants are enmeshing themselves in a web of social relations that will "force" them to keep the peace.[108]

Sixth, one of the main roles of the third party in *sulha* is to restore honour publicly because of the shame and rejection felt by all disputants. Shame and rejection were the main complaints shared by both pastors and the younger generation as a result of the splits. Phil, a third party, complained they failed because disputants took things too personally and both made harsh accusations. He told me, "Pastor A's party was focusing on his long history of sacrifice and service in the church as if the other party did not acknowledge that."[109] In *sulha*, interveners and disputants use honour tools during each stage to enable the parties to gradually go through transformation from anger (revenge) to willingness to contribute to communal healing (reconciliation). In the case studies, third parties did try to restore dignity by offering honourable solutions (such as keeping Pastor A as emeritus pastor), but they did not use honour in each stage, as ought to happen in *sulha*. It seems that the pastors' requests to be recognized by the ABC as "the Pastor," and eventually to control the church buildings, was one method they used in attempt to restore part of their lost honour.

Furthermore, in *sulha*, venting or emotional expression is equally important to resolving problems. Interveners may act as voluntary targets for the victim's family's sense of anger and frustration. Ignoring venting played a critical role in the case studies; third parties did not realize their critical role as anger or shock absorbers' and that they must enable grief work.[110] They perceived venting as an obstacle in achieving reconciliation. Phil, a third party, said, "We spent three hours hearing the same complaints again from both sides with no progress." Peter, a third party, gave up because of the harsh emotions expressed; he concluded a split was inevitable. Most third parties mentioned the issue of strong emotions controlling the process as a reason for failure. Jack, a deacon, asserted Pastor A's feeling of rejection after the split hindered any reconciliation.[111] Mary, a member at church A2, argued,

---

108. Lang, "*Sulha* Peace-Making Process."
109. Phil, interview with author, July 2014.
110. Jabbour, *Sulha*, 46–47.
111. Jack, interview with author, Apr. 2014.

"Since we live in intertwined community, tension escalates during conflict."[112] According to her, the parties were not able to reconcile after so many insults and injuries. She added, "They burned bridges behind them. There were very hard accusations from both groups."[113]

Finally, time is a critical element in *sulha*, and the amount required is measured in relation to the interconnections between the conflict, participants and society; this dimension is critical in order to publicly restore dignity. However, in the case studies, third parties did not dedicate enough time and that was problematic. According to most interveners, they met with the disputants only once; the process usually ended at the first joint meeting as the emotional reaction was very strong and the meeting exploded.

In sum, *sulha* approach include different social codes of future relationships, compromise, deference to clergy, honour and saving face. It focuses on being a good witness and maintaining unity, with divorce as not an option. Disputants and third parties did not comprehensively apply the stages of *sulha* and did not fully address emotions and honour. They focused on externality (appearance) rather than internality, and the preservation of an imbalanced power relationship rather than change. *Sulha* attitude led to pacification, or "diplomatic reconciliation,"[114] rather than reconciliation. Its implicit theology of reconciliation lacks internal forgiveness and justice.[115] Apparently, Palestinian Baptists felt trapped: they faced a new reality of church conflict where their traditional model failed (either because it was not fully implemented or because it became ineffective); they had no central authority such as the traditional churches to force a solution; and no external coercion was possible.

5.4.2 Alternative-Legalistic Approach

This approach was mainly used by the younger generation. I use the term alternative-legalistic approach to denote the method of using only part of the techniques of alternative-legalistic conflict resolution to bring about change, such as confrontation and a legalistic framework as I elaborate below. The

---

112. Mary, interview with author, Apr. 2014.
113. Mary, interview with author, Apr. 2014.
114. I will discuss "diplomatic reconciliation" in chapter 7.
115. I will discuss that in more detail in the next chapters.

younger generation in the case studies mixed this approach with *sulha* when they showed deference to clergy, compromised their rights and did not seek help in secular courts.

I focus on the interplay between the creativity with which the younger generation, with its commitment to individual rights, challenged patriarchal and traditional limitations to expand their life opportunities on the one hand and were inclined to identify with the values of their own culture on the other. To a degree, my observations have been informed by an implicit expectation that they should serve as agents of change.

5.4.2.1 Alternative-legalistic techniques identified in case studies
Confrontational technique

When the younger generation confronted the pastors, this was an act of rebellion against the patriarchal system. The young laity admitted the conflict happened because of their enthusiasm for change and for a new vision that would include them in church life. For pastors, however, change was not an option, and conflict escalated. I find three different types of confrontations in the case studies.

First, the younger generation, using the constitution, confronted their pastor and refused to submit to him. They repeatedly requested that the pastor operate according to the constitution; they persisted in their right to bring in a younger pastor; they sent a petition letter which escalated the conflict; they appealed to the BCI and requested a separate service in the church building. After they failed to enact change, they split the church. Rima, a member of church A2, said, "When we started to question Pastor A, we did not get any response and we started to feel rejected and felt the division in the air."[116] Rima, who also rebelled against compromise and saving face for a clergyman in a patriarchal community, said, "God does not teach us to overlook wrong and to compromise. . . . When we mentioned that this was perceived as very rude and crossing the line, especially as a woman . . . I felt as if our patriarchal society was flowing into the church, in the very place where it shouldn't be accepted."[117]

---

116. Rima, interview with author, Mar. 2014.
117. Rima, interview with author, Mar. 2014.

The younger generation challenged patriarchal and traditional limitations in order to be able to respond to God's calling upon their lives through the church. They tried to act legally and respectfully, and they agreed to bring in a young pastor to work alongside Pastor A. In order to reach an agreement, they used rational measures with creative options, focusing on interests and mutual gain, but they also focused on relational measures and tried to retain a good relationship with Pastor A and the rest of the church. After the split, they welcomed third-party intervention; they were open to compromise by giving Pastor A the opportunity to become pastor emeritus and continue his salary, and they left without using legal means to force him to share the building.

Nonetheless, at times the younger generation insulted Pastor A, acting disrespectfully towards a clergyman. For example, some of them criticized the pastor and his preaching ability. Another example was sending the petition letter via a delivery service to Pastor A's house. For Pastor A, individuals are integral parts of a conflict and its solution; resolving the problem meant replacing the deacons, rejecting the "rebellious-group" and electing his family and friends to different positions.

In case B, the opposing party also confronted Pastor B and were ready to start their new church immediately. Three weeks after the split, church B2 was formed. Elias, a church leader, in his letter to one of the interveners, stressed that he saw no problem with them starting their own church, just as church A2 did nine years earlier. The split in case A was seen as a precedent for insisting on change.[118]

I identify a second type of confrontation in case B, when the ABC confronted Pastor B directly.[119] Pastor B, who felt rejected and betrayed, refused to be reconciled or to accept church B2 into ABC membership. For him, acceptance of the "rebellious-group" would amount to disregarding his thirty years of service, and he warned that it would encourage divisions.

---

118. Letter to the ABC, 17 Dec., and open interview with David. In cases A and B, the ABC gave legitimacy to the churches that split by accepting their membership; some argued that this attitude of the ABC indirectly encouraged members who opposed the pastor to leave church (Majd, Pastor B and Pastor C). Some even saw the split in case A as a precedent that gave a green light to future church splits. Pastor C and Elias explicitly said that they did not see a problem in starting a new church after a split, referring to other cases at ABC.

119. Some younger generation leaders were recruited in the ABC ten years after the split in case A.

He explained that being submissive to one another is a "Christ-like" quality, whereas rebellion is not.[120]

Pastor B's attitude was confronted by two young leaders who were part of a "rebellious-group" in their churches. Aaron, an ABC-representative, responded in another letter, confronting Pastor B directly. He wrote, "The submissiveness God expects from us is different from what is found in the papal church." He added that, biblically, not every disagreement between members and a pastor counts as rebellious and demonic, referring to the famous dispute between the Apostle Paul and Barnabas. He stressed that, since the ABC could not help achieve reconciliation because of distrust between the parties, each wanting to serve God differently, *divorce* was inevitable, referring to Abraham and Lot and emphasizing a belief in "pluralism in unity." However, the ABC recommended keeping positive relationships and being open to merging later. He ended by saying that the ABC was aware of the warfare and that both parties had been wounded; but the ABC had confronted Pastor B in a direct way, bringing it back to confrontation.[121]

One year later, the ABC was struggling with whether to accept church B2 into membership because of different opinions within ABC. Rami, a young ABC leader, told me the ABC was divided; most pastors were against church B2 becoming a member, claiming that accepting church B2 would encourage future splits. Lay leaders were supportive.[122] Sami, a member of the "rebellious-group" in case A, sent a letter to the ABC, expressing his resentment concerning this attitude. He insisted, since Baptists in Israel are a small community, it was important to keep these churches under the umbrella of the ABC for their protection, and if pastors would have shared power with church members, they would not have split. He added that this kind of attitude would turn the ABC into a "pastors' club" that would help them keep their status.[123] Rami also decided to confront Pastor B respectfully in a seven

---

120. His letter to the ABC, 23 Apr.
121. Letter, 27 Apr. It is noteworthy that the splits solved parts of the conflicts at church. Although split is not the optimal resolution, but reintegration is, we still live in a fallen world where optimal solutions are hard to achieve and pain will be healed completely in the world to come.
122. Open interview with Rami, Oct. 2016.
123. Letter, 27 May.

hour face-to-face meeting, after which he concluded that Pastor B was also hurt by the ABC stance.[124]

A third type of confrontation, accompanied by submissiveness to the pastor, was identified in case C. This was not a traditional "papal submissiveness" without questioning. Members of church C2 decided not to split the church. Nonetheless, their submissiveness was accompanied by questioning Pastor C. This young, third generation was more committed to principles of congregationalist ecclesiology. It was also directed by the American-Arab pastor who encouraged them to stay submissive and cooperate with the ABC committee during the conflict.

These three different types of confrontations caused a shift in the ABC approach to conflict management, from traditional reasoning to a modern approach. In 2007, as a result of the splits in cases A and B, the ABC constitution was changed to allow for greater influence and power for the ABC over-pastors and churches going through conflict.[125] Another change was to make the acceptance of a new church resulting from a split conditional upon its receiving a blessing from the church it split from.

Legalistic framework technique

The findings indicate that the younger generation consciously operated within a legalistic framework: behaving in accordance with professional codes, using letters to negotiate directly with their pastors, demanding to work in accordance with the constitution and appealing to the BCI. Using these techniques with pastors caused huge resistance and escalated conflicts, as both models (hierarchical and alternative-legalistic) have contradictory values (patriarchal versus democratic). I present some examples from the case studies.

In case A, a group of frustrated young men drafted a petition letter to Pastor A, calling on him to take immediate action to discuss introducing a new pastor, as this should be the decision of the whole church, and hinting that not taking these steps would cause a split. This letter was signed by nineteen church members.[126] Pastor A's letter in response, drafted jointly with

---

124. Rami, interview with author, May 2007.
125. See appendix 4, section 9, "The Ministry Committee," in the constitution. Also see chapter 3.
126. Nabil, Sami and Ramiz in interviews with author.

Waleed, a young member, was signed by forty-one people, many of whom were not active members in the church but were asked to sign. Pastor A's letter expressed his hurt at the disrespectful manner of sending the petition letter using a delivery service, and it stated that insisting on addressing the issue of a future pastor would lead to chaos and confusion in the church.[127]

In case B, a group of frustrated members, led by seven professional men and women, tried to change Pastor B's philosophy of individual church leadership to a pastor-and council-led church. Two years before the church split, and after many requests to have a church committee, pastor B agreed but then ignored it. Elias said, in explaining the importance of formality when dealing with the pastor, "We need *formality* so the pastor wouldn't say that he didn't know about the meetings of the committee."[128] When the committee insisted on having a constitution, they started to work on drafting one. The committee met several times without the pastor being present. When they handed the proposed constitution to him, the pastor, who was hurt by their attitude, did not accept it. They tried to call for a general meeting, ignoring the pastor, but he called a meeting without them; the committee was dismissed, and the church lock was changed.[129]

5.4.2.2 *The reason for the failure of the alternative-legalistic approach*

Confrontation and the use of legal framework techniques were familiar and common for the younger generation. Nonetheless, this approach was not acceptable for the pastors and the older generation; people such as Jack, a deacon, who did not fully agree with their techniques. He said, "The optimal thing would be that the opposing group would grow so they can change the pastor. . . . The church members have the authority. . . . There was only one attempt but it failed."[130]

---

127. Pastor A's letter suggested several issues: (1) the Holy Spirit raises up spiritual leaders according to the Lord's timing, (2) a more urgent subject was the need to activate the church, as the spiritual leaders (hinting at the deacons) were not participating in their spiritual roles, and (3) the need for new leaders who could work in harmony with Pastor A instead of opposing him.

128. Elias, interview with author, Aug. 2015.

129. Elias, interview with author, Aug. 2015.

130. Jack, interview with author, Apr. 2014.

Waleed, from Pastor A's party, spoke about the deacons' responsibility, saying, "The deacons should have stayed at church, served and won Pastor A's trust again; they are the pillars of the church. . . . It was their responsibility to solve the conflict without leaving."[131] Pastor Majd, who exited from church A, suggested, "If splits were inescapable, the group should leave silently, meet in a different place without taking members."[132] Paul, a missionary, agreed with Majd and added, "There would not have been the hurt and pain for those involved or the poor testimony in the community."[133]

Interestingly, the younger generation viewed confrontation and the use of legalistic techniques as kind and normal. They did not see their actions as intimidating to their pastors. Sami explained the petition letter as follows: "We sent Pastor A a very kind letter asking him to bring a pastor for the youth, just as Paul trained Timothy."[134] Dan, a deacon, explained that the idea was to convene a general assembly for the whole church to discuss the issue of bringing another pastor when Pastor A did not cooperate. However, Pastor A and Pastor B viewed some of these techniques (sending letters, writing petition letters, calls for a general meeting and appeals to BCI to use the building) as disrespectful and felt deeply rejected and insulted. Pastor A and Pastor B told me that even at the time of their interviews they still did not understand the reason for the splits.

These examples are evidence that the use of the alternative-legalistic approach by the younger generation burned bridges with their pastors. Church A2 fought Pastor A by splitting, staying in the same venue and talking unsympathetically about him. Church B2 fought Pastor B by splitting and speaking unsympathetically about him. Nonetheless in case C, although members confronted Pastor C, they did not oppose him by splitting, which allowed for reintegration (although accompanied by challenges, as discussed in section 5.4.4).

---

131. Jack, interview with author, June 2014.

132. Majd, interview with author, Mar. 2014.

133. Paul, Aug. 2014. George, who was supposed to replace Pastor A, spoke about the difficulty the deacons had acting as spiritual authorities at church A where the pastor should be accountable to them: "The problem is the deacons did not operate in their capacity as spiritual authorities. It would have been solved biblically if there had been spiritual authority in the church. Since churches are independent, pastors should be accountable to elders and deacons. The deacons should have written a letter to the church requesting Pastor A to resign, and they should have maintained this request until the end, even if that meant going to court."

134. Sami, interview with author, Feb. 2014.

In response to the use of the alternative-legalistic approach, pastors started to indirectly rebuke the parties wanting change from the pulpit, using Bible passages and sermons, and even blamed them for the poor spiritual state of the church. This step contributed to conflict escalation between the two groups. This was also seen in case C.

This method of rebuke was used by other members – not only pastors and some family members. For example, Sami, a young leader, received threatening phone calls from a church member who claimed he was hurting "the anointed from God" with his aggravating letters. Sami informed Pastor A in a letter that, for the sake of saving the face of the church, he would not approach the police about the intimidation he was experiencing; however, he did request that this person should be disciplined.[135] Eventually, Jack, a deacon, convinced Sami to drop his complaint in order to prevent an escalation in the conflict (*sulha* attitude).[136] This is another clear example of how the younger generation navigated between two cultures, using a legalistic framework based on the alternative-legalistic approach and Baptist theology, as well as being sensitive to some cultural limitations (saving face and respect to clergy).

It should be mentioned that there is some overlap between the values of Baptist theology (discussed below) and the alternative-legalistic approach familiar to the younger generation who made use of it. These techniques were rejected by the older generation and pastors. Eventually, it also escalated the conflict, since some of its values contradicted the values of the traditional *sulha* model. The implicit theology of reconciliation in the alternative-legalistic approach prioritizes justice and rights over relationships.

In sum, we can see that a shift occurred from case A (1995) to case C (2016), from the "anointed" pastor to a "confronted" pastor, from traditional "papal submissiveness" to "submissiveness" with questioning, and split became an option. However, the code of compromise, saving face, good witness and loyalty to clergy played a role in the cases. The younger generation navigated between the contradictions and tensions that could be summarized in the polarities of *theology and culture*: hierarchical versus congregationalist and traditional-patriarchal versus modern-democratic. The younger

---

135. Letter, 12 Aug.
136. Sami, interview with author, Feb. 2014.

generation required both the practice of adjusting to a contradictory situation and the practice of boundary maintenance between two different contradictory sets of values: democratic and traditional. The *habitus* oriented them to consider carefully the limitations of their worldview and motivation even while they also constantly modified their stance. This is also the place where people negotiate meaning, interest, and power in order to achieve change and reproduction.

5.4.3 Hierarchical Approach

The hierarchical approach was mainly used by pastors who acted as spiritual fathers. The behaviour of the pastors in the case studies was seemingly influenced by the non-evangelical, traditional Palestinian churches both theologically and culturally. Pastors understood that their position could grant them the power to act as a bishops in traditional Palestinian churches and made decisions to solve conflicts by dismissing deacons (case A) and committee members (case B) from office or trying to appoint a successor after they resigned (case C). Additionally, Pastor A and Pastor B did not recognize the authority of the ABC who tried to intervene, emphasizing their individual authority and the autonomy of the local church. This approach was discussed in-depth in chapter 4.

In the three case studies, pastors tended to see conflicts in their churches as spiritual problems (members were not submissive to clergy). In case C, when Pastor C requested ABC's help, he was hoping they would give him complete support as *the pastor*; this was also seen in case B when Pastor B requested ABC to recognize that he was *the pastor*. All pastors made the claim "God told me to . . ." to increase their power by claiming a high spirituality. Ron, a missionary who served among Palestinian Baptists for many years, concluded, "Pastors always have the power in the end; culture and society affirms the conservative approach to leadership."[137] The hierarchical approach's implicit theology of reconciliation seems to suggest that the patriarch is the one who implements justice and offers forgiveness, as I elaborate in the next chapters.

This approach also failed to solve the conflicts. Church members felt desperate with the authoritarian style of their pastors, voicing their frustration

---

137. Ron, interview with author, June 2014.

and complaints through confrontation and letters and eventually escalating the conflicts which led to splits.

5.4.4 Western-Baptist Approach

This approach is another way of managing conflict. Like the other approaches it was not used in a *pure* form but was mixed with *sulha* and alternative-legalistic approaches. This approach failed to resolve the conflicts in the case studies since it did not take into consideration elements of the local culture; the majority of the interveners were either Southern Baptist missionaries (from America or the West) or Western-minded Palestinians. Nonetheless, it succeeded in case C's second phase (see section 4.2.3). This approach is more individualistic and does not take family and emotions into account during the process. It exists in two major shapes: fundamentalist and pragmatic.

When I asked people what it meant to resolve conflicts biblically, many answered, "It is to pray and fast and seek God's guidance"[138] or to "continue to serve at church until God intervenes and brings the solution."[139] Some, who saw church conflict as a spiritual problem, said spiritual problems should be dealt with spiritually not culturally.[140] However, a few said it was to contact the other party through a mediator, and, if this failed, then each should go their own way; there was also an awareness that compromises are necessary in order to reach an agreement.[141]

I will examine the process of the Western-Baptist approach in two interventions in case A and case C.[142]

5.4.4.1 *The process*
The formation of a third party
In case A, after a few weeks of consultation, the ABC and BCI initiated a retreat between the disputants and invited a few highly respected ministers, such as the BCI coordinator, the ABC chairman, an evangelical leader and a

---

138. Rima, Mary, Amal, interviews with author, 2014.
139. Majd, interview with author, Mar. 2014.
140. Rima, interview with author, Mar. 2014.
141. Jack, Ramiz, interviews with author, 2014.
142. In case B, Pastor B rejected all intervention.

senior pastor, to act as facilitators. Seven representatives, determined respectively by the two groups themselves, were invited to attend.[143]

In case C, when Pastor C decided to leave church C2, he invited the ABC to lead the church. The ABC committee became the third party trying to mediate between Pastor C and church C2. After the ABC constitution was changed, this committee gained more power. This committee included five local pastors, two of whom were Western-minded, educated, influential pastors who had lived in western countries for many years.

Bible study and prayer meetings

In case A, the group was given a few worksheets (formulated by Paul, the BCI coordinator) about biblical peace-making in preparation for the meeting. They met for two days in a BCI retreat centre. The purpose of this gathering was to discuss the problems and see how they could be resolved. During the meetings, there were sermons and Bible studies based on what Scripture says about unity and reconciliation (with a focus on Matthew 18).[144] Two themes were addressed: relationships between believers and seeking the good of others over one's own desires.[145] Around nine prayer meetings and Bible studies took place during the retreat. While one group met with facilitators, the other group had prayer meetings.[146]

In case C, the ABC committee met with each party separately in around ten meetings, talking about forgiveness, grace, good witness and acceptance of others (they also studied Matthew 18 and Galatians 6).[147]

---

143. The pastor group included: the pastor, his son, three young leaders and two others. The other group included: young leaders who persisted in change and the deacons (BCI report, 13 Apr.).

144. Paul, interview with author, Aug. 2014.

145. Based on Scripture such as Matthew 6:33, Hebrews 12:1-2 and Philippians 2:3-8. They also studied the following themes: commitment in Matthew 28:19-20, cooperation in Ephesians 4:10-16, interpersonal relationships in Colossians 3:12-17, communication in Ephesians 4:15 and unconditional acceptance in Colossians 3:13 (BCI report, 13 Apr.).

146. The invitation to this retreat included these words: "These prayer times can be as important, perhaps more important, than the meetings with the facilitators. If we cannot hear God's voice, how can we hear our brother's voice?" They also encouraged calling a twenty-four hour prayer marathon during this meeting. "The BCI will also be praying. . . . Others will be enlisted throughout the Middle East, North Africa and the world to pray for us; we want everything that happens during our time together to be under the leadership of the Holy Spirit" (BCI report, 13 Apr.).

147. David, interview with author, Aug. 2015; George, interview with author, Mar. 2014.

Separate meetings

In both cases, Pastor A and Pastor C cooperated as third parties met separately with each group to discuss their requests. Additional joint discussions were held between third parties and both groups.

Preliminary agreement and honour restoration

As a result of the retreat in case A, a preliminary agreement was drafted that included the appointment of a nine-person committee from both parties to work on uniting the church and looking for a pastoral candidate. This new committee included five from Pastor A's new church committee, two deacons from the original four and two from the opposing group. The outcome would then go to the church assembly for a final decision.

Some of those I interviewed said there was a verbal suggestion, accepted by Pastor A, that he would become the "Pastor Emeritus" and continue his salary. The retreat ended with a prayer time and follow-up meeting. This was also an attempt at honour restoration for Pastor A, which, as I elaborate in the next chapters, he later rejected.

In case C, it was agreed Pastor C would leave the church and focus on pastoring church D.[148] The ABC committee met with the opposition group and requested that they be submissive to their spiritual father who had also served them for many years. The ABC committee suggested that Pastor C would stay at church C2 for a few more months and leave the church respectfully with a church organized party held in his honour. Thus, his departure would not be shameful in the community's eyes. This was another attempt to restore honour for Pastor C, which he rejected. Pastor C refused to drop his membership in church C2 for his family's sake. The ABC committee insisted he drop his membership and requested that his family stay at church C2. Pastor C became angry and decided to leave the church with his family.

In both cases these agreements failed.

5.4.4.2 *The reason for the failure of the Western-Baptist approach*

The findings show that studying Scripture together was not sufficient to deal with the conflict. Interveners (missionaries and Western-minded Palestinian pastors) focused on how to act and relate to God and others. However, this

---

148. Pastor C has been pastoring church D for the last ten years in a nearby village.

approach ignored the pastors' struggles, such as how to deal with feelings of rejection, anger, insult and loss of dignity. Also, it did not take into consideration that the parties were deeply related and influenced by their families, so any agreement was incomplete until approved by the family. Another important element was the internal struggle of the third party (ABC committee), mainly in case C, around issues concerning authority, confidentiality, theological disagreement within the committee and other limitations. We will now look at each struggle in turn.

Pastors' struggles

The pastors believed their long years of service earned them the privilege to decide what was right at church; they felt ownership of the churches they founded. As clergy with a high view of ordination, they expected members to be submissive. They felt a huge pain of rejection and betrayal by people they had long served. This led them to rebuke and finally dismiss those who were not "loyal" to them. This also led to their overreactions and refusal to accept help. Rebellion against pastoral hierarchy was perceived by pastors as sin, and, thus, they felt these members had to repent. When the younger generation left, pastors lost their honour publicly since this action indicated public rejection of the spiritual father in a religious town full of religious symbols. Under *sulha*, lost honour can only be restored publicly.

As I shall elaborate, three important issues were not addressed properly which contributed to unsuccessful management of the conflict: emotional, familial and economic factors.

First, failure to address *emotions*. Venting is an indispensable part of every *sulha* since it helps the disputants move beyond their immediate grief and anger to agree to give reconciliation a chance.[149] All pastors expressed in their letters to the ABC the pain and hurt they had experienced during the splits.[150] One of the pastors signed his letters with the phrase "your wounded brother." During my interviews with the pastors many years after the split, I could feel the pain and shame they had experienced as they sometimes became tearful; some even mentioned becoming ill. John, an evangelical leader, initiated a conversation with Pastor A eighteen years after the split and told me Pastor A

---

149. See section 5.2.1.
150. Pastor C's letter, 14 May; Pastor B's letters, 23 Apr., 7 Dec., and 9 Dec.

was still hurt. John explained, "There is no address for these people [pastors] to cry and express their hurt.... They need God's intervention to be healed."[151]

Another example of the power of emotions in case A was the follow-up meeting after the retreat, which aimed to approve the outcome of the retreat. The chairman of the ABC and Paul, the BCI coordinator who led the retreat, were present as observers. A young leader, who had not been present at the retreat, showed up in this meeting unexpectedly. The meeting began by reviewing the summary of what was agreed in the first meeting, but they could not agree on the results. This young leader then spoke impolitely to the chairman of the ABC and Jack, a deacon. As a result, the meeting "exploded" and no progress was made. The opponents left the meeting and the mediators remained to try to soften Pastor A's group. They failed and decided to give up. Paul (the BCI coordinator) also perceived strong emotions as a barrier to reconciliation, saying, "It is the attitude and emotions of those involved and not the means for conflict resolution that is the root problem."[152] He added, "In church conflicts I have observed people do not really act rationally... but it was very strong emotionally in this case [case A]."[153]

In case C, a committee of two respected leaders (a lawyer and a Western-minded pastor) were authorized to deal with the evangelistic ministry conflict that eventually caused church C2's split. They led the mediation sessions using mediation techniques, taking cultural codes into consideration. After spending long hours trying to convince Pastor C and Bishara to reconcile for the sake of good witness in the community, they tried to push for a resolution honouring Pastor C. To their surprise, Pastor C rejected the process and the agreement. When I asked if the issue of hurt had been addressed, they explained that would be dealt with next – after resolving the conflict. It is likely that not addressing the issue of emotions and hurt prior to a solution prevented them from giving reconciliation a chance. George, a member of the ABC committee, viewed emotions as a barrier to achieving reconciliation in case C; he argued that the main challenge to receiving reconciliation was what he called the "emotional mentality."[154] Seemingly, interveners viewed venting

---

151. John, interview with author, Apr. 2014.
152. Paul, interview with author, Aug. 2014.
153. Paul, interview with author, Aug. 2014.
154. Focus group, June 2016.

as spiritual immaturity and "acting according to the flesh," and thus emotions were not given legitimacy and were viewed as a barrier to, and rejection of, reconciliation, therefore leading interveners to give up.[155]

Second, failure to address the centrality of the *family*. As already mentioned,[156] in the same manner that the family may be the key to resolving conflicts, they could also cause the eruption or quick expansion of conflicts. In case A, it was common knowledge that Pastor A's decisions were influenced by his family. This resulted in conflict escalation as he would frequently change his mind even with third parties, as happened in the follow-up meeting after the retreat.

In case C, since the ABC committee did not address the needs of Pastor C's family after he left church C2 at their (ABC committee) request, the result was Pastor C ended up founding a new church for his family and relatives who left church with him. It is likely that this factor was critical in causing the split, as we read in Pastor C's letter to the ABC committee:

> After praying and consulting my family regarding closing the meeting at my mother's house [at the request of the ABC committee] and despite the fact that according to the Baptist faith . . . each church is independent . . . and that no institution can force or control independent churches . . . and despite the fact that this decision will cause injustice to my family's right for religious freedom and for the sake of good witness . . . we decided to stop this meeting and my family would join church D, despite the expenses and transportation [to its location in a different village]. . . . We would bear this cross for God's glory . . . and to show submissiveness to one another in God's fear.[157]

Later on, Pastor C decided to start church C3 since his family was not able to continue to travel to church D during difficult weather. He met with the ABC committee, but they insisted that starting a new Baptist church in the same town was unacceptable. According to Pastor C, he decided to resign from the ABC so he could pastor his family.[158]

---

155. Peter, Phil, Paul, Jack, Ramiz and Nabil in interviews with author.
156. See section 1.3.1 and section 5.2.1.
157. Letter, 23 Feb.
158. Letter, 7 Apr.

Third, failure to address the *economic* factor. Culturally, talking about economic factors is unacceptable; it would be perceived as "unspiritual" and worldly. Thus, although the economic factor was essential to conflict management, pastors and third parties did not mention it. Issues of salary and funds to pay for renting and so on remained important but were not dealt with. Indirectly, this made church conflicts more complicated and unresolvable. Interestingly, younger-generation interviewees did mention these issues as an important element in the conflict.

Third-party struggles
Based on the research, third-party struggled with five areas:

First, *late stage of intervention*. In the case studies, intervention came late; the conflicts had existed at least five years before the split. Most third parties said they felt helpless since the disputants had already burned their bridges and it was difficult to intervene. Jack, a deacon (case A) explained, "If dissatisfaction in church is not dealt with immediately, it will mostly lead to a split."[159] Albert, a church leader, mentioned that since the conflict in case C was not managed early on it was followed by many mistakes, becoming complex and involving many other members.

Second, *lack of third-party authority*. In *sulha*, the third party acts as arbitrator. According to the ABC-constitution, the ABC committee acts as a mediator and cannot force a resolution. In the case studies, interveners could not reconcile the disputants, since, ultimately, the pastor or the church could reject the agreement if they did not like it. This happened in case A when Pastor A's family intervened and in case C when Pastor C refused to listen to the ABC committee and founded church C3. David, an ABC committee member, argued that since there is no accountability, and the committee acts as a mediator (not an arbitrator), resolving conflicts would take a very long time. He suggested third parties should be arbitrators because it is impossible to achieve consensus in every conflict resolution and it is hard to satisfy everybody.[160]

Third, *lack of confidentiality*. In *sulha*, third parties are obliged to keep the information they collect confidential as they meet and interview witnesses

---

159. Jack, interview with author, Apr. 2014.
160. David, interview with author, Aug. 2015.

and members of disputants' families.[161] In case C, David, a third party, complained, "In the midst of negotiation we felt we were in a war zone; we were trying to make peace during war. There were members from both sides 'shooting.'"[162] He was hinting regarding the chatter that was going on, which, in his opinion, was destroying their reconciliation work. As a result, they had to invest considerable time into building trust between the parties at every meeting.

Forth, *lack of third-party consensus.* Another level of confidentiality in *sulha* is the decision-making process of the committee when it reflects on its verdict.[163] Since different third-party members may have various views as the process evolves, it is critical to maintain confidentiality about the committee's discussions and its members' positions and opinions, so as to reduce their exposure to pressures following a verdict that may be sensed to be unfair by one or more disputants.[164] In *sulha,* members of the committee keep discussing until they achieve consensus.

The ABC constitution has no clear instruction on church-conflict management.[165] For example, the third party in case A acted differently from the third party (ABC committee) in case C. The mechanism they used was the personal subjective opinion of committee members.

In case C, the lack of instructions on how to deal with the conflict caused tension between Pastor C and one of the ABC committee members. I attended one of the ABC committee meetings. The tension was obvious in the committee itself and its attitude towards both the conflict and Pastor C. Some preferred not to take a stance in order to maintain a good relationship with Pastor C or church C2; for them, relationships were more important

---

161. See chapter 5, section 5.2.1.1, for further information on the importance of confidentiality in *sulha.*

162. David, interview with author, Aug. 2015.

163. See section 5.2.1.

164. Jabbour, *Sulha*; Pely, "Where East Not Always Meets West."

165. George, Albert, Shirin, David. Section 4 in the constitution deals with the procedure for dealing with disputes: "The procedure for dealing with disputes shall be first to ask the various disputants to meet in private and seek reconciliation and agreement as to the way forward. If this fails, the Ministry Committee shall appoint a delegation to call together the disputants for the same ends. If this fails, the Ministry Committee shall decide any terms it may deem appropriate for the disputants to settle matters or otherwise. Refusal to accept this judgment shall be deemed an act of resignation from the ABC by the Church or pastor concerned, with the loss of all rights and privileges of membership."

than resolution to the conflict. Others thought that the church was more important than Pastor C. The rest thought that both Pastor C and church C2 were equally important.

I find that two approaches could be seen in use during that meeting, as well as through interviews and documents: fundamentalist and pragmatic.[166] These differed according to the attitudes of people involved in the attempts at conflict resolution.[167]

According to the fundamentalist approach, there is one interpretation to any problem; the problem is seen from the perspective of the law. The issue is viewed in terms of right and wrong, and the Bible is seen to be clear about attitudes. Every wrong attitude is viewed as a sin; for example, Pastor C's lack of submissiveness to spiritual authority (the ABC committee) was interpreted as a spiritual problem.[168] The opposing side evaluated Pastor C according to his personality, not his attitudes. They also tended to generalize. In order to convince the committee regarding their resolution, they tried to bring his past patterns of behaviour as evidence. Because of their attitude, they did not take into consideration his hurt emotions and family. As a result, Pastor C's relationship with one of the committee members became tense and he did not cooperate with the committee. However, they believed they were very tolerant with Pastor C and made many compromises for the sake of their future relationship. In the ABC constitution there is no clear mechanism to evaluate a pastor's ministry, so this was done according to personal subjective opinions, and the decision was made that this case would be an example to other churches of how to resolve problems with splits. They also disagreed with Pastor C coming to one of the meetings, despite his desire to do so. They viewed relationships as more important than ministry, while Pastor C viewed ministry as more important. According to this view, sometimes called evangelical Biblicism, there is only one way to deal with conflict and that is God's way. All problems of faith, life and theology are solved simply by use

---

166. Fundamentalism is a type of militantly conservative religious movement characterized by the advocacy of strict conformity to sacred texts. Christian fundamentalists vigorously opposes theological modernism which attempts to reconcile traditional Christian beliefs with modern science. Fundamentalism as a movement arose in the United States. Munson, "Fundamentalism Religious Movement."

167. Field note, May 2014.

168. George, interview with author, Aug. 2015.

of the Bible and no other considerations are needed; neither psychology nor sociology must be consulted, the Bible alone is sufficient.[169]

People using the pragmatic approach see problems as an opportunity to grow by looking for common ground and finding constructive ways to solve problems; they separate the person from the problem. They tried to see Pastor C's humanity and believed their job was not to evaluate his life and ministry but to deal with a specific problem. They were able to see his hurt and need to be healed. They suggested there should be an objective mechanism to evaluate the problem. For them, the purpose of the law was to serve mankind and not vice versa. They saw Pastor C as being in an unhealthy situation and in need of help and support. They saw Pastor C's problem as a complex of problems, not one big problem, and thus saw some of his attitudes as positive. They said he should be part of that meeting since he was still open to negotiations. They believed that their role was to help him make better decisions and not force him to obey rules. Accordingly, there could be a number of different godly resolutions and not only one. The purpose of canonical discipline is to restore relationships, not to punish. It is likely that this approach is close to transformative mediation, where conflict is looked at not as a problem but as an opportunity for growth and transformation, and where anger and venting are seen as contributing to empowerment, recognition and the making of outcome-related decisions.[170]

By the end of this meeting a letter was drafted to Pastor C concerning his request to resign from the ABC (since they insisted he could not start church C3). Adherents of the fundamentalist approach wanted to draft an assertive, hard letter, while those with a pragmatic theological approach wanted to invite Pastor C to that meeting and keep negotiating. They also proposed bringing in professional help. Disagreements at this meeting were obvious; finally, they drafted a letter that focused on the problem not on the person. They accepted his resignation from the ABC, and, nonetheless, welcomed him to rejoin the ABC when his attitude changed.[171]

Eventually, what helped Pastor C was being surrounded by loving pragmatic people who rejected his attitude but supported him (such as Rami,

---

169. Fulkerson, *Places of Redemption*, 182.
170. Bush and Folger, *Promise of Mediation*.
171. ABC letter, 23 May.

David and the American-Arab pastor). One year later, Pastor C started to negotiate to rejoin the ABC. This also led to the reconciliation retreat that took place a year after. Four months later, church C2 and church C3 reintegrated.

Fifth, *no post-ceremony activities to ensure the durability of the agreement.* Members of church C2 felt the ABC committee did not continue to work with them as they should have following the merger between the two churches. Some believe the merger was too early since church C2 was not yet ready to accept Pastor C back. According to some church C2 leaders, the ABC committee expressed weariness and dissatisfaction with both Pastor C and church C2 members since this conflict management had taken so long (five years). This also explained the third party's limitations. First, the limitation of time meant they were not available when needed. Second, the ABC committee members were neither unified nor working together; they had different attitudes and were not kept up to date with each other about what some of them had done. Third, not all of them were suitable for this position.[172]

5.5 Conclusion

In this chapter, I identified two cultural approaches and two theological approaches at work in the case studies. These approaches were unproductive in resolving intra-church conflict because of the contradiction between the cultural approaches (namely, *sulha* and alternative-legalistic) and a contradiction between the theological approaches (namely, hierarchical and Western-Baptist). Stated differently, the traditional power of the pastor in a patriarchal, hierarchical community, the movement towards modern culture and democratic congregationalist ecclesiology by the new generation, and the newness of the Palestinian Baptist churches that have not yet institutionalized their church-conflict management practices are the main reasons for the failure of the four approaches. Nonetheless, this process of conflict management is polyphonic and dynamic and includes an ongoing and internal dialogue between the four approaches.

The *sulha* approach was used by all disputants, either solely or combined with other approaches. For *sulha*, conflict is a negative interaction; social codes of non-confrontation, compromise, deference to clergy, shame, saving

---

172. Albert, interview with author, Oct. 2016; Shirin, interview with author, July 2016.

face and good witness are critical. Disputants and third parties used some elements of *sulha* but did not comprehensively apply its stages and rituals. They also did not fully address emotions and dignity and had no authority and experience. They faced a new reality of church conflict where their traditional model (in the way they applied it) failed.

However, we also saw the creativity of the younger generation who mainly used the alternative-legalistic approach, alongside *sulha* and/or a Western-Baptist approach. In addition to identifying with the values of their own culture, they focused on individual rights and used confrontation and a legalistic framework to seek change and power, challenging patriarchal and traditional limitations to expand their life opportunities. To a degree, they were agents of change. Between case A (1995) and case C (2016), we saw the following shifts: (1) from the pastor as the "anointed one" to a pastor confronted directly by congregants and the ABC; (2) from members being passive at church to members exercising their right to lead the church with the pastor; (3) from traditional "papal submissiveness" to submissiveness with questioning; and (4) splits became an option as the ABC gave legitimacy to churches that split by accepting them as members.

It seems that the pastors and laity held different implicit theologies of forgiveness and reconciliation which were all imperfect in some respects. *Sulha* lacks internal forgiveness and justice since it preserves imbalanced power which often contradicts the value of justice and individual rights. The alternative-legalistic approach prioritizes justice and individual rights over relationships. In the hierarchical approach, the pastor is the one who implements justice and offers forgiveness and laity must obey; this approach often resulted in pastors making one-sided decisions. Western-Baptist theology is more individualistic and only partly succeeded in solving the conflicts since it did not take into consideration some elements of Palestinian culture. This approach could not sustain justice.

This calls for a more rounded and comprehensive theology of forgiveness and reconciliation. Volf may help in this direction, which is the subject of the next chapters.

CHAPTER 6

Theology of Remembrance

6.1 Introduction

Thus far, in the first half of the thesis, I have described the context of Palestinian Baptists in Israel (chapter 1), explained my methodology (chapter 2), described the environment and the potential factors that contributed to conflict in the Palestinian Baptist churches (chapter 3), identified the nature and causes of intra-church conflict in three case studies (chapter 4) and explored the four conflict management approaches used during church conflicts in the case studies (chapter 5). In chapters 6 to 9, I theologically evaluate the four approaches using Volf's model of reconciliation.[1] I also evaluate the applicability of his model within a Palestinian Baptist context. In these chapters we see the fundamental significance of the combination of *theology and culture* in the solution.

In this research, Volf's themes cannot be adequately discussed if his model is addressed as an abstract concept; it must be contextualized. How is reconciliation understood in the Palestinian Baptist context? How might culture or religious beliefs influence reconciliation both in understanding and in its enactment? Some offences are considered more seriously depending on the cultural context: does this have a bearing on remembrance, forgiveness, justice and embrace? A key issue in the analysis has to do with understanding the spoken and enacted language of these themes.

My main argument in the second half of the thesis is that Palestinian Baptists in Israel are in the process of conceptualizing and integrating new

---

1. See chapter 1, section 1.5.

meanings into their theology of reconciliation. As we will see in the case studies, they are also experiencing a shift from what I call a "diplomatic reconciliation" that involves divorce, ceasefire, shaking hands and superficial cooperation to beginning a reconciliation that takes the form of reintegrating churches that had split.

The splits within the local Palestinian Baptist churches in Israel arise from multiple characteristics that uniquely define them, which can be summarized as follows:

1) Church members are a threefold minority, second-class citizens with an identity crisis, living in a legally uncertain environment that mirrors their insecure feelings in church life.
2) Church structure is flat, with no patriarch, yet exists in a patriarchal community.
3) The churches consist of a scattered field of very small churches lacking an organic community and consisting of different generations distinct from one another.
4) There is a low level of institutionalization in these churches.
5) The pastors hold a high view of ordination and face struggle over livelihood and power, which are constantly being threatened by young laity.
6) There is a lack of economic capital, and few churches have church buildings.
7) There has been an influx of very educated young leaders with a commitment to individual rights, individualistic-oriented competitiveness and an attitude of "rebellion" against patriarchal leadership though still maintaining some aspects of their patriarchal culture.
8) Most importantly, they are Christian believers but have no clear Christian model to deal with church conflict – their conflict management practices are complex and dynamic, involving an internal dialogue between their traditional practices (*sulha* and traditional churches) and innovative practices (alternative-legalistic approaches and Western-Baptist theology).

Because Palestinian Baptists are caught between all of these characteristics, in what follows I try to explain how I contribute through Volf's model to overcome this trap. I argue that Volf's model needs cultural translation in order to be applicable in this context.

In the next four chapters I will analyse and evaluate the four conflict management approaches used by Palestinian Baptists during their cases of church conflict in terms of Volf's four basic elements for reconciliation between people:[2] (1) remembrance, (2) forgiveness (repentance and apology), (3) justice and (4) embrace.

I begin by describing Volf's theme of remembrance, then, using his theme, I evaluate remembrance as demonstrated in the four approaches. I also evaluate Volf's theme of remembrance in light of each approach and present some recommendations.

6.2 Volf's Theology of Remembrance

The theme of remembrance is drawn mainly from Volf's book *The End of Memory: Remembering Rightly in a Violent World*. His thesis is that choices made in remembrance have the power to stem evil and thus to support or counter reconciliation between peoples. He argues we should remember a past wrong for the sake of both the victims and perpetrators, and the proper goal of such remembering is in fact non-remembrance – or, more precisely, the state of being reconciled in which memories of wrongdoing will not come to mind for either victims or perpetrators.[3] His central questions in this book are (1) How do we "remember rightly"? and (2) How long should we remember?

6.2.1 How Do We "Remember Rightly"?

Memory, Volf argues, is essential both to human functioning and to our sense of identity. Without memory, we could not recognize ourselves or each other as temporally continuous beings: "To be human is to be able to remember. It is as simple as that: no memory, no human identity."[4] Given the importance

---

2. The four conflict management approaches being those described in chapter 5.

3. Volf shares the personal account of his own struggle with remembrance as a result of the intimidation and interrogation he received at the hands of the communist Yugoslavian military in the mid-1980s. As a Christian married to an American, a pacifist and an expert on Marxist socialism, he was perceived to be a security threat to communist Yugoslavia. Long after these events, Volf has remained haunted by the memories of his interrogation. This led him to write his book *The End of Memory: Remembering Rightly in a Violent World*.

4. Volf, *End of Memory*, 147.

of memory to our human identity, argues Volf, the question is not whether we should remember our past or forget it, but how, what and for how long should we remember the past wrongdoing?[5]

According to Volf, our identity is not just shaped by our memories; we also shape the memories that shape us. What we do with our memories will depend on how we see ourselves in the present and how we project ourselves into the future.[6]

Volf argues that only reconciliation can liberate us from the poisoning effect of past wrongdoing upon the present and the future. At the same time, freedom from this poisoning is the condition of reconciliation. He suggests we need to remember rightly, an act which involves four elements essential to reconciliation: remembering truthfully, therapeutically, responsibly and in reconciling ways. These elements involve three different levels concerned with oneself, those who have done wrong and the broader society.[7]

6.2.1.1 *Remembering truthfully*

It is important for all those involved in reconciliation to have what Volf calls "truthful remembering," since victims tend towards exaggeration, and, at the same time, perpetrators' memories tend to be short and exculpating.

Volf suggests the word "remember" contains within itself two obligations: an obligation to truthfulness and a moral obligation to remember truthfully.[8] However, since our ability to complete this obligation is limited (because we remember partially and do not have control over our memories),[9] our goal should be to remember as truthfully as possible, regardless of our perspectives and interests. Another reason for truthfulness in remembering is to treat others justly; every untruthful memory is an unjust memory. "Obligation to do justice" is important to avoid fuelling further conflict or allowing wrongdoing to be repeated. An additional obligation for remembering truthfully is that it is a necessary precondition of reconciliation between disputants, "for peace can be honest and lasting only if it rests on the foundation of truth and justice."[10]

---

5. Volf, 148.
6. Volf, 25–26.
7. Volf, *End of Memory* and *Flourishing*.
8. Volf, *End of Memory*, 51.
9. Volf, 51–52.
10. Volf, 56.

For Volf, "remembering truthfully" has two aspects: one negative and one positive. In its negative aspect it is necessary not to speak falsely about the past.[11] In its positive aspect it is to "speak lovingly the truth about the past."[12] Volf argues "remembering truthfully is part of the larger obligation to speak well of our neighbours and thereby to sustain and heal relationships."[13] He adds that if someone seeks to be fair he should not only remember a person's evil deeds, but also remember his good deeds. In the same way, those who love should not remember a perpetrator's wrongdoing without also considering their own failings (Gal 6:1–2).[14]

6.2.1.2 Remembering therapeutically

The rule "remember truthfully" is insufficient, argues Volf, because it does not address the use of memory. The use of memory is important since what we do with our memories places restrictions on what we are willing to remember and that truthfulness constitutes a just use of memories and constrains their misuse.[15] Truthfulness is also important for inner healing. Memories which deeply trouble us "must pass through the narrow gate of truth to become memories which allow us to live at peace with ourselves."[16] Volf suggests three

---

11. Volf notes that truthful remembering amounts to an application of the ninth commandment: "you shall not bear false witness" (Exod 20:16). He suggests, "The rule provides an indispensable presupposition for employing memories as a shield rather than wielding them as a sword." (Volf, 66). For Martin Luther, argues Volf, the ninth commandment not only prohibits false witness; it is also a manner of speech that urges us to speak well of our neighbour and "benefits everyone, reconciles the discordant, excuses and defends the maligned" (as cited in Volf, 63). Based on the statement of the Apostle Peter, "love covers a multitude of sins" (1 Pet 4:8), Luther goes further, stating that we are to be "Christ" to our neighbours "by covering their sins in a way that reflects Christ's covering of our sins by means of his atoning death" (Volf, 64).

12. Volf, 66

13. Volf, 63.

14. Volf, 64.

15. Volf, 71.

16. Volf, 72. Volf argues that, "In most cases by far, we remember mistreatment rather than repressing it. But in memory we distort it, mostly giving its intolerable content a more acceptable form. . . . It takes knowing the truth to be set free from the psychic injury caused by wrongdoing. . . . We must name the troubling past truthfully – we must come to clarity about what happened, how we reacted to it, and how we are reacting to it now – to be freed from its destructive hold on our lives" (Volf, 74–75).

requirements for remembering therapeutically: integration, new identity and new possibilities.[17]

Regarding "integration," he explains that we try to integrate events into our life-story by giving them positive meaning within that story by understanding how they contribute to the goodness of the whole and how they have made us better people.[18] However, not everything in our lives can be integrated into a good wholeness. That is one of the reasons for non-remembrance. In Volf's words: "Our judgments on how such events contribute to some good are always provisional. For tomorrow may reveal insights about yesterday that are hidden from us today; and we can understand any given event adequately only from the perspective of the whole, which is to say when our lives and history have run their courses."[19]

"New identity" means that we remember wrongs as a self with a new identity defined by God, not as wrongdoers' evil deeds and their echo in our memory.[20] Volf argues, "When wrongdoing defines us, we take on 'distorted identities, frozen in time and closed in growth.' . . . The wrongdoing may not define us fully; yet it lodges in our core self and casts a dark shadow on everything we think and do."[21] Jesus Christ gives a new identity. Instead of being defined by wrongdoing or how others define us, we are defined by how God relates to us, "By opening ourselves to God's love through faith, our bodies and souls become sanctified spaces, God's 'temples,' as the Apostle Paul puts it (1 Corinthians 6:19)."[22]

"New possibilities" are important because, for Christians, future possibilities do not grow simply out of the reality of the past and present. As Jurgen Moltmann argues in *Theology of Hope*, the future comes from the realm of what is not yet, "from outside" – from God – rather than from what is. God's promise engenders new possibilities.[23]

---

17. These three elements of healing memories draw their basic content from the memory of the passion understood as a new exodus, a new deliverance. Volf, 103.
18. Volf, 77.
19. Volf, 78.
20. Volf, 79–80.
21. Volf, 79.
22. Volf, 79.
23. Volf, 82.

Volf speaks about the "identity-healing" use of memory whose primary concern is our own well-being: to construct a plausible narrative of the wrongdoing, to understand its effects on us, to condemn the wrongdoer and to recover and stabilize identity.[24] Without remembering therapeutically, we take two risks: allowing the wrongs suffered to control our lives and poison our future expectations. Remembering therapeutically is remembering the past but expecting something new will come.

To complete healing, argues Volf, the relationship between the disputants needs to be repaired. For Christians, this is what reconciliation is all about. Yet remembering so as to relate well to the self and to others are two different activities.[25]

6.2.1.3 Remembering responsibly

Remembering truthfully and therapeutically are not sufficient to help us remember rightly, notes Volf. It is necessary to think about the impact of our remembering on people not yet involved in the cycle of abuse. People who are defined by victimization can cause the perpetuation of the cycle of abuse on a third party.[26]

When we remember responsibly we are forced to move beyond our concern for our own wellbeing by learning lessons from the past to apply in new situations. This is in contrast to the identity-healing use of memory. On account of the injustice we have suffered, we decide to fight injustice done now to others.[27] Volf identifies two weaknesses: the difficulty of identifying a situation in which to apply the lessons of memory and not knowing exactly what a particular past situation exemplifies.

Volf concludes that the rules "remember truthfully," "remember therapeutically" and "remember responsibly" are all essential but insufficient. Volf suggests that we need to place the action of remembering in a larger ethical and theological framework.[28] He focuses on ways we are encouraged to remember the two central events of redemptive history: the exodus and

---

24. Volf, *End of Memory*, 87.
25. Volf, 84.
26. According to Volf, this is why the Old Testament keeps returning to Israel's remembering of slavery in Egypt.
27. Volf, *End of Memory*, 88.
28. Volf, 93.

the passion. Volf points out four important features shared by the sacred memories of the exodus and passion:[29] (1) they shape identity,[30] (2) they are embraced and deployed in community,[31] (3) they are defined in a horizon of expectations[32] and (4) they are primarily concerned with God.[33] When the people of God remember wrongs suffered, they remember them out of a sense of identity and community, out of expectations and ultimate trust derived from the sacred memory of the exodus and passion.[34]

The implications of the exodus memory for ordinary memories of wrongs suffered are (1) the imperative to remember – "no deliverance without memory," (2) the imperative to remember truthfully, (3) the imperative to remember so as to help those in need and (4) concerning God and the future, to link the memory to a redeemed future.[35] However, the exodus memory, argues Volf,

---

29. Volf states that we operate in a framework comprised of four components: Who are we? Where do we belong? What do we expect? What/who do we ultimately trust?

30. Identity: memory defines the identities of Jews when they remember the exodus, and Christians when they remember the passion (Volf, *End of Memory*).

31. Community: "religious communities sustain sacred memories and revitalize them in new contexts just as sacred memories define religious communities. Take the community away and sacred memory disappears; take the sacred memory away and the community disintegrates" (Volf, 99–100).

32. The future: The story of the exodus tells not just what happened, but also what will happen in our future. Similarly, in remembering Christ we remember not just his past but also,our future (Volf, 100–101).

33. God: The memories of the exodus and passion are most basically memories of God (Volf, 101).

34. Volf, 102. There are two significant things about remembering the exodus. First, the Passover Seder of Jewish memory is a ritual meal planned to memorialize Israel's deliverance from slavery in Egypt. This ritual meal is intended to make present the past event of redemption. Second, there is the idea of God's involvement; God heard the cries and God liberated his people. Israel's memory of this event, therefore, reinforces Israel's obedience to God and, inversely, Israel's obedience to God takes the form of right remembering.

Obedience and memory are the commandments that link Israel's former slavery in Egypt with Israel's present treatment of slaves and aliens in Deuteronomy (15:12–15). Memory here strengthens the commands, and the commands help them to know how to remember. The lessons of memory seem different, however, for Israel's enemies. The memory of Amalek's treatment in Deuteronomy (25:17–19) would teach the punishment of the violent, rather than God's compassionate protection of the weak. Volf concludes with a dual memory in the exodus: what Israel has experienced in terms of suffering, enmity, and liberation and what God has done. From this dual memory, two lessons can be drawn: (1) A lesson of solidarity – act in favour of the oppressed as God acted in your favour when you were oppressed.(2) A lesson related to retributive justice: oppose oppressors and punish them just as God opposed and punished those who oppressed you (Volf, 107).

35. Volf, 108.

is not a fully adequate framework for remembering rightly from a Christian perspective,[36] and he suggests remembering in reconciling ways.

6.2.1.4 Remembering in reconciling ways

In the passion memory, Christ's death and resurrection are obviously a past event, but, when we remember them, we remember both past and future. We remember in Christ what will happen to all humanity in the future. What implications does Christ's passion have for our ways of remembering evil suffered? Volf considers two topics: suffering and reconciliation. Regarding suffering, the New Testament lesson is continuous with the Old. For reconciliation, on the other hand, there is a significant difference between the Old and New Testaments.

Christ's death is never remembered for its own sake;[37] it is remembered as the death and resurrection of Christ. We remember deliverance in Christ. Therefore, the remembrance of suffering is a hopeful remembering, open to a transformed future. This pattern of *suffering – deliverance* is similar to the memory of the exodus. Israel suffered, and God delivered them. People suffer, and Christ's death in solidarity with them lifts them to resurrection and liberation.[38]

Volf addresses two problems with seeing Christ's passion solely as an act of deliverance: (1) Christ's act of liberation is a universal event, including both the offender and the perpetrator, so any memory of suffering or liberation has to be included in this larger picture of Christ's death for all humanity; (2) memory is put to its most deadly uses precisely by those who have suffered in the past – in the process, new victims are created, and the cycle of violence continues. For these two reasons, the axis of *suffering – deliverance* is insufficient; Volf suggests that we organize our memory along the axis *enmity – reconciliation*.[39]

Volf speaks of three practical lessons of the passion memory. First, there is a need to remember that we are all sinners. Consciousness of that principle can help us to avoid seeing ourselves, in our victimhood, as inherently

---

36. Volf, 110.

37. The same is true of exodus as it is remembered in the OT and the way Jews remember it today. The key novelty is universality and grace to perpetrators.

38. Volf, 114.

39. Volf, *End of Memory*, 115.

innocent. Second, wrongdoing having been atoned for assumes both affirmation of the valid claims of justice and not counting them against the perpetrator.[40] Third, Volf instructs us to aim for communion and reconciliation and remember every wrongdoing in the light of future, final reconciliation with the wrongdoer.[41]

The death and resurrection of Christ suggests that we and the other are reconciled and form one community; our relationships will be healed; and we ought to remember each other as those who will be both healed and ultimately reconciled in Christ's presence forever.

In sum, Volf concludes, "Communities of sacred memory are, at their best, schools of right remembering – remembering that is truthful and just, that heals individuals without injuring others, that allows the past to motivate a just struggle for justice and the grace-filled work of reconciliation."[42] The struggle to "remember rightly" is the very struggle to do justice and show grace to the wrongdoer.

6.2.2 How Long Should We Remember?

Volf argues against the widespread assumption that wrongdoings should be remembered forever as we worry that, if we were to forget wrongs committed, we would lose a sense of identity. Volf suggests Karl Barth's worry is different, "If we were to remember the wrongs we have committed, we may not be able to live with ourselves."[43]

Volf distinguishes between forgetting and non-remembering. According to him, forgetting is the inability to recall an event, even when one makes an effort to do so. In non-remembering, the event can still be recalled if desired but no longer presents itself without being intentionally recalled.[44] For Volf, non-remembrance is a divine gift, a fruit of successful reconciliation rather than a precondition of it. He explains, "Since no final redemption is possible

---

40. Volf centred on Paul's assertion in the New Testament that Christ died for all and therefore all have died – including those who have wronged us (Rom 5:9–10).

41. Volf, *End of Memory* 118–125. In the Eucharistic feast, we remember Christ's act of reconciliation between God and humanity and we enact the memory of each other as those who are reconciled to God and each other in Christ (Volf).

42. Volf, 128.

43. Volf, 134.

44. Volf, 145-146.

without the redemption of the past and since every attempt to redeem the past through reflection must fail because no theodicy can succeed, the final redemption is unthinkable without a certain kind of forgetting" – namely, non-remembrance.[45] However, for Volf this event is ultimately eschatological. It can indeed be anticipated in real life, though in an incomplete and never fully stable and accomplished way. This is seen most in more intimate relationships such as family and church. Volf refers to Isaiah 65:17, "See, I will create new heavens and a new earth. The former things will not be remembered, nor will they come to mind (NIV)." There are four features of this gift: (1) wrongdoers do not deserve it; (2) we give it to imitate God; (3) it presupposes that those who suffered have forgiven and the wrongdoer has repented, received forgiveness and mended his way; (4) the gift can be given irrevocably only in God's new world.[46]

But how does the future non-remembrance of wrongs suffered inform the way in which we should live in the here and now?[47] Volf explains that in the here and now non-remembrance rarely happens; in this world, the memory of wrongdoing is needed mainly as an instrument of justice and as a protection against injustice. Yet, Volf asserts: "Every act of reconciliation, incomplete as it mostly is in this world, stretches itself toward completion in that world of love. Similarly, remembering wrongdoing now lives in the hope of its own superfluity then. Even more, only those willing to let the memory of wrongdoing slip ultimately out of their minds will be able to remember wrongdoing rightly now. For we remember wrongs rightly when memory serves reconciliation."[48]

To understand the tension between remembering rightly and the promise of non-remembrance, Volf explains the difference between this world and the world to come. In this world, it is rare to see justice attained; threats continue, therefore, we remember wrongs suffered. In the world to come, justice will

---

45. Volf, 135–143.

46. Volf, 142–143.

47. Volf notes, "By showing how reconciliation reaches completion: a wrongdoing is both condemned and forgiven; the wrongdoer's guilt is cancelled; through the gift of non-remembrance, the wrongdoer is transposed to a state untainted by the wrongdoing; and bound in a communion of love, both the wronged and the wrongdoer rejoice in their renewed relationship" (Volf, 149).

48. Volf, 149–150.

have been done, and threats will no longer be present. Therefore we will finally be able to let go of memories of wrongs suffered.[49] Volf asserts that a journey from this world to the world to come must be taken: "We take this journey partially and provisionally here and now when we forgive and reconcile – and on rare occasions release the memory of wrong suffered. We undertake it once again, definitively and finally, at the threshold of the world to come."[50]

While conventional wisdom says that we would lose our identities if we stop remembering, Volf presents an alternative construal of personal identity. Volf distinguishes between "person" and "personality." In terms of personhood, as Christians we do not live within ourselves; we live outside ourselves – in God. Therefore, we receive our identity from "outside ourselves"; we are located in God, and our identity is found in God.[51] We are not the sum of our deeds and sufferings; we are as God relates to us. In terms of personality, our identity is shaped by how we relate to what we did and what happened to us, including not remembering even some of the most formative things in our lives. Thus, the non-remembrance of past wrongs does not violate our identity and personhood. On the contrary, being in God frees us from the unchangeable past exercises. The God who redeems the past "does not take away our past; God gives it back to us – fragments gathered, stories reconfigured, selves truly redeemed, people forever reconciled."[52]

Volf asserts that each wrong suffered will be exposed, its perpetrators condemned, the repentant transformed and its victims healed. Then, after evil has been condemned and overcome, we will be able to release the memories of wrongs suffered. Volf insists that we will not "forget" so we can rejoice; we will rejoice and therefore let memories of wrongs suffered be removed from our minds which will be rapt with the goodness of God.[53]

In sum, Volf presents a new interpretation of the concept of memory. When we remember rightly, we imitate "the enemy-loving God" in forgiveness

---

49. Volf, 150–151.
50. Volf, 151.
51. Volf, 198.
52. Volf, 201.
53. Volf, 214.

and reconciliation.⁵⁴ The goal of this remembering is love that remembers no wrongs.

Makant argues against Volf's claim that there are some memories so horrible as to be irredeemable. For Volf, the memory of suffering is antithetical to the notion of heaven to the extent that the memory of suffering limits the eternal experience of joy. Makant suggests that there is no suffering which is irredeemable, and, rather than limiting joy, "the memory of redeemed suffering" becomes a different type of memory.⁵⁵ Makant explains that Volf understands non-remembrance as a gift because he sees the recession of painful memories as an important step in the healing of memories, particularly those he sees as irredeemable; she sees Volf's account of memory as only considering memory as *a cognitive* event.⁵⁶ Volf's response is that, although the cognitive dimension of memories is central in his account, memory also has emotional and bodily dimensions.

Regarding the Palestinian context, it is not clear how Palestinians can remember rightly. The memory of trauma carried by Palestinians as members of the wider traumatized society of Israel/Palestine, each with their collective experience of collective national catastrophe (Holocaust and *nakba*) and who live in a continual state of conflict, means that it is difficult to determine how Palestinians can remember rightly. This is different from situations of post-conflict such as the Balkans, Northern Ireland and South Africa.

Another area of criticism concerns Volf's discussion of the relationship between memory and forgetting, which assumes a more or less linear structure – we have a duty to remember rightly up to a certain point when forgiveness takes place and the parties are reconciled, and what follows is a purposeful letting go of the memory of the offence.⁵⁷ Huebner also critiques Volf's treatment of memory and forgetting, as if they are primarily individual activities rather than aspects of larger social practices and cultural performances. In response, Volf argues that this linear structure is a trajectory of a cycle, not a sequence of one-time finished acts; this cycle is how we participate in the eschatological non-remembrance in the here and now. However, I find this

---

54. Volf, 9.
55. Makant, "Re-Membering Redemption," 4.
56. Makant, 83.
57. Huebner, "Review of *The End of Memory*."

linear structure, although a cyclical process, challenging to Palestinian Baptists whose reconciliation does not have a linear frame. Many times, they practise a "diplomatic reconciliation" – an action that is "forced" by the community to achieve social order. This does not necessarily happen after remembering rightly, repentance or forgiveness.

The theme of remembrance seems to be an important element of reconciliation to other scholars such as Tutu and Jones who also emphasize the necessity of dealing with the past and remembering, although they would address this using the language of forgiveness and forgetting.[58] Jones sees the problem of "forgive and forget" as threefold: psychologically impossible, morally difficult and theologically unfaithful.[59] Like Volf, Jones argues that the risen Christ does not come to ask us to forget the past but to allow it to be redeemed. Shriver says that the past is indeed "unchangeable," but one's relationship to it is not, though what is first required is "uncovering its dreaded secrets" and so to "remember and forgive."[60]

In South Africa, the Truth and Reconciliation Commission (TRC) created forums for contact and remembering together in order to acknowledge crimes committed during the apartheid era, seek truth about the past and facilitate national reconciliation.[61] Tutu practised the application of remembering truthfully during his term with the TRC post-apartheid, promoting truth-telling in exchange for less harsh sentencing, to encourage repentance and forgiveness. However, it was acknowledged by those recording the proceedings that this version of reconciliation did not include an apology from those responsible, or forgiveness by the victims.[62] For kairos theologians, reconciliation had been manipulated in South Africa since justice also was not represented, and thus the remaining concept was truth. TRC advocates, on the

---

58. See Tutu, *No Future without Forgiveness*, and Jones, *Embodying Forgiveness*.

59. It is psychologically impossible for us to control what we remember and what we forget – therefore when people retain that idea of "forgive and forget" as part of what they think they have to do, they think it is impossible to forgive if they cannot forget. It is morally difficult and problematic, since those who forget the past are condemned to repeat it. It is theologically unfaithful as it means that we end up worshipping Christ un-crucified rather than Christ crucified and risen (Jones, *Embodying Forgiveness*).

60. Shriver, "Where and When," 26–8; Goins, "Place of Forgiveness," 47.

61. DeGruchy, *Reconciliation*.

62. *The Truth and Reconciliation Commission of South Africa Report*, Vol. 5 (London: MacMillan Reference Limited, 1999), 400, cited in Robinson, *Embodied Peacebuilding*.

other hand, see this as necessary for the peace process.[63] Interestingly, TRC resonates more with *sulha* and its goal of achieving peace and coexistence even when justice and genuine forgiveness are not present. In section 6.4, I will explain in more detail the Palestinian position regarding remembrance.

6.3 Remembrance in the Case Studies

In dealing with remembering the wrongdoing, findings show that most Palestinian Baptists in the case studies struggled to forget wrongdoings and relied on the concepts of "forgive and forget" and "time will heal."[64] Almost all interviewees said forgiveness means *forgetting* the wrongdoing. Many others said we have to forget wrongdoing as "God throws our sins in the sea of forgetfulness." This saying is very common among Christian Arabs in the Middle East, and it is often heard in their hymns. They interpret "the former things shall not be remembered, or come into mind" (Isa 65:17) as God's forgetting. It is thus clear my interviewees relate forgiveness to forgetting.

Interviewees also emphasized the difficulty of forgetting because of close and intimate interconnections between people in the community that sometimes result in deep wounds and resentments. Some interviewees used Arabic poems stressing how hard this is, particularly when the issue is injustice: "injustice with proximity is tougher for oneself than the impact of a sharp sword,"[65] and "the sorrow is not to be forgotten."[66] Others relied on time to heal their wounds. Nonetheless, there were a few interviewees, especially from case C, who believed that forgiveness is not about forgetting the wrongdoing

---

63. Robinson, *Embodied Peacebuilding*.
64. Forgetting in these cases implies a disconnection with a past where people may be held captive. In this case, there is no healing possible (Hamber, "Does the Truth heal?").
65. The name of the poet is Tarafa ibn al-Abd. https://www.almrsal.com/post/776709.
66. Hiyam and Tamer, interviews with author, Mar. 2014.

but rather remembering it without pain, and requires divine intervention.[67] According to them, this happens gradually and as a result of healing.[68]

I will explain how each conflict management approach relates to Volf's theme of remembrance. These are rough guidelines; they do not necessarily describe the remembrance of a particular individual using the relevant conflict management approach.

6.3.1 Hierarchical Approach

This approach is associated with the pastors' way of dealing with conflict. When I describe Pastor C's attitude below, this refers to his attitude *before* the act of reintegration; since then his attitude has changed and he has transitioned to the use of a Western-Baptist approach.

The pastors who still felt hurt could not remember rightly in terms of Volf's theme of remembrance. For the pastors, right and wrong are defined by acts and duties.[69] They remembered and described the dishonouring actions of the "rebellious groups" with great pain and spoke unsympathetically about them.[70] It is likely these memories shaped the pastors' view of themselves as victims: they were broken and felt deeply humiliated; they remembered the conflict with a sense of shame for being rejected as the spiritual fathers (theologically inappropriate); and they experienced disloyalty from "rebellious groups" who wanted to replace them (culturally inappropriate). They defined these actions as wrong and unrighteous, believing they themselves did nothing wrong, and conditioned forgiveness upon a public repentance of the "rebellious groups."[71] These memories occupy their present with shame as

---

67. Shirin, a young leader at church C2, believed, "Real reconciliation happens when I don't remember the details of conflict anymore and this is hard. Only God can help in that." She also views forgetting (or some kind of forgetting, such as not remembering) as an essential element in dealing with the past, something that probably requires divine intervention. Rana, a member at church B2, also said, "In forgiveness we might not forget the wrongdoing, but we need to get to the point that when I remember, this incident will not affect me or cause me sadness or anger any more.... This happened gradually" (Rana, interview with author, Aug. 2015).

68. It is worth noting that interviewees in the three case studies remembered the other party's wrongdoing in detail but only briefly described their contribution to the conflict, providing some justifications.

69. Deontology ethical theory.

70. Although pastors said they tolerate them.

71. As explained in chapter 7 ("Theology of Forgiveness").

they are still feeling pain.⁷² They have not felt able to cooperate with past or present reconciliation attempts, and their churches have shrunk. This seems to support Volf's point, "When wrongdoing defines us, we take on 'distorted identities, frozen in time and closed in growth.'"⁷³

Additionally, pastors remembered and focused on their church's past glory and their contributions. They wondered how the "rebellious groups" could forget these past contributions. Pastor A spent 90 percent of the interview describing in detail the glory of church A during the 1970s–1980s revival. Pastor A's wife told me, teary-eyed, "When I remember [the split] I get sad and so does Pastor A who has served the church all his life."⁷⁴ Rami, an ABC leader, told me that history is still alive in people's minds; pastors expected that members would not forget their decades of service, and thus expected that their past contributions must influence the church's present decision-making.⁷⁵

I will evaluate the pastors' memory in light of Volf's four elements of remembering rightly.

1) *Remembering truthfully*. We can argue, in Volf's terms, it is not clear whether the pastors remembered truthfully or not. They did not believe they had contributed to the conflict and entirely blamed the "rebellious-group," conditioning forgiveness upon their repentance. The pastors evaluated the actions of the "rebellious groups" as sinful and thus their decisions to "fire" them from church were held to be ethically correct. Additionally, the pastors' *truth* was influenced by their belief that members should submit to their spiritual fathers. Thus, the pastors felt their actions were justified since they were directed to protect their pastoral (sacramental) role and the church.

2) *Remembering therapeutically*. Pastors could not remember therapeutically in terms of Volf's requirements for inner healing. They still seemed hurt when I interviewed them and could neither integrate these conflicts into their life-stories by giving them positive meaning nor understand how conflict could contribute to their growth as pastors. Sadly, they remembered

---

72. According to Volf, "Wrongdoing suffered is never dead; with the help of individual and communal memory, it reaches through the present and into the future, and occupies both with shame." Volf, *Flourishing*, 175.

73. Volf, *End of Memory*, 79.

74. Suhad, interview with author, Apr. 2014.

75. Rami, open interview.

the conflict as one of the worst events in their lives, causing them deep sorrow and, possibly, hindering church growth. They could not remember wrongs in terms of a new identity defined by God; rather, they seemed to view themselves as victims unable to see how God would engender new opportunities and growth from these conflicts.

Without remembering therapeutically, pastors take two risks: they allow their suffering to (1) control their lives and (2) poison their expectations of the future. If pastors remember therapeutically, they should remember the past but expect that something new will come. The impression I have from my observations post-split is that most pastors and many church members who experienced splits in fact experienced a traumatic event. They seemed broken and sad; had lost their zeal; and could not remember hopefully. This could be seen through their preaching, through the dramatically weakened church ministries to children, women and others and through the fact that less financial giving was taking place and membership had decreased.

3) *Remembering responsibly*. It was difficult for the pastors to remember responsibly since their pain seemingly remains unhealed. Although they appointed friends and family members in church positions to help strengthen and protect their pastoral (sacramental) role after the split, they seemed unable to bring significant change about in their churches, and the churches declined in numbers.

4) *Remembering in reconciling ways*. Most pastors did not remember in reconciling ways as they felt unable to cooperate with many reconciliation attempts.[76] They adhered to their obligations and duties to protect their (sacramental) position and churches from the "evil" actions of the "rebellious groups." It seems pastors considered that not responding to reconciliation attempts was morally right for them. It is noteworthy that the duties of the pastors were in conflict when some of them overrode the constitution in order to protect their positions and churches, which could be seen as being in opposition to their obligation to work according to the constitution.

---

76. See chapter 4.

6.3.2 *Sulha* and Alternative-Legalistic Approaches

Advocates of *sulha* were mainly the older, more traditional generations who used elements of *sulha* in dealing with the conflicts.[77] Advocates of the alternative-legalistic approach were the younger generation who used some alternative-legalistic conflict resolution techniques. Results show that advocates of both *sulha* and alternative-legalistic approaches *partly* remembered rightly; they struggled in remembering therapeutically and responsibly, and their remembrance did not lead to reconciliation. I distinguish between these approaches in the following analysis.

1) *Remembering truthfully*. Advocates of the alternative-legalistic approach sought change at their churches for the greater benefit of the church community and used a legal framework to achieve that end.[78] However, their prediction of the outcomes was inaccurate. The unexpected results made their decision appear unethical to pastors and the broader community. Some members of the "rebellious groups" in these cases said they were enthusiastic about bringing change and might have wronged their pastors by their behaviours, realizing the dishonour only later. In case A, Sami, a church A2 leader, admitted some of their ways were not appropriate. In case B, some voices confessed they were mistaken to leave church B. Elias, a church B2 leader, explained, "We insisted on doing things our way; we did not take Pastor B's interests into account. The communication was poor."[79] In case C, Albert, a church C2 leader, said he could not solely blame Pastor C; members of church C2 had contributed even more to the conflict. In a sense, they remembered "truthfully"; as they could somewhat see their contribution to the conflict and were willing to restore relationships with their pastors, they, perhaps, showed some kind of repentance.

Advocates of the *sulha* approach gave weight to the consequences in evaluating the rightness and wrongness of actions.[80] For them, peace and social order were right and a split was wrong, and both parties contributed to the wrong. Advocates of *sulha* also remembered truthfully; they blamed themselves for compromising and keeping the status quo that eventually led

---

77. See chapter 5.
78. Utilitarian ethical theory.
79. Elias, interview with author, Aug. 2015.
80. Teleology ethical theory.

to the split. Jack, a deacon, wrote to Pastor A, "Our compromise for many years is the reason for the hardships of today."[81]

2) *Remembering therapeutically*. In terms of Volf's three requirements for inner healing, the alternative-legalistic approach, used by most members of church A2 and church B2, integrated conflict events into their life-story, as they admitted they were young, enthusiastic and wanted to shape the church's future. They had learned from that experience and were willing to reconcile. Church B2 even expressed its willingness to reintegrate, and members expected to have positions at church B, but Pastor B did not agree. Some interviewees were hesitant to talk negatively about the pastors and stressed that they had no resentment towards them.[82]

Nonetheless, churches A2 and B2 were seeking their wellbeing too, for they did not want to live in shame (which might explain why they agreed to participate in joint church services). For many years some pastors boycotted churches A2 and B2 and would not agree to attend or preach in them since their split had caused shame within the community.[83] Sami, a church A2 leader, explained the importance of joint services: "We tried to bring about 'normalization' and to forget the past. God taught us to forgive, and time will help us to ignore our resentment."[84] They did not want to live in the prison of bitterness. As Pastor Mark, a third party, noted, "If we don't forgive, our heavenly father will not forgive us; we forgive for our sake so we can be blessed."[85]

In the *sulha* approach, members were more *accepting* of their suffering as part of their past and more willing to *let it go*;[86] they were ready to compromise

---

81. Jack's letter, 14 Apr. Again, split is viewed as an acceptable, although not optimal and preferable, solution. See chapter 5, footnote 121 page 155.

82. In case A, Mary (the wife of George, who pastored church A2 after the split) told me, "At the beginning [after the split], each time members of church A2 gathered they remembered the wrongdoing against them and were very hurt, but forgiveness is a continual process and gradually God healed their wounds" (Mary, interview with author, Apr. 2014).

83. See chapter 5.

84. Sami, interview with author, Feb. 2014.

85. Mark, interview with author, Aug. 2014.

86. Makant presents three common responses to suffering within the popular self-help genre: (1) to remember that things could have been even worse, (2) to believe the suffering has made one a stronger and wiser person, (3) to think suffering is something which a person should be able to quickly "get over" in order to "move on" – there is an unspoken expectation that once this acceptable time has passed any continued recognition of suffering is seen as a form of self-pity ("Re-Membering Redemption," 84–85).

for the sake of peace and social order. Seemingly, in both the alternative-legalistic and *sulha* approaches members *partly* remembered therapeutically. They continued to rely on *time and forgetting* to deal with the past, accepting their suffering as part of their past; they are moving on, but they are not necessarily healed.

3) *Remembering responsibly*. In the alternative-legalistic approach, for more than ten years following the split, churches A2 and B2 did not appoint new pastors. On the one hand, from their point of view, they remembered responsibly because they did not want to repeat their harsh experience. On the other hand, they possibly replicated the pastors' attitudes by creating a situation in which church leaders were not given authority, and so they, the church leaders, left (church A2 experienced four exits, and church B2 suffered two exits). We can argue they did not remember responsibly.

Advocates of the *sulha* approach did not remember responsibly either, for they became passive after the split (perhaps they felt they failed to prevent the split), and allowed the younger generation to lead the new churches (churches A2 and B2) that were established as a result of the splits.

4) *Remembering in reconciling ways*. In both the alternative-legalistic and *sulha* approaches, members remembered in a reconciling way. For many years church A2 welcomed all attempts to reconcile with Pastor A, albeit with no success. As of 2018, members of church B2 are open to reintegration, but Pastor B is sceptical.

6.3.3 Western-Baptist Approach

This approach was mainly seen in case C after the split.[87] In evaluating the memories of members of church C2 and Pastor C in terms of Volf's four elements of remembering rightly, I find that they remembered rightly. Even though they struggled in remembering therapeutically, their remembrances led to the beginnings of reconciliation (reintegration).

1) *Remembering truthfully*. Many members of church C2 remembered Pastor C's past wrongdoing in detail, but they also admitted their own wrongdoing (even while justifying it). During the reconciliation retreat, Pastor C publicly apologized from the pulpit for the wrongs he had committed against

---

87. See chapter 5.

church C2.[88] Pastor C's truthful confession was a very crucial step towards reconciliation. We can conclude that members of church C2 and Pastor C remembered the wrongdoing "truthfully."

2) *Remembering therapeutically*. Church C2 judged Pastor C by his old character rather than by his later actions towards motivating reconciliation. Their evaluation of his desire to reintegrate was based on his character as shaped by his past wrongdoings.[89] The ABC committee also judged Pastor C based on his character and past reputation.

Findings indicate that most members of church C2 and church C3 believed the reconciliation retreat was a "divine work" where God intervened, brought forgiveness and *healed* hurt emotions and broken relationships.[90] For participants, the Spirit was present in some kind of tangible way. Emotionally, they felt love towards the other group; they prayed for hours in tears, apologized and forgave one another. They believed this was led by the Spirit. Nonetheless, after the reintegration, members of church C2 realized that they were still displeased with Pastor C and that healing was not complete despite the reconciliation retreat. Members still struggled to forget the wrongdoing and thus interpreted Pastor C's behaviour based on his past wrongdoings. In terms of Volf's requirements, they integrated a new meaning to their story post-reconciliation, but they still could not see new possibilities and felt stuck again with Pastor C. This time the ABC committee could not help (it had recommended Pastor C should not pastor church C2 post-reintegration) since Pastor C insisted he must repair what the conflict had caused. Nonetheless, members of church C2 gave him a chance, predicting his failure as they did not trust he was changed despite his retreat apology. According to Volf, when we remember the past, we allow it to come into the present together with the feelings associated with the memory, and, since memories shape present identities, we cannot be redeemed without the redemption of our remembered past.[91] Since members' memories regarding Pastor C as being controlling still captured their thoughts and interpretation, we can conclude that they only partly remembered therapeutically.

---

88. See chapter 4.
89. Virtue ethical theory.
90. This is also discussed in chapter 7.
91. Volf, *Exclusion and Embrace*, 133.

It is likely that Pastor C remembered therapeutically as he integrated a new meaning into his life after his repentance, seeing God's hand in the reconciliation, seeing a new opportunity and even insisting on pastoring church C2 again despite the challenges he was facing.[92]

3) *Remembering responsibly.* Members of church C2 said they forgave Pastor C, but they did not trust he was changed and kept examining his motivation in every action. They also believed he should not pastor post-reintegration. We can conclude that this attitude is remembering responsibly since they admitted their distrust in Pastor C could cause more conflict at church C2. Furthermore, some leaders told me they had learned from the splits in cases A and B, and they did not want to replicate these mistakes. Apparently, their attitude was also influenced by the American-Arab pastor who mentored them to not leave church, to pray, to forgive and to act lovingly towards Pastor C. My observation and impression during the interviews was that the American-Arab pastor's instructions and influence on church C2 affected the whole dynamic of this conflict and its management.

Pastor C remembered responsibly. He remembered his old conflict (of twenty-five years ago) with the former pastor of church C.[93] He told me that, in his conflict with church C2, he did not want to follow the former pastor's model and attempted to learn from his former pastor's mistakes. This was the main reason he decided to reconcile with church C2. Interestingly, both members of church C2 and Pastor C sadly mentioned that, spiritually, they believe the first split with the former pastor still follows them as they are facing a third split, as if history keeps repeating itself. We can argue that Pastor C and church C2 remembered the conflict in a responsible way.

4) *Remembering in reconciling ways.* Members of church C2 remembered in a reconciling way even while struggling. Despite their reintegration, they struggled to forget; they still remembered the wrongdoings, blamed Pastor C and interpreted his motivations based on his character and past. However, they did not resist the reintegration, and a few of them cooperated with Pastor C. Pastor C remembered in a reconciling way. He insisted on reconciling

---

92. I will discuss this argument in more detail later.
93. See chapter 4.

despite the ABC committee's recommendation. He told me that for a whole year before the reintegration he was planning for this reconciliation.

In sum, when reflecting on the remembrances of the Palestinian Baptists concerning the three cases, it is evident that all struggled to forget the wrongdoings. In terms of Volf's remembering rightly, in the hierarchical approach, pastors struggled to remember rightly. Those of *sulha* and alternative-legalistic approaches *partly* remembered rightly (while struggling to remember therapeutically and responsibly), but their remembrances led to "diplomatic reconciliation" (pacification). In the Western-Baptist approach, Pastor C remembered rightly. Members of church C2 remembered rightly (somewhat struggling in remembering therapeutically) – indeed, their remembrances *led to the beginning of reconciliation* in the form of reintegration, as illustrated below:

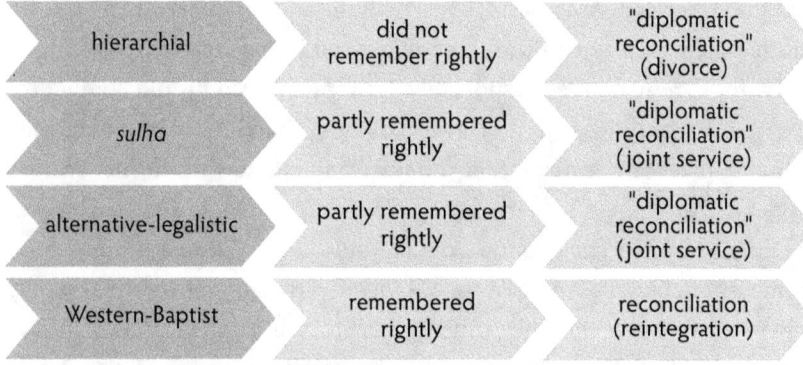

Figure 6.1: Remembering rightly in the case studies

6.4 Challenges and Recommendations

As we have seen in the four approaches, there are two common issues posing a challenge for Palestinian Baptists when dealing with cases of church conflict: (1) *forgetting* the wrongdoing and (2) *remembering therapeutically*. I begin by listing some general factors challenging Palestinian Baptists in practising the theme of remembrance and then move to discuss how I deal with these challenges by proposing some recommendations through adjusting Volf's theory.

Several factors from the Palestinian Baptists' context affect the process of backgrounding their memories. First, church buildings function as continual reminders of conflicts. Second, the disputants stand in intimate relationships with each other. Third, they belong to a broader traumatized society (Israeli-Palestinian) with a traumatized memory, each with the experience of a collective national catastrophe (Holocaust and *nukba*). These communities continually call for these catastrophes to never be forgotten. I will look at each issue briefly.

First, the church building itself was an important factor in the conflicts, particularly in case A. It is constantly present; seeing it continually reminds the disputants of their past pain, making it difficult to forget. Every Sunday, as church A2 meets next door to church A, they can see the conflict is alive since church A's building was one of the main reasons for the unresolved conflict.

Second, people cannot run away from their past because of the relatedness and closeness between them. Part of the problem is that the Palestinian Baptist community is very small and concentrated within the Galilee region. Due to several factors, the churches and ministries are confined physically in the area, and people live in close proximity to one another, and all they do is more or less interconnected. Even when people want to forget their past, they are not "allowed" to since they are being constantly reminded of it. Pastor C complained, "The old conflict [with the former pastor] still follows me even after I ran away from it."[94] It is likely this old conflict, although twenty-five years old, is still alive and influences Pastor C's present and, perhaps, future. When the ABC committee discussed the conflict in case C, some committee members mentioned Pastor C's past conflict in order to evaluate his present attitude.

Third, living in unforgetting, traumatized communities with unhealed memories makes it even harder to deal with a past memory of suffering. In moving towards reconciliation, we cannot bypass the difficulty of struggling with forgiveness in relation to memory. Generally, traumatized people are bothered by intrusive thoughts and memories. Unless memories connected to trauma are reframed or "healed," they can be a source of recurring emotional

---

94. See chapter 4, section 4.2.3.

distress.[95] Within the confines of this dissertation, it is not practical to develop the subject of trauma, but it is important to note that a clear understanding of what is involved in living in traumatized societies is essential for understanding how Palestinian Baptists view the theme of remembrance.

In light of these factors, how can Palestinian Baptists deal with forgetting? If they relate forgiveness with forgetting – and since forgetting is not a liberating act to be associated with forgiveness in this context – how can they then be reconciled? How can they, as a closely intertwined community who belong to broader traumatized society, remember truthfully and therapeutically?

Regarding the Palestinian Baptist struggle to forget, Volf's theory of remembrance provides a helpful perception of forgetting. Forgetting does not serve healing and should not be connected with forgiveness for several reasons:

1) We cannot control what we can forget and what we can remember.
2) Forgiveness presupposes remembering – we cannot forgive if we have already forgotten. (We condemn the wrongdoing and then do not count that against the wrongdoer, both of which require remembering.)
3) Non-remembrance is a fruit of forgiveness, not part of forgiveness itself.
4) We have the imperative to remember so that the wrong will not be repeated.
5) No deliverance and no healing can happen without attending to the past; thus, forgetting will not help in healing, only *redeeming the past* will.

The question is not whether or not one ought to remember, but *what to do with the memories* – those explicit and implicit memories which continue to shape identity whether they are recognized or not.

I agree with Volf that the focus should be on remembering rightly (or in a redeeming way) rather than forgetting. Since Palestinian Baptists live in an unforgiving environment politically, socio-culturally and religiously,[96] I suggest that it would be beneficial for them to focus on the language of

---

95. See Goins, "Place of Forgiveness." Even though thoughts and memories associated with trauma are culturally interpreted.

96. See chapter 7.

transformation rather than on that of forgetting the wrongdoing which poses a challenge in their specific context. Stated differently, how can Palestinian Baptists transform the saying "the sorrow is not to be forgotten" to "the past sorrow is to be transformed to a redeemed sorrow"?[97]

Volf's theme of remembrance is insightful and compelling, offering helpful insights on forgetting and remembering for the Palestinian Baptist context. Nonetheless, his theory seems to miss some aspects that relate to the Palestinian Baptist cultural context as I will explain.

First, on *remembering truthfully*, I agree with Volf that it is necessary to lovingly speak the truth about the past, and I agree that our goal should be to seek truth and remember the facts as truthfully as possible, regardless of our perspectives and interests. However, it is not clear exactly how we can evaluate the narratives of pastors and laity regarding the conflict in terms of truthfulness. Culturally and theologically, pastors viewed their decision to "fire" church leaders/deacons as morally correct. The pastors' truth was influenced by their religious belief that members should submit to their spiritual fathers who implement order. Emotionally, for pastors, the trauma of the church splits became a formative part of their identity, and thus it is hard to evaluate their reactions during the conflict as truthful or untruthful. The laity's truth was also influenced by the theological-cultural beliefs of congregationalist-democratic principles.

Second, in relation to *remembering therapeutically*, the difficulty in forgetting has forced Palestinian Baptists to develop a kind of therapeutic remembering which *accepted the suffering* and was oriented towards *moving on*.[98] However, this is different from Volf's theory of remembering therapeutically (that is, integrating a new story into their lives, a new identity and

---

97. This is similar to Gregory Jones' point that the emphasis should be more on healing memories rather than forgetting or erasing memories, since "healing" language better serves the need for "continuity in the stories of our lives" and fits the biblical imagery, assuming that deleting memory would seem more connected "to 'un-crucifying' Christ." He notes, in this life, we are called not to forget but to remember differently. God's gift in Christ enables us to be freed from the burden of a broken past, to see it as a redeemed past. Jones, "Behold, I Make All Things New," 178.

98. In case C, in the reconciliation retreat, there was collective repentance, forgiveness and the beginnings of reconciliation that led to reintegration. However, after this reintegration, members still struggled with remembering the past wrongdoings. Members of church C2 missed the old days and blamed Pastor C, and this was an obstacle towards real reconciliation – one in which the past is freed from poisoning the present and the future.

new possibilities). *Acceptance and moving on* is putting up with the past, *not redeeming it*.[99] Nonetheless, Volf's theory of remembering therapeutically lacks an essential factor of healing in the cultural model of *sulha* – namely, *venting*. Venting must be enabled in the reconciliation process to make way for peace, and there has to be a place where anger will be *publicly expressed*: naming wrong as wrong and blaming the wrongdoer (an indispensable aspect of forgiveness). This will enable the reversal of dignity violation through public acknowledgement of the moral standing of the victim – a form of symbolically reinstating the victim back to the status from which the injury has taken them down. This makes the future possible, as the victim is freed from fear that the future will be like the one of humiliation and wrongdoing suffered. I thus suggest adding this *venting* process to Volf's theme of *remembering therapeutically*.[100]

Third, although Volf mentions the significance of the society and community, seemingly, for Volf, the task of dealing with one's memories ultimately rests on the shoulders of the individual who has suffered wrong. Given the communal nature of Palestinian Baptists and, as we will see, given that community is a crucial element in achieving forgiveness and repentance,[101] I suggest adding the *community* as an essential participant in the process of redeeming the past's wrongdoings, in which the community will support the offended in bearing the burden with them.

Fourth, Volf's theory of remembrance does not suggest *concrete practical actions* for how past sorrow is to be remembered in a redeemed way. I find that case C provides a significant insight into how to transform past sorrow into redeemed sorrow while also involving the community – namely, *church practices*. As noted in case C, a transformation in remembering the past occurred between the two conferences. In the second conference another "wall fell down," and some members started to view Pastor C with a different lens. They could see repentance in his life and started to trust him

---

99. Therapeutic approaches to suffering focus on making those who have suffered feel better about themselves, and the suffering they have experienced, but do little or nothing to actually make better the past, present or future of the person.

100. Another important issue is the need to repent as victims. When victims repent, they resist sinful values and practices and let the new order of God's reign be established in their heart, which will bring about social change. Volf, *Exclusion and Embrace*, 116–117.

101. See chapter 7.

again. Apparently, what contributed to the transformation in their remembering of the past were some *communal church practices* done repeatedly over seven years: (1) the ABC committee engagement with church C2 in prayer meetings; (2) individual/group consultations and having their pain listened to post-split (venting); (3) worship meetings; (4) conferences; (5) studying Scripture and thereby allowing the word of God to work in their minds and hearts in reshaping their memory; (6) communion – remembering the promise of redemption as an eschatological reality and the recognition of partial redemption now;[102] and (7) foot-washing.[103] The participation in these church practices enabled church members to partly experience redemption of past sorrow. Church practices contribute to the transformation and reshaping of memories if they happen repeatedly and continually.

Fifth, according to Volf, we cannot be redeemed without the redemption of our remembered past.[104] The final redemption is unthinkable without non-remembrance, which is an eschatological gift. It is the fruit of real reconciliation which takes place in a *linear structure* in the trajectory of a cycle: remember rightly, forgive, reconcile and then let go of the memory of the offence. I find this *linear structure* to be challenging to Palestinian Baptists because their own reconciliation methods tend to take place outside of a linear time frame. They often practise "diplomatic reconciliation," an action that is "forced" by the community to regain social order, and this does not always need to take place after remembering rightly, repentance or offering forgiveness. The process of forgiveness and remembering rightly can take place after the "diplomatic reconciliation." In case A, for example, there was a "diplomatic reconciliation" between the two churches, but forgiveness was external and they only partly remember rightly.[105]

In sum, Palestinian Baptists can learn from Volf's theme of remembrance that remembering in a *redeeming way* is more persuasive than *forgetting*

---

102. Boulus, the interim pastor, told me that, during the conflict, church C2 did not practice communion.

103. Foot washing was done by David, a member of the ABC committee, during the conflict.

104. Volf points out that to reconcile is to attend to the past in order to keep it from colonising the future. Volf, *Flourishing*.

105. For more information about "diplomatic reconciliation," see section 5.4.1.2 and section 7.2.2.

suffering (the focus on transformation language in Palestinian culture is more applicable than forgetting language) and that the gift of non-remembrance is a fruit of forgiveness. Although redemption and non-remembrance will only be final in an eschatological reality, they can experience partial present redemption. However, Volf's theory can be informed by several elements from Palestinian culture: (1) *venting* is an essential factor in redeeming past sorrow;[106] (2) *community* is a fundamental participant in the process of redeeming past sorrow; (3) repeated *church practices* are helpful ways to redeem past sorrow, to gain community involvement and to provide a space for interaction; (4) reconciliation does not necessarily happen in a *linear structure* – "diplomatic reconciliation" may precede forgiveness and remembering rightly; and (5) given the Palestinian Baptist religious beliefs, culture and traumatized society, it is not clear how they can evaluate the truthfulness of one's narratives regarding the conflict in terms of Volf's remembering truthfully.

God's gift in Christ allows us to be freed from the broken past and to redeem it. Forgiveness does not simply involve looking back to the healing of the past; it also continues to look forward to new and different ways of living into the future. By becoming free from the burden of the past, we can begin the challenging and complicated process of redeeming the past. It is a difficult process because of the many layers of trauma and suffering as well as because of the ambiguities and complexities of memory, but it is a vital task nonetheless.[107]

Forgiveness, which is the subject of the next chapter, is the only way to deal with memories.

---

106. Though it was done privately and not intentionally as part of the formal process. See chapter 5.

107. Jones, *Embodying Forgiveness*.

CHAPTER 7

Theology of Forgiveness

In this chapter, I first describe Volf's theme of forgiveness, then explain four different perceptions of forgiveness demonstrated in the four approaches in the case studies. I also evaluate Volf's forgiveness in light of these approaches and propose several recommendations.

7.1 Volf's Theology of Forgiveness

The theme of forgiveness is drawn mainly from Volf's book *Free of Charge: Giving and Forgiving in a Culture Stripped of Grace*. Volf writes that the key to learning how to give and forgive in a godly way is to look at how God gives and forgives. Volf correctly presents the inevitable connections between doctrine and practice and between the nature of God and the nature of the Christian.

7.1.1 Understand God's Forgiveness

Volf argues that there are two reasons we can neither undo nor disregard wrongdoing and therefore need to do the hard work of forgiving. First, the metaphysical structure of the world; time does not run backwards. Second, the abiding effect of guilt; wrongdoing sits like a burden on the shoulders of the one who has committed it.[1]

According to Volf, to forgive is to name wrong in the sense that it entails it, but the heart of forgiveness is not naming and blaming. Forgiveness is a special kind of gift, and by forgiving we release others from the burden of

---

1. Volf, *Free of Charge*, 128–129.

their wrongdoing.² As for Christians, forgiving always takes place in a triangle involving the wrongdoer, the wronged person and God. In this regard, Volf argues that if we forgive because God forgives, then we should forgive *as* God forgives, by echoing God's forgiveness. Thus, to understand our own forgiveness we should understand God's.³

In understanding how God forgives, Volf highlights the difference between doing justice and forgiving. He argues, "To be just is to condemn the fault and, because of the fault, to condemn the doer as well. To forgive is to condemn the fault but to spare the doer. That's what the forgiving God does."⁴ But God does not merely spare sinners the penalty for sin, God also separates their sin from them.⁵ Our unforgiveness, explains Volf, may make manifest the fact we have not allowed ourselves to receive and be shaped by God's forgiveness.⁶

In sum, to receive forgiveness means to receive both the accusation and the release from debt. To receive release from debt, we simply believe and rejoice in gratitude for the generous gift. To receive the accusation, we confess our offence and repent.⁷

---

2. Volf, 130.

3. Volf, 131. Volf continues to explain two common misconceptions of God: God is an "implacable judge" (or tough divine negotiator) and God is a "doting grandparent" (or a soft, heavenly Santa) (131). Volf argues, if God is an "implacable judge" then he would deal with wrongdoing by punishment. If he is a "doting grandparent" then he would leave our wrongdoing alone and take care of our well-being. However, Volf concludes, "the world is sinful. That's why God doesn't affirm it indiscriminately. God loves the world. That's why God doesn't punish it in justice" (140).

4. Volf, 141.

5. God can do that because: first, Christ who died for our sins is one with God, and second, Christ who died for our sins is also one with humanity. It is because of Christ's union with humanity that God can separate sinners from their sin (Volf, 146). Volf mentions two effects of the union with Christ: (1) we are freed from the power of sin, and the life we live is God's life in us. (2) God does not count our sins to us but instead counts to us Christ's righteousness (2 Cor 5:17). So, in fact, God does not only forgive us; he transforms us into Christ-like figures (Volf, 148–151).

6. This is how Luther explained forgiveness in the Lord's Prayer: "The outward forgiveness that I show in my deeds is a sure sign that I have the forgiveness of sin in the sight of God. On the other hand, if I do not show this in my relations with my neighbour, I have a sure sign that I do not have the forgiveness of sin in the sight of God and am still stuck in my unbelief" (as cited in Volf, *Free of Charge*, 156).

7. Volf, 153.

7.1.2 How Should We Forgive?

According to Volf, in discussing forgiveness we can distinguish between three corresponding modes in which we relate to offenders and their offence: revenge, the demand for justice and forgiving.[8] He affirms that revenge is morally wrong; "In its zeal to punish, it overindulgently takes from the offender more than is due."[9] In Romans 12:19-20, the Apostle Paul wrote that we should not avenge ourselves; instead of revenge we should give gifts to those who have offended us. But why is forgiveness, rather than retributive justice, a Christian duty? Volf claims, "Consistent enforcement of justice would wreak havoc in a world shot through with transgression. It may rid the world of evil, but at the cost of the world's destruction." Additionally, the line between vengeance and justice is often hard to draw.[10]

Then why do we forgive instead of giving in to vengeance? Volf explains, we should forgive because "saving" our enemies matters more to us than punishing them, just as God reestablished communion with us by forgiving our sin.[11] He adds, we cannot forgive exactly as God does, but, because we were created to be like the God who forgives, we should imitate God in our own way as an instrument of God.[12] Since God is in us and Christ lives through us, God forgives and we make God's forgiveness our own and so pass it on.[13]

For Volf, to forgive means doing the following activities:

To condemn. Condemnation and blame are intrinsic to the process of forgiveness: "we accuse when we forgive, and in doing that, we affirm the rightful claims of justice."[14]

---

8. Volf, 158.
9. Volf, 159.
10. Volf, 160.
11. Volf, 162.
12. Volf, 165. Volf argues, "Revenge multiplies evil, retributive justice contains evil – and threatens the world with destruction. Forgiveness overcomes evil with good. Forgiveness mirrors the generosity of God whose ultimate goal is neither to satisfy injured pride nor to justly apportion reward and punishment, but to free sinful humanity from evil and thereby re-establish communion with us. . . . This is the gospel in its stark simplicity – as radically countercultural and at the same time as beautifully human as anything one can imagine." Volf, 161.
13. Volf, 165.
14. Volf, 166–169.

To not shrug off. We should forgive primarily for the other's sake, not our own, as a gift we give to the one who has wronged us. Emotional healing is not the main purpose of forgiveness.[15]

To release debt. (1) Not to press charges against the wrongdoer, (2) to forgo the demand of retribution, (3) to absorb the injury, (4) to blame but not to punish.[16]

To release guilt. Punishment cannot release us from guilt. Only forgiveness can. "Christ didn't only bear our punishment on account of his oneness with God; Christ also separated us, the doers, from our evil deeds and released us from guilt on account of his oneness with humanity."[17] Those who forgive see the forgiven offenders as innocent, not guilty.

To forgive indiscriminately. Before we existed, God's forgiving was already there.[18] "God's forgiveness is not reactive-dependent on our repentance."[19] It is original and conditioned by nothing on our part.

To apologize and repent. To apologize is to say we are sorry for committing the wrongdoing and for causing suffering. We also commit ourselves to not repeating the wrong in the future and repairing the damage. For an apology to be honest, repentance must be truthful. In the Christian sacrament of confession, repentance of the heart accompanies confession of the mouth. The only way to freedom from the wrongdoing leads through repentance and confession, through apology.[20]

Restitution. Repentance will prove sincere only if the wrongdoer is willing to repair what wrongdoing took away from the victim.[21]

Reconciliation. We forgive in hope that forgiveness will bring repentance, reparation and restoration of relationships.[22]

---

15. Volf, 168.
16. Volf, 169–170.
17. Volf, 172.
18. Volf, 180.
19. Volf, 179.
20. Volf, *Flourishing*. Volf explains that without faith and repentance we are not forgiven because, "forgiveness is stuck in the middle between the God who forgives and humans who don't receive." Repentance is a necessary consequence of forgiveness and not a condition of forgiveness, but it does help make repentance possible. Volf, *Free of Charge*, 182–186.
21. Volf, *Free of Charge*, 187.
22. Volf, 188–189.

Forgiveness is an important factor in the God-humanity restoration.[23] We forgive because we love even our enemies. This love, that motivates forgiveness, "pushes forgiveness not just from exclusion to neutrality, but from neutrality to embrace."[24] Volf concludes that forgiveness is embedded in a way of life that is committed to overcoming evil by doing good.[25]

7.1.3 How Can We Forgive?

Volf argues that we have the *power* and the *right* to forgive. Since every wrong committed against a creature is a sin against the creator, God has the power to forgive all sins, and he has already forgiven sinful humanity.[26] When we forgive, we make God's sending of the "forgiveness package" our own. This is why we have the power to forgive, "Whether the package will be received depends on the recipients, on whether they admit to the wrongdoing and

---

23. Volf points out that, in Scripture (Rom 5:1) peace is not the absence of war. Peace is the flourishing of the community and its people. And "Peace with God is our delight in communion with God. . . . God forgives by indwelling us and indwells us by forgiving us." Volf, 189.

24. Volf, 189.

25. Forgiveness is frequently thought of as a conscious shift in *feelings, attitude and behaviour* towards the offender. Psychologically, the process of forgiveness begins as an internal process of overcoming any negative feelings towards the offender – resentment, anger, avoidance and revenge (Worthington, *Dimensions of Forgiveness*, 108). For Enright, Freedman, and Rique, forgiveness should also include the development of undeserved positive qualities of compassion, generosity and love (Enright, Freedman, and Rique, "Psychology of Interpersonal Forgiveness"). Philosophers such as Murphy and Hampton and Govier suggest that forgiveness involves trying to replace any negative feelings towards the offender such as anger, hatred and resentment, with feelings of compassion and love (Murphy and Hampton, *Forgiveness and Mercy*; Govier, *Forgiveness and Revenge*). Biggar believes that forgiveness means overcoming resentment, encouraging compassion towards the offender and finally a desire for "friendship." In this way, the intrapersonal process which involves shifting in attitude and emotions may progress to the interpersonal process of the restoration of broken relationships (Biggar, "Forgiveness in the Twentieth Century"). For some, forgiveness is incomplete if this intrapersonal process stops from becoming interpersonal. Empathy has to do with entering the world of the other and responding accordingly (Rogers, *Way of Being*). Some see empathy as entering God's point of view, through prayer and through an honest assessment of one's own weaknesses (Adams, "Forgiveness"; Biggar, "Forgiveness in the Twentieth Century"; Govier, *Forgiveness and Revenge*; Jones, *Embodying Forgiveness*; Volf, *Free of Charge*). Empathy may reduce the injustice gap by causing the offended to see himself as less innocent and to view the offender as less evil (Armour and Umbreit, "Paradox of Forgiveness"). Forgiveness also can be seen as a shift in *behaviour*, for example, through the action of "opening the arms" for the embrace of the offender (Volf, *Exclusion and Embrace* and *Free of Charge*). Jones views forgiveness as a craft that one practises throughout a lifetime, an embodied way of life; it is practised in such a way that "the art" cannot be separated from "the artist." Jones shows, this requires consistent practice in shifting ones attitudes/behaviours for the sake of others/community (Jones, *Embodying Forgiveness*). See also Goins, "Place of Forgiveness."

26. Volf, *Free of Charge*, 196–197.

repent."²⁷ We too have the right to forgive because God has forgiven. We do not have that right on our own, "But we have the right and the obligation to make God's forgiving our own – to forgive on our part what has already been forgiven by God," so we have a derivative authority. Without this authority, the Bible could not urge us to forgive and God's warning not to be forgiven if we do not forgive others would only mock us.²⁸

Regarding the relationship between God's forgiveness and ours, Volf illustrates the idea that God forgives, and we take this divine forgiveness and put our own signature under God's. This activity is God's work, so when we forgive it is Christ who forgives through us. In comparing our forgiving with God's, Volf states:

> All our forgiving is inescapably incomplete. That's why it's so crucial to see our forgiving not simply as our own act, but as participation in God's forgiving. Our forgiving is faulty; God's is faultless. Our forgiving is provisional; God's is final. We forgive tenuously and tentatively; God forgives unhesitatingly and definitely. As we forgive, we always wrong the offender by inadequate judgment and pride; God forgives with justice and genuine love. The only way we dare forgive is by making our forgiving transparent to God's and always open to revision. After all our forgiveness is only possible as an echo of God's.²⁹

How can we let that echo become full of our own real voices? Volf proposes that when things go well forgiveness gives birth to forgiveness. When things go ill, forgiveness remains barren. That's the impotence of forgivers; they can "knock at the door" by forgiving, and wait, "trusting that the Spirit of the resurrected Christ will make the seed of their forgiveness bear fruit."³⁰

---

27. Volf, 197.
28. Volf, 199.
29. Volf, 220.

30. Volf, 205. Sometimes, Volf notes, we practise prideful forgiveness. Volf suggests the source of such a pride: (1) we feel we have been sinned against; (2) forgiving, like giving, can be a source of pride. Sometimes we forgive for the wrong reason and in the wrong way, as when we feel we are right, superior, on the side of the light, and the offender is the wrong, inferior, on the darkness side (215). Volf argues, "In forgiving we sometimes put on a display of our righteousness, magnanimity, and greatness, and in the process, insult, demean, and diminish the offenders. It is possible to forgive so wrongly that it can seem that we need to be forgiven for forgiving" (215). In this regard, Volf suggests that it is good to remind ourselves that "we are

In relation to the burden of mending relationships resting on the shoulders of victims, Volf agrees that although it is unfair for victims to bear it, they should.[31] We bear the burden of forgiveness because (1) Christ forgave in such a way, and, (2) when we are forgivers, "we are restored to our full human splendour. We were created to mirror God."[32] However, as long as victims do not forgive (due to death, mental illness, etc.), even if we have received God's forgiveness, we will have to live with a small wound of unforgiveness. In the world to come, all partial forgiveness will be made complete.[33] Forgiveness is a social relationship, not an act of a solitary individual. God works in the lives of forgivers "not through the isolated decision of self-enclosed individuals but through a life lived in response to the God of grace and through a community that makes the practice of forgiveness meaningful."[34]

Volf advocates an *unconditional* view of forgiveness; it is unilateral and is a process within a person and between persons. A unilateral act aiming at response so that it is always interpersonal, like giving, has the structure of giving and receiving. Ideally, forgiveness is also bilateral.[35] Therefore, we forgive even without repentance. To do that, "We shield the tender plant of

---

always sinners ... victims included. ... We always remain God's good creatures ... offenders included. No wrongdoing is an isolated act ... it is nourished by our sinful inclination and reinforced by a sinful culture" (216). Pride subverts what forgiveness seeks to achieve "because forgiveness is not a private act, it's part of a larger strategy of overcoming evil with good and bringing about reconciliation" (217). In this regard we achieve two victories: (1) when we forgive and (2) when we reconcile.

31. Volf explains, "Because that's what it means to be followers of Christ. Forgiving the unrepentant is not an optional extra in the Christian way of life; it is the heart of the thing." Volf, 209.

32. Volf, 209.

33. Volf also explains that we should always forgive humbly and provisionally. Sometimes what we considered to be an offence against us is actually an offence that we need to apologize far more than we need to forgive. We do not need to know exactly what the nature and extent of the offence, argues Volf, since God knows, and "we join God in forgiving," Volf, 211.

34. Volf, 214. Sometimes the reason we do not forgive is that we live in an unforgiving culture. "Since we are social beings, shaped by our environment, what we in fact think and choose often merely echoes the choices of a group to which we belong and a wider culture in which we live.... Once a culture has become litigious, forgiveness starts making less and less sense" (Volf, 212). Volf concludes that, in order to forgive, we need an environment in which forgiveness is valuable and nurtured (212).

35. The central question is whether that bilateral relationship has the nature of exchange or some kind of equivalent (so that forgiveness is dependent on adequate repentance, and if repentance is not there forgiveness is withdrawn), or whether it has the nature of a gift. Volf advocates the latter.

forgiveness from the frigid winds that blow from unrepentant perpetrators, and we nourish it with the food of God's goodness."[36] Even when offenders are unrepentant we can and should forgive. There are better ways to protect ourselves than the refusal to forgive. For Volf, forgiveness is not a reaction to something but the beginning of something new.[37]

As mentioned in section 1.5.1, Schreiter and Liechty, in the context of Northern Ireland, associate reconciliation with forgiveness and repentance.[38] Tutu also explains that there is no future for an interdependent world without forgiveness and that the act of forgiveness declares faith in the very future of relationship. For Tutu, forgiveness is an unconditional gift that frees our own minds from the prison of hatred as it is not dependent on repentance. The spirit of unconditional forgiveness was behind the TRC, which was chaired by Tutu post-apartheid.[39]

Some Palestinian scholars also advocate unconditional forgiveness in action. Abu El-Assal and Younan highlight the importance of relationships, focusing on coexistence and avoiding confrontations.[40] Massad sees that only confession, repentance, forgiveness and love lead to reconciliation.[41] Munayer also asserts that forgiveness is unconditional and reconciliation is unattainable without forgiveness.[42]

For advocates of *conditional* forgiveness, forgiveness is bilateral.[43] It is conditioned by the offender's repentance and should include remorse, confession and restitution. Without repentance, the offended is obligated to withhold forgiveness.[44] For conditional forgiveness, reconciliation automatically

---

36. Volf, *Free of Charge*, 209.
37. Volf, 209.
38. See Schreiter, *Ministry of Reconciliation*, and Liechty, "Putting Forgiveness in Its Place."
39. Tutu, *No Future without Forgiveness*.
40. See Abu El-Assal, *Caught in Between*, and Younan, *Witnessing for Peace*.
41. See Massad, "Theological Foundation for Reconciliation."
42. See Munayer and Loden, *Through My Enemy's Eyes*.

43. According to Nelson, two passages are commonly used to support conditional forgiveness. The first is Colossians 3:13, "Forgive as the Lord forgave you" (see also Eph 4:32). The second passage is Luke 17:3, "If he repents, forgive him." Nelson, "Exegeting Forgiveness."

44. Ardel Caneday comments, "We would be mistaken to suppose that we are obligated to forgive the sins of those who will not repent in violation of the order of the gospel." Caneday, *Must Christians Always Forgive?*, 10.

follows forgiveness.[45] Forgiveness is modelled after God's forgiveness, which is conditioned on repentance.[46] Biggar, in his work on the Northern Ireland conflict, advocates conditional forgiveness, his proposal of forgiveness being a two-part process: "The Two Moments of Forgiveness." The first moment he calls "forgiveness-as-compassion," where the offended allows his feelings to be moderated by sympathy and love for the offender. The second moment is "forgiveness-as-absolution," where the offended says, "I forgive you," but the absolution waits for signs of the offender's repentance.[47] One important challenge with conditional forgiveness is to decide when there is enough demonstration of repentance for forgiveness to finally be given and when we think repentance is truly genuine. Conditional forgiveness is consistent with our natural inclinations and cultural climate. We believe that we have the right – indeed the obligation – to withhold forgiveness from those who wronged us. In a sense, withholding forgiveness seems to border on vengeance.[48]

Nelson notes conditional and unconditional forgiveness have many common aspects: (1) The offence was wrong, and the injury was real. By forgiving, the offended agrees to release the offender from any moral liability. (2) A personal offence harms the relationship. (3) Playing the victim or seeking vengeance are both wrong. (4) There are natural and legal consequences to wrongdoing, even when forgiveness has been granted. (5) Our forgiveness of others should be modelled after God's forgiveness of us. (6) The final goal is reconciliation. Since conditional and unconditional forgiveness have much in common, while differing in their method of the realization of reconciliation, Nelson suggests the focus should be on reconciliation.[49]

Although I advocate unconditional forgiveness, I agree with Nelson that conditional and unconditional forgiveness have much in common and suggest

---

45. See Brauns, *Unpacking Forgiveness*.

46. See Adams, *From Forgiven to Forgiving*. Although not all advocates of conditional forgiveness would agree, Sande allows for unconditional forgiveness only in the case of minor offences (Sande, *Peace Maker*).

47. Biggar, "Forgiving Enemies in Ireland."

48. See Nelson, "Exegeting Forgiveness," and Adams, *From Forgiven to Forgiving*. According to Adams, "Refusal to forgive is a decision for vengeance. It is taking vengeance into your own hands. . . . Because the Lord has said, 'Vengeance is Mine; I will repay,' to take vengeance of any kind – even the withholding of forgiveness – is an attempt to arrogate God's work to oneself." Adams, *From Forgiven to Forgiving*, 25.

49. Nelson, "Exegeting Forgiveness."

that Palestinians focus on achieving reconciliation and restoring relationships whether they practice conditional or unconditional forgiveness, as I will explain in section 7.3.

7.1.4 A Cultural Critique of Volf's Theme of Forgiveness in Light of Local Culture (*Sulha*)

Sulha functions as a social mechanism for the promotion of forgiveness. When a conflict breaks out, dignitaries recruit the victim's clan into the *sulha* process, achieve a ceasefire and generally convince the disputants that their honour will be restored and increased if they forgive much more than if they seek vengeance. In a public reconciliation ceremony, dignitaries become communal guardians of the reconciliation.[50] The final ceremony is centred on forgiveness, peace and compromise for the greater good of society.[51] In *sulha*, forgiveness is obligatory, since only with forgiveness can the torn social fabric be mended. "*Sulha* is first and foremost based on forgiveness. If the offended side does not forgive, there will be no *sulha* and there will be no peace";[52] in a similar way Volf states that forgiveness is the only solution to vast conflicts.[53] Forgiving strengthens communal bonds and restores relationship.[54]

As mentioned in chapter 5, a *sulha* ceremony involves three symbolic rituals: (1) *Musafaha*, the handshake; (2) *Musamaha*, declaring forgiveness; (3) *Mumalaha*, the ceremonial meal. *Musamaha* (declaring forgiveness) is demonstrated by both parties: the offender's family humbly accepts the wrongdoings and offers compensation on behalf of their family member; the bereaved family respectfully forgives the offender's family as an act of humility. These cultural symbols and rituals are necessary for societal constructions of peaceful coexistence, even if they are done with resentment.

More importantly, in *sulha* forgiveness (unlike revenge) demands the participation of the whole community with the rituals, otherwise restoration

---

50. Leaders from different religions are always present at the reconciliation ceremony to symbolize the coming together of the community.
51. Smith, "Reward of Allah." See chapter 5.
52. Jabbour, *Sulha*, 31.
53. Volf, *A Public Faith*.
54. Volf, *Free of Charge*.

of honour will fail.⁵⁵ In *sulha*, forgiveness is not divine;⁵⁶ it is human. It is a mostly external, decisional and communal process that takes place in a triangle consisting of the offender's family, the offended family and the community. Without the involvement of the *community, sulha* fails. Given that religious dignitaries are part of the *sulha* process, it is likely God has a role in this process; however, it is not a clear role as in Volf's conception. Volf's definition of forgiveness is a divine gift. It is also human; internal, decisional and individualistic process (compared to *sulha*) and takes place in a triangle of the offender, the offended and God. "Take God away," Volf argues, "and the foundations of forgiveness become unsteady and may even crumble."⁵⁷ I am aware Volf distinguishes between social agents and social arrangements. While he argues the latter are important, his focus is on social agents. However, in Arab culture this distinction cannot be so easily made.⁵⁸

Additionally, Volf's theme of forgiveness does not require *public restoration of dignity* as in *sulha*, although, for Volf, it is part of a "larger strategy of overcoming evil with good and bringing about reconciliation."⁵⁹ Volf speaks about restoration of a lost human identity, an individual's own "dignity"; in his words, "When we are forgivers we are restored to our full human splendour."⁶⁰ For Volf, the good is primary and dignity is secondary. In *sulha*, it is also related to the primacy of the good; however, restoration of dignity is a significant tool to achieving forgiveness.⁶¹

In *sulha*, forgiveness covers past, present and future generations and has a declaratory nature. The *sulha* ceremony transforms forgiveness from a

---

55. According to Pely, theorists have viewed forgiveness through frames similar to those of revenge (Pely, "When Honor"). Some have argued that revenge is like forgiveness in having an evolutionary function; just like revenge, the capacity to forgive is authentic, intrinsic to human nature and a result of natural selection. The authors investigated whether within-person increases in rumination about an interpersonal transgression were associated with within-person reductions in forgiveness. Results supported this hypothesis (McCullough, "Rumination, Emotion, and Forgiveness").

56. It means that human beings, apart from acknowledging or invoking deity, still do practise forgiveness, which is a necessary invention for living – but not, in this case, a process of transcendence as in Volf's conception.

57. Volf, *Free of Charge*, 131.

58. See chapter 1, section 1.3.

59. Volf, *Free of Charge*, 217.

60. Volf, 209.

61. See chapter 5, section 5.2.1.

private affair to a public, formal one involving the community and multiple witnesses. The formal text in the *sulha* ceremony says: "This peace is valid for all those who are present here, and all those who are absent, for every embryo in the womb of its mother or for every sperm from the back of the father."[62] This means the community (in particular the victim's family) has a ritualistic and practical obligation to forgive – though, of course, not the duty to *forget* – and the act of reconciliation is binding for all of the victim's "circles of responsibility."[63] Volf's forgiveness covers past, present, and future. For Volf, God works in the lives of forgivers through a life lived in response to God and a "community that makes the practice of forgiveness meaningful."[64] Compared to *sulha*, Volf's forgiveness is binding by virtue of an internal personal obligation to imitate God and not an external obligation binding through the community the way we see in *sulha rituals*.

In *sulha*, the victims absorb the wrongdoing to maintain the social order and communal peace and be freed from *shame*.[65] However, for Volf, the victim should absorb the wrongdoing in order to transform the wrongdoer and to release him from the burden of *guilt*; the same way God has freed us from sin's guilt. The goal is a community of love.

The practical meaning of forgiveness in *sulha* is, first and foremost, pacification and the decision not to seek revenge – and also the restoration of relationships on different levels. The psychological component of forgiveness means the disputants will not view the "others" as enemies but will treat them as equal members in the community and rise above the dispute and its memory of conflict. If a member of the victim's family does not forgive the offender and his clan, any revenge from his side will bring dishonour on his family, community and the regional dignitaries who signed the forgiveness agreement. Even though Volf's forgiveness is aimed at stopping the circle of revenge and restoring relationships, and is connected with the affirmation of common humanity, it is not about the affirmation of common belonging

---

62. Jabbour, *Sulha*, 53.
63. Pely, "When Honor."
64. Volf, *Free of Charge*, 214.
65. Forgiveness is a fundamental value in Arab culture. It is related to honour and shame, and forgiveness is the only replacement of revenge that can redeem the disputant's honour.

to a specific group. Again, Volf's forgiveness has the primacy of the good over dignity.

In sum, forgiveness processes in *sulha* are initiated by the community. Forgiveness in *sulha* is obligatory; its aim is to transform revenge to forgiveness through the tool of a public restoration of honour. This forgiveness is human, not divine. It is decisional and an external process. It demands the participation of the whole community with the rituals; without this, restoration of honour will fail. It has a declaratory nature and transforms forgiveness from a private to a public affair, covering past, present and future generations. The victim's family has both a ritualistic and practical obligation to forgive. This act of reconciliation is binding. Practically, forgiveness in *sulha* is a pacification, which also includes restoration of relationships.

Volf's definition of forgiveness, like *sulha's*, is decisional and a process needing to be nurtured. While in *sulha* forgiveness is human, and conditional on achieving reconciliation, Volf's forgiveness is divine *and* human; it is unconditional and yet it aims at the reception of itself in repentance and restitution and is not complete until that happens.[66] Its aim is not pacification but restoration of the offended and the offender to the communion of love. It is a social event and involves God, the offended and the offender who can receive forgiveness by repentance, apology and restitution. The community has a role in encouraging forgiveness but not a role in "imposing" forgiveness or becoming guardians of its practical application as in *sulha*. This has implications for justice as well.

---

66. According to Volf, 'We forgive because Christ has forgiven us and because Christ forgives through us." Volf, *Free of Charge*, 206.

Table 7.1: **Forgiveness in Volf's theory and *sulha* model: A comparison**

Volf	*sulha*
Obligatory	Obligatory
Unconditional	Conditional
Internal process	External process (rituals)
Private individualistic process	Public communal process
Initiated by the offended	Initiated by the community
Burden on the offended	Burden on the community
Triangle of offender, offended, God	Triangle of the offender's family, offended family and community
Restoration of lost human dignity	Restoration of a group dignity
Binding by virtue of a personal obligation to imitate God	Declaratory binding by community
Divine and human	Human

7.2 Theology of Forgiveness in the Case Studies

In this section, I introduce the concepts of *internal, external and collective-public forgiveness*. *Internal forgiveness* is an internal process of overcoming negative emotions and attitudes towards the offender, such as resentment, anger, avoidance, and vengeance. *External forgiveness* is an external expression of the forgiveness process aimed at restoring social order and is realized in the broader community. *Collective-public forgiveness* is public and involves members of the community in apology and forgiveness.[67]

I argue that Palestinian Baptists in the three case studies are experiencing a shift in a growing understanding of forgiveness as a divine gift. The shift is from internal and/or external forgiveness (with private apology), as in *sulha* and alternative-legalistic approaches (case A and case B), to internal, divine,

---

67. Literature from different disciplines emphasizes the intrapersonal nature of forgiveness – involving only one party to the offence – or the interpersonal nature of forgiveness – involving both parties to the offence. Others consider it in the collective, political, spiritual and cultural context (Biggar, "Forgiveness in the Twentieth Century"; Jones, *Embodying Forgiveness*; Murphy and Hampton, *Forgiveness and Mercy*; Shriver, *Ethic for Enemies*; Volf, *Exclusion and Embrace*; Worthington, *Dimensions of Forgiveness*).

collective-public forgiveness (with public apology) in the Western-Baptist approach (case C). This understanding of forgiveness as a divine gift can reasonably lead to reconciliation in terms of the reintegration of churches which had split.

I identify four different perceptions of forgiveness in the four approaches.

7.2.1 Hierarchical Approach

Results show that for the pastors, granting forgiveness was *conditioned by public repentance directed to restore their dignity*.[68] Seemingly, this is affected by how pastors perceive their identity as clergy (sacramental). Pastors were influenced by traditional churches where the priest was the one who declared forgiveness (*ghofran*) based on divine authority given to him by God (and any wrong committed against them was perceived as wrong and committed against the church). Also, pastors' conditional forgiveness was influenced by the broader cultural context.

When evaluating the Palestinian pastors' attitudes in relation to their view of their identity as clergy (remembering they were raised in traditional churches), it would be helpful to understand the meaning of *ghofran* in its Middle Eastern Christian context. In the ancient Middle East, *ghofran* was a priestly purification reality, and the idea of *ghofran* is still practised by priests in traditional churches in the Middle East, where the priests declare *ghofran* based on divine authority given to them by God.[69] This might explain why the pastors viewed their role as being the ones to extend God's forgiveness.[70]

Regarding sin against the pastor, pastors tended to see church conflicts as spiritual problems. They often struggled to see the two different points of view and emphasized that the problem was that members were not submissive to their spiritual fathers. They perceived the questioning of their authority

---

68. Dignity is important to every human being and any threat provokes a strong reaction. When a relationship has been broken, affirmation of dignity in others is essential for releasing the pain – especially when conflict was caused by dignity violations (Hicks, *Dignity*). I discussed the importance of pastors' dignity restoration in chapter 5.

69. In the OT, *ghofran* includes the removal of sin and restoration to the community – or peace with God and peace with human beings. Forgiveness does not necessarily exclude punishment (see Num 14:19–25). There are places in Scripture where God refuses to offer forgiveness (2 Kgs 24:4; Deut 29:19–20; Jer 5:7; Lam 3:42).

70. In Palestinian traditional churches, clergy can also forgive sins of dead members during their funeral.

by the younger generation as disrespect for clergy and a "sin." Additionally, splitting their churches brought shame on them. This burden of shame and humiliation at being the object of offences, their loss of status and reputation and the failures in one's own and other's eyes have caused them deep pain.

It is likely that each pastor viewed his church as his domain and any "sin" against the pastor was perceived as being against his church. As a result, when members wrong the pastor this might lead to a church split as seen in the three cases; however, a split will not occur when two members wrong one another at church. Bassam,[71] an ABC leader, claimed pastors believe they must not compromise their ministry (church) for the sake of their members. David,[72] a third party, argued that pastors perceive themselves as ruling a small "kingdom" and are thus the ones implementing justice and order. According to David, the absence of clear church policies and the weak theology of justice caused them to act in monarchical ways. Thus, they struggled to offer forgiveness, preferring punishment.[73] This raises a question about church discipline, which is generally understood in a negative rather than a positive way.[74]

Pastors believed apology and repentance should be done publicly to restore their and their churches' dignity, which they felt was violated by the "rebellious groups." Pastors emphasized the importance of repenting (for not submitting to clergy) if anyone wanted to rejoin the church.[75] Pastor C said that if Bishara (regarding the evangelistic ministry conflict) repented the conflict would be resolved. Pastor B stated, "I tolerate them . . . but I cannot have them back unless they repent."[76] Pastor A's wife said forgiveness is conditioned by repentance. Some interviewees told me that Pastor A cannot forgive church A2 because of its location next door to his church, and thus he did not welcome any reconciliation. The interviews with the pastors left me with an impression that they felt the "rebellious groups" did not deserve to be forgiven unless they repented. For example, they used the word "tolerate" and not "forgive." For pastors, repentance included leaving the church

---

71. Focus group, June 2016.
72. Open interview, David, 2017.
73. David, interview with author, Jan. 2017.
74. This will be discussed in chapter 8.
75. David, Pastor B, and Pastor C in interviews with author.
76. Pastor B, interview with author, Aug. 2015.

location (as in case A) and apology/repentance done publicly and not privately (cases A, B, C).

Concerning *apology*, I find two different levels of apology in the cases: *private* and *public*. Pastors rejected private or public apology not directed to the restoration of their dignity. For example, in case C, in a private meeting mediated by the ABC committee, Bishara and Pastor C apologized to one another (each told me this was "false reconciliation"). Afterwards, Bishara was asked by the ABC committee to apologize in front of the church. Since Pastor C was not present during this church meeting, he did not accept Bishara's apology and the church split. It is noteworthy that the ABC committee did not ask Pastor C to apologize even though he could also be seen to have contributed to the conflict. This shows that the community, whose members were also converted from traditional churches, holds a deep respect for clergy, and thus the pastor's own actions were perceived differently (overlooked or not highlighted) than those of church members.

The need for *public* apology or repentance was an essential tool for dignity restoration for both the pastor and his church. This was evident when Pastor A and Pastor B did not accept any attempt from the "rebellious groups" to connect with them or to apologize privately. Elias, a leader at church B2, initiated a conversation with Pastor B requesting to visit him in order to apologize. He noted, "Pastor B told me, I tolerate you but there is no need to meet"[77] (private apology). He added, "Seven years after the split we initiated a joint service during Christmas, but Pastor B refused to join."[78] This might indicate that, for the pastor, accepting this invitation would imply an act of accepting apology. Apparently, the reason for not forgiving is because the pastors, still hurting and feeling dishonoured, conditioned forgiveness on *public apology and repentance*. Pastors perceived their decision for repentance to be a precondition to forgiveness as an ethical decision since they evaluated the actions of the "rebellious groups" as wrong and thus requiring public repentance or punishment.

Seemingly, the pastors' perception of forgiveness as being conditional was also shaped by the broader cultural context in which they live. In Arab culture,

---

77. Elias, interview with author, Aug. 2015.
78. Elias, interview with author, Aug. 2015.

there is a saying that "the sorrow should not be forgotten," and Palestinian culture has additionally been shaped by many assumptions from the surrounding Muslim culture, such as the belief in Islam that forgiveness is conditioned by repentance.[79] Similarly, among the Jewish communities in Israel there is a Hebrew saying, "never forgive, never forget." According to Volf, sometimes the reason we do not forgive is that we live in an unforgiving environment. As social beings shaped by our environment, our choices and thoughts echo the choices of a group to which we belong and the culture in which we live.[80]

There are three main differences between the hierarchical approach and that of Volf concerning forgiveness. First, in the hierarchical approach forgiveness is conditioned by public repentance; in contrast, Volf's theme of forgiveness is an unconditional gift that seeks to elicit repentance. Second, pastors are confused between their own act of forgiveness and the reception of forgiveness by the "rebellious groups". According to Volf, while pastors ought to forgive even without reparation (restoration of dignity) the "rebellious groups" can receive forgiveness only through apology and reparation. Volf highlights the difference between doing justice and forgiving: to be just is to condemn both the fault and the doer; to forgive is to condemn only the fault and release the doer. Third, pastors did not see their need for repentance even as "victims." They sincerely believed they had committed no wrong and blamed the "rebellious-group." This is in contrast to Volf's theory, as he argues that even as a "victim" one needs to repent – based on Jesus' demand for a pure heart – for letting one's own character and practices be shaped by wrongdoing.

7.2.2 *Sulha* Approach

I find that in *sulha* forgiveness is decisional, *external and a public process*. Its goal is to restore social order and to be apparent to the broader community as a form of "diplomatic reconciliation."[81]

---

79. The Quran recommends, whenever possible, it is better to forgive another Muslim. However, forgiveness is not recommended in the relationship between Muslims and non-Muslims (Quran, Surah Ash-Shuraa 42:36–39).

80. Volf, *Free of Charge*. According to Volf, other traditions, Jewish and Islamic, generally make repentance and apology a condition of forgiveness (see Auerbach, "Forgiveness and Reconciliation"). In recent years, some prominent Christian philosophers have argued that, in Christian thought as well, repentance is a condition of forgiveness. Volf, *Flourishing*.

81. See chapter 5, section 5.4.1.2, where I first introduce this term.

Different interpretations of forgiveness were identified here. Interviewees used the terms *musamaha* (tolerance) and *ghofran* (forgiveness) interchangeably,[82] as if they were synonyms. A few interviewees used the word "tolerance" (*musamaha*) in the sense of "to forgo our claim against the wrongdoer";[83] some said it means "to condemn no more." Most interviewees stated forgiveness means *forgetting* the wrongdoing.[84] They highlighted the following Scripture to explain their beliefs: "But one thing I do: forgetting what lies behind and straining forward to what lies ahead" (Phil 3:13). They asserted that we have to forgive as we were forgiven. Others related forgiveness to loving God,[85] since love is patient and tolerates everything (1 Cor 13:4–7), or they argued that loving others is a motivation to forgive.[86] Seemingly, in case A and case B, this kind of love pushed those involved to neutrality, not to embrace as in case C.[87]

Many interviewees stressed how hard it is to forgive and forget because of intimate relationships between disputants. Hiyam, a church A2 member, explained, "Forgiveness means to forget, but we can't forget. . . . It is like a tape in our mind taking us to the past. The hardest thing is to forgive." Both Hiyam and Tamer, a deacon, referred to the Arab saying, "The sorrow should not be forgotten." Tamer added, "We heard this saying from our pastor during his sermons! This means the conflict will remain an obstacle between us."[88]

---

82. *Musamaha* means tolerance, which refers to the capacity to endure the existence of someone you may not agree with, and *ghofran* means forgiveness.

83. Majd, interview with author, Mar. 2014.

84. Bishara, Tamer, Hiyam, Dan, Nabil, Amal, Ramiz, Jack, Pastor B, and Jack in interviews with author.

85. Emily, Michel, Boulus in interviews with author.

86. Boulus, interview with author, Aug. 2015.

87. "In a Christian account of things, we forgive because we love – specifically, because we love our debtors, our offenders, and even our enemies. The same love that motivates forgiveness pushes forgiveness not just from exclusion to neutrality, but from neutrality to embrace. Forgiveness between human beings is one crucial step in a large process whose final goal is the embrace of former enemies in a community of love. . . . Forgiveness is embedded in a way of life that is committed to overcoming evil by doing good." Volf, *Free of Charge*, 189.

88. Tamer, interview with author, Mar. 2014.

Forgiveness in *sulha* does not answer how to deal with *forgetting* the wrongdoing.[89] This will remain an issue that might leave forgiveness as external and not address all the issues.[90]

A few interviewees told me that they reconcile, but they do not forgive (pacification). I do not agree. There is no "peace" without some kind of forgiveness – whether seeds of forgiveness, conditional forgiveness, external forgiveness, internal forgiveness or divine forgiveness. It is likely that different kinds of forgiveness lead to different forms of peace, as I will discuss in chapter 9. In this chapter, I argue that external forgiveness leads to "diplomatic reconciliation."

In the Arab social and cultural context, "reconciliation" (*sulha*) might be a condition for achieving forgiveness. However, reconciliation rituals (*sulha*) do not always incorporate conditions for promoting forgiveness.[91] We can identify patterns of ongoing relationships despite imperfect forgiveness. For example, joint church services between church A and church A2 (post-split) were partly parallel to the *sulha* ceremony. Members of both churches shook hands (the first step in a *sulha* ceremony)[92] and participated in a service, although they chose to skip declaring forgiveness/apologizing (the second step in a *sulha* ceremony).[93] Joint church services can be interpreted as a form of "diplomatic reconciliation" for several reasons: they are a declaration of continuous relationships, a softening of deep resentments, a cessation of hostilities and a form of "repentance."[94]

First, engagement in worship services is indirectly a declaration that those who worship together are brothers and sisters in Christ and not enemies;

---

89. Forgetting was discussed in depth in chapter 6.

90. The more formal the process is the more external forgiveness becomes.

91. Nasser and Abu-Nimer, "Perceptions of Forgiveness."

92. These symbols were seen in the case studies. Although the conflict was not resolved, many interviewees in the three cases told me that when they met with the other party after the split, they shook hands although they wouldn't talk much.

93. As noted in chapter 5, in the three cases, third party were not authoritative enough to become the communal guardians of a settlement.

94. Bryan, who also initiated a joint service between churches A and A2, said, "certain bitterness remained on both sides, which may still be lying under the surface today, even though they are talking to one another much more easily and readily" (interview with author, Mar. 2014).

it is an indication that there is at least *moderation and softening of deep resentments.*[95]

Second, joint services reflects realism about existing realities; for example, church A2 is not going to win church A's building. Reintegrating church A and A2, though ideal, is unlikely, at least in the foreseeable future. The practical meaning was achieved in all three cases: there is a cessation of hostilities and no seeking of revenge. No one is to be completely determined by the wrongdoings of the past.

Third, church B2 tried to initiate a joint church service with church B. According to some church B2 members, there was a sense of guilt: "perhaps we were wrong when we decided to split the church and leave." The thought to initiate a joint service can be interpreted as a kind of "repentance," a turning away from former methods in pursuing their goals and positions.

Finally, every Sunday church A2 sees the church they renovated and remember they were "fired" by Pastor A and yet still did not seek revenge. This lack of action demonstrates a kind of forgiveness or transcendence.[96] It is likely that their acceptance of participation in joint church services demonstrated a public, external forgiveness that would open possibilities for internal forgiveness.[97]

---

95. Resentment (feeling bitter or angry about something) is a normal emotional reaction to an offence and an indication of self-respect and respect for the moral order (Biggar, "Forgiveness in the Twentieth Century"; Murphy and Hampton, *Forgiveness and Mercy*; Murphy, "Forgiveness, Self-Respect"; Volf, *Free of Charge*). Resentment is seen as an obstacle to forgiveness (Govier, *Forgiveness and Revenge*, 144). Some believe that struggling with resentment might be an indication that some forgiving has not happened (if we understand forgiveness as a process). Yet others advocate maintaining resentment for the sake of one's self-respect, especially when repentance has not taken place (Biggar, "Forgiveness in the Twentieth Century"; Lamb and Murphy, "Women, Abuse and Forgiveness"; Murphy and Hampton, *Forgiveness and Mercy*). Scriptures such as "Do not let the sun go down on your anger" (Eph 4:26) could be understood as against maintaining resentment. Some argue that overcoming resentment would have a positive effect on one's wellbeing, promote relationships and increase self-respect (Govier, *Forgiveness and Revenge*; Schimmel, *Wounds Not Healed*). According to Volf, unforgiving means to disrespect oneself and the Creator's spirit within. As he puts it, "When we are forgivers we are restored to our full human splendour" (Volf, *Free of Charge*, 209). See Goins, "Place of Forgiveness."

96. Müller-Fahrenholz talks about an aspect of forgiveness that can bring freedom from shame, guilt and anger, allowing people to forgive and be reconciled with one another. He calls this a transcending element, which requires a moment of trust and courage as the heart opens up. In this way, the heart can cross over boundaries and the dividing walls can be broken. Müller-Fahrenholz, "On Shame and Hurt."

97. I will explain that in my discussion of the Western-Baptist approach.

Other examples of external forgiveness and "diplomatic reconciliation," outside of these joint services, were instances of mutual help between both parties. The closeness and interconnectedness between Palestinian Baptists oriented them to develop a kind of forgiveness (external) that was reasonable and enabled them to connect despite unresolved conflicts. Pastor A, for example, requested assistance from members of church A2; at the same time, he allowed church A2 to use the church building for different occasions. On several occasions, relationships were restored to a limited degree for the sake of mutual interests but not for the sake of the relationship itself. Nonetheless, people still remember these acts and say there was "forgiveness." Although, seemingly, this forgiveness is imperfect and incomplete, it still is a kind of forgiveness – a forgiveness that is external and public, demonstrated in action although not by declaration.

This kind of forgiveness might make sense in a communal society.[98] This explains why *sulha* advocates focus on the outcomes in evaluating the rightness and wrongness of actions – for them split (divorce) is wrong so both parties should come together and demonstrate some kind of external forgiveness.

Cultural and religious beliefs guide the forgiveness process, and it may be difficult to determine whether the order of this process begins intrapersonally or interpersonally.[99] As demonstrated in case C, the intrapersonal process of shifting in attitude and emotions leads to the interpersonal process of relational restoration.[100] However, in the *sulha* approach people first "forgive" publicly in a ritual performance (external) and later have to struggle through forgetting and dealing with internal forgiveness. The decisional and external forgiveness in this relational approach opens a space and opportunity for internal forgiveness and renewing of relationships. It is important to see forgiveness as a process further or closer towards completion. The internal

---

98. *Sulha* highlights commonality between different groups so as to maintain the social order, especially as Palestinian Christians are a minority between Muslims and Jews. Research on forgiveness in Arab communities shows that the majority of Muslim religious scholars and theologians have emphasized justice as a central and primary value in Islam, while the majority of Christian theologians have emphasized forgiveness in the New Testament and Christ's life as a defining value (Abu-Nimer, *Nonviolence and Peace Building*).

99. Intrapersonal forgiveness means unilateral forgiveness in the literature, which is not complete. The term interpersonal forgiveness means forgiveness involving the offender and offended.

100. Generally, forgiveness and acceptance come at the end of a long emotional process.

work of forgiveness meets the felt needs of those involved in the process. The external work of forgiveness is realized in joint services/reintegration. Both are important in the transformation process, yet joint services/reintegration are not simply external programmes, they are internal processes.[101]

7.2.3 Alternative-Legalistic Approach

I find that forgiveness here is *external* and involves *private apology*. Its main goal is to "move on," seek mutual gain and promote *normalization* between the two churches that split; it is a form of "diplomatic reconciliation" but not necessarily reintegration.

While forgiveness in *sulha* is obligatory, it is not a critical element in the alternative-legalistic approach. The literature on this approach includes references to "apology" as part of a dispute resolution process but is largely silent on forgiveness.[102]

The "rebellious groups" using this approach sought to benefit the church community by trying to become part of the church leadership in order to shape the church future. They evaluated the church conflict and conflict management in terms of secular, rational measures and mutual gain and interests using a legalistic framework. Seemingly, they failed to predict the consequences and caused a church split. After the split, because of the shame they experienced in the broader community, along with the boycott by some pastors who refused to preach in their churches, perhaps due to experiencing similar problems in their new churches, they realized they might have wronged their pastors. All this influenced their decision to apologize and their desire to seek normalization. However, they preferred to apologize *privately*.[103] This attitude was expected since the alternative-legalistic approach is individually oriented. Similar to Volf, those using this approach also believe the only path to freedom from wrongdoing is through confession, apology, repentance and forgiveness. The "rebellious groups" realized refusal to apologize would highlight the shame on their image in front of their broader community. As Volf puts it, "Genuine apology makes the stain begin to fade."[104]

---

101. I will elaborate in section 7.2.4.

102. However, the transformative reconciliation model includes forgiveness as a component of the process.

103. See section 7.2.2.

104. Volf, *Flourishing*, 180.

Generally, forgiveness in this approach is benefit oriented. (There are some exceptions of members who demonstrated internal forgiveness.) The potential advantages of pleasure and healing gained by offering forgiveness are realized to be the reason for forgiveness. These advantages are greater than the emotional costs of withholding forgiveness. Volf agrees that when we forgive we find inner peace and freedom. However, he asserts that we should forgive primarily for the other's sake, not our own, as emotional healing is not the main purpose of forgiveness, but it is for the transformation of the wrongdoers so that reconciliation can take place – a community of love is the goal.

Forgiveness in the alternative-legalistic approach is in tension with justice. This approach focuses on rights and is oriented in a rational, calculative manner. External forgiveness appears to be one way "rebellious groups" chose to reduce the tension between forgiveness and justice.[105] Perhaps, for them, external forgiveness should be sufficient in order to restore relationships based on mutual interests, especially relationships they cannot escape in such a small, interconnected community.

Volf's theme of forgiveness could enrich this approach in several aspects. First, Volf argues that forgiveness is a divine gift but also a form of suffering. Second, one becomes aware that God is both love and justice only in the presence of God, and forgiveness provides a framework in which justice can be pursued.[106] Third, forgiveness is not to replace justice. Because the framework of strict restorative justice can never be satisfied, no reconciliation is possible without the framework of forgiveness.[107]

In sum, forgiveness in *sulha* and alternative-legalistic approaches can, at their best, achieve "diplomatic reconciliation" (pacification). The closeness and interconnectedness between the Palestinian Baptists oriented them to develop *external* forgiveness that involved *public* actions (such as shaking hands and joint church services). In this way they could "restore relationships," although this might still involve a feeling of resentment/blame and not forgetting the wrongdoing.

---

105. This tension is discussed in chapter 8.
106. Volf, *Free of Charge*, 123.
107. Volf, 122–123.

7.2.4 Western-Baptist Approach

In this approach, the findings show two main stages and perceptions of forgiveness. First, forgiveness is an *internal*, gradual process and relates to personal *healing*. Second, forgiveness is a *divine* work which gradually heals broken relationships. Given the fact that the Palestinian Baptist churches are influenced by the charismatic movement,[108] it is likely the above perceptions are also influenced by charismatic teachings (which focus on emotional and relational healing) such as those taught by George (a Western-minded pastor who pastored church A2 post-split), the American-Arab pastor (who mentored church C2 during and post-split) and the ABC committee (who pastored church C2 post-split and included George, David and two charismatic pastors). These teachings are not necessarily exclusively charismatic, but the focus on healing highlights the charismatic influence.

I begin with describing the two stages and perceptions and then compare them with Volf's theme of forgiveness.

7.2.4.1 Forgiveness is an internal process

Some interviewees viewed forgiveness as an *internal process* and tended to relate it to healing gradually. Others said forgiveness and healing happened in parallel. Rima, a member at church A2, spoke about the internal process of forgiveness she went through: "I was struggling in forgiveness and prayed a lot; I wanted to forgive, to be released and not keep holding against Pastor A each time I greeted him. Today, I can meet Pastor A and greet him gladly and have no resentment against him."[109]

Rana, a member at church B2, said forgiveness includes gradual healing, explaining that "in forgiveness we might not forget the wrongdoing but we need to get to the point that, when I remember, this incident will not cause me sadness or anger anymore. . . . This happened gradually."[110] She added that this forgiveness is Jesus-like and includes healing. Others said forgiveness comes after healing. Albert, a leader at Church C2, explained, "Forgiveness happened as a result of healing and healing happened when we stopped

---

108. See chapter 3.
109. Rima, interview with author, Mar. 2014.
110. Rana, interview with author, Aug. 2015.

getting upset when we remember the wrongdoing."¹¹¹ Boulus, the interim pastor of church C2, said forgiveness is a continuous action: "Forgiveness is an attitude I have to adopt every day; it is to act as Jesus acted on the cross." He referred to Jesus' cry on the cross: "Father, forgive them, for they know not what they do" (Luke 23:34 ESV).¹¹²

In this perception, forgiveness is an internal, gradual and continuous process linked to personal healing. This view of forgiveness was identified in case A (by a few members from church A and some members from church A2) and in case B (some members from church B2).

7.2.4.2 Forgiveness is a divine work

After the reintegration between churches C2 and C3, interviewees became more aware of forgiveness as a *divine* action and tended to relate it to relationship restoration. Shirin, a church C2 leader, explained there are levels in forgiveness and only divine forgiveness given by God is able to completely restore a broken relationship. David, an ABC committee member, differentiated between forgiveness and tolerance, saying, "Tolerance is done by the offended, while forgiveness needs divine help to happen."¹¹³

As mentioned, during and after the split, church C2 was pastored by the ABC committee, most of whose members were influenced by charismatic teaching and focused on forgiveness and healing. Additionally, leaders of church C2took direct consultation from the American-Arab pastor (a charismatic Arab evangelical), who also focused on healing. He insisted church C2 must forgive Pastor C, respect him, act in love and pray for him. He told them God is in control and brings justice.

Another important charismatic element that shaped the perception of forgiveness, besides the focus on healing, was *experiencing* a "divine presence" in a tangible way during the two conferences: the reconciliation retreat and the American-Arab pastor's conferences.¹¹⁴ Interviewees perceived these conferences as "divine presence" which brought healing and forgiveness, although partial. Pastor C and his wife told me that, a few months before the

---

111. Albert, interview with author, Aug. 2015.
112. Boulus, interview with author, Aug. 2015.
113. David, interview with author, Aug. 2015.
114. The American-Arab pastor was the main speaker in this conference.

reconciliation retreat, they were praying and fasting for reconciliation. She added, "People from both churches were praying for reconciliation, and God answered the prayer. This indeed was a divine work; humans cannot do that."[115]

Pastor C, who went through the repentance process himself, decided to apologize and reconcile. He told me that during the burial of the former pastor of church C he was in shock for a few minutes and suddenly understood when this pastor died that "even his grave was not his own; he begged it from another person." Pastor C explained, "This was a lesson for me and I decided to reconcile with church C2."[116] Pastor C's wife added that a few months earlier one of their guests had a dream and wrote it in their guest book. He dreamed that two groups were fighting, and in both groups there were hidden people praying; afterward he saw the two groups peacefully having dinner together. This "prophetic dream," as she called it, encouraged her to gather women from both groups to pray for reconciliation.[117]

It is likely that in the three cases there were some individuals who forgave, repented and apologized but not publicly and collectively as a church. Nonetheless, collective-public, internal and divine forgiveness was achieved in case C when Pastor C took his church (church C3) to visit church C2 during its retreat and there apologized from the pulpit. This was followed by members of both churches apologizing and forgiving one another, praying with tears throughout the evening. In describing the reconciliation retreat, Pastor C spoke about a *breakthrough*: "It is hard to explain what happened in the reconciliation retreat conference.... In that meeting we all cried, there was a breakthrough, we experienced a real healing and this has nothing to do with feeling alone – it was real! I apologized to everybody from the pulpit. I told them we had all wronged each other, we had all gossiped, and now we needed to reconcile and mend the relationships."[118]

This approach is close to Volf's concept of forgiveness as a divine gift. In case C, although the conflict and church split involved wrongdoing from both sides, and their forgiveness was incomplete, both parties transcended,

---

115. Susan, interview with author, July 2015.
116. Pastor C, interview with author, July 2015.
117. Susan, interview with author, July 2015.
118. Pastor C, interview with author, July 2015.

they "knocked at the door"[119] by not rejecting a reconciliation attempt; they were open to the work of the Spirit and waited. Two years post-split the reintegration took place. We can conclude that they trusted that "the Spirit of the resurrected Christ will make the seed of their forgiveness bear fruit."[120] They also realized the need to nourish the "seeds of forgiveness" with the food of God's goodness.[121] This is what church C2 did post-reintegration in order to maintain the reconciliation. Nonetheless, this was not the attitude of all members of church C2; some members were opposed but did not fight the process.

There are two differences between this Western-Baptist approach and Volf's. First, most advocates of this approach linked forgiveness with healing. For them, forgiveness was a result of healing (both forgiveness and healing took place at the conference). According to Volf, forgiveness is decisional, processual and we forgive mainly because we love and seek to transform the wrongdoer and restore community. Second, interviewees were aware they should forgive because God forgives. However, it was not obvious whether they fully understood why they had the power and the right to forgive. Concerning the power to forgive, Volf asserts that, when we forgive, we make God's sending of the "forgiveness package" our own. In relation to the right to forgive, Volf explains, "It is a derivative authority, dependent completely on God's."[122]

Forgiveness in this approach potentially achieved more than "diplomatic reconciliation" (as in the *sulha* and alternative-legalistic approaches). It made possible a reintegration after a split as in case C. However, personal agency seemed to contribute to this reconciliation, as I will discuss in section 9.4. Reconciliation needed the contribution of both church members and the pastor, which might explain why reconciliation did not take place in cases A and B even though some church members perceived forgiveness as internal and divine.

---

119. Volf, *Free of Charge*, 205
120. Volf, 205.
121. Volf, 209.
122. Volf, 199.

In sum, between case A (1995) and case C (2016), we noticed a shifting of beliefs from external and/or internal forgiveness with private apology towards internal, divine, collective-public forgiveness. Forgiveness in the hierarchical approach is conditioned by public repentance. Forgiveness in *sulha* is an external, public action. In the alternative-legalistic approach, forgiveness is also external but involves private apology. However, in the Western-Baptist approach Palestinian Baptists in case C viewed the first stage of forgiveness as internal and public, leading to reintegration, and the second stage as divine and collective-public, leading to the beginning of reconciliation. This is illustrated in the following diagrams:

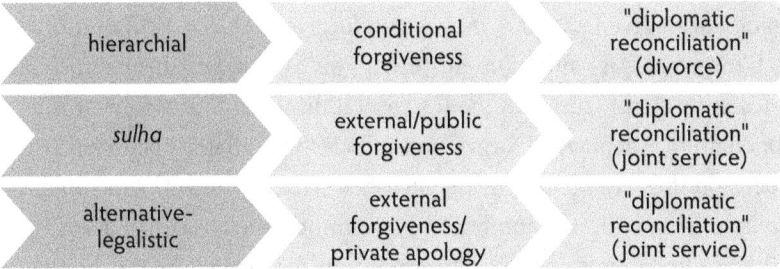

Figure 7.1: Forgiveness in the case studies

Figure 7.2: Case C stages of forgiveness

7.3 Challenges and Recommendations

How might Palestinian Baptists in Israel, whose context is very complex, living as a threefold minority with an identity crisis in a traumatized society, fulfil the requirements of Volf's theology of forgiveness? In addition, how can they forgive unconditionally when they live in an unforgiving environment in terms of culture and context? How can the concepts of shame and dignity, which are critical to Palestinian culture, be integrated in forgiveness? How can forgiveness be sustained when conflicts remain unresolved and when living together in a closely intertwined community within the contradictory frameworks of congregationalist churches in a patriarchal, hierarchical tradition?

Volf's theory offers valuable elements that can enrich a Palestinian Baptist theology of forgiveness. First, in order to forgive, we need a community in which forgiveness is valued and nurtured. This can happen through preaching/teaching that focuses on the horizontal dimension of forgiveness and reconciliation. Theology of forgiveness in Palestinian Baptist churches tends to focus on the vertical dimension and one's relationship with God and less on relationship with one another.[123] More importantly, reconciliation rituals (like *sulha*) should incorporate conditions for promoting a theology of forgiveness. Second, in order to forgive we need to understand forgiveness as a divine gift so that we have the power and the right to forgive. Third, forgiveness is decisional, processual and presumes and enacts a transformation that is nurtured in the context of communities of forgiveness. Fourth, we can *receive* forgiveness only through apology and reparation. Fifth, even as "victim" one needs to repent for letting one's own character and practices be shaped by wrongdoing. Finally, forgiveness is a form of suffering, but it does not replace justice; forgiveness provides a framework in which justice can be pursued.[124]

While Volf's theory is persuasive, several aspects important to Palestinian culture are missing in his theory or require cultural translation. The key to developing a successful framework of forgiveness in the Palestinian Baptist context is to build it from within the cultural values and social structure of the

---

123. See chapter 3.
124. I discuss justice in chapter 8.

community. I have identified five important aspects: conditional forgiveness, formality, venting, dignity and community. I will discuss each aspect in turn.

First, *conditional forgiveness*. Many interviewees said they forgave the other party, and some were even hesitant to share negative things about them, but they still saw the wrongdoer as guilty. After we forgive, are guilt, shame or blame removed – or just anger? If to forgive is merely to forgo revenge and resentment, then that does not necessarily seem to remove shame or guilt. This question is important, especially in situations of unresolved conflicts. If we decide to forgive without repentance from the other side, then how can we nourish the seeds of forgiveness with God's goodness, as Volf suggests?[125] For Volf, we are obliged to forgive even without repentance; such forgiveness, though deeply meaningful, is not complete.

The issue of repentance has been addressed in church discipline as well as in religious courts in Palestinian traditional churches. Both church discipline and religious courts are absent in Palestinian Baptist churches. This issue has a large impact on pastors' forgiveness, which they understand as conditional. Additionally, the Palestinian traditional model (*sulha*), and the approaches identified in the cases, view forgiveness as conditional. This issue might provide a challenge for them to be able to practise unconditional forgiveness.

One important challenge with conditional forgiveness is to decide when there is enough of a demonstration of repentance for forgiveness to finally be given and when we think that repentance is truly genuine. Conditional forgiveness is consistent with our natural inclinations and cultural climate. We believe that we have the right, indeed the obligation, to withhold forgiveness from those who wronged us. In a sense withholding forgiveness seems to border on vengeance.[126]

I suggest to follow Nelson's recommendation not to focus on whether forgiveness is conditional (consistent with natural human instinct) or unconditional (consistent with Jesus' countercultural message).[127] Since both have much in common,[128] while differing in the means by which reconciliation is

---

125. Volf, *Free of Charge*, 209.

126. See footnote 48 page 211.

127. Nelson, "Exegeting Forgiveness." While there are no conditions to unconditional forgiveness, there still may well be consequences, both natural and judicial.

128. See section 7.1.3.

realized, *the focus should be on reconciliation.* Forgiveness can be unilateral, but reconciliation is bilateral, requiring the best efforts of both parties. If the offender is a Christian who refuses to be reconciled, then the offended can use a formal process, such as church discipline, which aims at restoration rather than punishment.

Second, *formality*. While forgiveness may begin as an intrapersonal initiative (Volf's theory), it may also be worked out intrapersonally and interpersonally in the collective as it is expressed by the community in rituals, religious practices and other public activities as seen in the *sulha* ceremony. Churches should rely on internal and external resources; both of which can lead each party to realize forgiveness even though it may be imperfect. I suggest framing reconciliation and declarations of forgiveness by formal, ritualized, public action, culminating with the Lord's Supper followed by a common meal. The Lord's Supper and a common meal were not separated clearly in the early church. The Lord's meal is an appropriate ritual for the community to confirm the completion of the process of forgiveness because it celebrates God's reconciliation with us as the foundation of human reconciliation. The Aramaic word for forgiveness has the root "table."[129] Augsburger argues that Christ transformed the sharing of a meal (table) into a metaphor for realized forgiveness.[130] Interestingly, this is also an actual sign of forgiveness and reconciliation in Palestinian culture (*sulha* ceremony). This ritual would transform forgiveness from a private affair to a public, formal and binding one; one involving the church community and multiple witnesses. Another important ritual might be the creating and authorizing of a third party, as in *jaha*,[131] who would have the role of bringing ceasefire and transforming revenge/resentment to forgiveness/compassion.

Third, *venting*.[132] Volf's theory of forgiveness does not offer practical suggestions of how resentment can shift to compassion towards the offender. I suggest adding venting to the process. It allows condemning the wrongdoings as well as the expression of negative feelings such as hatred, resentment and

---

129. Jesus invited unrepentant sinners to "table fellowship" (Wright, *Jesus and the Victory*).
130. Augsburger, *Helping People Forgive*.
131. See chapter 5.
132. See chapters 5 and 6.

pain in order to transform them into tolerance and compassion. These are essential elements in achieving forgiveness. It is important that this process is overseen by a third party who can act as "anger absorber." Since to forgo revenge and resentment does not necessarily remove *shame*, it is important to add another element – namely, dignity restoration.

Fourth, *dignity restoration*. I recommend adding another public expression of forgiveness, integrating the concept of dignity restoration as a tool to achieve forgiveness. Since being embraced back into right relationship and community is what heals shame, the process of *musayara* (see section 5.2.1) temporarily places the offended in a position of "patronage" over the most respected figures in the community (*jaha*). This process is vital in helping to further calm the feelings of humiliation, in contributing to dignity restoration, and finally, embracing the offended back into the community.

Fifth, *community*. We need a more collective and public forgiveness involving a whole church community. The community can offer support to its members, both offended and offender, through bearing the burden of the wrongs done together. I suggest combining Volf's triangle of God, offender and offended, with the *sulha* triangle as follows:

As discussed, forgiveness in *sulha* takes place in a triangle consisting of the offender's family, the offended family and the community:

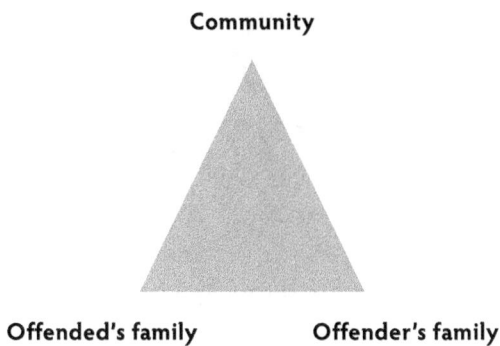

Figure 7.3: Forgiveness in *sulha* model

Volf's theory of forgiveness takes place in a triangle of the offender, the offended and God:

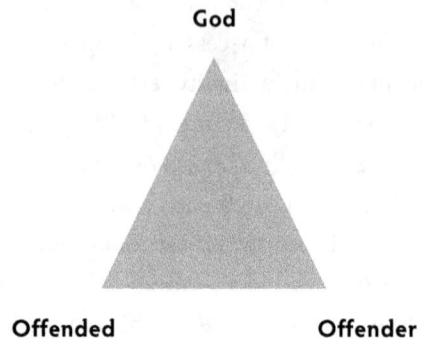

Figure 7.4: Forgiveness in Volf's theory

I suggest adding a fourth element to Volf's triangle – namely, the community – and adding the offended and offender's families to the process. The outcome will be that forgiveness takes place not in a triangle but in a rhombus as follow:

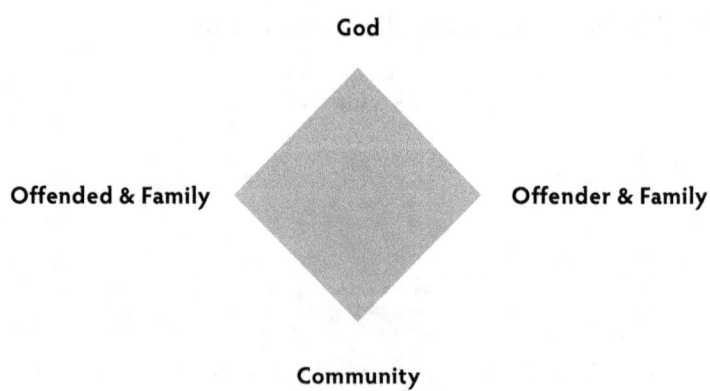

Figure 7.5: Proposed model

I find two important advantages to including the community as a fundamental participant in the process of forgiveness. First, the use of inclusive language such as "we" may help forgiveness interpersonally and in the collective, as members of the community influence and give courage to one another to practise forgiveness. Second, adding community to the process will help in that the burden of remembering rightly, forgiving and mending relationships will not rest alone on the offended/offender but will also be carried by the community. It is suggested that the key way for forgiveness to be demonstrated is through family, community and deity each supporting and recognizing the practice of forgiveness. Nonetheless, forgiveness is an act of a person and person's heart. Although community can promote, sustain and nourish the forgiveness process, community cannot forgive on one's behalf.

So far, forgiveness is the only way to deal with remembrance. Forgiveness is also the framework in which we seek justice, which is the subject of the next chapter.

CHAPTER 8

Theology of Justice

In this chapter, I describe Volf's theme of justice in which he proposes how to seek justice; I then explain how the four approaches perceived justice and relaxed the tension between justice and forgiveness. Afterwards, I evaluate how they sought justice using Volf's themes. Finally, I evaluate Volf's justice in light of the four approaches and propose several recommendations.

8.1 Volf's Theology of Justice

The theme of justice is drawn from Volf's book *Exclusion and Embrace* and his article "The Social Meaning of Reconciliation." Volf's intention is not to specify what justice is but to propose how to seek justice in a world of plurality and enmity.[1] For Volf, justice is broader than removing damage; truthfulness is concerned with justice,[2] forgiveness is concerned with justice,[3] and apology is concerned with justice. He sees justice as having two dimensions: a natural

---

1. Volf, *Exclusion and Embrace*, 197. Volf examines three dominant ways of dealing with the issue of clashing justice: (1) the universalistic affirmation that claims justice is one, (2) the postmodern claim that justice bears many names, and (3) the communitarian which places justice within a tradition (197). Volf concludes that since we are inescapably particular, our account of justice cannot be universal, and "justice" continues to struggle against other "justice." Postmodern thinkers believe that the struggle of justice against justice can end sooner, but then we are risking giving up the search for the one and only justice. In traditions, "one tradition struggles against another, its justice against the justice of another tradition, until one defeats the other by proving itself rationally superior" (Volf, 207).

2. Untruthful memories are unjust memories (see chapter 6).

3. We identify wrong committed against the backdrop of affirmation of what is just; not counting wrong against a person has to do with transcending the demands of justice without invalidating them (see chapter 7).

sense of justice in terms of restoration of balance and righteousness – doing what is right – which can be identical with love.[4]

8.1.1 Seeking Justice

Volf suggests that to achieve reconciliation a wrongdoer must make an effort to remove the damage he has caused.[5] Although apology removes the harm of having been disrespected, without the willingness to repair other damages the wrongdoer's apology remains mere words. In seeking justice, Volf makes three recommendations: practise "double vision," pursue smaller agreements and live life filled with the Spirit.

First, to practise "double vision," Volf suggests that since no one is neutral and we all stand within a hybrid of traditions, the proper response is to try to see things through the eyes of "the other."[6] Volf argues Christians are shaped by (1) the beliefs and practices of the community they belong to, (2) its biblical traditions and (3) the surrounding larger culture they inhabit. Volf concludes that since we cannot avoid living in "overlapping and rapidly changing social spaces we must rest satisfied with holding on to basic commitments. . . . It is better to give up on 'coherent tradition' and, armed with basic Christian commitments, enter boldly the ever changing world of modern culture."[7] We will be able to make these commitments only if we develop "double vision" by allowing the perspectives of others to resonate within ourselves, seeing them and ourselves from their perspective and readjusting our perspective by taking into account their perspectives – hoping that competing justices may become converging justices and finally issue in agreement.[8]

---

4. Volf, "God, Justice, and Love" and "Reconciliation, Justice, and Mercy." As Volf puts it, "My sense is that we have to ground human rights in an account of divine love that bursts the boundaries of love as attachment and that comes closer to a particular form of benevolence. First, human beings come to be because Love, which is God, has 'projected' itself outside the rim of the Trinitarian circle so that there would be both objects and agents of love other than God. The love out of which human beings come to be as bearers of worth is fecund delight in there being additional objects and agents of love – delight in the sheer 'thatness' of such creatures. Second, the divine love with which human beings are loved as created is care for the flourishing of these objects and agents of love – their flourishing as both recipients of love and givers of love." Volf, "God, Justice, and Love."

5. Volf, *Flourishing*.
6. Volf, *Exclusion and Embrace*, 213.
7. Volf, 210.
8. Volf, 213.

Volf confirms that the life of Jesus Christ offers the best biblical example for "double vision"; as Jesus Christ unconditionally embraced us, the godless perpetrators, so we should embrace even our enemies and be able to see from their perspective.[9] Volf concludes that the search for justice must ultimately be a search for embrace, as we practise "double vision."[10]

To practise "double vision," Volf proposes that we (1) step outside ourselves, (2) cross a social boundary and move into the world of the other to inhabit it temporarily, (3) take the other into our own world and (4) repeat the process. By repeating this process, we can bring about a common human understanding and a common language.[11]

Second, to pursue smaller agreements rather than overall victories, he suggests that we lower our sights over the issue of justice in conflicts, and instead of seeking overall victory, we should look for piecemeal agreements.[12]

Third, to underscore the necessity of a grand vision for life that is filled with the Spirit inspired by Acts 2 and Acts 6, Volf says:

> Along with the grand vision we need stories of small successful steps of learning to live together even when we do not quite understand each other's language. . . . The grand vision and the small steps will together keep us on a journey towards genuine justice between cultures. As we make space in ourselves for the perspective of the other, in a sense we have already arrived at the place where the Spirit was poured out on all flesh. As we desire to embrace the other while we remain true to ourselves and to the crucified messiah, in a sense we already are where we will be when the home of God is established among mortals.[13]

8.1.2 Justice as a Dimension of Embrace

Volf urges a moving away from justice as a central focus, to embrace, arguing that, although the struggle for justice is indispensable, in this way the

---

9. Volf, 215. In relation to embrace see section 8.1.2 and chapter 9.
10. Volf, 220. See chapter 9 regarding Volf's theory of embrace.
11. Volf, 251–252.
12. Volf, 207. Volf suggests that, "Agreement on justice depends on the will to embrace the other and that justice itself will be unjust as long as it does not become a mutual embrace" (197).
13. Volf, 230–231.

struggle becomes part of the pursuit of reconciliation. However, the pursuit of justice should not be about revenge, restitution, equity or liberation, but it should be about the restoration of communion. Such repositioning provides a framework for the pursuit of justice.[14]

Volf builds his argument on Paul's encounter with Christ and Paul's teaching in 2 Corinthians 5:17–21. He suggests that, "Though grace is unthinkable without justice, justice is subordinate to grace."[15] On the road to Damascus, Saul was "still breathing threats and murder against the disciples of the Lord" (Acts 9:1). Jesus named the injustice by its proper name, "persecution," and made the accusation "in the very act of offering forgiveness and reconciliation."[16] Paul's conversion was therefore not the result of the pursuit of strict justice. If God used strict justice, argues Volf, Paul never would have become an apostle of the very church he was persecuting. By confronting and reconciling, a greater justice was achieved.[17] Volf's argument is not so much that forgiveness should complete justice but that forgiveness should come before justice. Volf concludes, "At the core of the doctrine of reconciliation lies the belief that the offer of reconciliation is not based on justice done and the cause of enmity removed . . . but to open up the possibility of doing justice and living in peace whose ultimate shape is a community of love."[18]

Volf argues that *embrace* should be the central category for Christian social engagement in reconciliation and *justice* an essential dimension of embrace. His suggestion is to understand the struggle for justice as a dimension of the pursuit of reconciliation, whose ultimate goal is a community of love.[19] According to him, reconciliation is not simply the result of a successful

---

14. Volf, "Social Meaning of Reconciliation." Volf provides the following two examples of how embrace serves justice within the context of oppression: firstly embrace enables grace to deal with the constantly changing differences between humans, and second, that it is only through the forgiveness of injustice that true reconciliation is possible, because "justice" alone is powerless to deal with past injustice whereas forgiveness is able to call for the unjust causes to be removed. Additionally, Volf speaks about identity and its relation to justice. According to him: "If our identities are shaped in interaction with others, and if we are called ultimately to belong together . . . true justice will always be on the way to embrace." Volf, *Exclusion and Embrace*, 224–225.

15. Volf, "Social Meaning of Reconciliation," 10.
16. Volf, 10.
17. Volf, 9–10.
18. Volf, 10.
19. Volf, 9.

struggle for justice. Rather, the move towards reconciliation precedes the achievement of justice and is a means towards greater justice. Reconciliation is seen both as a result of justice and as an instrument of justice. However, Volf's intention is mainly to caution those who would give superiority to justice above reconciliation.[20] According to him, not to recognize justice as a means of the broader goal of reconciliation will encourage situations where the single-minded pursuit of justice gives up reconciliation.[21] Full embrace or complete reconciliation can take place only when matters of justice have been attended to. Without the commitment to justice under the umbrella of love, the pursuit of reconciliation will become a pursuit of cheap reconciliation.[22] Volf sees justice as a dimension of love. Love (as a particular kind of benevolence) precedes justice.[23]

Tutu does not construe the struggle for justice as an end in itself. Tutu advocates restorative justice, meaning the restoration of a right relationship between victim and perpetrator with the greater goal of restoration of community.[24] Volf is of a similar mind when he talks about justice as a dimension of embrace. Tutu practised the application of restorative justice during his term with the TRC.

As mentioned in section 1.5.1, DeGruchy, in the South African context, sees justice as the primary element in reconciliation.[25] Ateek also focuses on justice, arguing that peace begins with doing justice and ends by opening

---

20. Volf, 11.

21. Volf believes that there is no paradox in the fact that pursuing reconciliation results in greater justice. According to him, in situations of significant difference in power, such as in apartheid South Africa where the struggle for justice was indispensable, the weaker party must often engage in struggle to bring the stronger party to the point of wanting peace with justice rather than pacification of the oppressed. At the same time the Kairos Document was being written, tentative secret talks were under way between Nelson Mandela and the government of South African (Volf, 11).

22. Volf, "Social Meaning of Reconciliation."

23. Volf, "God, Justice, and Love."

24. Tutu explains: "Restorative justice, which was characteristic of traditional African jurisprudence. Here the central concern is not retribution or punishment but, in the spirit of *ubuntu*, the healing of breaches, the redressing of imbalances, the restoration of broken relationships. This kind of justice seeks to rehabilitate both the victim and the perpetrator, who should be given the opportunity to be reintegrated into the community he or she has injured by his or her offence." Tutu, *No Future without Forgiveness*, 51.

25. DeGruchy, *Reconciliation*.

the possibility of reconciliation, forgiveness, healing and love.[26] Volf argues against these approaches, seeing that a focus on only justice will lead to injustice and thus justice should be at work under the greater structure of reconciliation.[27] However, both DeGruchy and Volf agree that the meaning of the main concepts in a theology of reconciliation is related to each social context, DeGruchy in the South African and Volf in the Croatian contexts.

Another Palestinian perspective, regarding Christian-Muslim relationships, sees justice as subordinate to peaceful coexistence, such as Abu El-Assal and Younan.[28] Massad even goes further and makes justice unnecessary to reconciliation in regard to the relationships between Messianic Jews and Palestinian evangelicals;[29] Munayer, contra Massad, suggests that pursuing justice and restoration is a natural part of the reconciliation process, which needs to take place in the context of relationship.[30]

In these writings we notice a recurrent tension between seeking justice and offering forgiveness. As I will illustrate in the next section, this tension was also identified in the case studies, mainly between the young generation who make justice primary and the older generation who view justice as secondary. While justice for the older generation means the restoration of relationships, for the younger generation it is more about achieving one's rights than emphasizing the relational aspect.

Marshall, contra Volf, El-Assal, Younan and Massad, does not see justice as subordinate to grace or love. He also, contra DeGruchy and Ateek, does not view justice as primary to love. He suggests there is no tension between divine justice and grace; they should not be separated or one take precedence over the other. He argues that mercy is an expression of justice; if we understand justice in terms of restoring relationships, then mercy will help to bring justice.[31]

Philpott agrees with Volf that justice is a matter of rights; however, for him, biblical justice is wider than rights: it includes the obligation to give others

---

26. Ateek, *Justice and Only Justice* and *Palestinian Theology of Liberation*.
27. Volf, "Social Meaning of Reconciliation."
28. See Abu El-Assal, *Caught in Between*, and Younan, *Witnessing for Peace*.
29. See Massad, "Theological Foundation for Reconciliation."
30. Munayer, "Relations between Religions."
31. Marshall, *Little Book of Biblical Justice*.

what is not deserved – generosity, mercy, forgiveness. He suggests the best way to render biblical justice is via "comprehensive right relationship," understood as a restoration of broken relationship.[32] It is through grace and mercy that justice is transformed from being about rights alone to become something wider and richer. God's justice is a saving, healing, restorative justice.[33] For Volf, however, both justice and mercy together define right relationship among people and are best termed righteousness that is equivalent to love.[34]

I agree with Marshall. Rather than viewing justice as primary or subordinate to love, it is more compelling to view divine justice as compatible with divine love, and thus the two should not be separated during conflict. Therefore, I suggest that Palestinian Baptists understand justice in terms of restoring broken relationships; justice that brings peace and right order. In a sense this kind of justice seems to resonate with *sulha*, their cultural model, as I explain in section 8.2 and 8.3.

8.2 Theology of Justice in the Case Studies

How did Palestinian Baptists in the case studies perceive justice? How did they seek justice? How did they relax the tension between seeking justice and offering forgiveness? Most interviewees shared two common understandings. First, justice is subordinate to love, and second, God brings justice.[35] I argue the four approaches view justice differently.[36] For the hierarchical approach, justice is about the restoration of honour publicly (to restore power).[37] For *sulha*, justice is restoration of relationship and reestablishment of social order (to sustain power). The alternative-legalistic approach focuses on the

---

32. Philpott, *Just and Unjust Peace*, 54.
33. See Philpott, *Just and Unjust Peace*; Marshall, *Little Book of Biblical Justice*; and Wright, *Evil and the Justice of God*.
34. Volf, "Reconciliation, Justice, and Mercy."
35. In contemporary Christianity, believers are to leave vengeance to God, acknowledging that personal revenge is not appropriate.
36. Marshall suggests that justice is an inclusive term that embraces a variety of meanings, involving at least four key ingredients: distribution, equity, power and rights. Marshall, *Little Book of Biblical Justice*.
37. Justice involves the exercise of legitimate *power* to implement social benefits, order or sanctions. Marshall, *Little Book of Biblical Justice*, 6.

members' constitutional right to lead church as justice (to gain power).[38] Finally, the Western-Baptist approach navigates between both rights and restoration of relationships.

8.2.1 Hierarchical Approach

How did the pastors perceive justice? The findings indicate that for the pastors justice meant *public restoration of honour* – and God brings justice. For them, public restoration of honour was the main thing needed to repair the rejection and shame they experienced by church leaders who split the church. Restoration of honour involves, first, apology and public repentance; as one of the pastors put it, "I don't close the church in front of anybody but if they come back they will not be given position at church. . . . The prodigal son has to repent before he comes back. . . . I don't seek my own *right*." In a sense, for him justice was to receive a sincere apology and repentance from those who "sinned" and rejected him as their spiritual father (this was expected also as pastors focused on actions in evaluating right and wrong). At the same time, he suggested this request had nothing to do with seeking his "own right," but it was merely about accepting the "rebellious group" back as the father in the prodigal son story accepted his rebellious son. Second, restoration of honour involved both being *accepted* and seen by the broader community as the "church" and *rejecting* the "rebellious group" as a "church." This explains the conflicts happening at ABC meetings when both church A2 and church B2 requested membership in the ABC, and the two pastors fought against that. At the beginning, when the ABC did not accept Pastor B's attitude, this was perceived by him as, "you [ABC] undermine me and my integrity."[39] Obviously, for the pastors, acceptance of the "rebellious groups" by the ABC was perceived as a rejection of the pastors.

How did the pastors seek justice? Although the pastors claimed God brings justice, they had active roles in achieving their justice. Seemingly, punishment was one way to achieve justice. They changed the lock of the churches to indicate not welcoming back the "rebellious-group," they fought against accepting

---

38. Justice gives moral legitimacy to the rights of those who have legitimate moral or legal claim on some good. Marshall, *Little Book of Biblical Justice*, 7.

39. Letter, 9 Dec.

the "rebellious group's" membership in the ABC,[40] and they were also seen to be punishing the "rebellious groups" by not accepting reconciliation attempts.[41] Pastor B saw punishment as justice and part of God's judgment, insisting that God brings justice, and since the "rebellious group" rejected him, "God had rejected them from church."[42] Pastor A's wife also confirmed this belief that God "fired" the "rebellious group" from the church. Put differently, pastors believed God brought their justice in the form of judgments, but they seemed to have active roles in achieving that. Pastors' attitudes and sayings could be translated to express retributive justice – a predictable theme from an unforgiving/non-forgetting environment.

When evaluating how pastors *sought justice* using Volf's theme of justice, it seems both their pain and perception of the problem prevented them from practising "double vision." For them, there was a spiritual problem at church related to young laity being unsubmissive that was treated as sin. As one of the pastors put it, "Unsubmissiveness is Satan-like behaviour."[43] Pastors could not understand the attitudes of the younger generation and their need for change. They viewed members' disagreements with them as disloyalty and a conspiracy to "fire" them from church. In Volf's terms, they could not step outside themselves, could not enter the younger generation's world and could not make the younger generation understand their need. This attitude, however, did not bring the pastors and youth to a common understanding. Nonetheless, the pastors pursued small agreements, such as when Pastor A and Pastor B eventually accepted the membership of churches A2 and B2 in the ABC, or when Pastor A agreed for joint church services with church A2 and allowed the use of the church building for several occasions.

How did pastors relax the tension between justice and forgiveness? When pastors feel pain and humiliation because of the "wrongdoings," asking them to come to forgiveness without justice can add hurt to their suffering for not being taken seriously as community religious leaders. For the pastors, conditioning forgiveness on public repentance was a way to not only achieve justice but also to relax the tension between justice and forgiveness.

---

40. However, after a few years they were "forced" to accept them.
41. Some view this attitude as revenge. Adams, *From Forgiven to Forgiving*.
42. Pastor B, interview with author, Aug. 2015.
43. Pastor B, interview with author, Aug. 2015.

Regarding *easing tension between justice and forgiveness*, Volf's theory might enrich the pastors' practices by the following. First, seeking justice should always be on the way to embrace, and the move towards reconciliation precedes the achievement of justice. Second, condemnation is not forgotten when forgiveness is offered; we accuse when we forgive. Third, disciplinary punishment does not contradict forgiveness; "disciplinary measures" (deterrence, prevention or rehabilitation) are compatible with forgiveness since they focus on bringing a better future.[44] Thus, combining forgiveness with disciplinary measures will remove obstacles from the past to create conditions for peace in the present.[45] Punishment often serves as a tool for protecting and restoring *shalom*.[46]

8.2.2 *Sulha* Approach

I find that advocates of *sulha* perceive justice as the *reestablishment of social order and restoration of relationship*, as justice is subordinate to love and God brings justice.

How did advocates of sulha perceive justice? In the *sulha* approach some members spoke about restoring relations and even reintegration as their justice. Hiyam, a church A2 member, said, "I wish one day we would all return to the mother church [church A]. . . . This church is our roots."[47] Interestingly, many interviewees, when asked about justice, paused and did not know what to answer; they said they did not think about justice. Instead many of the answers were similar to Dan, a deacon: "If we love we overlook. For the sake of peace at church I am ready to compromise. This is what Christ taught us, *to compromise*."[48] They compromise because they focus on the desired outcome – namely, social order.

---

44. Volf explains that retribution and reprobation are the two main rationales for punishment strictly understood. Forgiveness is incompatible with retribution (one purpose of punishment) because to forgive is to forego retribution. But forgiveness is compatible with reprobation, for to forgive is to implicitly condemn the forgiven deed. Volf, *Flourishing*.

45. Volf, *Flourishing*.

46. *Shalom* is a Hebrew word meaning "peace." It denotes the presence of harmony and wholeness, of health and prosperity, of integration and balance. *Shalom* is when everything is as it ought to be, and thus, it combines into one concept the meaning of justice and peace. Marshall, *Little Book of Biblical Justice*, 12–13.

47. Hiyam, interview with author, Mar. 2014.

48. Dan, interview with author, Mar. 2014.

How did advocates of sulha seek justice? *Sulha* advocates have an active role in seeking justice; they are peaceful, and when justice stands in contradiction with future relationships, they leave it completely to God, believing God will compensate them. Dan noted proudly, "I compromise *my right* for the sake of future relationships." Emily, a church A2 member, went further; she accepted injustice as a sacrifice for Christ, "Even if we were treated unjustly, we have to accept and sacrifice for the sake of Christ."[49] Jack, a deacon, spoke about compensation and divine justice, saying, "God is not content with the split, but God blessed church A2 and this is compensation. Right is a legal word and logically we had to accept that; however, the divine justice is different from the human. Humans cannot achieve that."[50]

When using Volf's theme to evaluate how *sulha* advocates sought justice, "double vision" appears to have been practised. They did not focus on resolving the problem as much as restoring the social order at church. For many years they compromised for the pastors' sake. They were able to see both viewpoints of hierarchical and alternative-legalistic approaches; they in fact acted as mediators between the advocates of the two approaches. *Sulha* was the approach that convinced Pastor A and Pastor B to accept the membership of churches A2 and B2 in the ABC. When there was disagreement, they compromised so as to seek right order. Using Volf's terms, they stepped outside themselves; they entered the world of the younger generation and the pastors and also understood their needs. Additionally, they frequently pursued small agreements and were very patient.

How did sulha advocates reduce the tension between justice and forgiveness? When there was tension between justice and forgiveness, justice immediately became subordinate to social order. This generally contributed to conflict de-escalation but only for a limited time. Eventually, this attitude escalated the conflict because of the culture clash between the traditional-patriarchal attitude (pastors) and the modern-democratic attitude (younger generation).[51]

Volf's theory could enrich a *sulha* approach in that the struggle for justice should be indispensable. Although Volf agrees with *sulha* that justice is not

---

49. Emily, interview with author, Mar. 2014.
50. Jack, interview with author, Aug. 2014.
51. See chapter 5 regarding the contradictory values of these two approaches.

a central focus but an "embrace," the struggle for justice should become part of the pursuit of embrace.

8.2.3. Alternative-Legalistic Approach

I find that advocates of the alternative-legalistic approach linked justice to *rights* and relaxed the tension between justice and forgiveness by divorce (split); they gave superiority to justice above reconciliation.

What is justice? Advocates of an alternative-legalistic approach presented a variety of definitions for justice: rights, reparation, social order and punishment.[52] I list some of these perceptions. Of justice as *rights*, Elias, a church B2 leader, said, "I take my rights in a peaceful way without seeking the court. Sometimes I compromise my right because I don't see any solution."[53] He admitted, "We sought our rights, but we did not think about Pastor B's rights and interests." Regarding justice as *reparation*, a church A2 leader said, "To reconcile we need to attend to justice. . . . In church splits reparation and healing must be attended to."[54] Concerning justice as *right order*, Nabil, a church A2 leader, said, "What do we need at church, to be just or to worship God? We struggled, but it is not appropriate to fight for my right at church."[55] As for justice as punishment, Majd, who exited from church A, said he did not seek justice since his sufficiency is in God; at the same time, he said, "I see justice is happening. . . . The absence of the anointing upon church A is a real judgment. We are not victims, but our competence comes from God [2 Cor 3:5]. I don't need to ask him for justice; God does what is best for me."[56]

How did the alternative-legalistic approach seek justice? How did they relax the tension between justice and forgiveness? Many said God brings justice and compensation. Nonetheless, they also played active roles in seeking justice. This approach was more one of seeking and evaluating rights and interests according to legal mechanisms.[57] When justice was in contradiction with

---

52. Apparently, the reason for this diversity is because people were interviewed a long time after the split, and their perception concerning justice had changed depending on how the split affected their lives.

53. Elias, interview with author, Aug. 2015.

54. Focus group, June 2016.

55. Nabil, interview with author, Mar. 2014

56. Majd, interview with author, Mar. 2014.

57. See chapter 5.

future relationships, they confronted the pastors and older generation. They struggled in the tension between justice and forgiveness, which eventually led to split. In a sense, they relaxed this tension by making justice primary and forgiveness external.[58] They chose to split the church to seek some of their rights. In this approach, members had a strong feeling of injustice; as Bryan, a third party, put it, "There was a strong feeling of injustice, and self-justification was the major force apparent." Sami, a church A2 leader, saw the success of church A2 after the split as a reward from God: "We felt deep injustice, but God rewarded us. Even if we don't reintegrate, it is a shame there is no reconciliation."[59]

When using Volf's theme to evaluate how this approach sought justice, seemingly they practised "double vision" in part, focussing on resolving the problem and achieving their rights and less on future relations. When there were disagreements, they tried to understand the pastor's viewpoint and find a way for mutual gain (for example, they agreed to keep Pastor A as pastor emeritus with salary); however, when they failed, they rushed into achieving their goals to seek change and power.[60] In Volf's terms, they stepped outside themselves; they entered the world of the pastors, but they did not take the other into their world or repeat the process. Seemingly, this approach did not take time to understand the real struggle between their pastors and themselves, with their differing theology and culture, or the pastors' struggle to earn a livelihood.[61] This approach pursued small agreements when they accepted some compromises such as their rights to use the church building.

Volf's theory differs from this approach in that the pursuit of justice should not be about revenge, restitution, equity or liberation; but it should be about the restoration of communion, of which liberation is an important element. Volf suggests understanding the struggle for justice as a dimension of the pursuit of reconciliation, whose ultimate goal is a community of love, rather than seeing reconciliation as the result of a successful struggle for justice.

According to Volf, in situations of significant power differences (as between pastors and members) the struggle for justice is important. How could

---

58. See chapter 7.
59. Sami, interview with author, Feb. 2014.
60. Elias, interview with author, Aug. 2015 and Jack, interview with author, Aug. 2014.
61. See chapter 4.

the younger generation seek justice in a traditional, patriarchal community which recognizes authority figures (clergy) and age? The weaker party must often engage in a struggle to bring the stronger party to the point of wanting peace with justice, rather than keeping the status quo.[62] The younger generation used techniques unacceptable to the older generation.[63] For them, justice preceded reconciliation. Volf speaks to this attitude when he cautions those who would give precedence to justice over reconciliation. According to him, not to recognize justice as a means of the broader goal of reconciliation will encourage situations where reconciliation is given up on altogether.[64] This was the stance of the hierarchical approach and some advocates of the alternative-legalistic approach.

8.2.4 Western-Baptist Approach

For advocates of the Western-Baptist approach, both *justice and love are required*. They navigated between both rights and restoration of relationships. They reduced the tension between justice and forgiveness by seeking *justice that brings right order* and relying on God to bring justice.

How did Western-Baptist advocates perceive justice? Interviewees spoke about both justice and love. Phil, a third party, explained, "Justice is inferior to love; justice seeks fairness, love goes beyond fairness. If we cannot practice justice at church then we cannot succeed in reaching love, since love is a virtue that rises upon justice." Similarly, David, an ABC committee member, stated, "Justice is the complete peace; there is no complete justice because of the broken relationships and wounds. I think if Pastor A retired, and the two churches reintegrated, this would be the justice that brings peace. There is no peace without justice and no justice without peace since justice brings the right order which God intended and only then peace happens."[65]

Boulus, church C2 interim pastor, said, "Our God is just and his work on the cross manifests this justice. As a Christian, I need to have a voice against injustice in society, but this should be addressed lovingly."[66] Others said God

---

62. Volf, "Social Meaning of Reconciliation," 11.
63. See chapter 5, section 5.4.2
64. Volf, "Social Meaning of Reconciliation."
65. David, interview with author, Mar. 2014.
66. Boulus, interview with author, Aug. 2015.

brings justice, and we should compromise justice for the sake of the church. Albert, a church C2 leader, said he tends to forgive and forsake his rights so he becomes a good witness for the other party. Bishara (regarding the evangelistic ministry conflict) used Psalm 37:6 – "He will bring forth your righteousness as the light, and your justice as the noonday" – to describe how God will bring his justice regarding the evangelistic ministry conflict with Pastor C. Bishara said, "When you walk in truth, even if you were wronged, God will bring back justice, even if it comes late." He added that he decided not to fight Pastor C in order to prevent a church split, and he trusted God would bring his justice. Bishara explained that he made some compromises for he knew God would reward him. However, he sought fair reconciliation, insisting he was ready to apologize at church for his part only and not for false accusations.

How did advocates of the Western-Baptist approach seek their justice? How did they relax the tension between justice and forgiveness? Members of church C2 did not split the church. Five years after the conflict they reintegrated, but how did they seek justice? They confronted Pastor C and sought help from different third parties (the American-Arab pastor and the ABC). The ABC used certain disciplinary tools against Pastor C, such as not allowing him to continue to be part of the ABC community if he founded a new church after he split church C2. Members of church C2 did not leave the church when they faced problems with Pastor C, and they told me that, when their personal rights contradicted the benefit of the church, they compromised their rights, trusting God to reward them. Two leaders decided to stop attending church C2 but did not establish a new church and did not fight Pastor C. Nonetheless, they used different ways to express their injustice, such as chatter (sharing frustration and complaints).[67] However, eventually their struggle in the tension between offering love and seeking justice led to reintegration.[68] This reintegration was not only because of their attitude. Pastor C was very active in such an endeavour. Both church C2 and Pastor C were influenced by the mentoring and teaching they received during and post-split. Similar to Volf's theme, their move towards reconciliation in this approach preceded the

---

67. See chapter 5.
68. As I explained in chapters 6 and 7.

achievement of justice. In case C, we can witness the beginning of reconciliation functioning both as an instrument of justice and as a result of justice, which nonetheless could have happened only when justice was sought in parallel with seeking the restoration of relationships.

In sum, each approach perceived justice differently. The hierarchical approach focused on the restoration of honour publicly as their justice; *sulha* focused on reestablishment of social order and restoration of relationship as their justice; the alternative-legalistic approach focused on rights; and the Western-Baptist approach navigated between both rights and restoration of relationships. All approaches struggled in the tension between seeking justice and offering forgiveness. In this struggle the hierarchical approach made forgiveness conditional; the *sulha* approach made justice subordinate to social order; the alternative-legalistic approach focused on justice and preferred divorce (split); and the Western-Baptist approach focused on embrace and preferred reintegration, compromising for the sake of right order at church and being a good witness. The following table summarizes the results.

Theology of Justice

Table 8.1: Evaluating the four approaches in terms of Volf's theory of justice

Approach	Justice	Seek justice	Relax tension between justice and forgiveness	Outcome
Hierarchical	Restoration of honour publicly	Punishment; no "double vision"	Conditioning forgiveness on public repentance	"Diplomatic reconciliation" (divorce)
Sulha	Re-establishment of social order	Compromise; "double vision" in part	Justice becomes subordinate to social order	"Diplomatic reconciliation" (joint service)
Alternative-legalistic	Rights	Confrontation and split; "double vision" in part	Justice becomes primary and forgiveness external	"Diplomatic reconciliation" (joint service)
Western-Baptist before re-integration	Rights and restoration of relationships	Disciplinary tools; "double vision"	Navigates between both rights and restoration of relationships	Reintegration
Western-Baptist after re-integration	Right order at church/ good witness	"Double vision"	Compromises for right order at church and being good witness (focus on embrace)	Reconciliation

8.3 Challenges and Recommendations

For Palestinians in general, justice is a fundamental issue – especially since the Israeli-Palestinian conflict remains unresolved.[69] Nonetheless, the works of Palestinian Christians have not focused on unpacking biblical justice in the Palestinian context. Instead they focused mainly on political justice. More work is needed in order to develop a Palestinian biblical theology of justice.[70] Some Palestinian theologians view justice as subordinate to love and reconciliation. Interestingly, this is also reflected in the data. Many interviewees, when asked about justice, were uncertain about the right answer, explaining they did not think about justice since it is less important than forgiveness and reconciliation. The preaching in most Palestinian Baptist churches tends to focus on the vertical dimension, with almost no teaching about justice – except for God's justice demonstrated on the cross. This attitude could be related to the tendency of the Palestinian Baptist churches to be apolitically pietistic,[71] with their hopes focused on the bodily return of Christ or on escaping from worldly issues such as the struggle to seek change and justice.[72]

In the Bible, doing justice conveys the idea of righting what has gone wrong, of restoring things to a condition of "rightness" or righteousness.[73]

---

69. Barakat points out, since the Ottoman times there has been a noticeable increase in the emphasis on justice in Arab society, rather than charity. Many Arabs believe that justice is a fundamental issue of human rights and that it is an important foundation of every society. There has been a growth in belief that it is important for societies to be able to ensure the well-being of all their citizens and to provide equal access to opportunities for the development of capabilities and improvement of living conditions. Barakat, *Arab World*, 204.

70. See Katanacho, "Palestinian Protestant Theological Responses."

71. *Dikaios*, the Greek word for justice used in the New Testament, is translated as righteousness and not justice in many translations. This might give the impression that the New Testament is less concerned with justice. Cannon argues that, "Contemporary evangelicalism has emphasized personal righteousness and piety and has missed much of the intended meaning bursting through the Scriptures about justice. . . . Righteousness and justice are interconnected in both Testaments. In the Old Testament righteousness was obedience to the Law of Moses. New Testament righteousness is received through faith in Christ. The demonstration of righteousness in our lives is *just* living – living out the justice of God . . . pursuing a life of justice motivated by love for God and love for his people." Cannon, *Social Justice Handbook*, 21.

72. See chapter 3, section 3.3.1.3.

73. In biblical usage, righteousness includes what we mean by justice. Often in the Hebrew Bible "righteousness" (*sedeqah*) and "justice" (*mishpat*) occur as a word-pair with virtually identical meanings. In modern English, "righteousness" carries the sense of personal moral purity and "justice" relates to public judicial fairness and equity. Marshall, *Little Book of Biblical Justice*, 11–12.

In the case studies, most interviewees did not assume this interpretation in the daily use. Many interviewees used the word "rights" to talk about justice. They expressed their individual rights at church. For pastors, their "right" is to restore their honour (restore power); for the young generation it is their constitutional right to lead church (gain power); for *sulha* it is to keep the status quo (sustain power). Generally, the word "right" is understood and used in legal, political and social contexts. A "right" exists when someone has a legitimate moral or legal claim on some good, which others have a duty to respect. This perception influences the way people perceive their "rights" at church too. Often conflicts are resolved but without taking into consideration God's "right" and the community's "right" (the good witness of the church). Theologically, "right" is not a biblical word. We talk about divine justice, and thus church conflict should be resolved taking into consideration honouring God; this is more about God's justice than "rights." When we think about "rights" from an individualistic perspective, the church loses its role in the community since we do not have the "right" to give up the "right" of the community or the "right" of God.

Besides the word "rights," another common saying from interviewees was "God brings justice." It is important to distinguish between our rights in a fallen world and our eternal rights in the Kingdom of God now and forever. God will restore our eternal rights as part of bringing forth the kingdom of justice. However, in the here and now, we are to act as *agents of justice*. Marshall sees God's coming justice as "the culmination of, not a substitute for, human striving for greater justice here and now." He adds, since justice is an attribute of God, those who bear God's image must also be agents of justice.[74]

With regard to the word "compromise" used by *sulha* advocates, we need to distinguish between wisdom and law. The moral law must be in place in strong, non-compromising ways, but implementing it must be done with wisdom and flexibility.

I suggest that Palestinian Baptists view justice in its biblical perspective, in which divine justice is seen as compatible with divine love and thus should not separate them during conflict. God's justice saves, heals and restores; however, disciplinary punishments often serves as a tool to achieve restoration.

---

74. Marshall, *Little Book of Biblical Justice*, 22–29.

Additionally, seeking justice should be a primary obligation of the church as a lifestyle which indicates holiness.

One challenge is related to disciplinary punishment, which is a tool to promote restoration, while *church discipline* is nonetheless viewed as a negative approach within Palestinian Baptist churches (as in many other contexts) and not as a tool to lead to reconciliation. This is why it is not practised and eventually "encourages" a split. At the same time, Palestinian traditional churches have religious courts in which the bishops authorize clergy judges to resolve conflicts using disciplinary measures. Do Palestinian Baptist churches need a similar system of religious courts to implement justice? David, an ABC committee member who was involved in some church conflicts, concluded that the only successful way to deal with conflict would be to have religious courts as in the traditional churches.[75] But how can this be applied in a congregationalist polity? How can the ABC, with its limitations, succeed in such a role?

Another challenge is how the younger generation can seek justice in a traditional-patriarchal community which recognizes authority figures (clergy) and age. The powerless party should often fight to bring the stronger party to recognize their rights. At the same time, how can pastors implement order at church in a congregationalist polity where unsatisfied members can easily exit?

Volf's theology of justice is indeed insightful and enriches each of the four approaches, as I explained. Nevertheless, it remains unclear how we should pursue justice in this world or how offenders are called to justice within the framework of the will to embrace. More importantly, after achieving justice, how can justice be sustained? Finally, repairing damage and restitution may take care of guilt, but what kind of justice deals with shame?

I suggest that Volf's theory of justice should be amended, in order to be applicable to this context, by adding the *community* as a fundamental factor in his theory, for the following reasons. First, as mentioned, the communal approach to conflict in *sulha* is based on the view that hurting an individual means hurting the entire community,[76] and injuries between individuals and

---

75. Focus group, June 2016.
76. Jabbour, *Sulha*.

groups will fester and expand if not acknowledged, repaired, forgiven and transcended.[77] *Sulha* rituals create the space for restoring dignity lost as a result of the offence. As an interpersonal strategy, *sulha* has the capability for micro- and macro-level restoration.[78] With that being said, I suggest the church community should become part of the process of seeking justice as well. As we partly saw in case C, this would support the offended to practice the will to embrace as they are embraced by the community throughout the whole process. Additionally, this would impact the offender in that the community's pressure would encourage repentance and repair of the damage. For example, Pastor C acknowledged the offence in a public setting (church community). The justice was minimal and partial in that no material reparations were made nor could the split be undone. Yet the possible restoration of dignity for both sides, inner peace and forgiveness were on the horizon, followed by the potential for a new relationship, bringing back the view of justice as restoration of broken relationships.

Second, regarding *sustaining justice*, the community could also be the best guardian to ensure the durability of the agreement post-conflict, since the third party (*jaha*-representative of the community) participates in post-ceremony activities to ensure the stability of the settlement. More importantly, the practices of justice and reconciliation are themselves strengthened and sustained by forgiveness. This also has to do with community.

Third, Shults and Sandage point out that paying a debt to justice might deal with the problem of guilt, but it does not remove shame.[79] What heals *shame* is to be re-embraced into relationship and community. What would truly satisfy the human heart is transformation that reshapes people and communities more than a transaction that brings justice. Stated differently, what heals shame is restorative *divine justice*. Thus, to embrace or to exclude is the main issue and is the subject of the next chapter.

---

77. Said, Funk, and Kadayifci, *Peace and Conflict Resolution*.
78. Gellman and Vuinovich, "From Sulha to Salaam."
79. Shults and Sandage, *Faces of Forgiveness*.

CHAPTER 9

Theology of Embrace

In this chapter, I describe Volf's theology of embrace, then, using Volf's theme, I evaluate embrace as demonstrated in the four approaches and evaluate Volf's embrace in light of them.

9.1 Volf's Theology of Embrace

9.1.1 The Social Construction of Identity

According to Volf, the expanding conflicts between cultures worldwide are "part of a larger problem of identity and otherness," and thus he claims that the future of our world will depend on how we deal with identity and otherness.[1] Therefore, to address the social meaning of reconciliation means unavoidably to address the issue of identity. Volf poses the following questions: how should one think of one's identity, and how should one relate to different people? How should one go about making peace with the other?

Volf addresses the problem of the "sacralization of cultural identity," which amounts to "captivity to our own culture, coupled so often with blind self-righteousness."[2] When churches give ultimate allegiance to their cultures, this leads to an incorrect dynamic between culture and self. When culture undermines faith, Christians lose the place from which to judge their own culture and find themselves unable to act on the gospel call to the ministry of reconciliation because their commitments are not ordered correctly.[3] Volf argues, "The universal claims of the Gospel of Jesus Christ are subordinated

---

1. Volf, *Exclusion and Embrace*, 16, 20.
2. Volf, 37.
3. Volf, 53.

to the claims of the particular social groups they inhabit instead of the claims of particular social groups being subordinated to the universal claims of the Gospel."[4]

Volf suggests the need for developing the proper relation between "distance from the culture and belonging to it," for Christians need to "depart" from their particular culture and give complete loyalty to the God of all cultures – to switch "from the particularity of 'peoplehood' to the universality of multiculturality, from the locality of a land to the globality of the world."[5] Volf argues that the distancing from a culture and belonging to it, when the self is situated "with one foot planted in their own culture and the other in God's future," will serve the self in two ways: (1) in creating space to receive "the other" and (2) in providing a vantage point to perceive and judge the self and the other in the light of God's new world, knowing there is an ultimate reality more important than one's culture.[6]

To avoid the risk that a local culture may lose its specificity for the sake of "universality," Volf draws upon the Pauline argument concerning the relation between various group identities within the Christian faith (Jew and Gentile, female and male, slave and free). He explains, "The Pauline move is not from the particularity of the body to the universality of the spirit, but from separated bodies to the community of interrelated bodies – the one *body in the Spirit with many discrete members*," where cultural specificity can be approved and yet at the same time each culture has to forsake its own "tribal deities."[7] Volf confirms that distance and belonging are necessary, expressing that "belonging without distance destroys and distance without belonging isolates."[8]

Volf uses the doctrine of the Trinity and the creation activity in order to explain the construction of identity. He argues the doctrine of the Trinity offers a paradigm concerning how Christians ought to think about identity – adjusted for the difference between God and the world. According to him, as

---

4. Volf, "Social Meaning of Reconciliation," 8.
5. Volf, *Exclusion and Embrace*, 37, 43.
6. Volf, 53.
7. Volf, 48; italics in the original. According to Volf, "Each culture can retain its own cultural specificities . . . at the same time, no culture can retain its own tribal deities; religion must be de-ethnicized so that ethnicity can be desacralized. Paul deprived each culture of ultimacy in order to give them all legitimacy in the wider family of cultures" (49).
8. Volf, 50.

human beings are created in God's image, they should seek to imitate God in their relationships. He concludes with two characteristics: (1) identity is "non-reducible" – and here is the importance of keeping boundaries; and (2) identity is "not self-enclosed" as the self always contains "the other" within itself.[9]

Volf uses the term "differentiation" to describe the creative activity of "separating-*and*-binding" that results in patterns of interdependence.[10] While separation alone would result in self-enclosed, isolated and self-identical beings, Volf suggests that identity is a result of distinction from the other and internalization of relationships with the other. We are who we are not because we are distinct from others but because we are both distinct and related; we are separate and connected to others. "Differentiation" is the complex process by which the self and the other negotiate their identities in interaction with one another – it is not based on opposition to and negation of the other – but rather a resourceful "taking in" and "keeping out."[11]

According to this definition of identity, Volf concludes that both cutting off the bonds that connect and removing separation lead to *exclusion*. Stated differently, exclusion occurs when the construction of one's identity is seen as "pure," without "the other": "Exclusion takes place when the violence of expulsion, assimilation, or subjugation and the indifference of abandonment replace the dynamics of taking in and keeping out as well as the mutuality of giving and receiving."[12]

9.1.2 The Self and Its Centre

After discussing the construction of identity, Volf discusses which kind of self is capable of making a "non-exclusionary judgment" between *legitimate* differentiation and *illegitimate* exclusion and what kind of centre such a self must have.[13]

Volf argues that, in Galatians 2:19–20, Paul de-centres his self when he states, "I have been crucified with Christ"; at the same time he re-centres his

---

9. Volf, "Trinity Is Our Social Program," 11.
10. Volf, *Exclusion and Embrace*, 65; italics in the original.
11. Volf, 66.
12. Volf, 67.
13. Volf, 68.

self around Christ when he states, "It is Christ who lives in me": "Paul presumes a centred self . . . a *wrongly* centred self that needs to be de-centred by being nailed to the cross."[14] Paul's new identity is based on Christ's self-giving love shown on the cross. This kind of "de-centred centre" is the "doorkeeper deciding about the fate of otherness. . . . From this centre judgment about exclusion must be made and battles against exclusion fought."[15] Volf argues that judgments must not be made between "innocent" and "non-innocent" as long as the practice of evil keeps re-creating a world without innocence. However, he adds, universality of sin does not mean equality of sins.[16]

Volf explains that the human tendency towards exclusion is connected to the tendency to found and support "exclusive moral polarities," which do not acknowledge this world as one in which "justice and injustice, goodness and evil, innocence and guilt, purity and corruption, truth and deception crisscross and intersect."[17] Volf states that a social reality based on moral polarities which assert, "Here, on our side, 'the just,' 'the pure,' 'the innocent,' 'the true,' 'the good,' and there, on the other side, 'the unjust,' 'the corrupt,' 'the guilty,' 'the liars,' 'the evil,'" must be denounced as *sinful*.[18]

Volf concludes that, since no one is innocent in a world where everyone falls captive to the inescapable system of evil and exclusion, "*No one should ever be excluded from the will to embrace.*"[19] Volf clarifies, "At the core of the Christian faith lies the persuasion that 'others' need not be perceived as innocent in order to be loved, but ought to be embraced *even when they are perceived as wrongdoers.*"[20] But what exactly will enable one to make the choice of a "will to embrace"? Volf suggests it is the Holy Spirit:

---

14. Volf, 69; italics in the original.

15. Volf, 71.

16. Volf, 82. Volf suggests that there is interdependence between the "universality of sin" and the "primacy of grace": "Solidarity in sin underscores that no salvation can be expected from an approach that rests fundamentally on the moral assignment of blame and innocence. . . . The question cannot be how to locate 'innocence.' . . . Rather, the question is how to live with integrity and bring healing to a world of inescapable non-innocence. . . . The answer: in the name of the only innocent victim and what he stood for, the crucified Messiah of God, we should de mask as inescapably sinful the world constructed around exclusive moral polarities" (84).

17. Volf, 84–85.

18. Volf, 84–85.

19. Volf, 85; italics in the original.

20. Volf, 85; italics in the original.

The Spirit enters the citadel of the self, de-centres the self by fashioning it in the image of the self-giving Christ, and frees its will so it can resist the power of exclusion in the power of the Spirit of embrace. It is in the citadel of the fragile self that the new world of embrace is first created. . . . It is by this seemingly powerless power of the Spirit . . . that selves are freed from powerlessness in order to fight the system of exclusion everywhere – in the structures, in the culture, and in the self.[21]

9.1.3 Embrace

Volf builds his argument around the notion of "embrace."[22] According to him, the basic argument is based on the story of the prodigal son and the Apostle Paul's command to the Romans (15:7), "Welcome one another, therefore, just as Christ has welcomed you."[23] Volf suggests that his thesis will enable life under conditions of enmity. He states that God's welcoming of hostile humanity into divine communion is an example for how human beings should relate to the other.[24] He argues, "Reconciliation with the other will succeed only if the self, guided by the narrative of the triune God, is ready to receive the other into itself and undertake a re-adjustment of its identity in light of the other's alterity."[25] We should embrace the other because others are part of our own true identity; we cannot live authentically without welcoming the other for we are created to reflect, in a creaturely way, the personality of the triune God.[26]

To describe the process of "welcoming," Volf employs the metaphor of "embrace." The metaphor symbolizes four requirements of reconciled life after a conflict:

---

21. Volf, 92.

22. The notion of embrace brings together three theological themes: the mutuality of self-giving love in the Trinity; the outstretched arms of Christ on the cross for the "godless"; and the open arms of the "father" receiving the "prodigal." Volf, 29.

23. Volf, 28–29. For Volf, the metaphor is helpful but not essential; "The most basic thought that it seeks to express is important: the will to give ourselves to others and 'welcome' them, to readjust our identities to make space for them, is prior to any judgment about others, except that of identifying them in their humanity. The will to embrace precedes any 'truth' about others and any construction of their 'justice.' This will is absolutely indiscriminate and strictly immutable; it transcends the moral mapping of the social world into 'good' and 'evil'" (28–29).

24. Volf, 100.

25. Volf, 110.

26. Gundry-Volf and Volf, *Spacious Heart*, 59.

1) *Opening arms*: a sign of creating space in oneself for the other and an invitation to enter.
2) *Waiting*: waiting for the other to come (an indicator of differentiation).
3) *Closing of arms*: when the reciprocity of "giving" and "receiving" is achieved (a symbol of unity).
4) *Opening of arms again*: affirmation of each person's discrete identity (a symbol of differentiation).

The embrace represents bilateral forgiveness. Movement is required on the part of the offender. For many settings, a handshake, connecting people while they are at a safe distance, is a form of embrace. Such an embrace will never be perfect, but partial and tension-filled, yet it will open possibilities of mutual cooperation and enrichment.[27]

Forgiveness is essential to the theme of embrace. Volf understands forgiveness as the boundary between exclusion and embrace and thus the lattice which holds an interdependent world in place. He explains that forgiveness falters when one excludes the enemy from the community of humanity and excludes the self from the community of sinners.[28] It is only through faith and repentance that one is freed to rediscover the wrongdoer's humanity and imitate God's love for that person.[29]

In sum, while "the will to embrace" is unilateral, unconditional and free, "the embrace" is a mutual and conditional process that requires repentance, confession, reparation. Volf's basic thesis is "there can be no justice without the will to embrace . . . no genuine and lasting embrace without justice."[30]

An area of criticism targets the practical level of Volf's theory. In the act of "opening arms" for the wrongdoer to come, how do we name the wrongs committed? Can the "will to embrace" be initiated, maintained and developed outside of a "community of embrace"?[31]

The TRC might resonate with Volf's theme of embrace. As Peter Storey argues in his article "A Different Kind of Justice: Truth and Reconciliation in

---

27. Volf, *Flourishing*.
28. Gundry-Volf and Volf, *Spacious Heart*.
29. Gundry-Volf and Volf.
30. Volf, *Exclusion and Embrace*, 216.
31. See Corneliu, "Exclusion and Embrace."

South Africa," the experiences of the TRC point "beyond conventional retribution into a realm where justice and mercy coalesce and both victim and perpetrator must know pain if healing is to happen. It is an area more consistent with Calvary than the courtroom."[32] Tutu also affirms the fundamental importance of relationship, using the word *ubuntu*, meaning, "The essence of being human. . . . It speaks about humaneness, gentleness, hospitality, putting yourself out on behalf of others, being vulnerable. It embraces compassion and toughness. It recognizes that my humanity is bound up in yours, for we can only be human together."[33] *Sulha* also resonates with embrace and its goal in achieving peace and coexistence.

9.2 Theology of Embrace in the Case Studies

I argue that Palestinian Baptists in the three cases experience a shift from conditional embrace, or embrace lacking "differentiation" (as identified in hierarchical, alternative-legalistic and *sulha* approaches), to an embrace including a process of "differentiation," which, although partial, nonetheless leads to reintegration (as seen in the Western-Baptist approach in case C).

I will explain how each approach relates to Volf's theme of embrace. These are rough guidelines which do not necessarily describe the embrace of an individual using the relevant approach.

9.2.1 Hierarchical Approach

In this approach, I find that pastors *conditioned their embrace on repentance* of the "rebellious-group." In terms of Volf's theme, although pastors declared "opening arms" (step 1) conditioned on the repentance of the "rebellious groups," it was not clear if they were truly waiting for their repentance (step 2) in order to close arms and finally welcome them back at church.

1) *Opening arms*. Interviewees from the "rebellious groups" felt rejected by their pastors when they insisted on taking part in church leadership. Pastors viewed this desire for change as rebellion and a "sin" against the pastor and the church. They also experienced dignity violation as a result of the behaviour of the "rebellious groups." For the pastors, opening arms for these groups

---

32. Storey, "Different Kind of Justice," 793.
33. Tutu and Tutu, *Words of Desmond Tutu*, 49.

required extra carefulness. They wanted to be sure the group repented and apologized before welcoming them back. In case A, apparently Pastor A felt that opening arms during joint church services was enough. He did not want them back to share the space of the church building, which was a factor in causing conflict.

2) *Waiting*. Pastors might be in the stage of waiting for the "rebellious group" to repent publicly in order to come in, but for Volf, waiting does not mean waiting for the other person to start the process of reconciliation. Pastor A might want a renewed relationship, but it could be seen that he would rather go his own way even after an apology, reparation and forgiveness. Reintegration is not an option for him, as mentioned above. Pastor B insisted he would welcome them back after repentance but without leadership positions.

3) and 4) *Closing of arms and opening arms again*: Pastors viewed the difference in ministry philosophies (individual leadership versus council-led church) between them and the "rebellious group" as unsubmissiveness and rejection.

In this approach, there was no process of "differentiation" by which pastors negotiated their identities in interaction with the younger generation. They perceived the younger generation's education and enthusiasm as a threat to their power. Thus, there was no resourceful "taking in" and "keeping out" but only keeping "the other" out by not allowing the younger generation to participate in church in their own style of leadership, accepting them only if they worked under their pastoral authority and style. Pastors evaluated the conflict as a spiritual problem of the "rebellious groups": they, as pastors, were right and good, and the "rebellious groups" were wrong and unrighteous. Some members from the three cases claimed pastors could not separate the people from the problem and tended to view members who did not agree with them as against them personally. For example, one pastor said, "Either me or them – you cannot accept both."[34] In Volf's terms, this way was more an exclusion, as pastors decided to cut the bonds connecting them with the younger generation, preferring divorce as a way to solve conflicts. Their *embrace* of

---

34. Pastor B in his letter to the ABC.

the opposing group was conditioned by repentance; they were excluded until they repented, and pastors had the power to exclude.

Volf bases his suggestion on how identities should be understood, in order to restore and embrace broken relationships, on the story of the prodigal son.[35] Volf argues relationships have priority over rules: "For the father, the priority of the relationships means not only a refusal to let moral rules be the final authority regulating 'exclusion' and 'embrace' but also a refusal to construct his own identity in isolation from his sons. He readjusts his identity along with the changing identities of his sons and thereby reconstructs their broken identities and relationships."[36] According to Volf, the father suffers being "un-fathered" by his two sons, so through this suffering, he may regain them both as his sons and help them rediscover each other as brothers.[37]

The pastors *struggled* in the tension between rules (requiring repentance or punishment) and relationships (they *suffered* the broken relationship with their church members); what they needed was public apology which could restore their dignity. Theologically, it is likely the pastors understood that the father's embrace was conditioned on the prodigal son's repentance. Since pastors saw the "rebellious group" as an *unrepentant* prodigal son who came to be embraced, they did not welcome them.

The pastors seemed to act as the older brother, who refused to celebrate the prodigal's return. The older brother's response is a metaphor for refused, and therefore unrealized, forgiveness.[38] The father has clearly communicated his forgiveness with the embrace before knowing his son repented. He felt the need for having his son in his life/identity. He had waited long for him to come back. His motivation was his deep desire to embrace and honour his son.

Although the father reminded his elder son that the younger son would not reinstate his former privileges (this was the condition of some pastors if the "rebellious group" came back), the elder son could not accept the father's embrace and did not even sit at the same table. Yet what if the prodigal was out raping and robbing? Is the warm, individual relationship between father and son all that matters? What about the victims of the prodigal son? Rules and

---

35. In Luke 15:11–32.
36. Volf, *Exclusion and Embrace*, 165.
37. Volf, 165.
38. Augsburger, *Helping People Forgive*, 13.

moral structures matter for relationships too. I think, if the pastors wanted to follow the father in his attitude, they should at least not have rejected private apology by the "rebellious-group."

9.2.2 *Sulha* Approach

My results show that *sulha* seems to resonate most with the theme of embrace because of the way in which it prioritizes the relationships. Nonetheless, it is an *embrace lacking "differentiation,"* since the older generation (mainly deacons) embraced the younger generation without "allowing" the process of "differentiation." They required the younger group to forsake their modern identity for the sake of deference to clergy and maintaining the social order.

1) and 2) *Opening arms and waiting. Sulha's* communal approach to conflict is based on the view that hurting an individual means hurting the entire community. This emphasizes the interrelationships and connections between people. In a sense, this approach does not exclude; it welcomes everybody. However, this approach does not welcome a change of power; rather, it prefers keeping the status quo, even if this results in compromising the other group's rights – such as seen in case A where the deacons compromised their rights and convinced the younger generation to forsake their rights to the church buildings. In Volf's terms, this approach did not exclude others. For them, there was no right and wrong, good and evil; for them, there was a desired outcome – namely, social order at church.

3) *Closing of arms.* There were no processes of "differentiation" by which older and younger generations negotiated their identities. Although they did not oppose or negate the other, there was no resourceful "taking in" or "keeping out," as Volf suggested. For *sulha*, we are who we are not because we are "distinct and related, separate and connected," but because we are interrelated; as such, the younger generation, in a patriarchal-traditional community, are expected to compromise for the sake of clergy and social order. Since divorce was not an option in this approach, the splits by the "rebellious groups" were perceived by the community as poor decisions resulting in their boycott by several pastors.

4) *Opening arms again.* There was no opening of arms again. There was no affirmation of the younger generation's distinct identity, as mentioned above. This is a kind of exclusion because exclusion happens when there is a

removal of the boundaries in such a way that the identity of the other cannot be recognized in a relationship.[39]

9.2.3 Alternative-Legalistic Approach

Results indicate that in this approach *embrace lacks "differentiation."*

1) *Opening arms.* One can argue that the participation of the "rebellious groups" in joint church services in case A, and their initiative in case B (although not welcomed by the pastor), were examples of opening arms as an invitation to the pastors to restore relationships.

2) *Waiting.* It started with opening arms and was stopped at the second step of waiting. In case A, Pastor A responded to joint services which were initiated by joint missionary friends; however, these initiatives did not develop any further interaction. In fact, these joint services took place several times and then stopped. In case B, the "rebellious groups" were left waiting for the pastor to respond.

3) and 4) *Closing of arms and opening arms again.* They started with the process of "differentiation" because they were ready to negotiate with the pastors, as they realized they were distinct from the older generation. They were ready to compromise to stay related. This negotiation failed because pastors saw themselves as "pure" without the "rebellious groups," and, as a result, the "rebellious groups" saw themselves as "pure" without the pastors and decided to split the church. We can conclude both the "rebellious groups" and the pastors excluded one another.

9.2.4 Western-Baptist Approach

I focus only on case C since this approach was mostly seen there. Embrace in case C went through a *shift from conditional to a welcoming* embrace. I identified two different stages of embrace between the two conferences: first, "forced" or rushed "differentiation" (leading to reintegration after the reconciliation retreat conference), and, second, welcoming embrace (leading to the beginning of reconciliation after the American-Arab pastor's conference).

9.2.4.1 *"Forced differentiation" embrace*

1) and 2) *Opening arms and waiting.* After the reconciliation retreat and the reintegration, church C2 struggled with having Pastor C as their pastor

---

39. Volf, *Exclusion and Embrace.*

again. As a result, they approached the ABC to agree that his return with church C3 would be conditional and not as the church pastor. Influenced by the American-Arab pastor and the ABC committee, they gave him a chance. Although church C2 had conditions, we can conclude it opened its arms and waited to see Pastor C change once back in the church. This was a conditional embrace, but it also included a "forced differentiation" process, as I will explain in the next step. How genuine are open arms with conditions? Looking back at the father's attitude in the prodigal son parable, he lovingly embraced his son before hearing any confession.

3) *Closing of arms.* Pastor C, who was embraced by a few leaders during the conflict, insisted on returning to church C2 as a pastor. Obviously, Pastor C and the ABC committee "forced," or rushed, a process of "differentiation" between Pastor C (church C3) and church C2. Church C2 did not fight this process, but they did not cooperate. Some members of church C2 did not participate in programmes Pastor C initiated in the church, such as baptisms, trips and conferences; they were reluctant to have Pastor C back and found it hard to trust him. They were passive and waited to see Pastor C fail. Shirin, a church C2 leader, said, "After the reintegration, we felt we were a church inside a church. . . . We did not feel we belonged."[40] Both groups opened arms partly, but not widely, and waited. They were suspicious, afraid and not ready to take the third step of *closing arms*.

This embrace lacked "differentiation" (step 4); no negotiation took place between the two groups.

9.2.4.2 Welcoming embrace

3) *Closing of arms.* After the American-Arab pastor's conference, a resourceful "taking in" and "keeping out" started between church C2 and Pastor C (and church C3), as some leaders from church C2 started to cooperate again with Pastor C and became more confident in taking the step of closing arms as their trust in him increased. However, this was not the attitude of the whole church.

---

40. Shirin, interview with author, 2016.

4) *Opening arms again.* Church C2 and Pastor C began this process; a transformation started to take place in the attitudes of Pastor C and some leaders from church C2.[41]

Two important elements contributed to this successful embrace: (1) *The Spirit* played a role during the two "divine presence" conferences, which caused the change in the attitude of embrace as participants felt its presence in different ways. This element is critical also since church C2 is a charismatic church. (2) An *identity grounded in Christ* prevailed, which was seen in Pastor C's repentance and apology and in members who were reminded (by the ABC committee and the American-Arab pastor) how they should act as Christians whose identity is centred in Christ. Members of the ABC committee told me that church C2 was taught to take the approach of interpreting everything out of love for Pastor C, taking the example of the self-giving love of Christ. The American-Arab pastor kept reminding them not to judge Pastor C but rather pray, love and forgive him. Similar to Volf's model, the American-Arab pastor mentored church C2 to embrace Pastor C even when he was perceived as a wrongdoer. These mentors were aware of the role of the Spirit in helping them to resist the power of exclusion and replacing it with embrace.

In sum, between case A (1995) and case C (2016), embrace shifted from conditional (as in hierarchical) or lacking "differentiation" (as in *sulha* and alternative-legalistic approaches) to an embrace which took the form of reintegration and, afterwards, reconciliation. This embrace was imperfect, however, as the reintegration "rushed" the process of "differentiation" and then embrace.

---

41. Case C confirms Volf's point, as he argues, "If we are able to exit a relationship, the pressure to reconcile lessens . . . we can walk away from them. But if we must live with those who have wronged us, we are pushed to reconcile. If we don't reconcile, we risk being either crippled by resentment or consumed by a cycle of revenge, and in either case being unable to cooperate with them." Volf, *Flourishing*, 9.

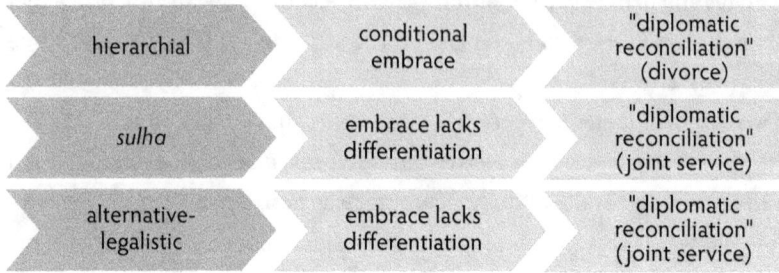

Figure 9.1: Embrace in the case studies

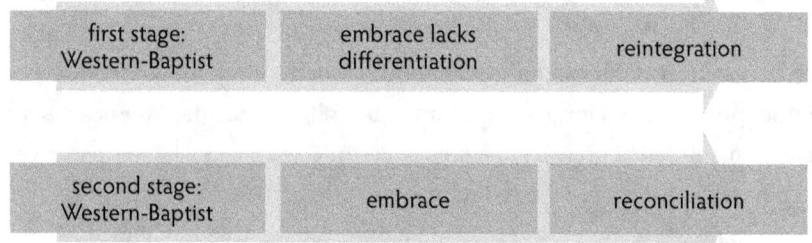

Figure 9.2: Two stages of embrace in case C (reintegration and beginning of reconciliation)

9.3 Challenges and Recommendations

The case studies provide an interesting insight into the relationship between forgiveness and embrace. When forgiveness is conditional, as seen in the hierarchical approach, then embrace is also conditional. When forgiveness is external, as in *sulha* and alternative-legalistic approaches, then embrace lacks "differentiation." In the Western-Baptist approach of case C, forgiveness was viewed as internal (first stage) and divine (second stage), and embrace in its first stage took the form of reintegration while in the second stage reconciliation started to take place.

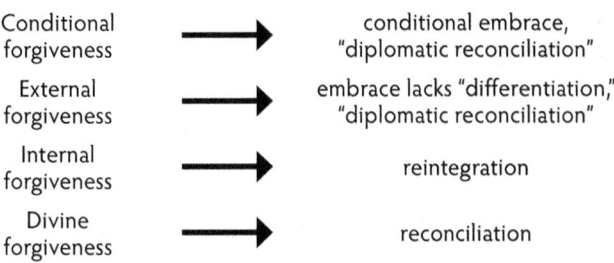

Volf argues there is a tight unity between forgiveness and embrace: "God forgives by indwelling us and indwells us by forgiving us."[42] In answering the question of whether to first forgive or embrace, Volf states that what is important is only to insist on the unbreakable unity of forgiveness and embrace. There can be no embrace of the former enemy without forgiveness, and forgiveness should lead beyond itself to embrace. The same love which motivates forgiveness pushes forgiveness from exclusion to embrace.

According to Volf, it is the responsibility of the church to create practical steps to live out the theme of embrace. However, it is not clear how this "will to embrace" is to be implemented in churches. How are pastors or church members to choose to embrace and not exclude? Volf suggests the use of a confession text to endorse embrace, the commitment to "double vision" and preparedness to make changes. Churches could develop a similar confession. Nonetheless, although the "will to embrace" is decisional, there are no practical indications of a process that may lead one to make the choice of the "will to embrace." Additionally, how do we name the wrongdoings in the act of "opening arms" for the wrongdoer to come?

Besides adding the "community" to remembrance, forgiveness and justice,[43] I suggest adding it to Volf's theology of embrace. Individuals who act from within a group do not stand alone as individuals but together as group members, though in all groups there is a distribution of power and authority that makes some members more persuasive or responsible than the others.[44] Groups make decisions and act on them, empowering their members to collective actions. This was demonstrated in case C where several

---

42. Volf, *Free of Charge*, 189.
43. See also Sections 6.4, 7.3, 8.3.
44. See Shriver, *Ethic for Enemies*.

key leaders influenced the overall attitude of church C2 and contributed to reconciliation (embrace).

Another suggestion is church practices. Long-term divorce (as in cases A and B) would not have provided a space for bilateral forgiveness or reconciliation. For both forgiveness and reconciliation to happen there must be some kind of interaction that can encourage the move beyond offence to the metaphorical embrace of forgiveness. This is evident in case C where reconciliation took place less than two years after the rushed reintegration. As mentioned in chapter 6,[45] church practices in case C played an important role in contributing to the transformation of attitudes and feelings.

Case C demonstrates that the process of reconciliation is not linear. Embrace took place (when the ABC rushed reintegration) before remembering rightly and genuine forgiveness. In other words, in this case the community had the power to force embrace, despite unforgiveness and not remembering rightly, which eventually encouraged the process of forgiveness and remembering rightly.

9.4 Personal Agency

If all approaches struggled in remembering rightly, forgiving, seeking justice and embrace, how could the Western-Baptist approach, in its second phase, lead to reconciliation whereas the other approaches could not?

Even when a refined contextualized model of reconciliation is in place and is known by all parties, reconciliation is not guaranteed. The parties involved will have to make a personal choice to effect reconciliation. Even in the absence of a refined model of reconciliation (as in many cases), personal agencies and good choices can facilitate the journey towards reconciliation. The ideal case is when a good model of reconciliation is understood by all who act personally in the way of *integrity, humility, courage* and *love*. I have identified the following examples of personal agency that seemed to contribute to the reconciliation in case C.

First, Pastor C's repentance and his persistence in reconciling influenced the result of reconciliation, as mentioned above. Pastor C's attitude was influenced by several events. (1) the death of his former pastor (church C), (2)

---

45. See section 6.4.

the "prophetic dream" his guest had in his sleep, (3) being embraced by a few leaders who allowed/accepted his *venting* process – such as David, Rami and the American-Arab pastor who did not cease loving and encouraging him – and (4) the prayers and fasting of some members from both church C2 and church C3, led by Pastor C's wife.

Second, coaching by a third party. The mentoring of the American-Arab pastor given to some laity in church C2, and his guidance to Pastor C, nurtured the seeds of forgiveness and love. As Shirin put it, "Without his [American-Arab pastor's] guidance, we would have lots of bitterness."[46] Additionally, the intervention by members of the ABC committee involved personal agency – such as David, George and another pastor who played a role in coaching church C2 post-split.

Third, the attitude of some church C2 leaders was towards restoring the relationship they were missing.[47] Shirin stated, "The pain of the members was connected to the brokenness of relationships. . . . Church members who loved Pastor C were hurt and wondered, 'Why did this happen to us?' We had had great times as a church; we missed the past."[48] She concluded that restoration of the broken relationship brought healing. Concerning trusting Pastor C again, some members remembered Pastor C's past good deeds, but church C2 needed to see proof of his repentance. Pastor C's transformation encouraged church C2 to trust and accept him again. Seemingly, if Pastor C had not changed, church C2 would have continued to struggle to accept and trust him, causing the conflict to escalate again.[49]

Fourth, a few members from both church C2 and church C3 were separately committed to praying for reconciliation.

---

46. Shirin, interview with author, 2016.
47. This is the only factor that was seen also in case B, where church members loved pastor B; interviewees said that they missed the past relationship and wished they could restore it.
48. Shirin, interview with author, Jan. 2017.
49. Apparently, it is easier to deal with forgetting after a divorce (split), as in cases A and B, than after reintegration, as in case C. The main difference here is the issue of trust. After a divorce, trust is no longer relevant; however, after reintegration, trust becomes the main struggle, as well as remembering therapeutically. The issue of trust was mentioned by some members from church C2 post-reintegration. They said they forgave and wanted reconciliation but trusting pastor C again was a different issue. As Boulus, the interim pastor at church C2 explained, "What church C2 needed was to gain trust and to see a real change in pastor C's behaviour" (Boulus, interview with author, Aug. 2015).

Another important element that influenced reconciliation in case C was the *charismatic* influence on members of church C2, Pastor C, the American-Arab pastor and the ABC committee.[50] This is an important factor in that it influenced the way they perceived the two conferences, where they referred to experiencing "divine presence": first, the reconciliation retreat conference, which was followed by reintegration, and, second, the American-Arab pastor's conference, which took place a year after the reintegration. In comparing the two conferences, Shirin explained:

> In the reconciliation retreat we experienced the beginning of forgiveness but there was no trust yet [in Pastor C]. The second conference was the continuation of the forgiveness and trust-building. Suddenly, I could see that Pastor C had changed; now when I look at him I see the pastor that everyone loved prior to the conflict. In this conference another barrier fell down. Today, when I remember the conflict, I see human weakness and God's grace lifting up the church again.[51]

Shirin mentioned several *practices* that showed continuation of the work of reconciliation in church C2 post-conferences. First, worship flows smoothly and members participate in worship. Second, after the service, members of church C2 and C3 have fellowship together at church, and sometimes Pastor C invites the church for coffee at his house. Third, generally church matters are flowing.

Another fundamental component to the reconciliation success was *humility*. Without the humility of the key actors mentioned above, especially Pastor C's public apology, no reconciliation could have happened. Given the fact that the local culture is patriarchal-hierarchical, it is *shameful* for a clergy to confess his wrongdoings as this might be an indication of deficient spirituality. Georges and Baker suggest that Christians should feel broken and *unworthy* before God, *ashamed* of sin (because our involvement in it was dishonouring God) and *humble* towards others.[52] Humility towards others is another way Christians should think lowly of themselves. Jesus calls his followers to be

---

50. This element was discussed in chapter 7, section 7.2.4.
51. Shirin, interview with author, Jan. 2017.
52. Georges and Baker, *Ministering in Honor-Shame Cultures*.

servants of all (Luke 14:7–11). This heart of service grows out of humility. In comparing between shame and humility, they state:

> Humility is the righteous counterpart to shame. Humility flows from a heart filled with divine honour, whereas shame is the absence of any honour. In one sense humility involves purposely taking on unearned shame for a righteous purpose or willingly setting aside one's honour for a greater good, such as Jesus did in his incarnation, life and crucifixion. Shame, on the other hand, perverts humility, as it hardly leads to serving others.[53]

Differentiation between honour and pride can further align our hearts with God's values. Pride is a feeling of delight derived from one's own achievements and is self-declared. Honour is recognition from others and is granted. The world equates shame with humility and honour with pride, however, in the kingdom of God pride produces shame and humility leads to honour.[54]

9.5 Summary Analysis of the Four Approaches in Light of Volf's Model (Table)

In the second half of the thesis (chapters 6 to 9), I theologically evaluated the four conflict management approaches (Hierarchical, *sulha*, Alternative-legalistic and Western-Baptist) used by Palestinian Baptists during their church conflicts in terms of Volf's reconciliation theology (Remembrance, forgiveness, justice and embrace). I also critically evaluated the applicability of Volf's theological model within a Palestinian Baptist context, I did cultural translation to his theory and proposed a *culturally-sensitive* model of reconciliation in chapter 10.

The following table summarizes the results of the analysis of the four approaches in light of Volf's model.

---

53. Georges and Baker, 125.
54. Georges and Baker.

Table 9.1: The results of the analysis of the four approaches in light of Volf's model

Approach	Remembrance	Forgiveness	Justice	Embrace	Outcome
Hierarchical	Didn't remember rightly. Struggled to remember • Truthfully • Therapeutically • Responsibly • In reconciling ways	Conditioned by repentance	Restoration of honour publicly	Conditioned by public repentance	"Diplomatic reconciliation" (divorce)
Sulha	Partly remembered rightly. Struggled to remember • Therapeutically • Responsibly	External, decisional, public	Re-establishment of social order	Embrace lacks differentiation	"Diplomatic reconciliation" (joint service)
Alternative-legalistic	Partly remembered rightly. Struggled to remember • Therapeutically • Responsibly	External, private apology	Rights	Embrace lacks differentiation	"Diplomatic reconciliation" (joint service)
Western-Baptist (before reintegration)	Partly remembered rightly. Struggled to remember • Therapeutically • In reconciling ways	Internal, public/private apology	Rights and restoration of relationships	Embrace lacks differentiation	Reintegration
Western-Baptist (after reintegration)	Remembered rightly. Struggled to remember • Therapeutically	Divine, internal, collective-public	Right order at church/good witness	Embrace	Reconciliation

CHAPTER 10

Recommendations and Conclusion

10.1 Findings and Recommendations

This research has investigated the environment, nature, causes and management of the Palestinian Baptist intra-church conflict in Israel between 1990 and 2016 and evaluated Miroslav Volf's theology of reconciliation in light of it. My basic argument was that the clash between the pastors and laity, which led to the church splits, was in fact a clash between each side's strong combination of its *theology and culture* working against the other side. This same clash was seen in the conflict management practices and contributed to the failure to bring any effective conflict resolution. Palestinian Baptists have also been experiencing a shift from traditional-patriarchal to modern culture, a shift in the position and influence of women and a shift in their theology of reconciliation from "diplomatic reconciliation" (a form of pacification that seeks social order and status quo) to reconciliation. I also argued that Volf's theory needs cultural translation in order to be applicable in this context.

It is noteworthy that my goal in this research was not to judge the attitudes of the pastors or the laity as right or wrong but to draw out some practical conclusions and recommendation as follows.

My analysis of the field mapping shows that the departure of the missionaries in the early 1990s, along with other generational, cultural, social, theological, structural and economic factors, led to divisions among Palestinian Baptist churches in Israel. The splits within Palestinian Baptist churches in Israel are caused by the various unique characteristics that define these churches and can be summarized in the following points:

1) Members of the church are a threefold minority with an identity crisis, who experience life as second-class citizens living within a legally uncertain environment that mirrors the insecurity they feel in their church life.
2) Despite the community being patriarchal, the church structure is flat and lacks a patriarch figure.
3) The churches do not constitute an organic community; instead, there are a variety of very small churches, each consisting of different and distinct generations.
4) There is a low level of institutionalization in these churches.
5) The high view of ordination held by pastors is constantly threatened by young laity, causing a struggle for the pastors over livelihood and power.
6) It is unusual for churches to have their own buildings due to the lack of economic capital.
7) There has been an influx of highly educated young leaders who are committed to individual rights and individualistic-oriented competitiveness, and who hold an attitude of "rebellion" against traditional, patriarchal leadership, while still holding on to some aspects of their patriarchal culture.
8) Most importantly, there is no clear Christian model on how to deal with church conflict.

My analysis of the nature and causes of intra-church conflict in three cases of church split indicates that the *primary* cause is the clash between pastors' strong combination of theology and culture working against the laity's strong combination of theology and culture. Since the pastor's authoritarian manner, derived theologically (they understand their position to be a lifelong sacrament – *hierarchical approach*), is also encouraged in the culture (*patriarchal approach*), their authoritarian stance is entrenched *theologically and culturally*. This "hierarchical-patriarchal" approach combined powerfully to strengthen pastors' desire to keep their position and power at church. On the other hand, the younger generation's "congregationalist-democratic" approach was influenced culturally by secular, Western ideas of individual rights and democracy (*democratic approach*), in which they justified their demands to share power theologically in terms of the "priesthood of all believers" (*congregationalist approach*). Since their claim for power, derived theologically, is also encouraged by their modern cultural components, their claim is also entrenched *theologically and culturally*. The clash between the pastors and laity reflects a deep generational clash between older and younger generations' worldviews, which encompass theology, cultural values and social relations.

Secondary causes for church splits are church buildings, women's informal power and economic factors. The symbolic meaning of a church building (power and its theological commitments) and its location grant the pastors honour and respect in the broader community. The informal power of women extended throughout the conflict in the three cases. The economic factors also influenced the way conflict was handled.

I also found that these same main factors of *theology and culture* contributed to the ways the conflicts were dealt with from the perspective of the pastor and the perspective of the laity. Again, because of the clash of those factors from each side, the conflicts were not resolved effectively. In managing church conflict, Palestinian Baptists engage in four different practices, all operating in the field, each with a distinct perception, tradition and approach to conflict resolution. My research identified and explored two *cultural* approaches: (1) the traditional Palestinian *sulha* approach and (2) the alternative-legalistic approach; and two *theological* approaches: (1) the hierarchical, traditional Palestinian church approach and (2) the Western-Baptist approach. The pastors' cultural-theological approach is a combination of *sulha* and hierarchical, traditional church ("patriarchal-hierarchical"). The laity's cultural-theological approach is a combination of alternative-legalistic and Western-Baptist approaches ("democratic-congregationalist"). These conflict management practices are complex and dynamic, involving an internal dialogue between the traditional practices (*sulha* and traditional churches) and innovative practices (alternative-legalistic and Western Baptist theology). In the case studies, a shift can be seen from the first generation, desiring to maintain status quo and power, to the younger generation, seeking change and power.

The research revealed that pastors and laity held different implicit theologies of reconciliation, which were all imperfect. *Sulha* lacks internal forgiveness and justice, which kept the conflict unresolved. The alternative-legalistic approach prioritizes justice over relationships, which led to splits. In the hierarchical model, the pastor is the one who implements justice and offers forgiveness, and the laity has to obey, which led unsatisfied laity to leave church. Western Baptist theology is more individualistic and lacks some aspects of Palestinian culture, such as family and emotions. This called for a more comprehensive theology of reconciliation, such as Volf's theory. Volf's reconciliation theology was developed in the Balkan context; it is culturally American-Croatian and theologically an evangelical perspective.

In the theological discussion, I showed that the combination of *theology and culture* was fundamental to providing the solution. I theologically evaluated the four conflict management approaches used by Palestinian Baptists in terms of Volf's four themes (remembrance, forgiveness, justice and embrace). I found that Palestinian Baptists in Israel are in the process of conceptualizing and integrating new meanings into their theology of reconciliation. They are also experiencing a shift from "diplomatic reconciliation" to the beginning of reconciliation taking the form of reintegrating churches that split.

I found that Palestinian Baptists in the case studies developed what I called a "diplomatic reconciliation"; an ethical response which echoed some of the major concerns of Palestinian Baptists – notably, living in a relational, closely intertwined community in an unforgiving environment within the framework of congregationalist churches in a patriarchal, hierarchical tradition. By walking a fine line between conflicting demands and possibilities, this "diplomatic reconciliation" allowed them to cooperate and live together in some kind of social order but lacked genuine internal and interpersonal forgiveness. Ceasefire, shaking hands, joint church services and cooperation based on mutual gain were external expressions of their *forgiveness* that was conditional, external and incomplete. They partly *remembered* rightly and struggled to forget the wrongdoings, and thus they struggled in remembering therapeutically and responsibly. They had different understandings of *justice*, and struggled in the tension between seeking justice and offering forgiveness, which left conflicts unresolved. Their *embrace* was conditional and lacked "differentiation" (a process by which the self and the other negotiate their identities).

Between case A (in 1995) and case C (in 2016), Palestinian Baptists experienced a shift in their theology of reconciliation, in terms of Volf's four themes, as follows:

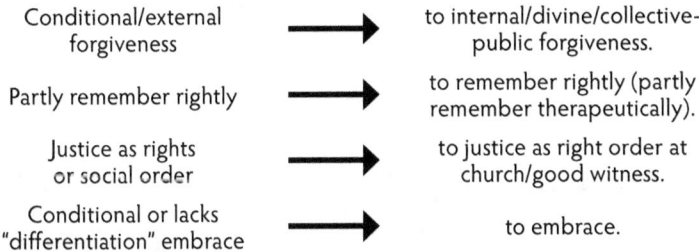

I also examined the relevance of Volf's theological themes within the Palestinian Baptist context and found that Volf's *theological* model is indeed pertinent to Palestinian Baptists. Yet, in order to be applicable to this context, it requires *cultural* translation. I found that there are some principles from *sulha* which can be embraced to modify Volf's model: (a) community, (b) formality, (c) venting, (d) dignity restoration, (e) nonlinear structure of the reconciliation process, (f) the focus on achieving reconciliation rather than focusing on whether forgiveness should be perceived as conditional or unconditional and (g) to view justice in terms of restoration of broken relationships, not only in terms of its socio-political understanding (rights). Needless to say that each one of these principles should be adjusted to fit the specific conflict.

1. Community

Although, for Volf, the community is important to make the practice of forgiveness meaningful, it is not an essential participant in achieving reconciliation as in *sulha*. The findings showed that we need a more collective and public reconciliation involving a whole church community. I suggested combining Volf's triangle (a theological model), in which forgiveness and reconciliation take place between God, offender and offended, with the *sulha* triangle (a cultural model) of the offender's family, the offended's family and the community. The outcome was a rhombus. Thus, I proposed that *effective* forgiveness and reconciliation, theologically and culturally relevant to Palestinian Christians, would now take place not in a triangle but in a rhombus as demonstrated in the following graph:

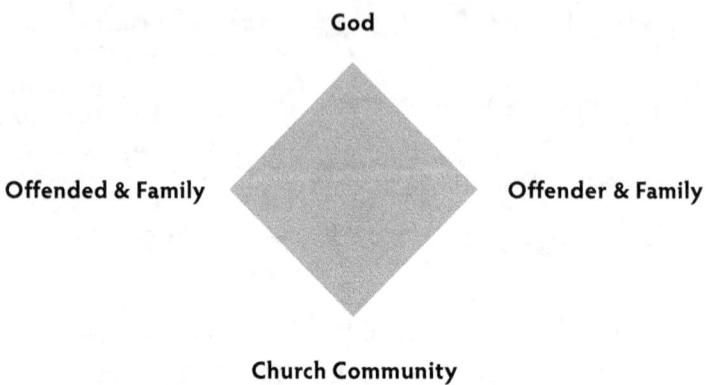

Figure 10.1: Proposed rhombus model

I found several advantages to adding the community as a fundamental participant in the process of reconciliation. The community helps to remove the obstacles and builds the bridge toward reconciliation by the following actions:

First, *bearing the burden of the wrongs done together*. When the community takes an active role in the forgiveness and reconciliation process, the psychological, emotional, and communal burden of the conflict will shift from the parties to the community, who has the ability to act as "anger absorber." The community can offer support to its members, both offended and offender, through bearing the burden of the wrongs done together in the process of redeeming the past wrongdoings, remembering rightly, forgiving, repairing and restoring broken relationships.

Second, *using forgiveness and inclusive languages*. The power of language (tongue) to destroy and heal is explained clearly in the bible.[1] Given the influence leaders have on the community members. The language of forgiveness that community leaders use is necessarily on behalf of and for the sake of the community. Additionally, the use of inclusive language such as "we" may help forgiveness interpersonally and in the collective as community members encourage one another to forgive and remember rightly.

Third, *seeking and sustaining justice*. The community can put pressure on the offender to encourage him/her to repent and repair the damage. James in his letter stresses the importance of being truthful with one another in

---

1. James 3:1–12.

order to name sin.[2] He invokes mutual accountability and support where members are required to speak truthfully with the erring person, for the sake of both the community and the erring person, which will be effective if there is a high level of trust, mercy,[3] and community practices. In addition, the community can be the best guardian to sustain justice and ensure the durability of the agreement post-conflict, as well as becoming the witness in which reconciliation takes place.

Fourth, *restoring and embracing*. The community has the potential for a powerful restorative influence in the life of its members, especially in healing the shame of both offender and offended by welcoming them back and restoring what was lost, in helping them to move from the painful past to a hopeful future, and to overcome present and future challenges. For example, community sensitization or awareness raising should be worked through community leaders who can influence community members in order to put a stop to a specific attitude or behavior towards offenders or offended.

2. Formality

When the community becomes active in the reconciliation process, the process becomes more formal and public. In this way forgiveness and reconciliation will be seen, heard and "binding." Formality (rituals) is another fundamental element of reconciliation in *sulha*, which is missing in Volf's theory. While forgiveness may begin as an intrapersonal initiative (Volf's theory), it may also be worked out interpersonally in the collective, as it is expressed by the community in rituals, religious practices and other public activities as seen in the *sulha* ceremony. As I elaborate below, churches could rely on internal and external resources or practices, both of which can lead the parties to realize forgiveness.

Ceremonial-covenant meal: A ceremonial-covenant meal of reconciliation is an ancient tradition could be seen in many covenantal ceremonies in scripture. Some examples are the covenant meal of reconciliation between Jacob and his father-in-law Laban;[4] the ceremonial meal the father prepared

---

2. James 5:19–20.
3. James 2:13.
4. Genesis 31:52–54.

for the Prodigal Son;[5] Jesus's invitation: "Behold, I stand at the door and knock. If anyone hears My voice and opens the door, I will come in to him and eat with him, and he with me."[6] In the Lord's Supper, Jesus chooses the fellowship meal of the Passover to celebrate God's redemption of his people. In addition, for thousands of years Eastern cultures throughout Asia, Africa and the Middle East, perceived sharing a meal together as a sign of genuine fellowship and a symbol of peace.

I suggested framing reconciliation and the declaration of forgiveness through ritualized, formal, public action, culminating with the Lord's Supper followed by a ceremonial common meal. As mentioned, the Aramaic word for forgiveness has the root "table"; Christ transformed the sharing of a meal (table) into a metaphor for realized forgiveness.[7] This is also an actual symbol of forgiveness and reconciliation in Palestinian culture (*sulha* ceremonial meal). Both internal and external resources and expressions can lead the disputants to realize forgiveness, even though it may be imperfect. Formality and rituals create the space for restoring dignity lost as a result of the offence. This would transform forgiveness and reconciliation from a private affair to a public, formal and binding one, involving the church community and multiple witnesses.

Church practices: the spiritual or eternal aspects of a community may be expressed in rituals, symbols, songs and music. These represent shared values such as love, compassion, and integrity. Volf's theory does not suggest concrete practical actions for how past sorrow is to be forgiven and remembered in a redeemed way. Church practices could be seen as ritualized formal public action for promoting forgiveness and remembering the past sorrow in a redeemed way. I suggested that repeated church practices such as communion, foot washing, singing, praying, and studying Scriptures are helpful for several reasons. First, it gains the community's involvement. Second, it provides a space for interaction that can encourage the move beyond offence so bilateral forgiveness and reconciliation can take place. Third, the participation in church practices also enables church members to partly experience redemption of past sorrow/wrongdoing as these practices contribute to the

---

5. Luke 15:11-31
6. Rev 3:20
7. Augsburger, *Helping People Forgive*.

transformation and reshaping of the offended's memories, as they happen repeatedly and continually. Studying Scripture allows the word of God to work in their minds and hearts in reshaping their memory. In communion, they remember the promise of redemption as an eschatological reality and the recognition of partial redemption now. Singing together unites; there is a responsibility to perform and to listen which open us to God, to one another and to ourselves.[8] Finally, these activities are significant to sustain Christian forgiveness since they focus on God's love as we repeatedly remember that we are *forgiven* and *forgivers* each time we confess, sing, pray, read scripture and eat together.

3. Venting

Volf's theory does not offer practical suggestions as to how resentment shifts to compassion towards the offender in the forgiveness process. I suggested adding venting to Volf's theory, as in *sulha*. First, venting names and condemns the wrongs. Second, it allows the expression of negative feelings, such as hatred, resentment and pain, in order to transform them into tolerance and compassion. Third, venting is an essential factor in redeeming past sorrow. It provides the place where anger will be publicly expressed, which will enable the reversal of dignity violation through a public acknowledgement of the moral standing of the offended, a form of symbolically restoring the offended back to the status from which the offence has humiliated and shamed them in the eyes of the community. This, then, makes the future possible, as the offended is freed from fear and from being shaped by the wrongdoing suffered and humiliation. These elements are essential in achieving forgiveness. It is important that this process is overseen by a third-party who can act as "anger absorber" and guide the process toward reconciliation. Since to forgo revenge and resentment does not necessarily remove shame, it is also important to add another element, namely dignity restoration.

4. Dignity restoration

Dignity restoration is another public expression of reconciliation that I suggested should be added to Volf's theory. Dignity is important to every human being and any threat provokes a strong reaction. When a relationship has

---

8. Jones, "Crafting Communities of Forgiveness."

been broken, affirmation of dignity in the other is essential for releasing the pain, especially when conflict was caused by dignity violations.[9] In *sulha*, dignity restoration acts as a tool to gradually achieve forgiveness. The process of *musayara* refers to the practice whereby the community (*jaha*) treats the victim's family, from the beginning to the end of the *sulha* process, with the great respect normally given to high status persons.

The *jaha* temporarily places the family in a position of "patronage" over the most respected men in the community (*jaha*). This process is vital in helping to further calm the feelings of humiliation, in contributing to the restoration of dignity and in *healing shame* by embracing the offended back into right relationship and community and finally transforming revenge to forgiveness.

5. Nonlinear structure

For Volf, reconciliation takes place in a linear structure, in the trajectory of a cycle: remember rightly, forgive, reconcile and then let go of the memory of the offence. Reconciliation in the Palestinian context does not necessarily have a linear nature; sometimes "diplomatic reconciliation" occurs before or without genuine forgiveness and remembering rightly. The community has the power to "force embrace" despite a lack of forgiveness and remembering rightly, which might, in some cases (as in case C), encourage the move to forgiveness and genuine reconciliation, but, in other cases (as in case A), forgiveness might stay external with "diplomatic reconciliation."

6. Conditional/unconditional forgiveness

Volf and Tutu in the Balkan and South African contexts, respectively, advocate unconditional forgiveness. Biggar, in a Northern Ireland context among others, advocates conditional forgiveness. Palestinian theology is also diverse. Nonetheless, given their unforgiving environment politically, socio-culturally and religiously, practising unconditional forgiveness might be challenging for Palestinian Baptists. Since conditional and unconditional forgiveness have much in common and differ in the way reconciliation is realized, I suggest following Nelson in that it might be more beneficial to focus on achieving reconciliation rather than focusing on whether forgiveness is conditional or unconditional.

---

9. Hicks 2011.

7. Justice as Restoration of Broken Relationships

I agree with Marshall that divine justice should be seen as compatible with divine love, rather than seeing justice as of primary importance, like DeGruchy and Ateek, or seeing it as subordinate to love, like Volf, El-Assal, Younan, Massad and Tutu. Divine justice and grace should not be treated as separate elements, with one being focussed on at the expense of the other, and thus should not be separated during conflict. Those who bear God's image must also be agents of justice, since justice is a divine attribute. Therefore, I suggest that Palestinian Baptists view justice not only in terms of its socio-political understanding (rights) but also as compatible with their own cultural model of *sulha*, in its biblical perspective in terms of restoration of broken relationships.

Additionally, at a practical level, several issues in Volf's theory are not clear. First, it is not clear how we can evaluate the truthfulness of one's narrative regarding the conflict in which this "truth" is influenced by religious beliefs, culture and emotions. This is important, especially, if the narrator was engaged in a past trauma that became an integral part of their identity. Second, although the "will to embrace" is decisional, there are no practical indications of a process that may lead one to make the choice of the "will to embrace." In addition, how do we name the wrongs committed, in the act of "opening arms" for the wrongdoer to come? Third, in which way are offenders called to justice within the framework of the "will to embrace"? Fourth, after achieving justice, how can it be sustained? Finally, repairing damage and restitution may take care of guilt, but what is the kind of justice that deals with shame?

Since there were no splits before the departure of the missionaries, does this mean that some entity should replace them to prevent and manage conflicts? What does this say about the role of the missionaries? Were they external peacekeepers, with authority from another culture, who were treated with respect as founders and outsiders? Who might take on this role now? Does this mean a stronger ABC is required? Or is there an inherent weakness in Baptist congregationalist polity which leads to church splits in general? If so, should Baptist congregationalist polity and its underpinning theology be questioned and revised according to context? Implicit in these questions is the question of the use and balance of power.

10.2 Contribution to Existing Body of Knowledge

This empirical study was conducted in the midst of ongoing conflict; the findings of such research are useful for conflict prevention and resolution and will add knowledge about the nature and sources of conflict in conflict zones in general and in the ongoing Israeli-Palestinian conflict in particular.[10]

This study is an original contribution to academic study on four levels:

1) On the *concrete level*, this study is the first not only to analyse conflict among Palestinian Baptist in Israel, but also, as far as I can discern, it is the first to critically evaluate their implied theologies and make a constructive theological proposal in the Palestinian context, which is contextually and biblically appropriate. I hope my research will contribute to the process of contextualization and institutionalization that Palestinian Baptists are experiencing in the last two decades.

2) On a broader *regional level*, this study provides a Palestinian Christian perspective on the professional discipline now being developed in Israel. The need for such an approach is increasing as the Israeli-Palestinian turmoil continues and tensions increase in the Middle East.

3) Concerning the *religious level*, the recent decline of Arab nationalism and the rise of Islamic fundamentalism have emphasized religious identity in the Middle East. The need for addressing conflict within religious communities from a religious perspective is escalating.

4) On a broader *theological level*, my research contributes to the theological discussion of a theology of reconciliation by *presenting a Palestinian perspective* to the body of knowledge in this field. I have examined the Palestinian theology of reconciliation in three cases, evaluated the applicability of Volf's theory in the Palestinian context and presented a proposal to adjust Volf's theory as stated in section 10.1.

---

10. There is currently growing interest in developing academic and professional expertise in the field of conflict resolution, and research projects have become common in institutions located in conflict zones.

It is my hope that this research will assist Arab churches in developing a greater *cultural* and *theological* awareness in order to resolve their conflicts in a more profound and lasting manner.

10.3 Limitation and Scope for Further Research

There is no doubt that there are some issues that I have not tackled adequately, where further research will be required. It follows that research of this sort, which focuses only on three case studies, calls for further research to expand on my own work. Further, given that the research is limited to a single country, I will be interested to follow subsequent research in other countries and regions and what that might reveal. Nonetheless, my work represents a significant contribution upon which other scholars may build upon as they look at different contexts and types of conflict.

The study investigates the phenomenon of church splits between 1990 and 2016. This phenomenon is *dynamic*, since Palestinian Baptists constitute a new denomination in Israel and are working on the issue of institutionalizing conflict management practices and conceptualizing a theology of reconciliation.

With regard to a theology of reconciliation, it was neither my intention to survey all contributions to this field nor explore its biblical and historical roots. Rather, I focused on Volf's theology of reconciliation as the theoretical model to be used to both evaluate the case studies and be evaluated by them. This choice also implies that the analysis has been undertaken from a Protestant perspective only. Further research could address church conflict in local Palestinian traditional churches.

APPENDIX 1

Arab Palestinian Baptists in Israel: A Threefold Minority

PALESTINIAN BAPTISTS IN ISRAEL

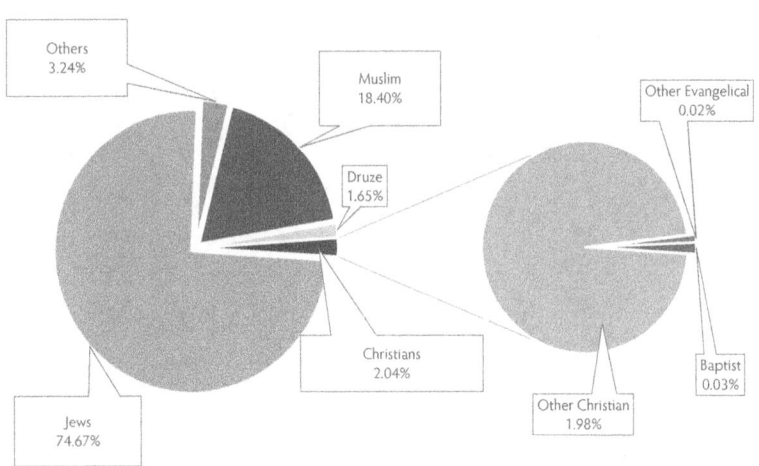

APPENDIX 2

Parachurch Members in the Convention of Evangelical Churches in Israel (CECI) Established between 1985-2015

1. Nazareth Evangelical College (NEC)
2. House of Light
3. LINGA – Christian Services – Light in the Galilee
4. Light for All Nations
5. Life Agape – Cru
6. Grace Ministry – Christian Holy Land Foundation (CHLF)
7. The Harvest
8. Back to Jerusalem
9. House of Prayer and Exploits (HOPE)

APPENDIX 3

List of Interviewees (In-depth Interviews)

Names have been changed to protect identities.

	ID	Date
Pastor	Pastor A	Apr 2014
Pastor	Samir	Apr 2014
Pastor	Mark	Aug 2014
Pastor	Majd	Mar 2014
Pastor	Amir	Apr 2014
Pastor	Nizar	June 2014
Pastor	Adam	Apr 2014
Pastor	George	Mar 2014
Pastor	Jonathan	Apr 2014
Pastor	Victor	Dec 2014
Member	Suhad	Apr 2014
Member	Nora	Mar 2014
Member	Rima	Mar 2014
Member	Emily	Mar 2014
Member	Mary	Apr 2014
Member	Amal	Mar 2014
Member	Hiyam	Mar 2014
Member	Sally	Mar 2014
Member	Mira	Apr 2014

	ID	Date
Deacon	Jack	Apr 2014
Deacon	Ramiz	Mar 2014
Deacon	Dan	Mar 2014
Deacon	Tamer	Mar 2014
Leader	Waleed	June 2014
Leader	Nabil	Mar 2014
Leader	Sami	Feb 2014 Aug 2015
Leader	Yosef	April 2014
Leader	Bilal	Nov 2014
Missionary	Ron	June 2014 July 2014
Missionary	Marcus	Aug 2014
Missionary	Paul	Aug 2014
Pastor	Chris	Sep 2014
Leader	William	July 2014
Pastor	Greg	Apr 2014
Leader	Jol	Mar 2015
Pastor	Pastor B	Aug 2015
Member	Ward	Aug 2015
Member	Lina	Aug 2015
Member	Rana	Aug 2015
Member	Anita	Aug 2015
Leader	Yasmin	22 Sep 2016
Leader	Nadia	Aug 2015
Pastor	Robert	Open interview 2013
Leader	Elias	Aug 2015
Leader	Michel	Aug 2015
Leader	Albert	Aug 2015 May 2016 Oct 2016

List of Interviewees

	ID	Date
Leader	Bishara	Aug 2015
Pastor	Pastor C	July 2015
Member	Susan	July 2015
Pastor	Boulus	Aug 2015
Leader	Shirin	Aug 2015
		Dec 2015
		7 Jul 2016
		Aug 2016
		Sep 2016
		12 Jan 2017
Third party	David	4 May 2015
		10 May 2015
		26 May 2015
		3 Aug 2015
Third party	Bryan	Mar 2013
Third party	Rami	Open interviews
		16 Mar 2014
		18 Mar 2014
		26 Mar 2014
Third party	George	Aug 2015
Third party	Peter	May 2014
Third party	Phil	July 2104
Third party	John	Apr 2014
Third party	Jack	August 2014
Third party	Dave	June 2016
Third party	Paul	Aug 2014

APPENDIX 4

Excerpts from the Constitution of the Association of Baptist Churches in Israel (ABC)[1]

6.6. Pastors and Elders

The Church Meeting shall appoint an Eldership (of males only) consisting of at least one person to be the Pastor, who shall thereby be the teaching elder and president of the Church. The Elders shall be mature believers in character, spirituality and biblical understanding, gifted to lead the Church and to explain the Christian faith either in private or public. They shall be responsible under God to the Church Meeting, to govern the Church's spiritual and practical life, to ensure that biblical standards are met in the Church's life and fellowship, to give pastoral care to the congregation, and to maintain the spiritual vision of the Church. In matters for which they have the authority of Scripture or the authority of the Church, Elders are to be given willing submission. Such matters will mainly concern acceptance of the Church's agreed doctrinal basis, or its rules and policies, or the moral standards required by Scripture. They shall not include matters of private judgment, in which a believer must make his or her own conscientious decision before God unless he or she freely agrees to limit that freedom, such as in a commitment to keep church rules.

---

1. 2007, used by permission.

6.7. Deacons

The Church Meeting shall appoint a Diaconate (open to all) to assist the Eldership as the need arises or as the Church Meeting decides in agreement with the Eldership.

6.8. Officers

The Church Meeting shall appoint a Church Secretary to head the church's administration, a Church Treasurer to head the Church's finance. They shall, for the time they hold office, become either a Deacon or an Elder as the Church Meeting may decide. The Church Meeting may appoint other Officers to do such work on such conditions as it may deem appropriate.

6.9 The Church Council

The Elders, Deacons and such other officers as the Church Meeting may decide, shall form a Church Council, which shall be responsible to the Church Meeting for the general conduct of Church business between Church Meetings, and shall refer appropriate business to it as set out above in Section 6.4. for its approval or otherwise.

6.10

The Church shall maintain involvement in local and world mission, through prayer, giving and action according to its ability, so that the Church possesses a larger vision than its own existence and ministry.

7. Membership of ABC

The ABC seeks to be a spiritual fellowship united in Christ and expressing spiritual attitudes, values and goals. What follows is necessarily legalistic as a careful statement of essentials, but the spiritual nature of fellowship and co-operation remains the ultimate desire of the ABC.

9. The Ministry Committee

9.1. The Ministry Committee, elected by the Annual General Assembly, shall consist of three recognized Pastors of the ABC, and four others in membership of an ABC Church, one of whom shall be the wife of a recognized Pastor of the ABC. Service shall be for three years, after which members may be re-elected once and be ineligible for further re-election for one year.

9.1.1. The Ministry Committee shall be responsible to deal with all matters pertaining to the recognition of Pastors and the exercise of their ministry within the ABC, in accordance with the provisions of the Ministerial Scheme (hereafter stated in the bylaws).

9.2. The Ministry Committee shall be responsible, and are hereby entitled, to intervene in any disputes within member Churches, between member Churches or between member Churches and their Pastors that are not previously resolved to the satisfaction of the Ministry Committee, as set out in the Ministerial Policy of the ABC.

9.3. The Ministry Committee shall advise the Executive Committee annually as to a *minimum recommended stipend* for full-time ministry in a local Church. The stipend shall be equivalent to a middle-range graduate teacher's stipend and shall include similar benefits such as in-service training and pension allowance. It shall be understood that this is a *minimum*, not a maximum, amount; and that part-time employment should be paid pro rata. The Executive Committee shall consider this and make its recommendation to the Council, who shall decide the annual amount.

Bylaw Two: Ministerial Scheme (a recommendation to the ABC churches)

1. The Nature of the Office of Minister or Pastor
1.1. Definition
Baptist Churches recognize two internal offices in the leadership and government of the local Church: Elders who direct the affairs of the local Church and provide its spiritual leadership (Gk: *presbuteros* or *episkopos*, having substantially the same meaning); and Deacons (Gk: *Diakonos* and *diakona*), who are assistants to the Elders in their work.

A Pastor holds

1.1.1 the office of Elder in the local Church (restricted to males only), which may be one of several;

1.1.2. the office within the Eldership of teaching Elder, that is, someone gifted to expound the Word of God to the Church and to the world;

1.1.3. the office within the Eldership of presiding Elder over the congregation and officers of the Church, the shepherd (hence Pastor) of the flock;

1.1.4. the office of representing his local Church to the wider Christian Church, especially fellow Baptists.

1.2. Authority

The authority of a Baptist Pastor is derived from his calling from God, recognized in his formal appointment by a local Church, which thereby authorizes him to fulfil his calling among them. Within this calling, a Pastor has the following authority to which the Church that has called him must give willing submission:

1.2.1 To have the right, or to delegate that right to a fellow Church member of his choice, to preside over his congregation, or any group within the congregation, whenever it meets, or to invite a visiting preacher to minister to the congregation.

1.2.2 To command obedience within the Church to the Word of God in all matters of faith and practice, on pain of God's displeasure and, if biblically necessary of Church discipline. In extreme cases disciplinary action may be taken before the formal proceedings (for example, to preclude someone from the Lord's Table), but such decisions shall be subject to confirmation by the disciplinary procedure established in the Church.

1.2.3. To exhort, rebuke, correct and encourage those under his Pastoral care so that he fulfils his calling to be a servant of Jesus Christ, a servant of the gospel, and a servant of the Church.

1.2.4. To approve the nomination of fellow officers (whether Elders, Deacons or other forms of leadership) of the Church before they are put to the vote of the Church Meeting.

1.2.5. To advise his Church on any matter before it is put to a vote in any meeting within the Church over which he presides by right.

1.2.6. To be acknowledged and honoured in all the Churches of the ABC as a recognized Pastor, but not to be given the function of Pastor or Elder in any congregation except by a proper Church decision, such as an invitation to give ministry, or some temporary advice, or a regular election to some office in the Church.

1.2.7. To claim recognition as a true minister of the Christian religion from the wider Christian community, other faith traditions and society at large.

1.2.8. A Pastor cannot exercise absolute authority over areas properly to be controlled by the Church Meeting or its other elected officers, such as Elders and Deacons and Church councils. Such areas include: the inclusion or exclusion of members, exclusive control of the Church's finances, requiring obedience of members in matters of private judgement. A Pastor may, however, act in accordance with a Church decision or policy previously recorded as agreed by the Church council or Church Meeting.

1.3. Responsibilities

1.3.1. To exercise leadership and to maintain vision and direction within the Church, including chairing meetings of the Church, and its various organizations (unless agreeing to a representative of his choice).

1.3.2. To ensure the Pastoral care of each Church member, including personal Pastoral ministry as far as is practicable.

1.3.3. To equip and release members of the Church to discover and use their personal spiritual gifting for the good of the Church.

1.3.4. To teach and preach at the Church's services, or to ensure a representative of his choice does so.

1.3.5. To ensure that his ministry is enhanced by further study and spiritual development.

1.3.6. To represent the Church to the wider Christian Church and the community, including attendance at ABC and other inter Church Meetings.

2. Qualifications

2.1. Gifting

A Pastor requires spiritual and natural gifts in three essential areas before holding a formal position: to be an effective and respected leader, to be a thoughtful and able communicator and preacher of God's Word, and to be a loving and wise Councillor to his people.

2.2. Calling

A person considering the Pastoral office must have a sense of God's calling in his heart, the substantial agreement to this of his wife if married, and thereafter must obtain the formal written agreement of his Pastor and any other Church Elders, and a vote of approval by secret ballot in his local Church's membership meeting.

2.3. Character

A person considering the Pastoral office must be stable in his emotional life and have a developed character in which the fruit of the Spirit is manifestly present: love, joy, peace, patience, kindness, goodness, faithfulness, gentleness and self-control. He must have, in addition, a humble spirit and servant heart like that of his Master, who came not to be served but to serve. Like Moses, he needs a meek spirit but still be someone who is looked to as a leader. No Pastor is perfect, however, and an essential quality of character is his openness to a lifetime of personal and spiritual growth as a man of God.

2.4. Training

Gifts and calling are not sufficient in themselves for the exercise of the Pastoral ministry. Our Lord Jesus Christ gave three years of training to His disciples after He had chosen and called into His circle the apostles. In like manner, Pastors (and all other leaders) need to be improved by sufficient study and training for the work they are called to do. Each Church, when considering a person for Pastoral ministry, is therefore advised to consider seriously and carefully, in consultation with the ABC Ministry Committee, the following areas at least.

    2.4.1. a demonstrable level of informal or formal theological development, including of Baptist History and Principles;

    2.4.2. the work of preaching and teaching;

2.4.3. the work of Pastoral ministry;

2.4.4. personal formation as a spiritual leader.

The ABC Ministry Committee shall consider these areas, and any others it believes appropriate, before giving formal recognition to a Pastor. The Ministry Committee shall require such measures as it deems appropriate for a Pastor to achieve those standards either before or after formal recognition. The Ministry Committee shall invite the Director, or his representative, of the NCCS to interview candidates for ministerial recognition and advise the Committee accordingly on matters of qualifications and training.

2.5. Beliefs

No person should be considered by the local Church for its Pastorate unless he sincerely affirms the doctrinal basis of the local Church, of the ABC, and also the principles and practices of Baptist Church life. Those who cease to do so shall be removed from the ABC list of recognized Pastors, and the local Church is advised to end the Pastorate of such people.

2.6. Ordination

Ordination to the Christian ministry is the act of laying on of hands upon a candidate, by authorized persons of the local and wider church, to recognize in him God's calling, set him apart to the Christian ministry, and to convey to him, his church, the wider Christian Church, and society, the authority and recognition of the churches of the same faith and order of his right and duty to fulfil the work of the Christian ministry.

Ordination should normally take place within the context of an appointment to service either in a local church or a specific wider ministry such as evangelism or chaplaincy, recognized by churches of the same faith and order (in this case, the ABC).

Ordination is an action of the local church, which should not, however, take place without the agreement of the wider fellowship of churches of the same faith and order (in this case, the ABC). Therefore, candidates for ordination must be acceptable to both bodies. Ordination shall be by the laying on of hands by representatives of the local and wider Church, not to convey grace, but to convey authority and recognition.

2.7. ABC recognition

The ABC shall maintain a list of recognized Pastors and lay Pastors, and establish such conditions for recognition as it sees fit. Recognition shall be given on the basis of the preceding sections, together with a reasonable affirmation of the moral and spiritual maturity and integrity of the candidate.

2.8. Probation

The first three years of ministry shall be a probationary period, during which the ordinand must confirm to the local and wider Church his fitness and calling. During this time, the ABC may require further studies both to develop the gifting of the ordinand and to enable him to establish good patterns of study for the future. Probation shall be ended and ordination permanently confirmed by a decision of the Ministry Committee.

2.9. Disqualification

A name shall be removed from the recognized list, and the fact shall immediately be reported to that person's local Church as well as to the next ABC Council, (and, if necessary, to the authorities) if, in the opinion of the Ministry Committee upon fair examination of the facts (including all the relevant procedures set out in this bye-law):

> 2.9.1. A Pastor commits a serious moral offence such that his character as a Christian and his work as a Pastor is seriously undermined. This shall certainly include instances of sexual immorality, criminal behaviour unless upholding the law of God above the laws of men, financial impropriety relating to Church funds, or the habitual verbal, physical or psychological abuse of those under his Pastoral care.
>
> 2.9.2. A Pastor ceases to uphold the doctrines stated in the ABC Basis of Faith.
>
> 2.9.3. A Pastor brings into serious and repeated public disrepute the life and witness of his Church.

2.10. Reinstatement

> 2.10.1. It shall not be guaranteed that a Pastor may gain reinstatement as a recognized Pastor.

2.10.2. The Ministry Committee may, at its discretion, consider a course of action to rehabilitate and reinstate a Pastor who has been disqualified. This may include a set period out of Pastorate or other spiritual service, a course of counselling, a course of study or training to deal with identified areas of need, and acts of reconciliation.

2.11 Lay pastors

2.11.1. A member church may appoint a lay person to fulfil the role of Pastor, but that person shall not identify himself to the local or wider church, or to the community, as an ordained Baptist Pastor.

2.11.2. The lay Pastor of a member church shall, on appointment, apply to the Ministry Committee for recognition by the ABC who shall determine any course of study or training it may deem appropriate for the better performance of his ministry. Failure to fulfil such conditions may result in his recognition being withdrawn and this fact being reported to his church and to the General Assembly.

2.11.3. A lay Pastoral appointment shall not be used to avoid the standards set out in this scheme for the proper training and recognition of the ordained ministry, or to avoid proper support by a church for a Pastor. If, in the considered opinion of the Ministry Committee, this becomes the case, recognition may be withdrawn of the lay Pastor or member church, as the case may be.

2.11.4. The lay Pastor of a member church shall, after two consecutive years' service, refer his ministry to the Ministry Committee for consideration of ordination and such training for that as the Committee may deem appropriate.

3. Conditions of Service for Pastors

3.1. It is the duty of a Church to provide as adequate support as possible for the Pastor in accordance to the full or part-time nature of his appointment. A Church should not ask a Pastor to live on less than the recommended rate established each year by the Ministry Committee and confirmed by the ABC Council.

3.2. There should be a fair exchange of work commitment for stipend between Pastor and Church. A full stipend should be in exchange for a full working week, which shall consist of serving the Church five days a week, including Sunday; with one further day being devoted to relevant private study to better equip the Pastor for his public ministry, and one day completely free of Church duties. Full-time service may be understood as serving the local Church in attending and leading meetings, giving Pastoral care individuals as required, and being the main preacher at services and other teaching events. In addition, every Pastor has a calling to the wider Church and a reasonable amount of time is needed to attend such things as inter-Church events, ABC meetings, preaching for other Churches, etc. Both the Church and the Pastor need to be responsible in their attitude to this, so that the Church is not neglected but the Pastor has time to benefit from outside influences as well as exercise a wider ministry.

3.3. The Ministry Committee shall provide advice to the ABC annually, in accordance with the constitution, as to a minimum recommended stipend for full-time ministry in a local Church, and a list of recommended expenses, equivalent to the stipend, pension, training budget, etc., of a middle-range teaching appointment. Larger or more affluent churches should consider a greater amount than the minimum recommendation.

3.4. A full-time Pastor should receive at least the recommended minimum stipend, the repayment of agreed expenses, (including telephone calls, mileage or public transport on official business, postage, etc) and contributions to a pension scheme. In proportion to the reduction of this package due to the Church's inability, the Church should reduce the nature of the appointment to an appropriate part-time one, so that the Pastor is free to seek other employment or income to meet his needs. Such employment shall be notified to the Church Council as to the hours involved.

3.5. The Pastor shall have the right to be provided by the Church with a suitable room and facilities for an office/study, free of cost to himself; or to receive an amount agreed between the Pastor and the Church, to use a room in his home.

3.6. If the Church provides living accommodation free of charge, the stipend may be reduced by an amount to be agreed between the Pastor and the Church. In the event of a dispute, the matter shall be referred to the Finance Committee of the ABC, whose decision shall be final.

3.6. The duty of support for a Pastor lies with the employing Church, which should call upon its members to give whatever stipend and other financial provision is agreed with the Pastor. Tithing should be encouraged as the norm among the members, who should give sacrificially and in acknowledgement that the Pastor is being sacrificial in return by his acceptance of less affluence than he might achieve in another profession, and by his willingness to serve the Church sacrificially in working long hours. If the Church is unable to provide at least the recommended minimum stipend, it should regard the Pastor as free from scrutiny as to his additional employment or income.

3.7. The ABC acknowledges that churches and Pastors are blessed by receiving gifts for the furtherance of their life and ministry. Pastors and member churches must act with transparent honesty and integrity in the manner in which such gifts are received, recorded and used, both in terms of Christian standards and the requirements of law. The ABC reserves its right and duty to refer churches and individuals to the Ministry Committee when a lack of integrity is discovered.

4. Pastors' Fellowship

4.1. There shall be a Pastors' Fellowship, open to any serving Pastor in the ABC, lay or ordained. This Fellowship shall meet together for the purpose of mutual support and encouragement, prayer and conference once in every two calendar months at least. The Fellowship shall elect a Chairman and Secretary, who shall together administer any necessary business for the Fellowship.

4.2. The Pastors' Fellowship shall have the right to place on the agenda of the Executive Committee, Council, or General Assembly, any one item in each year it deems appropriate for the doctrinal faithfulness, spiritual vitality or effective mission to society of the ABC. The Fellowship chairman or, in his place, another Pastor chosen by the Fellowship, shall have the right to address that agenda item. Unless otherwise provided within this constitution, that spokesman shall not have voting rights. The purpose of this provision is to better ensure that the ABC is open to God's constant calling to be reformed according to God's Word, renewed by His Holy Spirit, and relevant to society in the defence and proclamation of the gospel.

Glossary

amutot: non-profit organizations (Hebrew)

atwa: payment of good faith

edah moqeret: recognized community (Hebrew)

ghofran: forgiveness

hodna: ceasefire

intifada: uprising

jaha: notable elderly third party

millet: the word *millet* comes from the Arabic word *millah* which means "nation"; it refers to the separate court of "personal law" under which a confessional community was allowed to rule itself under its own laws during the Ottoman period

motajadideen: renewed

mumalaha: a ceremonial meal

musafaha: handshake

musamaha: tolerance

musayara: social etiquette and ingratiation

nakba: catastrophe

qawiyyi: strong female

shalom: peace (Hebrew)

shamas: deacon

sharaf: honour

sheikh: elder

sulha: "resolution" or "settlement" or "fixing" generally, in problem solving

taawid: compensation

taffwid: written authorization

wasta: the middle; the verb *yatawassat* means to direct parties towards a middle point or to mediate between them

Bibliography

Abu El-Assal, Riah. *Caught in Between: The Story of an Arab Palestinian Christian Israeli*. London: SPCK, 1999.

Abu-Nimer, Mohammed. "Conflict Resolution Approaches: Western and Middle Eastern Lessons and Possibilities." *American Journal of Economics and Sociology* 55, no. 1 (1996): 35–52.

———. "Conflict Resolution in an Islamic Context: Some Contextual Questions." *Peace and Change* 21, no. 1 (1996): 22–40.

———. "An Islamic Model of Conflict Resolution: Principles and Challenges." In *Crescent and Dove: Peace and Conflict Resolution in Islam*, edited by Qamar-ul Huda, 73–92. United States Institute of Peace Press, 2010.

———. *Nonviolence and Peace Building in Islam: Theory and Practice*. Gainesville: University Press of Florida, 2003.

Abu-Lughod, Lila. "Zones of Theory in the Anthropology of the Arab World." *Annual Review of Anthropology* 18 (1989): 267–306.

Adams, Jay. *From Forgiven to Forgiving*. Amityville: Calvary Press, 1994.

Adams, Marilyn. "Forgiveness: A Christian Model." *Faith and Philosophy* 8, no. 3 (1991): 277–304.

Adler, Patricia A., and Peter Adler. "Observational Techniques." In *Handbook of Qualitative Research*, edited by N. K. Denzin and Y. S. Lincoln, 377–392. Thousand Oaks, CA: Sage, 1994.

Ajaj, Azar, Duane Miller, and Philip Sumpter. *Arab Evangelicals in Israel*. Eugene: Pickwick, 2016.

Armour, Marilyn, and Mark Umbreit. "The Paradox of Forgiveness in Restorative Justice." In *Handbook of Forgiveness*, edited by E. L. Worthington Jr., 491–503. New York: Routledge, 2005.

Ateek, Naim. *Justice and Only Justice: A Palestinian Theology of Liberation*. Maryknoll, NY: Orbis, 1989.

———. *A Palestinian Theology of Liberation: The Bible, Justice, and the Palestine-Israel Conflict*. Maryknoll, NY: Orbis, 2017.

Auerbach, Yehudith. 2005. "Forgiveness and Reconciliation: The Religious Dimension." *Terrorism and Political Violence* 17, no. 3 (2005): 479–81.

Augsburger, David. *Helping People Forgive*. Louisville: Westminster John Knox Press, 1996.

Avnery, Uri. *Israel without Zionism*. New York: Collier, 1971.

Avruch, Kevin. *Culture and Conflict Resolution*. Washington, DC: United States Institute of Peace Press, 1998.

Avruch, Kevin, and Peter Black. 1990. "Ideas of Human Nature in Contemporary Conflict Resolution Theory." *Negotiation Journal* 6, no. 3 (July 1990): 221–228.

Badr, Habib. "The Involvement of the Evangelical Church in the Lebanon and Syria Context." *Middle East Association for Theological Education* 1, no. 6 (2011): 4–13.

Bailey, Betty J., and Martin J. Bailey. *Who Are the Christians in the Middle East?* Cambridge: Eerdmans, 2003.

Baker, Dwight. *Baptist Golden Jubilee: 50 Years in Palestine-Israel Baptist Village*. Israel: Baptist Convention in Israel, 1961.

Baker, William G. *Arabs, Islam, and the Middle East*. Dallas: Brown Books Publishing Group, 2003.

Barakat, Hatim. *The Arab World: Society, Culture and State*. Berkeley: University of California Press, 1993.

Barrett, Jerome, and Joseph Barrett. *A History of Alternative Dispute Resolution: The Story of a Political, Social, and Cultural Movement*. San Francisco: Jossey-Bass, 2004.

Barth, Karl. "Church and Culture." In *Theology and Church: Shorter Writings*, 334–354. New York: Harper & Row, 1962.

Bax, Josephine. *The Good Wine: Spiritual Renewal in the Church of England*. London: Church House Publishing, 1986.

Beasley-Murray, Paul. *Radical Believers: The Baptist Way of Being Church*. Swindon: Baptist Union of Great Britain, 1992.

Becker, Penny Edgell. "Congregational Models and Conflict: A Study of How Institutions Shape Organizational Process." In *Sacred Companies: Organizational Aspects of Religion and Religious Aspects of Organizations*, edited by N. J. Demerath, P. D. Hall, T. Schmitt, and R. Williams, 231–255. New York: Oxford University Press, 1998.

———. *Congregations in Conflict: Cultural Models of Local Religious Life*. Cambridge: Cambridge University Press, 1999.

Becker, Penny Edgell, Stephen J. Ellingson, Richard W. Flory, Wendy Griswold, Fred Kniss, and Timothy Nelson. "Straining at the Tie That Binds: Congregational Conflict in the 1980s." *Review of Religious Research* 34, no. 3 (1993): 193–209.

Behar, Ruth. *The Vulnerable Observer: Anthropology that Breaks Your Heart*. Boston: Beacon Press, 1996.

Bellah, R., R. Madsen, W. Sullivan, A. Swidler, and S. Tipton. *Habits of the Heart: Individualism and Commitment in America*. New York: Life Harper & Row, 1985.

Benziman, Uri, and Atallah Mansour. *Dayare mishneh* [Sub-tenants]. Jerusalem: Keter, 1992.

Bercovitch, J., V. Kremenyuk, and I. Zartman. "Introduction: The Nature of Conflict and Conflict Resolution." In *The Sage Handbook of Conflict Resolution*, edited by J. Bercovitch, V. Kremenyuk, and I. Zartman, 1–13. London: Sage Publications, 2009.

Berry, John. "Psychology of Acculturation: Understanding Individuals Moving between Cultures." In *Applied Cross-Cultural Psychology*, edited by R. W. Brislin, 232–253. Newbury Park, CA: Sage Publications, 1990.

Blalock, Hubert M. *Power and Conflict: Toward a General Theory*. Newbury Park, CA: Sage Publications, 1989.

Biggar, Nigel. "Forgiveness in the Twentieth Century: A Review of the Literature, 1901–2001." In *Forgiveness and Truth*, edited by A. McFadyen and M. Sarot, 181–217. Edinburgh: T&T Clark, 2001.

———. "Forgiving Enemies in Ireland." *Journal of Religious Ethics* 36, no. 4 (2008): 559–79.

Bonner, Ann, and Gerda Tolhurst. "Insider-Outsider Perspectives of Participant Observation." *Nurse Researcher* 9, no. 4 (2002): 7–19.

Bourdieu, Pierre. *The Logic of Practice*. Translated by Richard Nice. Cambridge: Cambridge University Press, 1995.

———. *Outline of a Theory of Practice*. Translated by Richard Nice. Cambridge: Cambridge University Press, 1977.

———. "The Sentiment of Honour in Kabyle Society." In *Honour and Shame*, edited by J. G. Peristiany, 191–241. London: Weidenfeld & Nicolson, 1965.

Bourdieu, Pierre, and Loic J. C. Wacquant. *An Invitation to Reflexive Sociology*. Chicago, IL: University of Chicago Press, 1992.

Brauns, Chris. *Unpacking Forgiveness*. Wheaton: Crossway Books, 2008.

Breen, Lauren J. "The Researcher 'in the Middle': Negotiating the Insider/Outsider Dichotomy." *The Australian Community Psychologist* 19, no. 1 (2007): 163–174.

Brown, Nathan. *The Rule of Law in the Arab World*. Cambridge: Cambridge University Press, 1997.

Brubaker, David. *Promise and Peril: Understanding and Managing Change and Conflict in Congregations*. Herndon, VA: Alban Institute, 2009.

Burton, John, ed. *Conflict: Human Needs Theory*. London: St. Martin's Press, 1990.

———. *Resolving Deep Rooted Conflict: A Handbook*. Lanham, MD: University Press of America, 1987.

———. *Violence Explained: The Sources of Conflict, Violence and Crime and Their Prevention*. Manchester: Manchester University Press, 1997.

Bush, R. A. B., and J. P. Folger. *The Promise of Mediation: Responding to Conflict through Empowerment and Recognition*. San Francisco: Jossey-Bass, 1994.

Caneday, Ardel. *Must Christians Always Forgive? A Biblical Primer and Grammar on the Forgiveness of Sins*. Mount Hermon, CA: Center for Cultural Leadership, 2011.

Cannon, Mae Elise. *Social Justice Handbook: Small Steps for a Better World*. Downers Grove: InterVarsity Press, 2009.

Corneliu, Constantineanu. "Exclusion and Embrace: Reconciliation in the Works of Miroslav Volf." *Kairos: Evangelical Journal of Theology* 7, no. 1 (2013): 35–54.

Cassell, Joan. "Ethical Principles for Conducting Fieldwork." *American Anthropologist* 82 (1980): 28–41.

Chacour, Elias, and David Hazard. *Blood Brothers*. 2nd ed. Grand Rapids: Chosen Books, 2003.

Chacour, Elias, and Mary E. Jensen. *We Belong to the Land: The Story of a Palestinian Israeli Who Lives for Peace and Reconciliation*. Notre Dame: University of Notre Dame, 2001.

Chavez, Christina. 2008. "Conceptualizing from the Inside: Advantages, Complications, and Demands on Insider Positionality." *The Qualitative Report* 13, no. 3 (2008): 474–494. Accessed November 2015. http://www.nova.edu/ssss/QR/QR13-3/chavez.pdf.

Chou, Hui-Tzu. "The Impact of Congregational Characteristics on Conflict-Related Exit." *Sociology of Religion* 69, no. 1 (2008): 93–108.

Clegg, Cecelia. "Between Embrace and Exclusion." In *Explorations in Reconciliation: New Directions in Theology*, edited by David Tombs and Joseph Liechty, 123–36. Aldershot: Ashgate, 2006.

Coe, Shoki. "In Search of Renewal in Theological Education." *Theological Education* 9 (Summer 1973): 233–43.

———. "Theological Education: A Worldwide Perspective." *Theological Education* 11 (Autumn 1974): 5–12.

Collins, Randall. *Conflict Sociology: Toward an Explanatory Science*. New York: Academic Press, 1975.

Coser, Lewis A. *The Functions of Social Conflict*. New York: Free Press, 1956.

Cragg, Kenneth. *The Arab Christian: A History in the Middle East*. Louisville: Westminster John Knox Press, 1991.

DeGruchy, John. "The Struggle for Justice and Ministry of Reconciliation." *Journal of Theology for Southern Africa* 62 (1988): 43–52.

———. *Reconciliation: Restoring Justice*. London: SCM, 2002.

Denzin, N. K., and Y. S. Lincoln, eds. *Collecting and Interpreting Qualitative Materials*. 2nd ed. Thousand Oaks, CA: Sage, 2003.

deSilva, David. *Honor, Patronage, Kinship and Purity*. Downers Grove, IL: InterVarsity Press, 2000.

Dodd, Peter. "Family Honor and the Forces of Change in Arab Society." *International Journal of Middle East Studies* 4, no. 1 (1973): 40–54.

Edwards, Rosalind. "An Education in Interviewing: Placing the Researcher and the Researched." In *Researching Sensitive Topics*, edited by Claire M. Renzetti and Raymond M. Lee, 181–196. London: Sage, 1993.

Emerson, Michael, and Christian Smith. *Divided by Faith: Evangelical Religion and the Problem of Race in America*. Oxford: Oxford University Press, 2000.

Enright, Robert, Suzanne Freedman, and Julio Rique. "The Psychology of Interpersonal Forgiveness." In *Exploring Forgiveness*, edited by R. Enright and J. North, 46–62. Madison: University of Wisconsin Press, 1998.

Farraj, Ziad. "An Analysis of Differences between Certain Open Brethren and Baptist Churches in the CECI Regarding Ordination and Church Leadership." Master's thesis, University of Wales, 2014.

Fiddes, Paul. "Ecclesiology and Ethnography: Two Disciplines, Two Worlds?' In *Perspectives on Ecclesiology and Ethnography*, edited by Peter Ward, 13–35. Grand Rapids: Eerdmans, 2012.

Fisher, Roger, and William Ury. *Getting to Yes: Agreement without Giving In*. Boston: Penguin, 1981.

———. *Getting to Yes: Agreement without Giving In*. Edited by B. Patton. 2nd ed. London: Arrow Business Books, 1997.

Flynn, Leslie. *When the Saints Come Storming In*. Wheaton: Victor, 1992.

Francis, Leslie J., David W. Lankshear, and Susan H. Jones. "The Influence of the Charismatic Movement on Local Church Life: A Comparative Study among Anglican Rural, Urban and Suburban Churches." *Journal of Contemporary Religion* 15, no. 1 (2000): 121–130.

Friedman, Edwin H. *Generation to Generation: Family Process in Church and Synagogue*. New York: Guilford Press, 1985.

Fulkerson, Mary McClintock. "Explorations in Ecclesiology and Ethnography." *Ecclesial Practice* 1, no. 1 (2014): 138–140.

———. *Places of Redemption: Theology for a Worldly Church*. Oxford: Oxford University Press, 2007.

Galtung, Johan. "International Development in Human Perspective." In *Conflict: Human Needs Theory*, edited by J. W. Burton, 301–335. London: Macmillan Press, 1990.

Gatson, Sarah, and Amanda Zweelink. "Ethnography Online: 'Natives' Practicing and Inscribing Community." *Qualitative Research* 4, no. 2 (2004): 179–200.

Gellman, M. and M. Vuinovich. "From Sulha to Salaam: Connecting Local Knowledge with International Negotiations for Lasting Peace in Palestine/Israel." *Conflict Resolution Quarterly* 26, no. 2 (2008): 127–148.

Georges, Jayson, and Mark Baker. *Ministering in Honor-Shame Cultures: Biblical Foundations and Practical Essentials*. Downers Grove: InterVarsity Press, 2016.

Giddens, Anthony. *The Constitution of Society: Outline of the Theory of Structuration*. Cambridge: Polity Press, 1984.

Ginat, Joseph. *Blood Revenge: Outcasting, Mediation, and Family Honour*. Brighton: Sussex Academic Press, 1997.

———. *Women in Muslim Rural Society: Status and Role in Family and Community*. New Brunswick, NJ: Transaction, 1982.

Goins, Stephanie. "The Place of Forgiveness in the Reintegration of Former Child Soldiers in Sierra Leone." PhD thesis, University of Wales, 2008.

Govier, Trudy. *Forgiveness and Revenge*. London: Routledge, 2002.

Greene, Melanie. "On the Inside Looking In: Methodological Insights and Challenges in Conducting Qualitative Insider Research." *The Qualitative Report* 19, no. 29 (2014): 1–13. Accessed November 2015. http://nsuworks.nova.edu/tqr/vol19/iss29/3.

Grillo, T. "The Mediation Alternative: Process Dangers for Women." *Yale Law Review* 100 (1990): 1545–1610.

Gundry-Volf, Judith, and Miroslav Volf. *A Spacious Heart: Essays on Identity and Togetherness*. Harrisburg, PA: Trinity Press International, 1997.

Gunnink, Jerrien. *Preaching for Recovery in a Strife-Torn Church*. Grand Rapids: Zondervan, 1989.

Gunton, Colin. "Towards a Theology of Reconciliation." In *The Theology of Reconciliation*, edited by Colin Gunton, 167–74. London: T&T Clark, 2003.

Halverstadt, Hugh F. *Managing Church Conflict*. Louisville: Westminster/John Knox Press, 1991.

Hamber, Brandon. "Does the Truth Heal? A Psychological Perspective on Political Strategies for Dealing with the Legacy of Political Violence." In *Burying the Past: Making Peace and Doing Justice after Civil Conflict*, edited by N. Biggar, 155–176. 2nd ed. Washington, DC: Georgetown University Press, 2003.

Hausken, Terje C. *Peace Making: The Quiet Power*. West Concord, MN: CPI Publishing, 1992.

Hellawell, David. "Inside-Out: Analysis of the Insider-Outsider Concept as a Heuristic Device to Develop Reflexivity in Students Doing Qualitative Research." *Teaching in Higher Education* 11, no. 4 (2006): 483–494.

Herman, Nancy. "Conflict in the Church: A Social Network Analysis of an Anglican Congregation." *Journal for the Scientific Study of Religion* 23 (1984): 60–74.

Herzog, Hanna. "Both an Arab and a Woman: Gendered, Radicalized Experiences of Female Palestinian Citizens of Israel." *Social Identities* 10, no. 1 (2004): 53–82.

Hewitt-Taylor, Jaqui. "Insider Knowledge: Issues in Insider Research." *Nursing Standard* 16, no. 46 (2002): 33–35.

Hicks, Donna. *Dignity: The Essential Role It Plays in Resolving Conflict.* New Haven: Yale University Press, 2011.

Himes, J. S. *Conflict and Conflict Management.* Athens, GA: University of Georgia Press, 1980.

Hirschman, Albert. *Exit, Voice and Loyalty: Responses to Decline in Firms, Organizations, and States.* Cambridge, MA: Harvard University Press, 1970.

Hofman, J. E., and N. Rouhana. "Young Arabs in Israel: Some Aspects of a Conflicted Social Identity." *The Journal of Social Psychology* 99, no. 1 (1976): 75–86.

Hoge, Dean. *Division in the Protestant House: The Basic Reasons behind Intra-church Conflicts.* Philadelphia: Westminster Press, 1976.

Horenczyk, G., and S. Munayer. "Acculturation Orientations toward Two Majority Groups: The Case of Palestinian Arab Christian Adolescents in Israel." *Journal of Cross Cultural Psychology* 38 (2007): 76–86.

Huebner, Chris. 2008. Review of *The End of Memory: Remembering Rightly in a Violent World*, by Miroslav Volf. Accessed 2015. https://onlinelibrary.wiley.com/doi/pdf/10.1111/j.1468-0025.2008.00476.x

Ibn Khaldūn. *The Moqaddimah: An Introduction to History.* Translated by F. Rosenthal. Edited by N. J. Dawood. Princeton, NJ: Princeton University Press, 1967.

Irani, George, and Nathan Funk. "Rituals of Reconciliation: Arab-Islamic Perspectives." *Arab Studies Quarterly* 20, no. 4 (1998): 53–74.

Isaac, Munther. *From Land to Lands, from Eden to the Renewed Earth: A Christ-Centred Biblical Theology of the Promised Land.* Carlisle, UK: Langham Monographs, 2015.

Isasi-Díaz, Ada María. "Reconciliation: An Intrinsic Element of Justice." In *Explorations in Reconciliation: New Directions in Theology*, edited by David Tombs and Joseph Liechty, 70. Aldershot: Ashgate, 2006.

Jabbour, Elias. *Sulha: Palestinian Traditional Peace-Making Process.* Montreat, NC: House of Hope, 1993.

Jaichandran, Rebecca, and B. D. Madhav. "Pentecostal Spirituality in a Postmodern World." Asian Journal of Pentecostal Studies 6 (2003): 39–61.

Jenkins, Philip. *The Lost History of Christianity: The Thousand-Year Golden Age of the Church in the Middle East, Africa and Asia.* Oxford: Lion, 2008.

Jones, Gregory. "Behold, I Make All Things New." In *God and the Victim: Theological Reflections on Evil, Victimization, Justice, and Forgiveness*, edited by Lisa Barnes Lampman, 160. Grand Rapids: Eerdmans, 1999.

———. "Crafting Communities of Forgiveness." *Interpretation* 54 (2000): 125.

———. *Embodying Forgiveness: A Theological Analysis*. Grand Rapids: Eerdmans, 1995.

Jones, Stanton L., and Mark A. Yarhouse. *Homosexuality: The Use of Scientific Research in the Church's Moral Debate*. Downers Grove: InterVarsity Press, 2000.

Joseph, Suad. "Gender and Family in the Arab World." In *Arab Women between Defiance and Restraint*, edited by S. Sabbagh, 194–202. New York: Olive Branch Press, 1996.

———. *Intimate Selving in Arab Families: Gender, Self, and Identity*. New York: Syracuse University Press, 1999.

Josselson, Ruthellen. "The Hermeneutics of Faith and the Hermeneutics of Suspicion." *Narrative Inquiry* 14 (2004): 1–28.

Kanaaneh, R. A. *Birthing the Nation: Strategies of Palestinian Women in Israel*. Berkeley: University of California Press, 2002.

Kassis, Riad, and Nabil Costa. *Sir Alhawkama Alnajiha* [The secret to successful governance]. Beirut: Dar Manhal al-Hayat, 2012.

Katanacho, Yohanna. *The Land of Christ: A Palestinian Cry*. Eugene, OR: Pickwick, 2013.

———. "Palestinian Protestant Theological Responses to a World Marked by Violence." *Missiology: An International Review* 36, no. 3 (2008): 289–305.

Khalidi, Walid, ed. *All That Remains: The Palestinian Villages Occupied and Depopulated by Israel in 1948*. Washington, DC: Institute for Palestine Studies, 1992.

Khūry, Jiryis. *A'rab masihiyūn: aṣālah, ḥuḍūr, infitāḥ* [Arab Christians: Authenticity, presence, openness]. Bethlehem: Al-Liqa, 2006.

Kraft, Kathryn Ann. "Community and Identity among Arabs of a Muslim Background Who Choose to Follow a Christian Faith." PhD thesis, University of Bristol, 2007.

Kriesberg, Louis. *Social Conflicts*. Englewood Cliffs, NJ: Prentice-Hall, 1982.

———. *The Sociology of Social Conflict*. Englewood Cliffs, NJ: Prentice-Hall, 1973.

Kurian, George T., ed. *The Encyclopedia of Christian Civilization*. Oxford: Blackwell, 2012.

Lamb, Sharon and Jeffrie Murphy. "Women, Abuse and Forgiveness." In *Before Forgiving: Cautionary Views of Forgiveness in Psychotherapy*, edited by S. Lamb and J. G. Murphy, 155–171. Oxford: Oxford University Press, 2002.

Lang, Sharon. "*Sulha* Peace-Making Process and the Politics of Persuasion." *Journal of Palestine Studies* 31, no. 3 (2002): 52–66.

Lanier, Chandler. *Can These Bones Live?* Hagerstown: Fairmont Books, 2000.
Leas, Speed, and Paul Kiitlaus. *Church Fights: Managing Conflict in the Local Church*. Philadelphia: Westminster Press, 1973.
Leas, Speed. *Moving Your Church through Conflict*. Washington, DC: Alban Institute, 1985.
Lederach, John Paul. *Building Peace: Sustainable Reconciliation in Divided Societies*. Washington, DC: United States Institute of Peace Press, 1997.
Liechty, Joseph. "Putting Forgiveness in Its Place: The Dynamics of Reconciliation." In *Explorations in Reconciliation: New Directions in Theology*, edited by David Tombs and Joseph Liechty, 59–68. Aldershot: Ashgate, 2006.
Lincoln, Yvonna S., and Egon G. Guba. *Naturalistic Inquiry*. Newbury Park, CA: Sage, 1985.
Lofland, J., and L. H. Lofland. *Analysing Social Settings: A Guide to Qualitative Observation and Analysis*. 3rd ed. Belmont, CA: Wadsworth, 1995.
Lustick, Ian. *Arabs in the Jewish State*. Austin: University of Texas Press, 1980.
Lybarger, Loren. "For Church or Nation? Islamism, Secular-Nationalism and the Transformation of Christian Identities in Palestine." *American Academy of Religion* 75, no. 4 (2007): 777–813.
Makant, Mindy. "Re-membering Redemption: Bearing Witness to the Transformation of Suffering." PhD thesis, Duke University, 2012.
Makdisi, Jean. *Teta, Mither and Me*. London: Saqi Books, 2006.
Mansour, Atallah. *Narrow Gate Churches: The Christian Presence in the Holy Land under Muslim and Jewish Rule*. Pasadena, CA: Hope, 2004.
Mansour, Bader. "A Brief Summary of Baptist History in the Holy Land: 1911–2011." Baptists in Israel. 2012. Accessed 2013. http://baptist.org.il/baptistdata/en-events/d/0/0/ev107/files/100-Years-of-Baptist-Witness-in-the-Holy-Land.pdf.
———. *Tarikh Al maamadaniyeen fe alarady almokaddasa baina 1867 and 1950* [Baptist history in the Holy Land between 1867 and 1950], Part 1, forthcoming.
———. *Tarikh Al maamadaniyeen fe alarady almokaddasa baina 1950 and 2020.* [Baptist history in the Holy Land between 1950 and 2020], Part 2, forthcoming.
Marshall, Chris. *Little Book of Biblical Justice: A Fresh Approach to the Bible's Teachings on Justice*. The Little Books of Justice and Peacebuilding Series. Intercourse, PA: Good Books, 2005.
Massad, Hanna. "The Theological Foundation for Reconciliation between the Palestinian Christians and the Messianic Jews." PhD thesis, Fuller Theological Seminary, 2000.
Mauthner, Natasha, and Andrea Doucet. "Reflexive Accounts and Accounts of Reflexivity in Qualitative Data Analyses." *Sociology* 37, no. 3 (2003): 413–431.

McCollough, Charles. *Resolving Conflict with Justice and Peace*. New York: Pilgrim Press, 1990.

McCullough, Michael, Giacomo Bono, and Lindsey Root. "Rumination, Emotion, and Forgiveness: Three Longitudinal Studies." *Journal of Personality and Social Psychology* 92, no. 3 (2007): 490–505.

Merriam, S. A., J. Johnson-Bailey, M.-Y. Lee, Y. Kee, G. Ntseane, and M. Muhamad. *Power and Positionality: Negotiating Insider/Outsider Status within and across Cultures*. International Journal of Lifelong Education 20, no. 5 (2001): 405–416.

Merry, S. "Mediation in Non-Industrial Societies." In *Mediation Research*, edited by K. Kressel and D. Pruitt, 68–90. San Francisco: Jossey-Bass, 1989.

Miles, Matthew B., and A. Michael Huberman. *Qualitative Data Analysis: An Expanded Sourcebook*. 2nd ed. Thousand Oaks, CA: Sage, 1994.

Moltmann, Jurgen. *Theology of Hope: On the Ground and the Implications of a Christian Eschatology*. London: SCM Press, 1967.

Morgan, David. L. *Focus Groups as Qualitative Research*. Newbury Park, CA: Sage, 1988.

Müller-Fahrenholz, Geiko. *The Art of Forgiveness: Theological Reflections on Healing and Reconciliation*. Geneva: WCC, 1997.

———. "On Shame and Hurt in the Life of Nations: A German Perspective." In *Reconciling Memories*, edited by A. Falconer and J. Liechty, 232–241. 2nd ed. Dublin: Columba Press, 1998.

Munayer, Salim. "Beyond Bells and Smells: The Gap Between Eastern and Western Christianity." Musalaha. 2 September 2016. Accessed 9 April 2017. http://www.musalaha.org/articles/2016/8/18/beyond-bells-and-smells-the-gap-between-eastern-and-western-christianity.

———. "The Ethnic Identity of Palestinian Arab Christian Adolescents in Israel." PhD thesis, University of Wales, 2000.

———. "Reconciliation from a Palestinian Point of View and the Challenge to the Jewish Believers." In *Seeking and Pursuing Peace: The Process, the Pain, and the Product*, edited by Salim Munayer, 103–106. Jerusalem: Musalaha, 1998.

———. "Relations between Religions in Historic Palestine and the Future Prospects: Christian and Jews." In *Christians in the Holy Land*, edited by Michael Prior and William Taylor, 143–150. London: World of Islam Festival Trust, 1995.

Munayer, Salim, and Gabriel Horenczyk. "Multi-Group Acculturation Orientations in a Changing Context: Palestinian Christian Arab Adolescents in Israel after the Lost Decade." *International Journal of Psychology* 49, no. 5 (2014): 364–370.

Munayer, Salim, and Lisa Loden. *Through My Enemy's Eyes: Envisioning Reconciliation in Israel-Palestine*. Milton Keynes, UK: Paternoster, 2014.

Munson, Henry "Fundamentalism." Encyclopaedia Britannica. Updated 6 December 2016. Accessed 3 November 2017. https://www.britannica.com/topic/fundamentalism#toc1191955main.

Murphy, Jeffrie. "Forgiveness, Self-Respect and the Value of Resentment." In *Handbook of Forgiveness*, edited by E. L. Worthington Jr., 33–40. New York: Routledge, 2005.

Murphy, Jeffrie, and Jean Hampton. *Forgiveness and Mercy*. Cambridge: Cambridge University Press, 1988.

Nader, Laura, and Harry F. Todd. *The Disputing Process: Law in Ten Societies*. New York: Columbia University Press, 1978.

Nagar-Ron, Sigal. "Al dibor, shtika ve-refleksiviout bezman imet" [On speaking, silence and "reflexivity in real time" in interviews with marginalized women]. In *Feminist Research Methodologies*, edited by Mikhal Kromer-Navor, Maia Lavy-Agay and Daphnah Haker, 112–133. Tel-Aviv: Hakibuts Hamiauhad, 2014.

Nagel, Joane. "Constructing Ethnicity: Creating and Recreating Ethnic Identity and Culture." *Social Problems* 41, no. 1 (1994): 152–176.

Narayan, Kirin. "How Native Is a 'Native' Anthropologist?" *American Anthropologist* 95, no. 3 (1993): 671–686.

Nasser, Ilham, and Abu-Nimer Mohammed. "Perceptions of Forgiveness among Palestinian Teachers in Israel." *Journal of Peace Education* 9, no. 1 (2012): 1–15.

Nelson, Randy. "Exegeting Forgiveness." *American Theological Inquiry* 5 (2012): 33–34.

Oswald, Roy, James Heath, and Ann Heath. *Beginning Ministry Together: The Alban Handbook for Clergy Transitions*. Washington, DC: Alban Institute, 2003.

Pappé, Ilan. *The Forgotten Palestinians: A History of the Palestinians in Israel*. New Haven: Yale University Press, 2011.

Parsons, George. *Intervening in a Church Fight: A Manual for Internal Consultants*. Alban Institute's Special Papers and Research Reports Series. Washington, DC: Alban Institute, 1989.

Pely, Doron. "Honor: The *Sulha's* Main Dispute Resolution Tool." *Conflict Resolution Quarterly* 28, no. 1 (2010): 67–81.

———. "Resolving Clan-Based Disputes Using the '*Sulha*,' the Traditional Dispute Resolution Process of the Middle East." *Journal of Dispute Resolution* 63, no. 4 (2008): 80–88.

———. "The *Sulha* (Israeli Arabs' Dispute Resolution Process) and Israel's Formal Legal System: A Tale of Tenuous, yet Mutually Beneficial Coexistence." Master's thesis, University of Massachusetts, 2008.

———. "When Honor Needs Trump Health and Safety Needs." *Negotiation Journal* 27, no. 2 (2011): 205–225.

———. "Where East Not Always Meets West: Comparing the *Sulha* Process to Western-Style Mediation and Arbitration." *Conflict Resolution Quarterly* 28, no. 4 (2011): 427–440.

———. "Women in *Sulha* – Excluded yet Influential: Examining Arab Women's Formal and Informal Place in Traditional Dispute Resolution, within the Patriarchal Culture of Northern Israel's Arab Community." *International Journal of Conflict Management* 22, no. 1 (2011): 89–104.

Philpott, Daniel. *Just and Unjust Peace: An Ethic of Political Reconciliation*. New York: Oxford University Press, 2012.

Poloma, Margaret. *The Charismatic Movement: Is There a New Pentecost?* Boston: Twayne Publishers, 1982.

Popielarz, Pamela, and McPherson, Miller. "On the Edge or In Between: Niche Position, Niche Overlap, and the Duration of Voluntary Association Memberships." *American Journal of Sociology* 101 (1995): 698–721.

Qualben, James. *Peace in the Parish*. San Antonio: LangMarc, 1991.

Rabinowitz, Danny. "The Palestinian Citizens of Israel, the Concept of Trapped Minority and the Discourse of Transnationalism in Anthropology." *Ethnic and Racial Studies* 24 (2001): 64–85.

Rabinowitz, Danny, and Khawla Abu-Baker. *Door zakoof* [The stand tall generation]. Jerusalem: Keter, 2002.

Raheb, Mitri. *Bethlehem Besieged: Stories of Hope in Times of Trouble*. Minneapolis: Fortress, 2004.

———. *I Am a Palestinian Christian*. Translated by Ruth Gritsch. Minneapolis: Fortress, 1995.

Ramon, Amnon. *Christianity and Christians in the Jewish State*. Jerusalem: Jerusalem Institute for Israel Studies, 2012.

Rantisi, Audeh, and Ralph Beebe. *Blessed Are the Peacemakers: A Palestinian Christian in the Occupied West Bank*. Grand Rapids: Zondervan, 1990.

Register, Ray. *Back to Jerusalem*. Enumclaw, WA: Wine Press, 2000.

Reynolds, Jeremy. "Baptists in Israel Celebrate 100 Years of Ministry." Assist News Service. 2012. Accessed 21 June 2014. http://www.assistnews.net/Stories/2011/s11040134.htm.

Robinson Leah. *Embodied Peacebuilding: Reconciliation as Practical Theology*. Oxford: Peter Lang, 2014.

Rogers, Carl. *A Way of Being*. Boston: Houghton Mifflin, 1980.

Roof, Wade. *Community and Commitment*. New York: Elsevier, 1978.

Rooney, Pauline. "Researching from the Inside: Does It Compromise Validity?" *Level3* 3, no. 1 (2005): 4.

Rothman, J., and M. L. Olson. "From Interests to Identities: Towards a New Emphasis in Interactive Conflict Resolution." *Journal of Peace Research* 38 (2001): 289–305.

Rowden, Rebecca. *Baptist in Israel*. Nashville: Field Publishing, 2010.
Russell, Bertrand. *Power: A New Social Analysis*. New York: W. W. Norton, 1938.
Sa'ar, Amalia. 1998. "Carefully on the Margins: Christian Palestinian in Haifa between Nation and State." *American Ethnologist* 25, no. 2 (1998): 215–239.
———. "Feminine Strength: Reflections on Power and Gender in Israeli-Palestinian Culture." *Anthropological Quarterly* 79, no. 3 (2006): 398–431.
———. "Lonely in Your Firm Grip: Women in Israeli-Palestinian Families." *Royal Anthropological Institute* 7 (2001): 723–739.
Sabella, Bernard. "Arab Christian Presence in Palestine." *Al-Liqa' Journal* 24 (2005): 76–90.
———. "Socio-Economic Characteristics and the Challenges to Palestinian Christians in the Holy Land." In *Christians in the Holy Land*, edited by Michael Prior and William Taylor, 31–44. London: World of Islam Festival Trust, 1994.
Said, Abdul Aziz, Nathan Funk, and Ayse Kadayifci, eds. *Peace and Conflict Resolution in Islam: Precept and Practice*. Lanham, MD: University Press of America, 2001.
Sande, Ken. *The Peace Maker*. Grand Rapids: Baker, 2004.
Scharen, Christian. *Fieldwork in Theology: Exploring the Social Context of God's Work in the World*. Grand Rapids: Baker, 2015.
Schimmel, Solomon. *Wounds Not Healed by Time: The Power of Repentance and Forgiveness*. Oxford: Oxford University Press, 2002.
Schreiter, Robert. *The Ministry of Reconciliation: Spirituality and Strategies*. Maryknoll, NY: Orbis, 1998.
Sharabi, Hisham. *Neopatriarchy: A Theory of Distorted Change in Arab Society*. Oxford: Oxford University Press, 1988.
Sharkey, Heather. "Middle Eastern and North African Christianity: Persisting in the Lands of Islam." In *Introducing World Christianity*, edited by Charles Farhadian, 7–20. Oxford: Blackwell, 2012.
Shehadeh, Imad. "A Comparison and a Contrast between the Prologue of John's Gospel and Qur'anic Surah 5." ThD thesis, Dallas Theological Seminary, 1990.
———. "Ishmael in Relation to the Promises of Abraham." ThM thesis, Dallas Theological Seminary, 1986.
Shihade, Magid. "Internal Violence: State's Role and Society's Responses." *Arab Studies Quarterly* 27, no. 4 (2005): 31–44.
Shin, Eui H., and Hyung Park. "An Analysis of Causes of Schisms in Ethnic Churches: The Case of Korean-American Churches." *Sociological Analysis* 49 (1988): 234–248.
Shorrosh, Anis. *Islam Revealed: A Christian Arab's View of Islam*. Nashville: T. Nelson, 1988.

———. *Jesus, Prophecy & Middle East*. Daphne, AL: Anis Shorrosh Evangelistic Association, 1979.

———. *The True Furqan*. 3rd ed. Duncanville, TX: World Wide Printing, 2002.

Shriver, Donald. *An Ethic for Enemies: Forgiveness in Politics*. Oxford: Oxford University Press, 1995.

———. "Where and When in Political Life is Justice Served by Forgiveness?" In *Burying the Past: Making Peace and Doing Justice after Civil Conflict*, edited by N Biggar, 23–39. Washington, DC: Georgetown University Press, 2001.

Shults, LeRon, and Steven Sandage. *The Faces of Forgiveness: Searching for Wholeness and Salvation*. Grand Rapids: Baker Academic, 2003.

Silbey, S., and S. Merry. "Mediator Settlement Strategies." *Law and Policy Quarterly* 7 (1986): 19–20.

Simmel, Georg. "Conflict." In *On Individuality and Social Forms*, edited by Donald Levine, 70–95. Chicago: University of Chicago Press, 1971.

Slaughter, M. M. "The Salman Rushdie Affair: Apostasy, Honor, and Freedom of Speech." *Virginia Law Review* 79 (1993): 141–198.

Smedes, Lewis. "Stations on the Journey from Forgiveness to Hope." In *Dimensions of Forgiveness: Psychological Research and Theological Perspectives*, edited by E. L. Worthington Jr., 341–354. Philadelphia: Templeton Foundation Press, 1998.

Smelser, Neil. *The Social Edges of Psychoanalysis*. Berkeley: University of California Press, 1998.

Smith, Andrea. "Murder in Jerba: Honour, Shame and Hospitality among Maltese in Ottoman Tunisia." *History and Anthropology* 15 (2004): 107–132.

Smith, Daniel L. "The Reward of Allah." *Journal of Peace Research* 26, no. 4 (1989): 385–398.

Smith, Linda Tuhiwai. *Decolonizing Methodologies*. London: Zed Books, 1999.

Smooha, Sammy. *Arab-Jewish Relations in Israel: Alienation and Rapprochement*. Washington, DC: United States Institute of Peace, 2010.

———. "Yaḥasy A'raveim yehodeim be Yeśrael ke medyna yehodyt demoḵraṭyt" [The relationship between Arabs and Jews in Israel as a democratic and Jewish state]. In *Trends in the Israeli Society*, edited by Ephraim Yaar and Ze'ev Shavit, 231–363. Tel Aviv: Open University, 2001.

Smyth, A., and R. Holian. "Credibility Issues in Research from within Organizations." In *Researching Education from the Inside*, edited by P. Sikes and A. Potts, 33–47. New York: Taylor & Francis, 2008.

Snyder, Timothy. "Theological Ethnography: Embodied." *The Other Journal: An Intersection of Theology and Culture* 23, no. 5 (May 2014). Accessed November 2015. http://theotherjournal.com/2014/05/27/theological-ethnography-embodied/.

Stake, R. E. "Case Studies." In *Strategies of Qualitative Inquiry*, edited by N. K. Denzin and Y. S. Lincoln, 86–109. Thousand Oaks, CA: Sage, 1998.

Starke, Frederick A., and Bruno Dyke. "Upheavals in Congregations: The Causes and Outcomes of Splits." *Review of Religious Research* 38 (1996): 159–174.

Stevens, David. *The Land of Unlikeness: Explorations into Reconciliation*. Dublin: Columba Press, 2004.

Storey, Peter. "A Different Kind of Justice: Truth and Reconciliation in South Africa." *The Christian Century* 114 (1997): 788–793.

Strauss, Anselm, and Juliet Corbin. *Basic Qualitative Research: Grounded Theory Procedures and Techniques*. 2nd ed. Newbury Park: Sage, 1998.

Swinton, John, and Harriet Mowat. *Practical Theology and Qualitative Research*. London: SCM, 2006.

Takayama, Peter. "Strains, Conflicts, and Schisms in Protestant Denominations." In *American Denominational Organization: A Sociological View*, edited by R. P. Scherer, 298–329. Pasadena, CA: William Carey Library, 1980.

Tarabeih, Hussien, Deborah Shmueli, and Khamaisi Rassem. "Towards the Implementation of *Sulha* as a Cultural Peace-Making Method for Managing and Resolving Environmental Conflicts among Arab Palestinians in Israel." *Peace Building and Development* 5, no. 1 (2009): 50–64.

Taylor, Jodie. "The Intimate Insider: Negotiating the Ethics of Friendship When Doing Insider Research." *Qualitative Research* 11, no. 1 (2011): 3–22.

Torrance, Alan. *The Theological Grounds for Advocating Forgiveness and Reconciliation in the Sociopolitical Realm*. Belfast: Centre for Contemporary Christianity in Ireland, 2006.

Tsimhoni, Daphne. "The Christians in Israel: Aspects of Integration and the Search for Identity in a Minority within a Minority." In *Middle Eastern Minorities and Diasporas*, edited by M. Ma'oz and G. Sheffer, 124–152. East Sussex: Sussex Academic Press, 2002.

Tutu, Desmond. *Battle, Reconciliation: The Ubuntu Theology of Desmond Tutu*. Cleveland: Pilgrim, 1997.

――――. *God Has a Dream: A Vision of Hope for Our Time*. New York: Doubleday, 2004.

――――. *No Future without Forgiveness*, London: Rider, 1999.

Tutu, Desmond, and Naomi Tutu. *The Words of Desmond Tutu*. London: Newmarket Press, 1989.

Unluer, Sema. "Being an Insider Researcher While Conducting Case Study Research." *The Qualitative Report* 17, no. 58 (2012): 1–14. Accessed November 2015. http://www.nova.edu/ssss/QR/QR17/unluer.pdf.

Volf, Miroslav. *After Our Likeness: The Church as the Image of the Trinity*. Grand Rapids: Eerdmans, 1998.

――――. *Against the Tide: Love in a Time of Petty Dreams and Persisting Enmities*. Grand Rapids: Eerdmans, 2010.

———. "The Church as a Prophetic Community and a Sign of Hope." *European Journal of Theology* 2 (1993): 9–30.

———. *The End of Memory: Remembering Rightly in a Violent World*. Grand Rapids: Eerdmans, 2006.

———. *Exclusion and Embrace: A Theological Exploration of Identity, Otherness and Reconciliation*. Nashville: Abingdon Press, 1996.

———. *Flourishing: Why We Need Religion in a Globalized World*. New Haven: Yale University Press, 2015.

———. *Free of Charge: Giving and Forgiving in a Culture Stripped of Grace*. Grand Rapids: Zondervan, 2005.

———. "God, Justice, and Love: The Grounds for Human Flourishing." Books and Culture. *Christianity Today*, 6 February 2009. Accessed 25 June 2017. https://www.booksandculture.com/articles/2009/janfeb/16.26.html.

———. *A Public Faith: How Followers of Christ Should Serve the Common Good*. Grand Rapids: Brazos Press, 2011.

———. "Reconciliation, Justice, and Mercy: An Alternative to 'Liberal Peace.'" Books and Culture. *Christianity Today*, 26 August 2013. Accessed 25 June 2017. http://www.booksandculture.com/articles/2013/sepoct/reconciliation-justice-and-mercy.html.

———. "The Social Meaning of Reconciliation." *Transformation* 16 (1999): 7–12.

———. "Soft Difference: Theological Reflections on the Relation between Church and Culture in 1 Peter." *Ex Auditu* 10 (1994): 15–30.

———. "Theology for a Way of Life." In *Practicing Theology: Beliefs and Practices in Christian Life*, edited by Miroslav Volf and Dorothy Bass, 245. Grand Rapids: Eerdmans, 2002.

———. "The Trinity Is Our Social Program: The Doctrine of the Trinity and the Shape of Social Engagement." *Modern Theology* 14, no. 3 (1998): 403–423.

Walker, P. "Concepts of the Self: Implications for Cross-Cultural Conflict Resolution." *ADR Bulletin* 2, no. 2 (1999): 17–24.

Wallace, John. *Control in Conflict*. Nashville: Broadman, 1982.

Ward, Pete. *Perspectives on Ecclesiology and Ethnography*. Grand Rapids: Eerdmans, 2012.

Watts, James. *Palestinian Tapestries*. Richmond: Foreign Mission Board, 1936.

Weber, Max. *The Theory of Social and Economic Organization*. Translated by A. M. Henderson and Talcott Parsons. International Library of Sociology and Social Reconstruction Series. London: Free Press of Glencoe, 1947.

Webster, John. "The Ethics of Reconciliation." In *The Theology of Reconciliation*, edited by Colin Gunton, 109–124. London: T&T Clark, 2003.

Wigg-Stevenson, Natalie. *Ethnographic Theology: An Inquiry into the Production of Theological Knowledge*. New York: Palgrave Macmillan, 2014.

Witty, Cathie. *Mediation and Society: Conflict Management in Lebanon.* New York: Academic Press, 1980.

Wood, James R. *Leadership in Voluntary Organizations: The Controversy over Social Action in Protestant Churches.* New Brunswick, NJ: Rutgers University Press, 1981.

Worthington, Everett L., Jr., ed. *Dimensions of Forgiveness: Psychological Research and Religious Perspectives.* Philadelphia: Templeton Foundation Press, 1998.

Wright, N. T. *Evil and the Justice of God.* Downers Grove: InterVarsity Press, 2006.

———. *Jesus and the Victory of God.* London: SPCK, 1996.

Ye'or, Bat. *Islam and Dhimmitude: Where Civilizations Collide.* Cranbury, NJ: Fairleigh Dickinson University Press, 2002.

Yin, Robert. *Case Study Research: Design and Methods.* 4th ed. Los Angeles: Sage, 2009.

Younan, Munib. *Witnessing for Peace: In Jerusalem and the World.* Edited by Frederick Strickert. Minneapolis: Fortress Press, 2003.

Yu, Carver. "Culture from an Evangelical Perspective." *Transformation* 17, no. 3 (2000): 82–85.

Zaky, Andryh. *Naḥwa lāhūt moʿāṣir* [Towards a contemporary theology]. Cairo: Dar El Thaqafa, 2007.

Langham Literature, with its publishing work, is a ministry of Langham Partnership.

Langham Partnership is a global fellowship working in pursuit of the vision God entrusted to its founder John Stott –

> *to facilitate the growth of the church in maturity and Christ-likeness through raising the standards of biblical preaching and teaching.*

Our vision is to see churches in the majority world equipped for mission and growing to maturity in Christ through the ministry of pastors and leaders who believe, teach and live by the Word of God.

Our mission is to strengthen the ministry of the Word of God through:
- nurturing national movements for biblical preaching
- fostering the creation and distribution of evangelical literature
- enhancing evangelical theological education

especially in countries where churches are under-resourced.

Our ministry

Langham Preaching partners with national leaders to nurture indigenous biblical preaching movements for pastors and lay preachers all around the world. With the support of a team of trainers from many countries, a multi-level programme of seminars provides practical training, and is followed by a programme for training local facilitators. Local preachers' groups and national and regional networks ensure continuity and ongoing development, seeking to build vigorous movements committed to Bible exposition.

Langham Literature provides majority world preachers, scholars and seminary libraries with evangelical books and electronic resources through publishing and distribution, grants and discounts. The programme also fosters the creation of indigenous evangelical books in many languages, through writer's grants, strengthening local evangelical publishing houses, and investment in major regional literature projects, such as one volume Bible commentaries like the *Africa Bible Commentary* and the *South Asia Bible Commentary*.

Langham Scholars provides financial support for evangelical doctoral students from the majority world so that, when they return home, they may train pastors and other Christian leaders with sound, biblical and theological teaching. This programme equips those who equip others. Langham Scholars also works in partnership with majority world seminaries in strengthening evangelical theological education. A growing number of Langham Scholars study in high quality doctoral programmes in the majority world itself. As well as teaching the next generation of pastors, graduated Langham Scholars exercise significant influence through their writing and leadership.

To learn more about Langham Partnership and the work we do visit **langham.org**

www.ingramcontent.com/pod-product-compliance
Lightning Source LLC
Chambersburg PA
CBHW052012290426
44112CB00014B/2210